The Kṛṣṇa Cycle in the Purāṇas

Themes and Motifs in a Heroic Saga

Benjamin Preciado-Solis, M.A., Ph.D.
Professor of Indian Studies, El Colegio de México

MOTILAL BANARSIDASS
Delhi □ Varanasi □ Patna

Published with the financial assistance of El Colegio de México

Bungalow Road, Delhi-110 007 (India)
Branches : 1. Chowk, Varanasi-1 (U.P.)
2. Ashok Rajpath, Patna-4 (Bihar)

First Edition : Delhi, 1984
ISBN: 0-89581-226-6

Printed in India
By Shantilal Jain, at Shri Jainendra Press,
A-45, Phase-I, Naraina, New Delhi-110 028.
Published by Narendra Prakash Jain, for Motilal Banarsidass, Delhi-7.

Table of Contents

(Figures are taken from V. Vitsaxis' *Hindu Epics, Myths and Legends in Popular Illustrations*, Oxford, Delhi 1977, plates 17 and 30.)

मल्लानामशनिर्नृणां नरवरः स्त्रीणां स्मरो मूर्तिमान्
गोपानां स्वजनोऽसतां क्षितिभुजां शास्ता स्वपित्रोः शिशुः ॥
मृत्युर्भोजपतेर्विराडविदुषां तत्त्वं परं योगिनां
वृष्णीनां परदेवतेति विदितो रङ्गं गतः साग्रजः ॥

श्रीमद्भागवतम् ॥१०॥ ४३॥ १७॥

Preface

When it was first suggested to me that I do research on Kṛṣṇa, my immediate reaction was to say that the topic had been very well covered. I was, however, asked to consider it and so I did, with the result that I found that the topic was indeed very far from having been covered. Contrary to my first opinion I found that a full study of Kṛṣṇa was still wanting. Many general—and in many cases superficial—accounts of Kṛṣṇa and the Kṛṣṇa-cult had been produced and there were also detailed studies of particular aspects of the topic—especially on Kṛṣṇa's teaching in the *Bhagavad Gītā*—but still it was obvious that a work covering in more detail the figure of Kṛṣṇa was needed. So I decided to take up the investigation in the confidence that there was still much to say on the theme. However, as the months passed and I examined more and more material, it also became evident that Kṛṣṇa alone was a very vast subject of research, and that anyone wanting to cover it in its totality, if he had all the necessary qualifications, would have to write a multi-volume work to do full justice to the topic. Thus I had to narrow the scope of my research to a manageable size. I chose to look into the stories that formed the Kṛṣṇa cycle and find more about them and their different versions. I would be dealing with the image of Kṛṣṇa that is presented by the stories of the Purāṇas, first trying to identify some of the sources where these stories could have had their origins, and then examining the earliest historical evidence on Kṛṣṇa and the Kṛṣṇa-cult to see if any of these legends could be placed chronologically. I would have to examine then in detail some of the most characteristic episodes in the legends to identify their underlying themes and motifs. Finally, to complement this analysis of the stories, I decided to look also into their plastic representation in the Iconography. This was to be the scope of my research.

The advice of Professor Basham, for it was he who suggested I research this topic, proved to be very fruitful, and I think that, with his help, I obtained some good results in the analysis of the materials and that some original views are presented in this investigation, as well as some new evidence put forward to add to the store of knowledge on the subject.

Earlier versions of parts of this research were presented to various Conferences. One part of chapter five was delivered as a paper at the Second National Conference of the Asian Studies Association of Australia, University of New South Wales, Sydney, Australia, May 1978; and parts of chapter three were delivered to the Staff Research Seminar, Faculty of Asian Studies, Australian National University, Canberra, Australia, 1978; the Second Congress of the Associación Latinoamericana de Estudios Afroasiáticos, Paipa, Colombia, April 1981; and the First International Symposium of the Sanskrit Language, Universidad Nacional Autónoma de México, February 1982. Modified versions of parts of chapter five and chapter two were published in Australia and Mexico : "Dark as a Cloud," *Hemisphere*, vol. 23.2, 1979, Canberra, Australia; "Los Múltiples Enigmas de Kṛṣṇa", *Diálogos* 90, Nov.-Dec., 1979, México; and "Primeras Evidencias Históricas sobre Kṛṣṇa", *Estudios de Asia y Africa*, vol. 15.4, 1980, México.

I regret that I could not profit during my research of the magnificent book of Prof. Priyatosh Banerjee

The Life of Kṛṣṇa in Indian Art (National Museum, New Delhi, 1978).

I would like to thank the authorities and staff of the National Museum, New Delhi; Indian Museum, Calcutta; Government Museum, Madras; Archaeological Museum, Mathura; Archaeological Museum, Bhuvanesvar; Archaeological Museum, Jodhpur; and Bharat Kala Bhavan, Banaras Hindu University. Also to the authorities of the Archaeological Survey of India in Kanchipuram, Mahabalipuram, Aihole, Badami, Pattadakal, Ellora, Khajuraho, Deogarh and Udayagiri; as well as to the American Institute of Indian Studies, Ramnagar, Varanasi, who kindly provided plates 15, 19 and 56.

I also have to thank the authorities and staff of the following libraries : Library of the Madras University; Kuppuswamy Shastri Research Institute, Madras; and Adyar Library, Madras; Deccan College Research Institute and Bhandarkar Oriental Research Institute, Poona; Archaeological Survey of India, New Delhi; Banaras Hindu University Library, Varanasi; Victoria State Library, Melbourne, Australia; Sydney University Library, Sidney, Australia; and especially to the staff of the Australian National University Library—both at the Menzies and the Chifley Libraries. Also, the National Library of Australia and the British Museum Library and the S. O. A. S. Library, London, as well as other Australian and American University libraries that kindly provided materials for research. I also thank the Universidad de Guadalajara for the economic support during my studies in India and Australia.

It is now my very agreeable duty to acknowledge the help received from many teachers, colleagues and friends during the time of my research. First and foremost, to Professor A. L. Basham through whose invaluable guidance I was able to start, follow up and finish this project. Then to Drs. B. J. Terwiel, K. H. J. Gardiner, R. Barz and T. Rajapatirana, all of the Australian National University, who helped me on numerous occasions. My thanks go also to Professor R. N. Dandekar, Dr. V. N. Shukla, Professor R. V. Joshi and the late Professor V. Raghavan for their advice and help. To Jackie Holyoake, Mary Hutchinson and Portia MacCusker for their kindness and help, and to my friends and colleagues K. Zysk, A. Galla, E. Perera, A. Ruelas, Carolyn Thornley and María and Carlos Amat for their advice and help with typing and reading. Also to Lic. Luis Echeverría, thanks to whose generosity and deep interest in learning and science, I have been able on two occasions, to visit and study in India. To the Australian National University my warmest thanks for their thorough support and liberality. To El Colegio de México and its Centre for Asian and African Studies as well as to Professors Victor L. Urquidi, Graciela De la Lama and Manuel Ruiz for their interest in this publication. Finally, most special thanks are due to my wife Magdalena and our daughters who have heroically, with love and understanding, put up with a very long research project.

Abbreviations

AB	Aitareya Brāhmaṇa.
ABORI	Annals of the Bhandarkar Oriental Research Institute.
ANU	Australian National University.
Apo.	Apollodorus Atheniensis, *The Library.*
AS	Artha Śāstra of Kauṭilya.
ASI	Archaeological Survey of India.
ASIAR	Archaeological Survey of India. Annual Report.
AV	Atharva Veda.
BC	Bālacarita.
BD	Bṛhad Devatā.
BDS	Baudhāyana Dharma Sūtra.
BEFEO	Bulletin de l'École Française de l'Extréme Orient.
BG	Bhagavad Gītā.
BhP	Bhāgavata Purāṇa.
BHU	Banaras Hindu University.
BSOAS	Bulletin of the School of Oriental and African Studies.
BSOS	Bulletin of the School of Oriental Studies.
Chand.Up.	Chāndogya Upaniṣad.
DBP	Devī Bhāgavata Purāṇa.
Dio.	Diodorus Siculus, *The Library of History.*
EFEO	École Française de l'Extréme Orient.
EI	Epigraphia Indica.
ERE	Encyclopaedia of Religion and Ethics.
GJ	Gaṭha Jātaka.
GOS	Gaekwad Oriental Series, Baroda.
HOS	Harvard Oriental Series.
HV	Harivaṃśa.
IA	Indian Antiquary.
IHQ	Indian Historical Quarterly.
IIJ	Indo-Iranian Journal.
JAAR	Journal of the American Academy of Religion.
JAOS	Journal of the American Oriental Society.
JASB	Journal of the Asiatic Society of Bengal.

JBBRAS	Journal of the Bombay Branch of the Royal Asiatic Society.
JBRS	Journal of the Bihar Oriental Research Society.
JDCRI	Journal of the Deccan College Research Institute.
JIH	Journal of Indian History.
JISOA	Journal of the Indian Society of Oriental Art.
JGJRI	Journal of the Ganganath Jha Research Institute.
JOIB	Journal of the Oriental Institute, Baroda.
JRAS	Journal of the Royal Asiatic Society.
JRASB	Journal of the Royal Asiatic Society of Bengal.
JUPHS	Journal of the United Provinces Historical Society, or Journal of the Uttar Pradesh Historical Society.
Mait.Sam.	Maitrāyaṇī Saṃhitā.
MarP	Mārkaṇḍeya Purāṇa.
MASI	Memoirs of the Archaeological Survey of India.
Mbh.	Mahābhārata.
OST	Original Sanskrit Texts by J. Muir.
Pan.	Pāṇini.
PP	Padma Purāṇa.
Ram.	Rāmāyaṇa.
RV	Ṛg Veda.
SB	Śatapatha Brāhmaṇa.
SBE	Sacred Books of the East.
SBH	Sacred Books of the Hindus.
SED	Sanskrit-English Dictionary, Monier-Williams.
Su.	Suśruta Saṃhitā.
TS	Taittirīya Saṃhitā.
VP	Viṣṇu Purāṇa.
VS	Vājasaneyi Saṃhitā.
VVRI	Vishveshvarananda Research Institute.
WRV	Wörterbuch zum Ṛig Veda, Grassman.
ZDMG	Zeitschrift der Deutsche Mörgenlandische Gesellschaft.

CHAPTER ONE

Vedic Antecedents

Kṛṣṇa, the hero and god of the Purāṇas, is considered to be an incarnation of the supreme god Viṣṇu or Nārāyaṇa. Although eventually he reaches the highest position within the Vaiṣṇava pantheon as in the *Brahma Vaivarta Purāṇa* and the Bengal Schools, in the early Purāṇas, and even in the *Bhāgavata Purāṇa*, he is just one more of the *avatāras* of the Vedic God. There are certain characteristics both in Viṣṇu and Nārāyaṇa that come down and permeate the personality of Kṛṣṇa, we could say that they have, or are, the essence of Kṛṣṇa, the very core of his character, without the particular incidents that form the Kṛṣṇa legend.

Previous to a study of the Kṛṣṇa cycle it is convenient to review briefly the main traits of these two gods to whom Kṛṣṇa is assimilated. We shall consider only the earliest accounts about them and not the later mythology that is really coeval with the Epic and Purāṇic Kṛṣṇa.

We have also to account for the use of the name Kṛṣṇa in the Veda, and we shall examine briefly the instances where it is mentioned and try to find out if our hero had any relation to the Kṛṣṇa or Kṛṣṇas in the Veda, as some authors hold. We shall examine their opinions and see if they can be valid.

i. VIṢṆU

For more than a hundred years many scholars have given their opinion on the meaning and significance of Viṣṇu's character, and this permanent interest in him is due mainly to his identification with Kṛṣṇa and with the other great Epic hero, Rāma, an identification that converts him at once into one of the most popular gods in the Indian pantheon, and perhaps the one with the largest number of followers.

What is surprising is that Viṣṇu, to whom only a very few hymns are dedicated in the *Ṛg Veda*, has been the object of interpretations so different and divergent as to fill many pages of discussion in an apparently unending dispute on the 'real' character of the god. As Jan Gonda has aptly said :

> it would appear that any effort to attain a detailed, complete and well-defined statement about the functions and sphere of activities of the ancient Indian divinities would be in vain. Beings and powers figuring in so-called primitive or semi-primitive religions and mythology, never having undergone a logical specification and systematization, are not clearly definable in accordance with modern standards.[1]

Here we shall present the Vedic texts that refer to Viṣṇu to try to find out what these texts really show about him.

In the very first hymn in the *Ṛg Veda* which mentions Viṣṇu we find many of the characteristics that had made him famous:

> May the gods protect us from there where Viṣṇu strode over the seven quarters of the earth.
> Viṣṇu strode over this, thrice set down his foot; [the world] was covered by his dust.
> Three steps strode Viṣṇu, the benevolent cowherd [or protector], hence establishing the injunctions.
> Look at Viṣṇu's deeds from which he contemplated the vows; Indra's fast friend.

1. Jan Gonda, *Aspects of Early Viṣṇuism*, Utrecht 1954; rep. Motilal Banarsidass, Delhi, 1969, p. 9.

That supreme step of Viṣṇu the *sūris* always see,
as an eye extended on the sky.
That the wise, inspired, kindle singing; Viṣṇu's
supreme step.[1]

Here we have the verb *vicakrame* 'to stride', and his strides are mentioned as three. He is a protector, *gopa*, and unconquerable or undeceivable, *adābhyaḥ*. Besides he ensures that the injunctions of the gods (or his own) are kept, *dharmāṇi dhārayan*; he is a friend of Indra, and his Supreme step or dwelling, *paramam padam*, is compared to an eye in the sky, *divīva cakṣur*. All these characteristics are elaborated later and combined in a mythology that still contains many obscure points.

Let us start with his wide stepping and his three strides. This is his most relevant feature and the one that the Vedic poets most often associate with him. There is almost no mention of his name without the epithets: *urugāya*, *urukrama*, etc. He it is 'who supported the high meeting-place [of the gods] the wide-striding of three steps',[2] 'who widely strode the earth in three paces for [granting us] a long life.'[3] That is, he is a deity that represents extensiveness and pervasiveness, his most typical feature being that of extending himself through space and covering the universe. This is a beneficent characteristic, as his spreading out means creation and protection, and it is specifically stated in the Veda that his strides are made for the sake of all creatures and that within his wide-extended paces all living creatures have their habitation.[4] He it is 'who alone has triply supported heaven and earth and all beings',[5] and because of this the Vedic people so adored him as to sing:

We sing this manly exploit of him, the powerful,
the saviour, harmless, generous.[1]

Viṣṇu, who thrice measured [with his strides] the terrestrial expanses for the afflicted man; in this your protection which is granted, let us rejoice in riches with our offspring.[2]

From the sky, from earth, from atmosphere, O Viṣṇu, fill thy hands abundantly with good things; and bestow them from the right and from the left.[3]

Most of the gods are prayed to for riches and wealth, it is true, but only in Viṣṇu are these features associated with spatial extensiveness, and this spreading was for the welfare of living beings. Certainly these traits of widespread motion are sometimes attributed to the sun (*RV* 5.47.3; 5.81.3) and, more aptly, to the sun's light, but we do not think that the Vedic hymns refer to a solar characteristic when they mention that Viṣṇu's striding is done to provide mankind with a dwelling: 'Viṣṇu swiftly strode the earth to grant it as dwelling to man. The people who sing his praises are firmly established, the benevolent one has made a wide abode [for men].'[4] To us this providing of a habitation means nothing less than the creation of the world, its expansion from a previous void or dead point. This is why he is the beneficent god and bountiful *par excellence*, and also this would explain his being associated with embryos and birth (*RV* 10.84.1) since he himself causes the Universe to be born.

Closely associated with his three steps but with a meaning in a different context we have Viṣṇu's highest step (*paramam padam*) or station, where the gods rejoice (*RV* 8.29.7) and where springs a well of honey or mead:

May I attain to that his beloved place, where pious men get inebriated; that is indeed the friendship of the wide-striding one. Verily in his supreme step there is a spring of honey.[5]

1. *RV* 1.22.16-21.
ato devā avantu no yato viṣṇur vicakrame / pṛthivyāḥ sapta dhāmabhiḥ // idaṃ viṣṇur vicakrame tredhā ni dadhe padam / samūḷham asya pāṅsure // trīṇi padā vi cakrame viṣṇur gopā adābhyaḥ / ato dharmāṇi dhārayan // viṣṇoḥ karmāṇi paśyata yato vratāni paspaśe / indrasya yujyaḥ sakhā // tad viṣṇoḥ paramaṃ padaṃ sadā paśyanti sūrayaḥ / divīva cakṣur ātatam // tad viprāso vipanyavo jāgṛvāṅsaḥ sam indhate / viṣṇor yat paramaṃ padam //

2. *RV* 1.154.1. yo askabhayad uttaraṃ sadhasthaṃ vicakramāṇas tredhorugāyaḥ.

3. *RV* 1.155.4. yaḥ pārthivāni tribhir id vigāmabhir uru kramiṣṭorugāyāya jīvase.

4. *RV* 1.154.2b. yasyoruṣu triṣu vikramaṇeṣvadhikṣiyanti bhuvanāni viśvā.

5. *RV* 1.154.4. yaḥ u tridhātu pṛthivīm utadyām eko dādhāra bhuvanāni viśvā.

1. *RV* 1.155.4. tad tad id asya pauṃsyaṃ gṛṇīmasīnasya tratur avṛkasya mīḷhuṣaḥ.

2. *RV* 6.49.13. yo rajāṃsi vimame pārthivāni triścid viṣṇur manave bādhitāya / tasya te śarmann upadyamāne rāyā madema tanvā tanā ca.

3. *AV* 7.26.8. divo viṣṇa uta vā pṛthivyā maho viṣṇa urorantarikṣāt / ustau pṛṇasva bahūbhir vasavyairāprayacha dakṣiṇādota savyāt. Tr. Whitney.

4. *RV* 7.100.4. vi cakrame pṛthivīm eṣa etāṃ kṣetrāya viṣṇur manuṣe daśasyan / dhruvaso asya kīrayo janāsa urukṣitiṃ sujanimā cakāra //

5. *RV* 1.154.5. tad asya priyam abhi pātho aśyāṃ naro yatra devayavo madanti / urukramasya sa hi bandhur itthā viṣṇoḥ pade parame madhva utsaḥ //

The mortal trembles if he sees just two steps of him who sees the sun. But the third step no one dares [to see], not even winged birds in flight.[1]

Viṣṇu the cowherd guards the supreme abode, sustaining loved, immortal dwellings.[2]

Some modern scholars would like to think of Viṣṇu's later pre-eminence as due mainly to this *paramam padam*, his highest site, but although partly true this is not, by any means, the complete explanation of Viṣṇu's supremacy. This, as we have seen, is not just a matter of later literature but is already perceptible in the *Ṛg Veda*.

Let us now look at the Brāhmaṇa literature and what is said there about Viṣṇu and his three strides. The Brāhmaṇas are treatises on the sacrifice, and in them the Vedic verses are explained in relation to the sacrifice. There is a special part in the concluding ceremony of the new-moon sacrifice when the priest has to take three steps, and these are given a meaning relating them to the three strides of Viṣṇu:

And again why he strides the Viṣṇu-strides, is: Viṣṇu, truly is the sacrifice, by striding (*vi-kram*) he obtained for the gods that all-pervading power (*vikranti*) which now belongs to them. By his first step he gained this same [earth], by the second this aerial expanse, and by his last [step] the sky. And this same pervading power Viṣṇu, as the sacrifice, obtains by his strides for him [the sacrificer]: for this reason he strides the Viṣṇu-strides. Now it is indeed from this [earth] that most [beings] go [upwards].[3]

Here we have two facts of great importance: first the unmistakable identification of the sacrifice with Viṣṇu and then the explanation of his three strides as covering earth, air and sky. We also notice that by his strides Viṣṇu won for the rest of the gods their all-pervading power. Another speculation of the Brāhmaṇas on the famous three steps occurs in the *Śatapatha Brāhmaṇa* (1.2.5.1-7). There is related how the gods and the demons, all sons of Prajāpati, were fighting for the supremacy, and how the demons appropriated the earth for themselves without sharing it with the gods. In view of this the gods, headed by Viṣṇu as the sacrifice, went to the demons and asked for their part of the earth, but the demons, teasing them, said 'we'll only give you a part as big as this Viṣṇu here can lie upon.'[1] The gods accepted and, with fire and Vedic hymns, proceeded with the ceremony of the sacrifice, thereby winning the whole earth for themselves alone. In another version of the myth the gods make a wager that whoever of them was first in encompassing the end of the sacrifice, through austerities, fervour, faith, sacrifice and oblations should be the most eminent of all the gods. As Viṣṇu won the contest he is the most eminent of gods and at the same time is the sacrifice himself.

Whatever be the importance of these Brāhmaṇic speculations—very great indeed for the future development of mythology—we can only note here that they are all afterthoughts, that is, even if the Brāhmaṇic priests knew the real meaning of the Vedic hymns, they were so fond of ritual that they simply did not care to interpret them in a faithful manner. Rarely, if ever, do the sages who composed the *Brāhmaṇas* seem to care about what the authors of the Vedic hymns really meant, and perhaps to them this was unimportant, since they found the greatest relevance in the new magical ceremonies. These priestly speculations, however, give us invaluable data on the characteristics and importance of each god. We see that, at least in some circles, Viṣṇu is already considered the supreme god, since a myth has been invented to explain his supremacy. Now, should we conclude, as some scholars have done, that Viṣṇu's supremacy is traceable to the Vedic hymns only on account of his *paramam padam* and his creative character there, forgetting the evident fact that Viṣṇu is, according to the number of times that his name is mentioned, relatively unimportant? Or can we maintain with Keith[2] that this number does not demonstrate anything, since the *Ṛg Veda* is a collection of hymns on the *soma* sacrifice, and Viṣṇu has but a minor role in that sacrifice? But in that case, how are we to explain his Brāhmaṇic identifica-

1. *RV* 1.155.5. dve id asya kramaṇe svardṛśo'bhikhyāya martyo bhuraṇyati / tṛtīyam asya nakir ā dadharṣati vayaścana papatayantaḥ patatriṇaḥ //

2. *RV* 3.55.10. viṣṇur gopāḥ paramām pāti pāthaḥ priya dhāmāny amṛtā dadhānaḥ /

3. *Śatapatha Brāhmaṇa* 1.9.3.9; yadveva viṣṇukramānkramate / yajño viṣṇuḥ sa devebhya imām vikrānti vicakrame yaiṣāmiyaṃ vikrāntiridameva prathamena padena paspārāthedamantarikṣam dvitīyena divamuttamenaitāmvevaiṣa etasmai viṣṇuryajño vikrānti vikrāmate tasmādviṣṇukramānkramate tadvā'jñāta eva parācīnaṃ bhūyiṣṭhā iva kramate // tr. Julius Eggeling.

1. *SB* 1.2.5.4. te'surāḥ asūyantaḥ iva ucur yāvad eva eṣa viṣṇūr abhiśete tāvad vo dadmaḥ iti.

2. A.B. Keith, *Religion and Philosophy of the Veda and Upanishads*, 1925; rep. Motilal Banarsidass, Delhi, 1976, v.1, p. 10.

tion with the sacrifice, and Bergaigne's assumption that Viṣṇu is closely related to *soma*?[1] We would rather say that the Vedic Religion, as a polytheistic one, had many different gods, each with his own priests and special worshippers, besides the general mass of the people who would adore any one of them on different occasions. We are not speaking here of sectarianism, but of the specialisation normal in any polytheism. The natural god, however, was the warrior Indra, and to him the greatest part of hymns were addressed. It may be true that Viṣṇu was from early times considered the supreme god, but this can only have been recognised by his own priests and a few devotees, while for the rest of the people he was merely the god of the three steps. We might speculate that his votaries tried to convince the rest of the people that their god had the highest station and was the comrade of Indra, and gradually their propaganda had some effect.

As a companion and helper of Indra it is not strange that Viṣṇu rose to prominence. But, even if subordinate to the warrior chief, his votaries ever make clear their favourite god's special position: 'The divine Viṣṇu hurried to accompany the benign Indra, [himself] more benign.'[2] Here, it is Viṣṇu who seeks Indra's company but in many other places (e.g. *RV* 8.100.12) it is Indra himself who pleads for the help of Viṣṇu in his strife with Vṛtra and, strangely enough, the help that he receives is not in striking the demon but, apparently, in clearing up the field for the battle by his three steps. 'Then, when about to kill Vṛtra, Indra said, O Viṣṇu my friend, stride widely.'[3]

In still other hymns Indra is addressed conjointly with Viṣṇu and together they are described as drinking *soma*, striding widely and fighting against the *asuras*:

> This is worthy of being sung, O Indra and Viṣṇu, that you, inebriated by soma, widely strode. You extended the atmosphere and broadened the space for us to live [in]. You both have defeated [others] and [yourselves] are not defeated. None of these two has ever been defeated. Indra and Viṣṇu, when you fought you triply set in motion a thousand [?][4]

What seems important in this hymn is the cooperation of the gods in stretching out the worlds for human existence. This, in my opinion, is a very clear indication of a cosmogonical myth. This is still more evident in this line: 'You [Indra and Viṣṇu] have extended space for sacrifice in begetting Sūrya, Agni and Uṣas / You have vanquished in battles, O heroes, the Māyā of Vṛṣaśipra.'[1]

In some other passages it is not Viṣṇu who helps Indra but it is the latter who provides the strength for the former's feat: 'When by your energy Viṣṇu widely strode three steps / Then your two loved horses grew up.'[2] At last it was recognised that without Viṣṇu's help in the battle against Vṛtra, Indra could not have defeated the demon, and the poets sang how Indra pleaded to Viṣṇu for help: 'Viṣṇu, my friend, stride widely; Dyaus, give space for the *vajra* to fall. Let us kill Vṛtra, let us release the rivers, let them flow released by the force of Indra.'[3] This theme was amply elaborated in the Brāhmaṇic literature. In *Taittirīya Saṃhitā* 2.14.12 Vṛtra comes out from the sacrifice, owing to the hatred of Tvaṣṭṛ towards Indra. The monster was so terrible, covering the whole universe, that the same Tvaṣṭṛ feared him and Indra was overcome by terror. So Tvaṣṭṛ gave Indra the consecrated bolt, but even this would not suffice to kill the demon. Then he called Viṣṇu. This god extended himself in three parts, one in earth, one in the air, and the third in the sky, to impede the growth of the monster. After this Indra dared to attack the demon with the force of Viṣṇu's third portion on earth, and Vṛtra feared him thus aided and tried to pacify him, giving him a part of his strength, which Indra handed to Viṣṇu. Then he raised again his thunderbolt against Vṛtra, using the force of Viṣṇu's second portion in the air and, through his help, a second time Vṛtra retreated and offered his strength, which Indra took and gave to Viṣṇu. And for the third time the same happened, till Vṛtra surrendered the power by which he was the entire world and Indra

1. Abel Bergaigne, *La Réligion Vedique*, 1878-83, rep. Bibliothèque de l'école des hautes Études, Paris, 1963, p. 417.

2. *RV* 1.156.5. ā yo vivāya sacathāya daivya indrāya viṣṇuḥ sukṛte sukṛttaraḥ.

3. *RV* 4.18.11. athābravīd vṛtram indro haniṣyan sakhe viṣṇo vitaraṃ vi kramasva.

4. *RV* 6.69.5 & 8. indrāviṣṇu tat panayayyaṃ vām somasya mada uru cakramāthe / akṛṇutam antarikṣaṃ varīyo'prathataṃ jīvase no rajāṃsi // ubhā jigyathur na parā jayethe na parā jigye katarāś canainoḥ / indraś ca viṣṇo yad apaspṛdhethāṃ tredhā sahasraṃ vi tad airayethām //

1. *RV* 7.99.4. uruṃ yajñāya cakrathur u lokaṃ janayantā sūryam uṣāsam agnim / dasasya cid vṛṣaśiprasya māyā jaghnatur nara pṛtanajyesu; see Gonda, *Aspects* . . .; p. 30.

2. *RV* 8.12.27. yadā te viṣṇur ojasā trīṇi padā vicakrame / ād it te haryatā harī vavakṣatuḥ //

3. *RV* 8.100.12. sakhe viṣṇo vitaraṃ vi kramasya dyaur dehi lokaṃ vajrāya viṣkabhe / hanāva vṛtraṃ riṇacāva sindhūṃ indrasya yantu prasave viṣṛṣṭāḥ //

again gave it to Viṣṇu. In this myth we find an explanation to both Vedic references, the one in which Viṣṇu helps Indra and the other in which Indra gives force to Viṣṇu.

In one other passage of the same Veda[1] Viṣṇu does not appear in the battle till Indra raises his bolt for the third time and then supports the warrior god and orders him to kill the demon[2] *tam viṣṇuran-vatiṣṭhata jahīti*. And in yet another text Indra and Viṣṇu expel a horde of demons from a sacrificial litany.[3] So we see that the Indra-Viṣṇu partnership became with time widely recognised, which makes us suppose that there was really some symbolic meaning in their alliance.

Let us now see what modern scholars have to say on all this material. We have already said that some Indologists have emphasised the mainly solar character of the god; this is due mainly to the ancient interpretations of the native commentators. So in the *Bṛhaddevatā* attributed to Śaunaka, a work that intends to give a summary of all the Vedic gods and myths, we find the name of Viṣṇu among those of the sun. There we see already quoted a previous authority, a certain Medhātithi, which indicates that this interpretation was current from very early times. The line in question reads: 'Because the three (*trīṇi*) regions (*rajāṃsi*) shine with brilliance as his footsteps, therefore Medhātithi pronounces him [to be] Viṣṇu of the three strides [*trivikrama*).[4] And at the end of the list of the sun's names the etymology of the name of Viṣṇu is given in the following manner :

> Viṣṇu may be [the root] *viṣ* (*viṣṇāti*—be active) or *viś* (*viśati* - to enter), [or] from *veviṣ* (*veveṣṭi*) (?) expressing pervasion: [he] is [thus] explained as the Sun who is everything and is contained in everything.[5]

This interpretation was sustained by Auguste Barth[6] who, however, notes that: 'Quand le soleil est invoquē comme dieu suprēme. c'est de préférence sous d'autres noms.'[1] In 1891 Hopkins admits[2] that all evidences in the Veda indicate that Viṣṇu is a solar God. Macdonell is of the same opinion[3] and after him Grierson,[4] Griswold,[5] Keith,[6] Mrinal Dasgupta,[7] Dandekar[8] and Gonda[9] all adhere to this interpretation, even if they emphasise at the same time one or more of the god's other characteristics.

Against this opinion we hear the voices of R.G. Bhandarkar,[10] who emphasises Viṣṇu's highest step as the main factor in his elevation to the supreme rank, Barnett,[11] who finds that the solar identification is an afterthought and believes that the god's identification with the sacrifice is his most important trait, Oldenberg,[12] and, more recently,[13] Kuiper,[14] who holds that Viṣṇu's main aspect is that of being a symbol of the centre and the totality of the cosmos.

What are the conclusions we can arrive at after reviewing the texts in dispute? As we saw, Viṣṇu's pre-eminent characteristic is that he strode thrice, and it is mainly because of this fact that many maintain that he is the sun. From the times of Yāska (500 B.C. approx.), and even earlier, since he quotes two authors who preceded him, this view has been held, the only discrepancy being about the exact place of each of the three steps. Śākapūṇi, quoted by Yāska, opined that the three strides referred to

1. *TS* 6.5.1.1-2.
2. Note the resemblance to the situation at the beginning of the *BG*.
3. *AB* 3.50.3: so'bravīd indraḥ kaś cāhaṃ cemān ito 'surān notsyāvahā ity ahaṃ cety abravīd viṣṇus.
4. *BD* 2.64: trīṇi bhānti rajāṃsyasya yatpadāni tu tejasā / tena medhātithiḥ prāha viṣṇumenaṃ trivikramam // tr. Macdonell.
5. *BD* 2.69: A.A. Macdonell, *The Bṛhad-devatā Attributed to Śaunaka*, 1904, rep. Motilal Banarsidass, Delhi, 1965, v. 1, p. 17; viṣṇāterviśatervā syād veveṣṭervyāptikarmaṇaḥ / viṣṇurnirucyate sūryaḥ sarvaṃ sarvāntaraśca yaḥ //; in Monier-Williams *SED* we find vevī-vevīte, to go, to pervade.
6. A. Barth, Les *Religions de l'Inde*, 1885, rep. in *Oeuvres Complètes d'Auguste Barth*, *Ernest Leroux*, Paris 1914, v. 1.

1. *Ibid.*, p. 150.
2. E.W. Hopkins, *The Religions of India*, Ginn & Co., Boston 1891, p. 41.
3. A.A. Macdonell, *History of Sanskrit Literature*, 1899, rep. Motilal Banarsidass, Delhi, 1971, p. 66.
4. G. Grierson, 'Bhakti', *ERE*, v. 3 1911, p. 541.
5. H.D. Griswold, *Religion of the Ṛg Veda*, 1923, rep. Motilal Banarsidass, Delhi 1971.
6. A.B. Keith, *Religion and Philosophy* ..., v. 1, p. 109.
7. M. Dasgupta, 'Early Viṣṇuism and Nārāyaṇīya Worship', *IHQ*, v. 7, 1931, p. 103.
8. R.N. Dandekar, 'Viṣṇu in the Veda', in *Studies in Indology, Commemorative Volume to P.V. Kane*, Poona Oriental Series, Poona 1941, p. 99.
9. J. Gonda, *Aspects* ..., pp. 25-28.
10. R.G. Bhandarkar, *Vaiṣṇavism, Śaivism and Minor Religious Sects*, 1913, rep. Indological Book House, Varanasi, 1965, pp. 33-3.
11. L.D. Barnett, *Hindu Gods and Heroes*, London 1922.
12. H. Oldenberg, *Die Religion des Veda*, Cotta'sche Buchhandlung Nachfolges, Stuttgart, 1923, p. 232.
13. Sten Konow (S. Konow and P. Tuxen, *The Religions of India*, Copenhagen 1949, p. 61f.) denies that Viṣṇu is the sun-god, even if he has some solar characteristics.
14. F.B.J. Kuiper, 'The three strides of Viṣṇu', *Indological Studies in Honor of W.N. Brown*, American Oriental Society, New Haven 1962, passim.

'a threefold existence, on earth, in the atmosphere, and in the sky.'[1] Aurṇavabha, also quoted by the author of the *Nirukta*, opined on his part that the strides were meant to refer to the hill where the sun rises, the meridian, and the hill where the sun sets.[2] But, as L.D. Barnett said,[3] how can we know that this is not an afterthought, a posterior elaboration to explain apparently unmeaningful Vedic verses? We can argue that the Brāhmaṇic myths were constructed in the same way. On the other hand there are a very few verses in the Veda that really support this interpretation, as the one where his highest position is compared to an eye in the sky,[4] and the hymns where the sun-god Savitṛ is referred to in the same terms as those addressed to Viṣṇu.[5] Therefore we conclude that though, despite these last references, Viṣṇu is not considered in the Veda as the sun, he certainly presents some solar characteristics in the same way as he presents fertility characteristics, vegetative characteristics and ritual characteristics, that is, according to his character as a universal god.

The passages referring to his other traits, especially to his association with Indra, have been overlooked. A scholar such as Dandekar even claims that this association 'is clearly superficial',[6] misunderstanding completely the cosmogonical significance of the myth of Vṛtrahan. It was Norman Brown[7] who first made clear the meaning of this creation myth, even if he did not emphasise the role of Viṣṇu in it. But, after seeing how Viṣṇu is the god of expansion and extensiveness, of pervasion and wide space, we can understand how he came to be associated with the Indra-Vṛtra cosmogonic myth, being a natural complement to Indra's function as the power that liberates the nourishing waters restrained by the demon Vṛtra.

Among the other interpretations on the symbolism of Viṣṇu relevant to us are those by Professors R.N. Dandekar and F.B.J. Kuiper. The first notices,

1. treddhā-bhāvāya pṛthivyām antarikṣe divi; *Nirukta* 12.19.
2. samārohane viṣṇupade gayaśirasi; *ibid.*
3. *Hindu Gods and Heroes*, 1922, p. 38.
4. divīva cakṣur ātatam; *RV* 1.22.20.
5. *RV* 4. 53 and 4. 54.
6. R.N. Dandekar, 'Viṣṇu in the Veda', in *Studies in Indology to P.V. Kane*, Poona 1941 p. 96: 'Obviously loose and artificial connection', p. 97.
7. W.N. Brown, 'The Creation Myth of the *Ṛg Veda*', *JAOS*, v. 1942; 'Theories of Creation in the *Rig Veda*', *JAOS*, v. 85, 1965.

on somewhat loose grounds, the phallic character of Viṣṇu.[1] That he has a generative aspect is amply known[2] but this is far from affirming that Viṣṇu is identified with the phallus on the basis of the epithet *śipiviṣṭa*. Despite this exaggeration Dandekar illuminates several aspects of Viṣṇu's symbolism. On the other side Professor Kuiper made a magistral study of Viṣṇu as a symbol of totality, emphasising his ambiguous character to demonstrate that he includes everything in himself. Kuiper also remarks on the importance of Viṣṇu in the creation myth. Gonda has more recently criticised Kuiper on minor details and technicalities, leaving, however, in our opinion, his main thesis untouched[3] and even, to some extent, adhering to it: 'there is much truth in the time honoured interpretation of the god's character as representing pervasiveness and spatial extensiveness, and especially that pervasiveness which is essential to the establishment and maintenance of our cosmos and beneficial to the interests of men and gods.'[4]

On the other hand Gonda's contribution to the study of this god[5] is at the moment unsurpassed both for its accuracy and its comprehensiveness. He surveys all the different aspects of Viṣṇu's complex mythology and symbolism, demonstrating the real impossibility of correctly interpreting him in just one sense. On our part we recognise the richness and complexity of the personality of Viṣṇu and would only like to emphasise his role as a creator and protector god as relevant to his later identification with Kṛṣṇa and the inclusion of this aspect in Kṛṣṇa's mythology.

ii. NĀRĀYAṆA

One of the first mentions of this deity is made in the tenth *maṇḍala* of the *Ṛg Veda* in the famous hymn to the Puruṣa (*RV* 10. 90); there however he does not appear in the hymn proper but only as the *ṛṣi* or seer who first sang it. This fact has led many to support the euhemeristic theory that affirms that originally there existed a person called by that name meaning 'son or descendant of Nara', who for some reasons was later deified. Another appearance of

1. Dandekar, 'Viṣṇu ...', pp. 108-110.
2. Gonda, *Aspects ...*, pp. 11-21.
3. Jan Gonda, *Viṣṇuism and Śivaism*, The Athlone Press, London 1970.
4. *Ibid.*, p. 5; also *Aspects of Early Viṣṇuism*, 1954, rep. Motilal Banarsidass, Delhi 1969, p. iii.
5. *Ibid., ibid.*

Nārāyaṇa occurs in the *Śatapatha Brāhmaṇa*, where he is called Puruṣa-Nārāyaṇa, thus identifying him with the deity of the Vedic hymn above mentioned (*SB* 12.3.4.1 and 13.6.1.1). Now it seems to us very improbable that, in so conservative a tradition as the Brāhmaṇic only a recognised *ṛṣi*, that is, a poet, a human person, could be promoted straight away to the ranks of the gods. That does not occur with any other name. But looking at the Veda itself we can see what could have happened. In the tenth book of the *Ṛg Veda* there appear another 22 hymns, in each of which the deity corresponds with the *ṛṣi* or poet that sang it. What does this mean? We suppose that these hymns were not kept in the hands of any of the families in charge of transmitting the sacred lore, the Āṅgirasas, Paulastyas, Vasiṣṭhas, Ātreyas, etc., so that they did not have any recognised author. In this case, what else could the compilers do than attribute them to the same deities as those to which they were dedicated? And we cannot admit that such names as Hiraṇyagarbha, Yama, Yamī, Viśvakarman or Prajāpati were common at that age, since these gods are given as family names the ones that correspond to them according to mythology. So Yama is called Vaivasvata or descendant of Vivasvat, that is, the sun; Hiraṇyagarbha is called Prājāpatya or descendant of Prajāpati; and Yajña, or the sacrifice is also called Prājāpatya; whereas Viśvakarman is called Bhauvana, that is 'proceeding or belonging to the world or creation'. And Indra, Indranī and Vāc are simply mentioned with no family name.[1]

This is what may have happened in the case of Nārāyaṇa, and so we have the hymn 10.90 addressed to Puruṣa-Nārāyaṇa and supposedly composed by the same Puruṣa, 'the descendent of Nara or Man' (another word for Puruṣa). And it cannot be argued that the name refers to a descendant of Nara, the *ṛṣi* of hymns 35 and 36 of the sixth maṇḍala of the same Veda, since that *ṛṣi* belonged to the family of Bhāradvāja[2] and thus Nārāyaṇa should be styled Bhāradvāja and not 'descendant of Nara'.

The Epic tradition of two sages Nara and Nārāyaṇa, of which the second is the most prominent, twin brothers and not father and son, could be just an elaboration of the established fact of the mention of both names as *ṛṣis* in the *Ṛg Veda*, although unrelated and included there for quite different reasons, as we have seen. Besides, in the Epic it is stated that Nara and Nārāyaṇa were the sons of *Dharma* (*Mbh.* 12.321.8-9; 16-18) without any reference whatsoever to any Bhāradvāja that would connect them to the Vedic *ṛṣi*. And in still another Vedic passage it is related how Nara was born from the austerities of Nārāyaṇa, so that in strict logic the roles of father and son are inverted and therefore we can conclude that the name Nārāyaṇa is not a patronymic.

An explanation of the name is given by Manu and in the *Mahābhārata* (*Manu* 1.10; *Mbh.* 1.328. 35 b, c), deriving it from a pseudo-word *nāras*, water, meaning 'he who dwells in the waters'. It seems to us that this is just an elaboration on the Vedic passage that mentions Hiraṇyagarbha or the primeval germ lying in the waters containing all the gods and all beings in a receptacle that rests in his navel—an image already used in the Epic for Nārāyaṇa (*RV.* 10.82.5-6; *Mbh.* 3.272.38). However, in the same passage of the Epic, in the previous line, a reasonable explanation of the name is given: *narāṇāmayanaṃ khyātamahamekaḥ sanātanaḥ*, 'I am known as the one eternal refuge [or goal] of men' (*Mbh.* 12.328.35a), an interpretation that fits well with the description of the Puruṣa in *RV* 10.90 as producing all men and beings from his body, and that also corresponds to the description given in the *Śatapatha Brāhmaṇa's* account of Nārāyaṇa's sacrifice by which he 'became all this.'

Leaving aside the problem of the name Nārāyaṇa, let us pay attention to the contents of the several versions of his myth. The Vedic hymn dedicated to him is connected with the sacrifice and with the cosmogony:

> A thousand heads had Puruṣa, a thousand eyes, a thousand feet; He, having covered the earth on all sides, extended beyond [it] by ten fingers [breadth].
> Puruṣa is verily this all, what has been and what will be. And he is the lord of immortality, which by food he outgrows.[1]

Here we can see in the description of the primeval man the rudiments of the Upaniṣadic conception of Ātman. Puruṣa has a thousand, i.e. infinite heads, eyes and feet. He fills the Universe and even so surpasses it by ten fingers. He is all the past and future.

1. T. Aufrecht, *Hymnen des Rigveda*, 1877, rep., Otto Harrassowitz, Wiesbaden 1968, v. 2, pp. 497-506.
2. *Ibid.*, p. 481.

1. *RV* 10.90.1-2; sahasraśīrṣā puruṣaḥ sahasrākṣaḥ sahasrapāt / sa bhūmiṃ viśvato vṛtvā aty atiṣṭhad daśāṅgulam // puruṣa evedaṃ sarvaṃ yad bhūtaṃ yacca bhāvyam / utāmṛtatvasyeśāno yad annenātirohati //

He is manifested and unmanifested, what we see and perceive is only a fourth of his whole being, the other three fourths being absolutely transcendent; 'With three quarters Puruṣa rose upwards, one quarter of him was here again. Then he extended everywhere to what eats and what eats not.'[1]

So we have this Universal Person comprehending the created and the uncreated, pervading all the Universe and transcending it. Now the poet gives us an obscure and symbolic genealogy of the world and the soul: 'From that was born Virāj and from Virāj again Puruṣa. When he was born he surpassed the earth in the back and the front.'[2] Who is this Virāj? It is a feminine entity whose name means: ruling far and wide, sovereign, excellent, splendid,[3] and therefore related to the later concept of *śakti*, but here just an example of the cosmogonies caused by the division of a first principle in two parts: a masculine and a feminine. From them a second Puruṣa is born. This evolved giant is sacrificed by the gods in order to bring out the rest of creation.[4]

> From his mind was born the moon, from his eye the sun was born, Indra and Agni from his mouth, from his breath Vāyu was born.
>
> From his navel was the atmosphere, from his head the sky was developed. The earth from his two feet, the directions from the ear. Thus they formed the worlds.[5]

So we see that since his first apparition Nārāyaṇa is connected both with the cosmogony and sacrifice. When he next appears in the Brāhmaṇic literature these themes accompany him. In *Śatapatha Brāhmaṇa* 12.3.4. he is already called by the compound name Puruṣa-Nārāyaṇa (*puruṣaṃ ha nārāyaṇam prajāpatir uvāca*) so making the pseudo-*ṛṣi* and the primeval man the same person. Here again we find Puruṣa-Nārāyaṇa identifying himself with the whole cosmos through the sacrifice. Prajāpati bids him sacrifice and tells him how to do it and to recite the following: 'In me be light, in me might, in me glory, in me everything.' Which words Prajāpati explains: 'Now light, indeed, is this [terrestrial] world, might the air, world, glory the heavens, and what other worlds there are, they are everything.' The next verses identify light, might and glory with the gods Agni, Vāyu and Āditya, with the three Vedas, and with speech, breath, and the eye, which identifications are also made in the Puruṣa hymn.[1] Lastly Nārāyaṇa ends this sacrifice saying:

> All the worlds have I placed within my own self, and my own self have I placed within all the worlds. All the gods have I placed within my own self, and my own self have I placed within all the gods. All the Vedas have I placed within my own self, and my own self have I placed within all the Vedas. All the vital airs have I placed within my own self and my own self I have placed within all the vital airs.[2]

In this litany the pantheistic tone is notable as well as the assumption that this universality is gained by means of ritual sacrifice. In the other passage in the *Śatapatha Brāhmaṇa* that mentions Nārāyaṇa this is no less emphasised. There we are told how Nārāyaṇa wished to become the whole cosmos and how he managed to obtain his wish:

> Puruṣa-Nārāyaṇa desired 'Would that I overpassed all beings, would that I alone were everything here [this universe].' He beheld this five days' sacrificial performance, the Puruṣamedha, and took it, and performed offering therewith; and having performed offering therewith he overpassed all being, and became everything here.[3]

Now, it is clear that Puruṣa-Nārāyaṇa is identified with the totality of the Universe in all three texts and that this is brought about through sacrifice. In the Vedic hymn and in this last passage quoted it is a human sacrifice that is prescribed, in the first

1. *RV.* 10.90.4; tripād ūrdhva udaitpuruṣaḥ pādo'syehābhavat punaḥ / tato viṣvaṃ vyakrāmat sāśanānasāne abhi //

2. *RV.* 10.90.5; tasmād virāḷ ajāyata virājo adhi pūruṣaḥ / sa jāto atyaricyata paścād bhūmiṃ atho puraḥ //

3. M. Monier-Williams, *A Sanskrit-English Dictionary*, 1899, p. 982.

4. Professor Basham suggests that these gods were also the product of Virāj i.e. younger brothers of Puruṣa. 'Review of Jan Gonda's *Viṣṇuism and Śivaism*', *IIJ*, v. 18, 1976, p. 289.

5. *RV* 10.90.13-14; candramā manaso jātaś cakṣoḥ sūryo ajāyata / mukhādindraścāgniśca prāṇādvāyur ajāyata // nābhyā āsīdantarikṣam śīrṣṇo dyauḥ samavartata / padbhyāṃ bhūmir diśaḥ śrotrāt tathā lokāṃ akalpayan //

1. *SB* 12.3.4.6-7; ... mayi bhargo mayi maho mayi yaśo mayi sarvamiti // ayaṃ vai loko bhargaḥ / antarikṣaloko maho dyauryaśo ye'nye lokāstatsarvam //

2. *SB* 12.3.4.11; sarvāṃllokānātmannadhiṣu sarveṣu lokeṣvātmānamadhāṃ sarvāndevānātmannadhiṣu sarveṣu deveṣvātmānamadhāṃ sarvānvedānātmannadhiṣu sarveṣu deveṣvātmānamadhāṃ sarvānprāṇānātmannadhiṣu sarveṣu prāṇeṣvātmānamadhamityakṣitā ....

3. *SB* 13.6.1.1 : puruṣo ha nārāyaṇo'kāmayata'atitiṣṭheyaṃ sarvāṇi bhūtānyahamevedaṃ sarvaṃ syām'iti / sa etam puruṣamedham pañcarātraṃ yajñakratum apaśyat tam āharat tenāyajata teneṣṭva'tyatiṣṭhat sarvāṇi bhūtānīdaṃ sarvamabhavat / atitiṣṭhati sarvāṇi bhūtānīdam sarvam bhavati yaḥ evaṃ vidvānpuruṣamedhena yajate yo vai etad evaṃ veda // tr. J. Eggeling.

case made by the gods and the *ṛṣis*, in the second probably self-immolation. There has been a great deal of speculation on the name of the sacrifice mentioned here, *pañcarātra sattra* or 'Sacrifice of five days [or nights]', due to the fact that a popular Vaiṣṇava sect later took that name probably from this source.

There is another reference to Puruṣa-Nārāyaṇa in the Vedic literature that agrees with our interpretation. It is the *Uttaranārāyaṇānuvāka*, an appendix added to the Puruṣa hymn in the White *Yajur Veda* and repeated in the *Taittirīya Āraṇyaka*:

> In the beginning he was formed, collected from water, earth, and Viśvakarman's essence. / Fixing the form thereof Tvaṣṭar proceedeth. This was at first the mortal's birth and godhead. // I know this mighty Puruṣa whose colour is like the sun, beyond the reach of darkness. / He only who knows him leaves death behind him. There is no path save this alone to travel. // In the womb moves Prajāpati: he never becoming born, is born in sundry figures. / The wise discern the womb from which he springeth. In him alone stand all existing creatures. // He who gives light and heat to the gods, first, foremost Agent of the Gods, Born are the Gods - to him the bright, the holy one, be reverence. / Thus spake the gods at first, as they begat the bright and holy one: the brahman who may know thee thus shall have the gods in his control. // Beauty and fortune are thy wives: each side of thee are Day and Night. The constellations are thy form: The Aśvins are thy open jaws. / Wishing, wish yonder world for me, wish that the Universe be mine. //[1]

The last verses are clearly related to the Puruṣa hymn: 'each side of thee are Day and Night. The constellations are Thy form: the Aśvins are thy open jaws' and the rest of the litany is likewise reminiscent of that imagery. He is called Prajāpati and special reference is made to the womb where he was born. This motif reminds us immediately of the Epic figure of Nārāyaṇa, born in the waters from a golden egg and producing from himself the world (*Mbh.* 3.272.44; 12.207.13). Now we will inquire whence proceeds this image, afterwards always associated with Nārāyaṇa. Does it come from the fanciful etymology given in *Manu* (1.10) and the *Mahābhārata* (12.328.35)? Or was it formed from a previous image in the mythology? We think that it proceeds from such poetic metaphors as those used in the *Uttaranārāyaṇānuvāka* to express cosmological and metaphysical conceptions, 'the wise discern the womb from which he springeth. In him alone stand all existing creatures.'

We are inclined to believe that with time the figure of Puruṣa-Nārāyaṇa, symbolic of the sacrifice and the origin of the Universe, was associated with the figure of Hiraṇyagarbha and other poetic images of the creation of the world in the primitive aquatic chaos, to form the representation of Nārāyaṇa that we know: a sleeping giant floating (usually on a serpent but sometimes on a fig leaf) over the waters of a primeval ocean and containing in himself the whole Universe. This is the image that the *Ṛg Veda* presents us in a hymn to Viśvakarman:

> That which is beyond heaven and beyond this earth, beyond the gods and the *asuras*. What primal embryo did the waters produce, where all the gods looked on?
>
> That primal embryo the waters bore where all the gods gathered. In the navel of the unborn was placed the One in which all beings stood.[1]

Here we have the *ur*-text of that iconic representation already described. We cannot make an interpretation of the symbols because the different versions differ widely in their presentation of the imagery and, as in all Indian mythology, the whole is a rather confused story. However, we can present the more evident points in a simpler structure for its analysis. In the verses quoted we see at least two elements, the waters and the germ that lies in them. It is valid to suppose that there is a third element which deposited the germ in the waters. This third element has to be Viśvakarman, 'the creator of everything', to

1. *VS* 31.17-22; tr. R.T.H. Griffith, *Hymns of the Yajur Veda* (1898) Chowkhamba, Varanasi 1963; adbhyaḥ saṃbhūtaḥ pṛthivyai rasācca viśvakarmaṇaḥ samavartatāgre / tasya tvaṣṭā vidadhadrūpameti tanmartyasya devatvamājānamagre // vedāhametaṃ puruṣaṃ mahāntamādityavarṇaṃ tamasaḥ parastāt / tameva viditvā'timṛtyumeti nānyaḥ panthā vidyate 'yanāya // prajāpatiścarati garbhe antarajāyamāno bahudhā vijāyate / tasya yoniṃ paripaśyanti dhīrāstasminha tasthurbhuvanāni viśvā // yo devebhya ātapati yo devānāṃ purohitaḥ / pūrvo yo devebhyo jāto namo rucāya brāhmaye // rucaṃ brāhmam janayanto devā agre tadabruvan / yastvaivaṃ brahmaṇo vidyāttasya devā asanvaśe // śrīśca te lakṣmīśca patnyāvahorātre pārśve nakṣatrāṇi rūpamaśvinau vyāttam / iṣṇānniṣāṇāmuṃ ma iṣāṇa sarvalokaṃ ma iṣāṇa //

1. *RV* 10.82.5-6; paro divā paraḥ enā pṛthivyā paro devebhir asurair yad asti / kaṃ svid garbhaṃ prathamaṃ dadhre āpo yatra devāḥ samapaśyanta viśve // tam id garbhaṃ prathamaṃ dadhre āpo yatra devāḥ samāgacchanti viśve / ajasya nābhāv adhy ekam arpitam yasmin viśvāni bhuvanāni tasthuḥ //

whom the hymn is dedicated and who is supposedly even the poet who composed it, 'Viśvakarman is wide-knowing, mighty, creator and controller, verily, the supreme appearance.'[1] In the hymn immediately preceding (*RV* 10.81) Viśvakarman is sung as making a sacrifice for the sake of creation and coming down to the world as an archetype of man, 'He the *ṛṣi*, our father, sat down as priest and offered in oblation all these beings; He, desiring wealth by his prayers, concealed the first [beings?] and entered the following [ones].'[2] This connects him beyond doubt with Puruṣa-Nārāyaṇa. And even more clearly, a few lines after, we find him described in the same terms as Puruṣa in the hymn (10.90) addressed to the latter, 'He had eyes on all sides, mouths on all sides, arms on all sides, feet on all sides',[3] i.e. represented as the primeval giant.

This Viśvakarman, otherwise called Prajāpati, is, no doubt, referred to in the hymns addressed to Ka, 'Who', the unknown god, 'He, the moon, who created the wide and bright waters',[4] 'He who by his might looked over the waters carrying dexterity, giving birth to sacrifice',[5] 'He sustained the earth, the heaven and this [all].'[6] And the golden germ is associated with Agni, the fire, 'When the great waters came bearing all [the universe] as a germ, generating Agni.'[7] So here we have the same pattern of the three elements : a first total, but rather diffused, creator or generator; a middle chaotic but fertile medium represented by the water; and a third person, a kind of universal giant whose body is the Universe. This pattern is again repeated in 10.129 as it was in 10.90, the Puruṣa hymn. There we find the first Puruṣa, Virāj, that is the waters, and the Adhi-Puruṣa or cosmic giant. In 10.129 we read :

Then even nothingness was not, nor existence. There was no air then, nor the heavens beyond it. What covered it?

Where was it? In whose keeping? Was there then cosmic water, in depths unfathomed?

Then there were neither death nor immortality, nor was there then the torch of night and day. The One breathed windlessly and self-sustaining. There was that One then, and there was no other.

At first there was only darkness wrapped in darkness. All this was only unillumined water. That One which came to be, enclosed in nothing, arose at last, born of the power of heat.[1]

Here again we have the triad father, mother, son in the first *Tad ekam*, 'That One', the waters, and the second *Tad ekam*, 'born by the great tapas'. In the last line we find the word *tucchya*, 'void' or 'nothingness' that can be read as 'husk' or 'shell'.[2] It is very probable that the Vedic poet had this double meaning in mind and was referring to the golden egg deposited in the waters. This is more plausible if we remember that Agni, 'the fire', was said to be born in the egg (*RV* 10.121.7) and here the One is born through *tapas*, a word that also means 'heat'.

We can turn now to that other symbol associated with the figure of Nārāyaṇa in the Epic and the iconic representations, the stem and flower growing from his navel, a vegetal symbol from which, in turn, will spring all creation. We have seen how this symbol has been already outlined in the hymn to Viśvakarman (*RV* 10.82.6), but it is in the *Atharva-Veda* where it takes a more definite form. There, in a version of the Puruṣa Hymn (*AV* 19.6), appears a verse that does not occur in the *Ṛg Veda* nor anywhere else. This verse seems to allude to a *soma* plant growing out of Puruṣa-Nārāyaṇa: 'Seven times seventy rays (*aṃśu*) were born from the head of the great god, of king Soma, when born out of Puruṣa.'[3] Here the word *aṃśu* alludes not only to the rays of the moon but mainly to 'a filament [especially of the soma-plant]'.[4] This is acknowledged

1. *RV* 10.82.2; viśvakarma vimanaḥ ad vihayaḥ dhātā vidhātā parama uta saṃdṛk.

2. *RV* 10.81.1; ya imā viśvā bhuvanāni juhvad ṛṣir hotā ny asīdat pitā naḥ / sa āśisā draviṇam icchamānaḥ prathamacchad avarān āviveśa //

3. *RV* 10.81.3; viśvatocakṣur uta viśvatomukho viśvatobāhur uta viśvataspāt.

4. *RV* 10.121.9; yaścāpaścandrā bṛhatīr jajāna.

5. *RV* 10.121.8; yaś cid āpo mahinā paryapaśyad dakṣan dadhānā janayantīr yajñam.

6. *RV* 10.121.1; sa dādhāra pṛthivīṃ dyām utemām.

7. *RV* 10.121.7; āpo ha yad bṛhatīr viśvam āyan garbhaṃ dadhānā janayantīr agnim.

1. *RV* 10.129.1-3; nāsad āsīn no sad āsīt tadānīṃ nāsīd rajo no vyomā paro yat / kim āvarīvaḥ kuha kasya śarmann ambhaḥ kim āsīd gahanaṃ gabhīram // na mṛtyur āsīd amṛtaṃ na tarhi na rātryā ahna āsīt praketaḥ / ānīd avātam svadhayā tad ekaṃ tasmād dhānyan na paraḥ kiṃ canāsa // tama āsīt tamasā gūḷham agré'praketaṃ salilaṃ sarvam ā idam / tucchyenābhv apihitaṃ yad āsīt tapasas tan mahināјāyataikam // tr. A. L. Basham.

2. J. Muir, *OST*, v.4, p. 4; M. Muller, *Vedic Hymns, SBE*, v.46, p. F.D.K. Bosch, *The Golden Germ*, Mouton 1960, p. 52; Monier-Williams, *SED*, takes it as 'void' but gives the alternate meaning of 'chaff' for *tuccha, tucchyaka.*

3. *AV* 19.6.16; Mūrdhno devasya vṛhato aṃśavaḥ sapta saptatīḥ / rājñāḥ somasyājayanta jātasyapuruṣādadhi // tr. Whitney.

4. Monier-Williams, *SED*, p. 1.

by the commentary attributed to Sāyaṇa but we should note that whereas nowhere else is it said that the moon surges from the body of Puruṣa, except as a part of the whole Universe and then manifesting only the giant's mind, it is frequent to find mention of the growing of a plant from the body lying in the waters.

So in the *Atharva-Veda* we find the verse: 'A great monster (*yakṣa*) in the midst of the creation (*bhuvana*), strode (*krānta*) in penance on the back of the water - in it are set whatever gods there are, like the branches of a tree round about the trunk.'[1] The imagery of the universal tree is here associated with that of the primeval waters for the first time, and we see that we are looking at a process of formation in religious imagery where diverse mythological metaphors are combined to form a new image. It is a process in which we cannot say what comes first, the mythological concept or the literary metaphor soon translated into plastic shapes till it becomes fixed in the iconology. We have another example of this process in the legend of the sage Vasiṣṭha, who in the *Ṛg Veda* (7.33) is said to have been born from the seed of Mitra-Varuṇa spilt at the sight of the nymph Urvaśī and deposited by the gods in a lotus floating in the primeval waters. In the *Bṛhad-Devatā* (approx. 6th century B.C.) we find this account of the myth: '... Then, as the waters were being taken up (*gṛhyamāṇa*), Vasiṣṭha was [found] standing on a lotus (*puṣkara*). There on every side the All-gods supported the lotus. Arising out of that water [Vasiṣṭha] then performed great austerity.'[2] Here all the gods are not set in the divine plant as in *AV* 10.7.38, but they themselves sustain the lotus, a variant of the Universal Giant from whose body the lotus grows.

It is evident that the Universal-tree motif was very widespread, as we see in these examples and in a few others taken from Iconography, such as these presented by Coomaraswamy[3] from Sanchi, Bhumara, and Amaravati, and by F.D.K. Bosch[4] from Sanchi, Barhut and Amaravati, where we can see a dwarfish *yakṣa* from whose mouth or navel grows a tree that embraces flowers, fruits, animals and men in its branches, suggesting in fact that even beasts and men are produced from the tree. In these representations and in those of Nārāyaṇa-Śeṣaśāyin that appear in the Gupta period (Udayagiri, Deogarh), where the motif is already combined with that of the serpent, we have the last evolution of the poetic image that began in the *Ṛg Veda* as the symbol of the first creation: the golden germ in the waters, associated successively with the *yakṣas*, the Universal tree, and the Cosmic serpent.

1. *AV* 10.7.38; mahadyakṣaṃ bhuvanasya madhye tapasi krāntaṃ salilasya pṛṣṭhe/tapasmin chayante ya u ke ca devā vṛkṣasya skandhaḥ parita iva śākhāḥ // tr. Whitney.

2. *BD* 5.154-155; .. tato'psu gṛhyamāṇāsu vasiṣṭhaḥ puṣkare sthitaḥ // sarvatra puṣkaraṃ tatra viśvedevā adhārayan / atthāya salilāttasmād atha tepe mahattapaḥ // tr. Macdonell.

3. A. K. Coomaraswamy, *Yakṣas*, (1931), Munshiram Manoharlal Delhi 1971, pt. ii, plates 29-5 and 30-1 and 3.

4. F.D.K. Bosch, *The Golden Germ*, plates 5a-b and 32b-c; vide also Pramod Chandra, *Stone Sculpture in the Allahabad Museum*, American Institute of Indian Studies, Poona 1970, plates 41b and 123.

Another association included in the Cosmic tree symbolism is its characterisation as *Axis Mundi* and its identification with the Vedic sacrificial post (*yūpa*) and the pillar-god Skambha of the *Atharva Veda* (10.7). This among other circumstances may have led to the identification of Nārāyaṇa with Viṣṇu, a god who also is assimilated to the symbolism of the centre and the *Axis Mundi*.[1] This characterisation suits very well Nārāyaṇa's aspect of Universal god, which we have tried to emphasise here. According to our views Nārāyaṇa is a deified priestly speculation of the time of the Brāhmaṇas on the lines of the Puruṣa Sūkta, and we dismiss the euhemeristic view as a later concoction of the time of the *Mahābhārata* and without any real historical basis.

iii. KṚṢṆA IN THE *ṚG VEDA*

Although the mentions of Kṛṣṇa in the *Ṛg Veda* are very few and rather dubious, several scholars have suggested that the Kṛṣṇa or Kṛṣṇas of those hymns are identical with the Kṛṣṇa of the later tradition or at least with a figure that precedes him.

In the first place we have a certain *ṛṣi* or poet bearing the name Kṛṣṇa who composed hymn 8.85. He was the father of one Viśvaka who sings the next hymn, dedicated to the Aśvins like that of his father. By the benevolence of these gods his son Viṣṇāpu was restored to Viśvaka, a fact that is mentioned in two other hymns to the Aśvins:[2]

> To the son of Kṛṣṇa, [who] supplicated you, praised you, strove after you, O Nāsatyas, by your powers, like a lost animal, gave [back] to see, Viṣṇāpu to Viśvaka.[3]

1. J. Gonda, *Aspects....*, p. 81; F. B. J. Kuiper, 'The Three Strides....', p. 144 .

2. *RV* 1.116 and 117.

3. *RV* 1.116.23; avasyate stuvate kṛṣṇiyāya ṛjūyate nāsatyā sacībhiḥ / paśuṃ na naṣṭam iva darśanāya viṣṇāpvāṃ dadathur viśvakāya //

Macdonell and Keith[1] suggest that 'this Kṛṣṇa may be identical with Kṛṣṇa Āṅgirasa mentioned in the *Kauśītaki Brāhmaṇa* (30.9)', the same as the seer who composed hymns 10.42, 43 and 44 of the *Ṛg Veda* dedicated to Indra. But the fact that the hymns first referred to are dedicated to the Aśvins and these latter ones to Indra tends to indicate that there were two different *ṛṣis*. So, we have in the first place one *ṛṣi*, or perhaps two, called Kṛṣṇa mentioned in the *Ṛg Veda* and the *Kauśītaki Brāhmaṇa* of the same Veda.

The next instance of the name in the *Ṛg Veda* is far more uncertain, since it is not sure even if it is a name at all.[2] The authority on which the word Kṛṣṇa in hymns 1.101 and 2.20 is interpreted as a name is the famous commentary on the *Ṛg Veda* by Sāyaṇa of the fourteenth century A.D., who explains it as the name of a demon killed by Indra. This identification has proved very attractive to many scholars, who saw in it an indication of the struggle between the oncoming Aryans and the resistant forces of the indigenous peoples. The first complete translation of the *Ṛg Veda*, that of M. Langlois in the middle of the nineteenth century, follows this interpretation and renders the first line of hymn 1.101 thus: 'Faites offrandes de vos hymnes et de vos libations a ce [dieu], auteur de tout bien, qui, avec Ṛidjiśwan, a tué les épouses enceintes de Crichna',[3] and adds a little note explaining: 'Le mot Crichna signifie noir; c'est le nom d'un Asoura.' Langlois agrees with Sāyaṇa, but then offers his own explanation according to the academic fashion of the day: 'Cette allegorie represente les nuages, gros et noirs de tempêtes, et percés par la foudre d'Indra',[4] leaving aside the interpretation of the scholiast of Vijayanagara.

Wilson, the first translator of the entire *Ṛg Veda* in English, followed exactly the views of Sāyaṇa, but Griffith, the next to make a complete translation in 1889, departed from the traditional Hindu interpretation in some points, following it in others. His rendering of the line in question says: 'Sing, with oblation, praise to him who maketh glad, who with Ṛjiśvan drove the dusky brood away', explaining then in a note: 'The dusky brood: the dark aborigines who opposed the Aryans',[1] subscribing thus to the euhemeristic theory that sees in the *asuras* the earlier inhabitants of India, something far from the mind of the medieval Hindu commentators.

The compound *kṛṣṇagarbhā*, 'black wombs' or 'black embryos' is explained by Sāyaṇa as foetuses in the pregnant women of the *asura* Kṛṣṇa[2], an interpretation that we find in the words 'les epouses enceintes de Crichna', used by Langlois in his translation. But at least one other medieval Hindu commentator, Skandasvāmin, a predecessor of Sāyaṇa, interprets these words as fortified places.[3] This interpretation is followed by D.D.Kosambi: 'The strongholds shattered by Indra are occasionally described as *kṛṣṇagarbhāḥ*, "bearing black [people] in the womb".[4] And the most recent rendering of the hymns of the *Ṛg Veda*, that of Louis Renou, also follows Skandasvāmin on this point, although relying also on internal evidence of the *Ṛg Veda*. Renou's translation of the same line reads: 'Entonnez la parole consistant en nourriture pour le [dieu] rejouissant qui avec Ṛjiśvan a chassé-et-demoli les [citadelles] ayant en leur sein la [race] noire', and explains his choice thus: 'traduction en accord avec 2.20.7, (elle a été préférée a un premier projet: a chasse-et-tue les [femelles] [ennemis] aus noirs embryons)'.[5]

RV 2.20.7 is translated by Renou as 'Lui briseur de resistances, Indra, demolit les [citadelles] des dāsa qui ont en leur sein [la race] noire, lui le briseur de citadelles.'[6] Here the words *kṛṣṇayoniḥ*, being interchangeable with *kṛṣṇagarbhāḥ* and both meaning the same, literally 'black womb' or 'black-in-the-womb', as Renou takes it, interpreting them as 'a fortification with black people inside' on the basis of Skandasvāmin's rendering. Most probably this interpretation is suggested by Indra's epithet *puraṃdara*, the 'fort-destroyer'. Very sensibly Griffith detaches this name of Indra from the words *kṛṣṇayoniḥ*

1. A. A. Macdonell and A. B. Keith, *Vedic Index of Names and Subjects*, 1958, rep. Motilal Banarsidass, Delhi 1967, p. 184.

2. *RV* 1.101.1; pra mandine pitumad arcatā vaco yaḥ kṛṣṇagarbhā nirahann ṛjiśvanā / avasyavo vṛṣaṇaṃ vajradakṣiṇaṃ marutvantaṃ sakhyāya havāmahe //; *RV* 2.20.7; sa vṛtrahendraḥ kṛṣṇayonīḥ puraṃdaro dāsīr airayad vi / ajayanaṃ manave kṣām apaś ca satrā śaṃsam yajamānasya tūtot //

3. M. Langlois, *Le Ṛig-Veda*, Firmin Didot, Paris 1848-51, v.1, p. 193.

4. *Ibid.*, p. 286 n. 22.

1. R.T.H. Griffith, *The Hymns of the Rig Veda* (1889), rep. Motilal Banarsidass, Delhi 1973, p.

2. kṛṣṇo nāma kaścidasuraḥ / tena niṣiktagarbhāḥ tadīyā bhāryāḥ nirahan avadhīt //

3. kṛṣṇo nāmāsuraḥ, sa garbhabhūto'ntargato yāsāṃ senānāṃ tāḥ kṛṣṇagarbhāḥ.

4. D. D. Kosambi, *An Introduction to the Study of Indian History*, Popular Book Depot, Bombay 1956, pp. 93-94.

5. L. Renou, *Etudes Vediques et Panineennes*, Institut de Civilisation Indienne de l'Universite de Paris, v.17, 1969, p. 35.

6. *Ibid.*, p. 66.

his translation: 'Indra the Vṛtra-slayer, Fort-destroyer, scattered the Dāsa hosts who dwelt in darkness' and in a note to this line reverts to the old 'atmospheric' theory: 'The Dāsa hosts who dwelt in darkness: the words thus rendered are variously explained. It is uncertain whether the aborigines of the country are meant, or the demons of air who dwell in the dark cloud.'[1]

Venkatamādhava, another pre-Sāyaṇa Indian commentator, gives to the word *kṛṣṇayoniḥ* its face value and explains the line in this manner: 'That Indra, the killer of Vṛtra, smote with the thunderbolt in the womb of the woman of the asura Kṛṣṇa; "he who killed the black embryos" so it is said'[2] quoting *verbatim* from hymn 1.101.1 that we have just discussed and therefore establishing their relationship. Sāyaṇa on his part tries to avoid this evident meaning, attributing to the words *kṛṣṇayoniḥ* and *dāsiḥ* the meaning: 'the armies of the evil-doers, the asuras'[3] when in fact there is no mention here of any army, being possible to translate the line in question as: 'That Indra, killer of Vṛtra, destroyer of forts, drove away the enemy women of black vulvae' without any more elaboration. It is only in the next verse that the forts of the *dasyus* are mentioned: 'When they put the *vajra* in his two arms, having killed the *dasyus*, he demolished the forts of iron.'[4] But this explicit mention of forts (*puraḥ*) here does not imply a veiled allusion to them in the other two cases.

This only brings us to the conclusion that the word *kṛṣṇa* in these two hymns has nothing to do whatsoever with the name of the hero-god of the Epic and the Purāṇas. Let us pass then to the other mention of the word *kṛṣṇa*. In hymn 8.96, verses 13-15, is described another feat of Indra, a great battle of the god against an army of ten thousand:

> Drapsa went down into the Aṃśumatī approaching it, the Black-one, along with ten thousand. Indra, the blowing one, helpfully assisted him; the battle was put off by the friend of men.
>
> I saw Drapsa, unsteady, wandering in the bosom of the Aṃśumatī River, black as a cloud that had come down. I command you, O bulls, fight in battle.
>
> Then Drapsa stood firm in the lap of the Aṃśumatī with shining body. The advancing godless tribes Indra has vanquished together with Bṛhaspati.[1]

These lines have been taken by several scholars to mean a conflict and war between the Aryans and the aboriginals, and have also been given as evidence of the non-Aryan origin of Kṛṣṇa the Epic hero, as well as of the legends that surround him, especially those referring to his childhood which seem very unorthodox. We have seen that one of these scholars was Professor D.D. Kosambi, but long before him S. Radhakrishnan, in his justly renowned *Indian Philosophy* of 1923, comments briefly on this passage:

> Another foe of Indra in the period of the *Ṛg Veda*, was Kṛishṇa, the deified hero of a tribe called the Kṛishṇas. The verse reads: "The fleet Kṛishṇa lived on the banks of the Aṃśumatī (Jumna) river with ten thousand troops. Indra of his own wisdom became cognisant of this loud-yelling chief. He destroyed the marauding host for our benefit." (8.85.13-15) This is the interpretation suggested by Sāyaṇa, and the story has some interest in connection with the Kṛishṇa Cult. The later Purāṇas speak of the opposition between Indra and Kṛishṇa. It may be that Kṛishṇa is the god of the pastoral tribe which was conquered by Indra in the *Ṛg Veda* period.[2]

It seems incredible that the learned Professor should have written so many inaccuracies. The passage in question does not even hint at a 'deified hero of a tribe called the Kṛishṇas'. Neither is it anywhere said that the ten thousand were a pastoral tribe, and least of all, Radhakrishnan's version of the passage is not even an approximate rendering of the Sanskrit.

One other supporter of this interpretation was D.R. Bhandarkar, followed by A.P. Karmarkar. The latter says in an article of 1942: 'that the origin

1. R. T. H. Griffith, *ibid.*, p. 143.
2. 'saḥ vṛtrahā indraḥ' kṛṣṇāsuro yāsām yoniṣu tāḥ asurastrīḥ 'puraṃdaraḥ' vajreṇa 'vi erayat' 'yaḥ kṛṣṇagarbhā nirahan' ityuktamiti.
3. nikṛṣṭa jātīḥ. . . .āsurīḥ senāḥ.
4. *RV* 2.20.8; prati yad asya vajram bāhvor dhur hatvī dasyūn pura āyasīr ni tārīt.

1. *RV* 8.96.13-15; ava drapso aṃśumatīmatiṣṭhadiyānaḥ kṛṣṇo daśabhiḥ sahasraiḥ / āvat tamindraḥ śacyā dhamantamapa snehitīrnṛmaṇā adhatta // drapsamapaśyaṃ viṣuṇe carantamupahvare nadyo aṃśumatyāḥ / nabho na kṛṣṇamavatasthivāṃ samiṣyāmi vo vṛṣaṇo yudhyatājau // adha drapso aṃśumatyā upasthe 'dhārayattanvaṃ titviṣāṇaḥ / viśo adevīrabhyācarantīrbṛhaspatinā yujendraḥ sasāhe //
2. S. Radhakrishnan, *Indian Philosophy* (1923), rep. George, Allen and Unwin, London 1962, v.1, p. 87; hymn 8.85 corresponds to 8.96 if the ten hymns of the *khila* to *maṇḍala* 8 are counted separately.

of Kṛṣṇa, the cowherd king of Mathurā, was non-Aryan becomes evident if we accept the most shrewdly logical argument put forth by Dr D.R. Bhandarkar in regard to the interpretation of a Ṛgvedic passage. According to him, the word Kṛṣṇa referred to in the expression *kṛṣṇa-drapsaḥ* in the Ṛgveda, denotes the very same Kṛṣṇa in the later literature.'[1] A little more cautious was D.D. Kosambi, who says on the verses in question: 'The legend of his [Kṛṣṇa's] enmity to Indra reflects in the Ṛgveda the historical struggle of the dark pre-Aryans against the marauding Aryans' and adds in a note: '*RV* 8.96.13-14, but sometimes interpreted as part of the Soma legend. The traditional explanation is that this Kṛṣṇa was an "Asura", i.e. non-Aryan, and the fighting against Indra on the banks of the Aṃśumatī river was real, not symbolic of something else.'[2] Of course Kosambi's 'traditional explanation' means Sāyaṇa's, but it is highly improbable, and there is nothing to suggest, that Sāyaṇa intended by Asura a non-Aryan. If anybody at all was aware that both the Devas and Asuras were sons of Prajāpati, it was Sāyaṇa. For example an Asura of the quality of Varuṇa would hardly be called non-Aryan.[3]

Kosambi, however, also felt the feebleness of this particular 'proof' to his theories and says in a later book: 'It is doubtful whether *RV* 8.96.13-15 is a *soma* myth or the straight record that it seems to be of a fight between Indra and a Kṛṣṇa.'[4] Gonda is still more cautious when he says: 'If this Kṛṣṇa actually was the same as the later hero and god—which is far from certain, 'the Black' being a common name - he may have been then already an adversary of the mighty god.'[5] But this interpretation is still a current one, as we see in the work of Suvira Jaiswal. She adheres wholeheartedly to it in the following lines:

> The cult of Vāsudeva-Kṛṣṇa discloses many non-Vedic and non-Aryan elements. According to a Ṛgvedic passage, Indra for the benefit of his favourite drink *drapsa* (diluted sour milk?) defeated a non-Aryan chief Kṛṣṇa, who was equipped with an army of ten thousand soldiers, on the banks of Aṃśumatī. Aṃśumatī is identified with modern Jamna, and the non-Aryan chief, explained as an asura by Sāyaṇa, with the epic god of the same name. Whatever may be the identity of the Ṛgvedic Kṛṣṇa, the name certainly indicates a non-Aryan genesis.[1]

Again we find here the gratuitous presuppositions of Radhakrishnan and Bhandarkar, and a few others contributed by Suvira Jaiswal herself, like the attribution of the involvement of Indra in the battle 'for the benefit of his favourite drink *drapsa*', when the *Ṛg Veda* does not specifically mention any drink. Jaiswal relies for her information on Gonda's monograph mentioned before,[2] but Gonda also does not say anywhere that *drapsa* is a drink. All we find in his study is that 'a certain Kṛṣṇa, black like a cloud, was destroyed by Indra for the benefit of his favourite Drapsa.'[3] And he on his part cites Geldner on this matter, translating as 'favourite' the German expression 'Ihm ... stand bei', a phrase that should literally be translated as 'assisting him' or 'supporting him', this in turn is the rendering of the Sanskrit *āvat* ... *śacyā*, 'assisted helpfully'.[4] What Suvira Jaiswal does not mention is that both Radhakrishnan and Bhandarkar, following Sāyaṇa, take *kṛṣṇa-drapsa* as 'the swift moving Kṛṣṇa', one asura, whereas the almost literal translation of Geldner interprets *drapsa* and Kṛṣṇa as separate entities. On the other hand the assertion of Jaiswal that 'the non-Aryan chief [is] explained as an asura by Sāyaṇa', is a *petitio principii*, since it is not Sāyaṇa who explains a non-Aryan chief as an asura but Radhakrishnan, Bhandarkar and Jaiswal who explain the asura of Sāyaṇa as a non-Aryan chief. And this against all evidence that indicates that the passage in question is nothing but a Soma myth misinterpreted by Sāyaṇa. We do not deny the fact of the Aryan invasion and the opposition of the previous inhabitants of India, but we believe that most probably this hymn does not refer to it and is therefore very unlikely to be a proof of the un-Aryan character of Kṛṣṇa.

As we have seen in our own interpretation of the verses in question there is no such asura Kṛṣṇa as

1. A. P. Karmakar, 'Some Nude Gods in the Hindu Pantheon', *ABORI*, v.23, 1942, p. 219, referring to D. R. Bhandarkar, *Some Aspects of Ancient Indian Culture*, University of Madras, Madras 1940, p. 82.
2. D. D. Kosambi, *Myth and Reality*, Popular Prakashan, Bombay 1962, pp. 24 and 39.
3. See W. N. Brown, *JAOS*, v.62.
4. D. D. Kosambi, *An Introduction*...., p. 94.
5. J. Gonda, *Aspects*..... p. 157.

1. S. Jaiswal, *The Origin and Development of Vaiṣṇavism*, Munshiram Manoharlal, Delhi 1967, p. 64.
2. S. Jaiswal, *ibid*, p. 64, n4.
3. J. Gonda, *Aspects*....p. 157.
4. K. F. Geldner, *Der Rig-Veda*, *HOS* vols. 33-35, 1951-53, v. 2, p. 423.

Sāyaṇa would have us believe, but rather *drapsa-kṛṣṇa*, the black drop, is the personified Soma who is fleeing from an enemy, who is none other than Vṛtra, the old opponent of Indra, according to Śaunaka. Drapsa takes refuge in the Aṃśumatī river and there is assisted by Indra and Bṛhaspati, who together defeat Vṛtra's forces.

That Drapsa refers to Soma is inferred from various indications. First, that Soma is referred to as such in *Ṛg Veda* 10.17.11-13.[1] These verses say:

> The drop has fallen to earth, to the sky,
> to this womb and to the one that was before.
> The drop that goes into the same womb
> I offer with seven invocations.
>
> Your drop that falls, your stem,
> shaken by the arms from the bosom of the press.
> Or from the Adhvaryu's filter,
> that I offer you heartily saying Vasat.
>
> Your drop fell, your stem,
> further down from the spoon.
> May this god Bṛhaspati
> sprinkle it for blessing.[2]

Here we see clearly that *drapsa*, 'the drop', is the Soma filtered by the Adhvaryu priest. Other hints of Drapsa's identity are the name of the river Aṃśumatī. *aṃśu* is usually associated with Soma[3] and *aṃśumatī* means 'rich in Soma plants or juice'. As a matter of fact it is only Sāyaṇa who says that this mystic river is the Yamunā.[4]

Also two of the epithets given to Drapsa are commonly used for the moon. The first is *viṣuṇe*, that we translate as 'unsteady' and Monier-Williams explains as 'changing [as the moon]', according to the usage in the *Ṛg Veda*.[5] The other is *titviṣāṇaḥ* that Monier-Williams gives as 'to shine, glitter' in precisely this verse.[6]

Besides this evidence we have the testimony of Śaunaka who, in his *Bṛhad-devatā*, one of the *Anukramaṇis* or Vedic indexes, gives the following story concerning the three verses that we are studying:

> In the second hymn of these (96) they say there is a story (*itihāsa*): Soma, oppressed by fear of Vṛtra, fled from the gods; and he betook himself to a river named Aṃśumatī in [the country of] the Kurus. Him approached, with Bṛhaspati only, the slayer of Vṛtra, being about to fight in company with the greatly rejoicing Maruts, armed with various weapons. Soma, seeing them approaching, stood in array with his forces, thinking Vṛtra was approaching with a hostile host, intent on slaying [him]. To him, arrayed and ready with his bow, Bṛhaspati spoke: "This is the Lord of the Maruts, O Soma; come back to the gods, O Lord." Hearing the speech of the preceptor of the gods, which was unavailing because he believed it was Vṛtra, he replied "No". [So] the mighty Śakra, taking him by force, went to the gods in heaven. The celestials [then] drank him in due form.[1]

Here Soma is identified with Drapsa, but it is not clear if by Vṛtra Śaunaka means the Kṛṣṇa of the hymn. In fact he seems to be identifying both Kṛṣṇa and Drapsa as the same Soma, the demon Vṛtra not appearing in the hymn but only in the explanation. This seems to us the most simple and logical explanation of the verses, since the other two—Sāyaṇa's and Geldners'—fail to account for the meaning of all the words or simply twist their sense. Sāyaṇa changes the significance of the words *āvat tam... śacyā*, 'helpfully assisted him', to *karmaṇā prajñānena*, 'with craft and guile', distorting the whole meaning of the story. As we have seen, his interpretation is that Drapsa-Kṛṣṇa, 'the swift Kṛṣṇa', is an asura enemy of Indra. In fact in his commentary to the next *ṛk* he specifically mentions him as such, counting him with Vṛtra and Namuci.[2] But this interpretation is not at all sustained by the words of the Veda.

1. And also in *RV* 9.78.4; 85.10; 89.2; 97.56; 106.8; 10.11.4 and 17.11-12.
2. drapsaś caskanda prathamām anu dyūn imaṃ ca yonim anu yaś ca purvaḥ / samānaṃ yonim anu saṃcarantaṃ drapsaṃ juhomy anu sapta hotrāḥ // yas te drapsa skandati yas te aṃśur bāhucyuto dhiṣaṇāyā upasthāt / adhvaryor vā pari vā yaḥ pavitrāt taṃ te juhomi manasā vaṣaṭkṛtam // yas te drapsaḥ skanno yas te aṃśur avaś ca yaḥ paraḥ srucā / ayaṃ devo bṛhaspatiḥ saṃ taṃ siñcatu rādhase //
3. M. Monier-Williams, *SED*, p.1.
4. *aṃśu* is moreover a cup used in the Soma rituals of the Vājapeya and Rājasūya sacrifices; A. B. Keith, *The Religion....*, pp. 328 and 339.
5. Monier-Williams, *SED*, p. 998.
6. *Ibid*, p. 464.

1. *Bṛhaddevatā* 6.109-115; sūkte dvitīya eteṣām itihāsaṃ pracakṣate / apakramya tu devebhyaḥ somo vṛtrabhayārditaḥ // nadīmaṃśumatīṃ nāmnābhyatiṣṭhat kurūn prati / taṃ bṛhaspatinaikena so'bhyayādvṛtrahā saha // yotsyamānaḥ susaṃhṛṣṭair marudbhirvividhāyudhaiḥ / dṛṣṭvā tānāyataḥ somaḥ svabalena vyavasthitaḥ // manvāno vṛtramāyāntaṃ jighāṃsumarisenayā / vyavasthitaṃ dhanuṣmantaṃ tamuvāca bṛhaspatiḥ // marutpatirayam soma prehi devān punarvibho / so'bravīnneti taṃ śakraḥ svarga eva balādbalī / iyāya devānādāya taṃ papurvidhivatsurāḥ// jaghnuḥ pītvā ca daityānām samare navatīrnava/ tadava drapsa ityasmin tṛce sarvaṃ nigadyate // tr. Macdonell.
2. aśatrubhyaḥ śatrurahitebhyaḥ saptabhyaḥ kṛṣṇa vṛtra namuci śamharādisaptabhyo balavadbhyaḥ....

Lastly, the much celebrated German translation of Geldner, otherwise very accurate, inexplicably takes Drapsa and Kṛṣṇa as two separate entities:

> Drapsa stieg in die Aṃśumatī hinab, Kṛṣṇa ist im Anzug mit zehntausend (kriegern). Ihm (dem Drapsa) stand bei, dem mit aller Kraft Blasenden. Der Mannhafte wendete die Heerhaufen (?) ab.
>
> "Ich sah den Drapsa in schlimmer Lage im schosse des Flusses Aṃśumatī, (Ich sah) den Kṛṣṇa, der schwarz wie eine Wolke hinabgestiegen war. Euch, bullen, biete ich auf: kampfet im Streite".[1]

Thus Geldner makes Drapsa both fly from Kṛṣṇa and be helped by Indra. But, as we have seen, the Veda seems to refer to a single Kṛṣṇa-Drapsa, fleeing from someone and being offered assistance by Indra. It is this Drapsa who rejects the army of the Maruts and not Indra the forces of Kṛṣṇa.[2] Only after this Indra commands his troops to fight and, despite Kṛṣṇa-Drapsa's resistance, captures him together with his followers, the 'godless tribes' (*adevīḥ*), godless not because they were un-Aryan aborigines as many have mistakenly believed, but because they had fled from the gods.

With this identification of Kṛṣṇa-Drapsa with Soma we come to the conclusion that in the *Ṛg Veda* there is no evidence whatever of Kṛṣṇa the Epic hero as such and under that name. We shall see later how Indra in certain instances prefigures some features of the Purāṇic Kṛṣṇa.

iv. CONCLUSION

As a conclusion we can say that, although the figure of Kṛṣṇa does not appear in the hymns of the Veda, very important traits later associated with him are conspicuously present there. Viṣṇu and Nārāyaṇa both share with Kṛṣṇa essential features in their personalities. In our brief outline of those two gods' characters we can discern a basic similarity, a fundamental relation, that connects them with the Purāṇic hero. Since Kṛṣṇa is supposed to be a terrestrial manifestation of that divine being—Viṣṇu and Nārāyaṇa combined—this agreement in their character is quite natural.

The Kṛṣṇa figure is associated with Viṣṇu due to the 'expansive' character of the latter. Let us remember Viṣṇu's description as a young boy with a giant body,[3] i.e. that has grown, has developed, which connects him with the Puruṣa that grows out of the Golden Germ. We have also the myth of the Brāhmaṇas where Viṣṇu is described as a dwarf who grows incommensurably, and we have also his epithets in the *Ṛg Veda*: *urukrama* and *urugāya*, 'the one of wide steps'. Everything indicates a symbol of universal expansion out of an infinitely small centre.

On his part Kṛṣṇa represents this in a more 'folkloric' way, in his adventures as a little child who destroys formidable monsters. It is the same universal force present in a small and insignificant object or person. The *Harivaṃśa* specifically compares the two instances when Brahmā tells Viṣṇu-Nārāyaṇa about his future birth on earth as the son of Vasudeva: 'There you will be a child having the marks of a cowherd, and you will increase as of old did Traivikrama.'[1] A clearer example of this we have in the episode when Yaśodā contemplates the whole Universe within the mouth of her naughty child.[2] Likewise Nārāyaṇa is also a symbol of Cosmic totality enclosed in a minimal point, he is *Hiraṇyagarbha*, the Golden Embryo, floating in the cosmic waters. The *Mahābhārata* explains the name Nārāyaṇa thus: 'The waters are called *nāras*, they have been so designated by me; therefore I am called Nārāyaṇa for the waters are forever my dwelling,'[3] and puts these words in the mouth of a babe floating on a banyan tree in an infinite ocean, inside whose body the sage Mārkaṇḍeya has just entered and seen the whole cosmos. This child Nārāyaṇa holds the entire world[4] just as Puruṣa does and as the baby Kṛṣṇa does. We will see later how this particular image of the floating child is also present in the story of Kṛṣṇa.

This imagery of the cosmic child is in our opinion a fundamental trait in the Vaiṣṇava mythology that connects at the roots the figure of Kṛṣṇa with those of his two Vedic predecessors, Viṣṇu and Nārāyaṇa; these two in turn were combined in a single character largely because of this same trait.

On the contrary the name Kṛṣṇa that appears in the Vedic hymns is almost surely not related to our hero. We have seen a few instances where the

1. Geldner, *Der Rig-Veda*, v 2, pp 422-23.
2. apa snehitīr nṛmaṇā adhatta.
3. *RV* 1.155.6; bṛhaccharīro....yuvā kumāraḥ.

1. *HV* 45.39; tatra tvaṃ śiśurevādau gopālakṛtalakṣaṇaḥ / vardhayasva mahābāho purā traivikrame yathā //
2. *BhP*. 10.8.37; sa tatra dadṛśe viśvaṃ jagat.
3. *Mbh*. 3.187.3; āpo nārā iti proktāḥ saṃjñānāma kṛtaṃ mayā / tena nārāyaṇo'smyukto mama taddhyāyanaṃ sadā //
4. *Mbh*. 3.186.114; kṛtsnamādāya vai jagat.

occurrence of this word has been interpreted as referring to the Purāṇic Kṛṣṇa and we have found that these interpretations are not warranted by any other evidence. Other instances of the word *kṛṣṇa* in the hymns of the Veda refer invariably to its general meaning as 'black', as in '[When] the black [night] stands among the red cows [the clouds at dawn ?], I praise you, O Aśvins, grandsons of the sky',[1] a passage that, because of its mention of cows, has also been adduced as a proof of the presence of Kṛṣṇa in the *Ṛg Veda*, in spite of the word being here feminine. It is clear, however, that the word is here used just to mean 'black' or 'dark' in a poetic image.[2]

Finally we have to mention that one figure in the Veda has very close similarities with Kṛṣṇa and, almost surely, served as a model on which some of the later Kṛṣṇa stories were developed. This is Indra, the most popular god of the Indo-Aryans. However, not being expressly described in the texts as a divinity of which Kṛṣṇa is a manifestation or avatāra, as of Viṣṇu or Nārāyaṇa, we have not discussed him here but shall deal in a later chapter with the parallelisms in his myths and the legends of Kṛṣṇa.

1. *RV* 10.61.4; kṛṣṇā yad goṣu aruṇīṣu sīdad divo napātāv aśvinā huve vām.

2. Likewise in *RV* 1.140.3; 1.164.47; 4.7.9; 8.43.6; 10.3.2 and 10.20.9.

CHAPTER TWO

Early Historical Evidence on Kṛṣṇa

For more than a hundred years scholars have been trying to give a clear picture of the early stages in the evolution of the Kṛṣṇa legend. Starting with the pioneering work of Lassen, Weber and Barth, followed by the efforts of Bhandarkar, Hopkins and Keith, to mention only a few, the Kṛṣṇa problem has puzzled several generations of Indologists and puzzled is quite an appropriate word here since it is to a jig-saw puzzle that we can very aptly compare this problem, a big jig-saw puzzle of which most of the pieces are missing. The few evidences that we have do not complement each other, and sometimes even contradict each other, so that the best picture that we can draw from them is anything but clear. We can number these evidences on our fingers: half-a-dozen lines in the Grammars of Pāṇini and Patañjali, and passing references in the *Chāndogya Upaniṣad*, in a Buddhist work and Kauṭilya's *Artha-śāstra* are, apart from the chronologically uncertain mentions in the *Mahābhārata*, the only literary records available on Kṛṣṇa in the centuries preceding the beginning of the Christian era. Besides this we have references to Kṛṣṇa in three or four inscriptions of the same time. Against this we have the fully developed story of the life of Kṛṣṇa as presented in the *Harivaṃśa*, the *Ghaṭa-Jātaka*, the Purāṇas and other texts, appearing in a more or less sudden manner in the first centuries after Christ. This is in brief the problem: how and when did the legend of Kṛṣṇa acquire the form that is known to us, what are the elements that entered in the formation of this legend, who originally was this Kṛṣṇa and for how long has he been a divine figure?

It is very difficult, not to say impossible, to solve all these questions definitely; all that the student can do is to try to present a plausible hypothesis or a theory that does not disagree with the available data and that at the same time gives a clear and probable picture of the events that led to the formation of the Kṛṣṇa religion as we know it from those later texts. In order to do this we will first present together all the evidence, literary and archaeological, with as little commentary as possible; secondly we will discuss this evidence together with the views presented by several scholars in the past; and thirdly we will try to give a hypothesis that will incorporate all the evidence in a coherent manner.

i. THE EVIDENCE

The first clear—although very brief—mention of Kṛṣṇa we find in the *Chāndogya Upaniṣad* 3.17, where it is mentioned that Kṛṣṇa was taught by one Ghora Āṅgirasa a secret doctrine on the meaning of Vedic ceremonial. He is there styled Devakī-putra, the son of Devakī, the same matronymic by which he is called in later texts. The *Chāndogya Upaniṣad* is attached to the *Sāma-Veda* and is roughly dated in the sixth century B.C. We give here a full rendering of the passage in question, which we shall discuss later:

1. When one hungers and thirsts and does not

enjoy himself that is a Preparatory Consecration Ceremony (*dīkṣā*).

2. When one eats and drinks and enjoys himself then he joins in the Upasada ceremonies.
3. When one laughs and eats and practises sexual intercourse then he joins in the Chant and recitation (*stuta-śāstra*).
4. Austerity, alms-giving, uprightness, harmlessness, truthfulness, these are one's gifts for the priests.
5. Therefore they say: "He will procreate (*soṣyati*)". He has procreated (*asoṣṭa*), that is his rebirth (*punar-utpādana*). Death is an ablution after the ceremony.
6. When Ghora Āṅgirasa explained—for he had become free from desire: "In the final hour one should take refuge in these three thoughts: 'You are Indestructible; you are the Unshaken; you are the very essence of life' (*prāṇa*)."[1]

The next reference to Kṛṣṇa, unfortunately a very brief one, is found in the most famous of the Sanskrit grammars, the Aṣṭādhyāyī of Pāṇini dated, very roughly too, in the fourth century B.C. There in 4.3.98[2] is mentioned a special form to call the devotees or followers of Vāsudeva, and Arjuna, the famous epic hero, thenceforth always associated with Kṛṣṇa. There has been, and still is, a strong controversy on the meaning of this sūtra and the word bhakti to which it refers, and we will review this below.

Besides this reference to Vāsudeva by name, Pāṇini also mentions the tribes to which Kṛṣṇa traditionally belonged, the Andhakas and the Vṛṣṇis.[3] The Vṛṣṇis particularly are also mentioned in the *Taittirīya Saṃhitā* (3.2.9.3), the *Taittirīya Brāhmaṇa* (3.10.9.15), the *Śatapatha Brāhmaṇa* (3.1.1.4), and the *Jaiminīya Upaniṣad Brāhmaṇa* (1.6.1).

1. *Chānd. Up.* 3.17.1-6; tr. by R. E. Hume in *The Thirteen Principal Upanishads*, Oxford Univ. Press, 1921 (7th rep. 1968), pp. 212-213;: sa yadaśiśiṣati yatpipāsati yanna ramate tā asya dīkṣāḥ /1/ atha yadaśnāni yatpibati yadramate tadupasadaireti /2/ atha yaddhasati yajjakṣati yanmaithunaṃ carati stutaśāstraireva tadeti /3/ atha yattapo dānamārjavamahiṃsā satyavacanamiti tā asya dakṣiṇāḥ /4/ tasmādahuḥ soṣyatyasoṣṭeti punarutpādanamevāsya tanmaraṇamevāvabhṛthaḥ /5/ taddhaitadghora āṅgirasaḥ kṛṣṇāya devakīputrāyoktvovācāpipāsa eva sa babhūva so'ntavelāyāmetattrayaṃ pratipadyetakṣitamasyacyutamasi praṇasaṃśitamasīti /6/
2. vāsudevārjunābhyāṃ vun.
3. 4.1.1.14 ṛṣyandhakavṛṣṇikurubhyaśca and 6.2.34 rājanyabahuvacanadvandve 'ndhakavṛṣṇiṣu.

Even before Pāṇini, in the *Nirukta*,[1] an etymological work by Yāska ascribed to the fifth century B.C.,[2] is quoted an example that presupposes a famous episode in the life of Kṛṣṇa. This is the incident around the Syamantaka jewel,[3] said by his own tribe to have been stolen by Kṛṣṇa and found and restored on two occasions by him. It was during the wanderings caused by the loss of the jewel that Kṛṣṇa obtained two of his wives, Jāmbavatī and Satyabhāmā.[4]

In the *Baudhāyana Dharma Sūtra*, a work ascribed to the fourth century B.C.,[5] we find an invocation to Viṣṇu where he is called by twelve different names, among which he is given three very well known names of Kṛṣṇa:

> Om, I satiate Keśava; Nārāyaṇa; Mādhava; Govinda; Vishṇu; Madhusūdana; Trivikrama; Vāmana; Śrīdhara; Hṛṣīkeśa; Padmanābha; Dāmodara; the goddess Śrī; the goddess Sarasvatī; Puṣṭi; Tuṣṭi; Viṣṇu; Garutmat; the male attendants of Viṣṇu; the female attendants of Viṣṇu.[6]

Here Keśava, Govinda and Dāmodara definitely point to Kṛṣṇa's early career according to the Purāṇic legends.[7]

1. *Nirukta* 2.1.2; akrūro dadāte maṇim : 'akrūra holds the gem' (see M.A. Mehendale 'Yāskas Etimology of Daṇḍa', *JAOS*, v.80, 1960, pp. 112-15).
2. A. A. Macdonell, *A History of Sanskrit Literature*, p. 227; A. L. Basham, *The wonder that was India*, Fontana, London 1971, p. 235.
3. *Mbh.* 16.4.22-23; *HV* 1.38 13 ff; *VP* 4.13.8 ff; *BhP* 10.56-57.
4. R. C. Hazra, 'Vasudeva Worship as known to Panini', in *Our Heritage*, Calcutta, vol.18, pt.1, 1970, pp. 41-42; B. B. Majumdar, *Kṛṣṇa in History and Legend*, Univ. of Calcutta, 1969, pp. 139-49.
5. Macdonell, *A History*...., pp. 218-19.
6. *BDS* 2.5.9.10; Georg Bühler, *The Sacred Laws of the Āryas*, pt. 2; *SBE*, v.14, p. 254.
7. R. G. Bhandarkar (*Vaiṣṇavism*...., p. 3) refers to the occurrence of a passage in the *Niddesa* of the Pali Canon where Vāsudeva and Baladeva are mentioned as divinities to some people. Bhandarkar did not specify the location of the passage and later writers who quote this evidence have not done so either, c. f. H. C. Raychaudhuri, *Materials for the Study of the Early History of the Vaiṣṇava Sect*, University of Calcutta, 2nd ed., 1936, p. 95; K. G. Goswami, *A Study of Vaiṣṇavism*, Oriental Book Agency, Calcutta 1956, p.1; S. Jaiswal, *Origin*...., p.72; P. Banerjee, *Early Indian Religions*, Vikas, Delhi 1973, p. 68. We have been able, however, to trace the passage as *Mahāniddesa* 1.4. 25, appearing in *Khuddaka Nikāya*, Nalanda Devanagari Pali Series, Nalanda 1960, v.4-1, p. 74 lines 15-16, equivalent to *Niddesa* ed. by Poussin and Thomas, Pali Text Society, London 1916, v.1, p. 89 (vāsudevavatikā va honti, valadevavatikā va honti).

Megasthenes, who was a Seleucid ambassador at the court of Candragupta Maurya at the end of the fourth century B.C., wrote in his *Indika*, according to Arrian, Diodorus and Strabo, that a tribe called the Sourasenoi specially worshipped Herakles and that in their land there were two great cities: Methora and Kleisobora and a navigable river, the Jobares.[1]

It is generally accepted among scholars that by 'Sourasenoi' Megasthenes meant the Śūrasenas (a branch of the Sātvata-Yādava-Vṛṣṇi tribes to which Kṛṣṇa belonged), by 'Herakles' he meant Kṛṣṇa Vāsudeva, by 'Methora' and 'Kleisobora' he meant Mathurā and perhaps Kṛṣṇapura (a town not yet identified), and by 'Jobares' he meant the river Yamunā. One other reference to Herakles is made by Quintus Curtius,[2] who mentions that when Alexander the Great confronted the forces of Porus by the river Jhelum (Vitastā) these soldiers were carrying in front of them the image of Herakles. On the identification of Kṛṣṇa with Herakles we will have more to say below.

Reputedly also from the fourth century B.C., is the *Arthaśāstra* of Kauṭilya; in this work we find a mantra or charm to make animals (principally dogs) sleep. One of the lines in the invocation mentions Kṛṣṇa and Kaṃsa and refers to the story of the birth of Kṛṣṇa (*kṛṣṇakaṃsopacāraṃ ca*).[3] Another line[4] mentions the Vṛṣṇis and seems to refer to the incident that led to the death of Kṛṣṇa and the destruction of all his family:

> A king, behaving in a manner contrary to that, [and hence] having no control over his senses, quickly perishes, though he be ruler right up to the four ends of the earth. For example, the Bhoja king Dāṇḍakya by name, entertaining a sinful desire for a Brahmin maiden, perished along with his kinsmen and kingdom.... Vātāpi trying to assail Agastya, out of foolhardiness, [perished]; and [so did] the clan of the Vṛṣṇis [trying to assail] Dvaipāyana.[5]

1. McCrindle, *Ancient India as Described by Megasthenes and Arrian* (1887), Chuckervertty, Chaterjee & Co., Calcutta 1960, p. 206.
2. McCrindle, *The Invasion of India by Alexander the Great* (1896)., rep. Barnes & Noble, New York 1969, p. 208.
3. *AS* 14.3.44.
4. *AS* 1.6.10.
5. *R. P.* Kangle, *The Kauṭilīya Arthaśāstra*, Pt. II, University of Bombay 1963, pp. 13-14. tadviruddhavṛttiravaśyendriyaścāturanto'pi rājā sadyo vinaśyati yathā harṣādvātāpiragastyamatyāsādayan vṛṣṇisaṅghaśca dvaipāyanamiti.

And in one last passage mention is made of ascetics consecrated to Balarāma, Kṛṣṇa's brother: '...an agent appearing as an ascetic with a shaven head or with matted locks and posing as a devotee of god Samkarsana, should overreach [the forest robbers] by using a stupefying liquid after holding a festival.'[1]

In the *Mahānārāyaṇa Upaniṣad* of the *Taittirīya Āraṇyaka*, ascribed to the third century B.C.,[2] appears a *gāyatrī* mantra in which Vāsudeva is identified with Nārāyaṇa and Viṣṇu.[3] The same mantra appears in the *Yajur Veda*,[4] without mentioning Vāsudeva.

In the *Mahābhārata*[5], parts of which are considered as old as the fourth century B.C., Kṛṣṇa plays a very important role as friend and advisor to the five Pāṇḍavas as well as an incarnation of the Supreme God. In the *Bhagavad Gītā*, generally reckoned as belonging to the second century B.C., Kṛṣṇa spectacularly reveals himself as the Absolute in human form. The early life of Kṛṣṇa, as traditionally told in the Purāṇas, does not appear in the *Mahābhārata*, but it is referred to on several occasions. In contrast his death is narrated in full in the *Mausala Parvan*.

Patañjali, the famous grammarian of the second century B.C., mentions Kṛṣṇa in several passages

1. Kangle, *ibid.*, p. 563. saṅkarṣaṇadaivatiyogo va muṇḍajaṭilavyañjanaḥ pravahaṇakarmaṇā madanarasayogamatisandadhyāt.
2. Jan Gonda, *Viṣṇuism and Śivaism*, p. 29; Jean Varenne, *La Mahānārāyaṇa Upaniṣad*, Paris 1960, v.2, p. 5f ascribes it to 400 B.C.
3. nārāyaṇāya vidmahe vāsudevāya dhī mahī tanno viṣṇuḥ pracodayāt. 10.1.6a.
4. *Mait. Sam.* 2, 9, 1.
5. *Mbh.* 2.38.1-15, the deriding of Kṛṣṇa by Śiśupāla, mentions the killing of Pūtanā, the killing of a bird, the killing of one horse and one bull, the overturning of a cart, the holding of Mount Govardhana, the eating of great amounts of food on its top, and the killing of Kaṃsa : pūtanāghātapūrvāṇi karmāṇyasya viśeṣataḥ / tvayā kīrtayatāsmākaṃ bhūyaḥ pracyāvitaṃ manaḥ //4// avaliptasya mūrkhasya keśavaṃ stotumicchataḥ / kathaṃ bhīṣma na te jihvā śatadheyam vidīryate //5// yatra kutsā prayoktavyā bhīṣma bālatarairnaraiḥ / tamimaṃ jñānavṛddhaḥ sangopaṃ saṃstotumicchasi //6// yadyanena hatā bālye śakuniścitramatra kim / tau vāśvavṛṣabhau bhīṣma yau na yuddhaviśāradau //7// cetanārahitaṃ kāṣṭhaṃ yadyanena nipātitam / pādena śakaṭam bhīṣma tatra kiṃ kṛtamadbhutam //8// valmīkamātraḥ saptāhaṃ yadyanena dhṛto'calaḥ / tadā govardhano bhīṣma na taccitraṃ mataṃ mama //9// bhuktametena bahvannaṃ krīḍatā nagamūrdhani / iti te bhīṣma śṛṇvānāḥ param vismayamāgatāḥ //10// yasya cānena dharmajña bhuktamannaṃ balīyasaḥ / sa cānena hataḥ kaṃsa ityetanna mahādbhutam //11//; *BG* 18.1, calls him Keśiniṣūdana, 'the slayer of Keśin'.

of his monumental commentary on the *sūtras* of Pāṇini, the *Mahābhāṣya*. Referring to the previously mentioned *sūtra* of Pāṇini,[1] Patañjali wonders why a separate *sūtra* has been written to include Vāsudeva and Arjuna when they would perfectly fit in the next sūtra without any change in the results since this sūtra deals with all famous Kṣatriyas, and everyone knows that Kṛṣṇa and Arjuna were of that class:

> Why is it that *vun* is affixed to the word Vāsudeva and it is not [included] in [the *sūtra*] "With [the names] of *gotras* or famous kṣatriyas *vuñ* is frequently used", when this is possible? And there is no difference whether we affix *vun* or *vuñ* to the word Vāsudeva, since even that form takes the same accent. This is then the motive: I will say [that] the word Vāsudeva is a *pūrvanipātaṃ*,[2] or [Vāsudeva] is not the name of a famous kṣatriya [but] it refers to the worshippable one.[3]

He first makes an hypothesis: perhaps they have been mentioned separately to show that in a compound where personal names are included the name of the more respectable person goes first even if it is longer, so differing from the general rule. Patañjali then suggests, considering that a sūtra has already been given on that matter, that in this instance Vāsudeva is not the name of a mere kṣatriya but the name of one worthy of respect.

A great deal of controversy has been raised by these lines of Patañjali, but that we will review later.

In his commentary on Pāṇini 3.1.26 Patañjali gives, as examples of a present causative form used to denote the name of a story or narration of a past event, the words *kaṃsavadha* and *balibandha* in the sense of 'the story of the killing of Kaṃsa' and 'the story of the subjection of Bali', so the expression *kaṃsaṃ ghātayati* means 'he narrates the story of Kaṃsa being killed' and not 'he causes Kaṃsa to be killed' and likewise in the case of the other,[4] and then Patañjali goes on to explain how this can be:

1. 4.3.98.

2. A case of irregular priority of a word in a compound.

3. vāsudevārjunabhyāṃvun / kimarthaṃ vāsudevaśabdādvunvidhīyate / nagotrakṣatriyākhyebhyo bahulaṃ vuñityeva siddham / nahyasti viśeṣo vāsudevaśabdādvuno vā vuño vā / tad eva rūpam sa eva svaraḥ idaṃ tarhi prayojanaṃ vāsudeva śabdasya pūrvanipātaṃ vakṣyāmīti // athavā naiṣā kṣatriyākhyā / saṃjñaiṣā tatrabhavataḥ //. *The Vyākaraṇa Mahābhāṣya of Patañjali*, ed. by F. Kielhorn, 3rd ed., Poona 1965, v. 2, p. 314.

4. In Patañjali's commentary to *vārtika* 6 of Kātyāyana, F. Kielhorn, *ibid.*, p. 34, lines 17-18.

> How is the present tense used here in "he causes Kaṃsa to be killed" and "he causes Bali to be bound", when Kaṃsa was killed long ago, and Bali bound long ago? But it is correct. How? First, those called *śobhanikas* visibly cause the killing of Kaṃsa and visibly cause the binding of Bali. And how in [the case of] the *citras*? In the *citras* are seen the threatened and the falling blows as well as the dragging[1] of Kaṃsa. And how in the [case of] the *granthikas* where only a superfluity of words is to be perceived? They [the *granthikas*] by telling their fortunes from birth to death cause [Kaṃsa and Bali] to appear in the scope of the mind as real beings and therefore they are seen as truly real. [So much so that] some become followers of Kaṃsa, some of Vāsudeva, and they even display coloration. Some become red-faced, some black-faced. And the three tenses are even heard among the people. "Come, Kaṃsa is being killed." "Come, Kaṃsa is going to be killed." "What [is the point in] coming? Kaṃsa is killed [already]."[2]

Besides this, there are other references to the story of Kṛṣṇa and Kaṃsa in the *Mahābhāṣya*. In the first[3] Kṛṣṇa is said to have been an enemy to his maternal uncle (Kaṃsa) (*asādhur mātule kṛṣṇaḥ*). And in the second one it is said that Vāsudeva killed Kaṃsa (*jaghāna kaṃsaṃ kila vāsudevaḥ*).[4]

One quotation by Patañjali in his explanation of

1. The use of the feminine plural *karṣaṇyaḥ* is strange. *karṣaṇi* means 'an unchaste woman' and has been taken as such in this context by Norvin Hein (*The Miracle Plays of Mathura*, New Haven 1972), but there is no reference elsewhere to Kaṃsa being dragged by women. His translation of *kaṃsakarṣaṇyaḥ* as 'the women dragging Kaṃsa to and from' (*ibid.*, p. 241) is obviously incorrect. See his discussion of the term on p. 254 (*ibid.*).

2. Patañjali, *Mahābhāṣya*, on *vārtika* 15 to Pāṇini's sūtra 3.1.26: iha tu kathaṃ vartamānakālatā kaṃsaṃ ghātayati baliṃ bandhayatīti cirahate kaṃse cirabaddhe ca balau. atrāpi yuktā. katham. ye tāvad ete śobhanikā nāmaite pratyakṣaṃ kaṃsaṃ ghātayanti pratyakṣaṃcabaliṃ bandhayantīti. citreṣu katham. citreṣvapy udgūrṇā nipatitāśca prahārā dṛṣyante kaṃsakarṣaṇyaśca. granthikeṣu kathaṃ yatra śabdagaḍumātraṃ lakṣyate. te'pi hi teṣām utpattiprabhṛtyā vināśād ṛddhīr vyācakṣāṇāḥ sato buddhiviṣayān prakāśayanti. ataśca sato vyāmiśra hi dṛśyante. kecit kaṃsabhaktā bhavanti kecid vāsudevabhaktāḥ. varṇānyatvam khalvapi puṣyanti. kecid raktamukhā bhavanti kecit kālamukhāḥ. traikālyaṃ khalvapi loke lakṣyate. gaccha hanyate kaṃsaḥ. gaccha ghāniṣyate kaṃsaḥ. kim gatena hataḥ kaṃsa iti.

3. On Pāṇini 2.3.36 Haryana ed., 1963, v. 2, p. 805 n. 1 (not included in Kielhorn's ed.).

4. Kielhorn, *ibid.*, v. 2, p. 119 line 7.

bahuvrīhi compounds on Pāṇini's sūtra 2.2.24[1] throws light on the cult of Kṛṣṇa and Baladeva. The half verse reads: 'May it increase the power of Kṛṣṇa with Saṃkarṣaṇa as second',[2] while another line quoted by Patañjali suggests certain theological developments in Kṛṣṇa's cult. The line appears under 6.3.6 and reads 'Janārdana (another name of Kṛṣṇa) with himself as the fourth.'[3] On Pāṇini sūtra 2.2.34 Patañjali quotes one quarter verse that mentions a palace, probably a temple, 'of the "Lord of *dhana*", Rāma and Keśava', where Rāma refers to Balarāma, the brother of Kṛṣṇa, and Keśava to Kṛṣṇa himself.[4]

Patañjali also mentions[5] followers of Akrūra, and followers of Vāsudeva (*akrūravargiṇaḥ* and *vāsudevavargiṇaḥ*). And finally there is one more reference to the tribe of Kṛṣṇa under 1.1.114[6] referring to the formation of the names of descendants of *ṛṣis* and of descendants of the tribes of the Andhakas, the Vṛṣṇis and the Kurus. There Patañjali gives as instances of Andhaka names Śvāphalka and Ugrasena, well known in the purāṇic tradition, and as instances of Vṛṣṇi names he mentions Vāsudeva and Baladeva.

We come now to the archaeological evidences bearing on the early development of the Kṛṣṇa cult. First we have the famous Besnagar column or Heliodorus column, at the village of Besnagar near Bhilsa in north-western Madhya Pradesh. It is a votive pillar originally with an eagle, the emblem of Viṣṇu, on the top, dedicated to Vāsudeva 'the god of gods'. The column has an inscription that reads:

> This Garuḍa column of Vāsudeva the god of gods was caused to be made by the Bhāgavata Heliodorus of Taxila, the son of Dion, who came as a Greek envoy of the great king Antialkidas to Kautsīputra Bhāgabhadra, the saviour, in the fourteenth year of his prosperous kingship. Three immortal steps when practised lead to heaven: charity, self-control and vigilance.[7]

The date of this inscription is generally recognised as c. 100 B.C.[1]

Two inscriptions from the Chitorgaḍh District in Rajasthan, having the same text, provide further evidence on the cult of Kṛṣṇa in the centuries before our era. The Ghosūndī and Hāthibāḍā inscriptions of the second half of the first century B.C., seem to refer to a temple of Saṃkarṣaṇa and Vāsudeva. The composed text of the parallel inscriptions reads:

> [This] stone enclosure, called the Nārāyaṇa Vāṭaka, for the worship of Bhagavān Saṃkarṣaṇa and Bhagavān Vāsudeva, the invincible lords of all, [was erected] by [the Bhāga] vata king of the line of Gāja, Sarvatāta, the victorious, who has performed an aśvamedha, son of a Pārāśarī.[2]

Another Garuḍa column from Besnagar dated c. 100 B.C.[3] refers to a temple of Bhagavat and to a king called Bhāgavata. The inscription in the column says:

> Bhāgavata, son of Gotamī caused a Garuḍa standard to be made in connection with the best temple of Bhagavat (Vāsudeva) when Mahārāja Bhāgavata had been crowned twelve years.[4]

From the Deccan, in the modern State of Mahārāṣṭra, we also have evidence of the cult of Kṛṣṇa. The inscription of Queen Nāganikā in the Nānāghaṭ cave, Thānā District, mentions the names of Saṃkarṣaṇa and Vāsudeva in the opening invocation, together with those of other deities.[5] This inscription is ascribed on epigraphical grounds to the second half of the first century B.C.[6]

From the beginning of the Christian Era we also find in Mathurā evidence of the Kṛṣṇa cult. One

1. *vārtika* 22.
2. saṃkarṣaṇadvitīyasya balaṃ kṛṣṇasya vardhatamiti. Kielhorn, *ibid.*, v. 1, p. 426 line 9.
3. Janārdanas tvātmacaturtha eva.
4. Prāsāde dhanapatirāmakeśavānām.
5. Under *vārtika* 11 to *sūtra* 4.2.104.
6. On *vārtika* 7 previously quoted.
7. (de)vadevasa vā(sude)vasa garuḍadhvaje ayam / karite i (a) heliodorena bhaga / vatena diyasa putrena takhkhasilākena/ yona-dūtena (a)gatena mahārājasa. / aṃtalikitasa upa(ṃ)ta sakāsam raña. / (ko)sīpu(tra)sa (bhā) ga bhadrasa trātarasa./ vasena ca (tu) dasemna rājena vadhamānasa. // trini amutpadāni (ia) (su) anuṭhitani neyaṃti (svagaṃ) dama cāga apramāda (//). *ASIAR*, 1908-9, p. 126.

1. A. K. Narain, *The Indo-Greeks*, Oxford 1957, p.119.
2. (karito ayaṃ rājnā bhāgava) (te) na gājāyanena pārāśarīputreṇa sa(rvatātena aśvamedha-yā) jinā bhagava(d)bhyāṃ saṃkarṣaṇa-vāsudevābhyāṃ (anihatābhyāṃ sarveśvarā)bhyāṃ pūja-śilā-prākāro nārāyaṇa-vāṭakā //. D. C. Sircar, *Select Inscriptions bearing on Indian History and Civilization*, 2nd ed., Calcutta 1965, v.1, pp. 90-91. (The parenthesis represent the words in the Hāthibāḍā inscription not readable in the one from Ghosūndī). ....
3. D. R. Bhandarkar, *ASIAR*, 1913-14, p. 190f.
4. Tr. Bhandarkar, *ibid.*, gotamī (?) putena bhāgavatena.. bhagavato prāsādota masa garuḍadhvaja kārita dvādasavasābhisite bhāgavate mahāraje.
5. (sidhaṃ...ne dhaṃmasa namo īdasa namo saṃkaṃsana-vāsudevāna caṃda sūrāna (mahi) mā (va) tānaṃ catuṃnaṃ caṃ lokapālānaṃ yamavarūna-kubera-vāsavānam namo.
6. D. C. Sircar, *Select Inscriptions*, v.1, p. 192.

sculpture found in a well at Mora, 11 km. from Mathurā, records the installation of the images of 'the five heroes of the Vṛṣṇis' in a stone temple by a lady called Toṣā during the reign of Mahākṣatrapa Śoḍāsa (c.10-25 A.D.) son of Mahākṣatrapa Rājūvula.[1]

Also from Mathurā and from the reign of Śoḍāsa is another inscription that records the erection of a doorway and a railing for a temple of Bhagavat Vāsudeva.[2]

ii. THE ASSESSMENTS

These are the evidences that we have to consider in connection with the early development of the Kṛṣṇa Cult. We have now to review the endless polemics that these evidences have provoked among the scholars. The tremendous importance of Kṛṣṇa in Indian Religion makes it unavoidable for anyone occupying himself with these matters to discuss the origins of this god. On the other hand the scarcity of the materials on which to base any investigation has brought a highly speculative character to all these attempts to trace the development of the Kṛṣṇa figure. One other consideration that we have to make in this respect is that many, or most, of the discussions on Kṛṣṇa that we shall review here are found in books or articles of a more general scope, since the works dealing exclusively with Kṛṣṇa and with this part of his career are, strangely enough for a figure of such magnitude, rather scarce. This perhaps also accounts to some extent for the speculative nature of the theories put forward.

We will follow the same order as in the previous section and start with the Kṛṣṇa of the *Chāndogya Upaniṣad*. The first question that comes to our minds is: is this Kṛṣṇa the same as the hero of the *Mahābhārata* ? The similarity in names and mainly the fact that both in the *Mahābhārata* and the *Upaniṣad* he is called 'son of Devakī', a name that occurs only in this instance, have led scholars to think that actually we are dealing here with the same personage. The first to acknowledge this was Colebrooke, as long ago as 1837,[1] followed by Weber in 1852.[2] The first to deny this possibility was Barth in 1879 who attributed the *Chāndogya* passage to a euhemerism:

> ... le culte de Krishna parait remonter assez haut. "Krishna le fils de Devaki" est nommé une fois du moins dans un écrit védique qui fait de lui purement et simplement le disciple d'un sage, et cette representation absolutement evhemerique parait deja moins originale que celle que montre l'épopée.[3]

Thus he wants to make the unknown authors of the Upaniṣad attribute to an original deity a human apprenticeship. Despite Barth, the identity of the *Chāndogya* Kṛṣṇa and the Epic Kṛṣṇa was still accepted by Hopkins, Müller, Garbe, Winternitz, Jacobi and Grierson;[4] but it was again questioned by Macdonell and Keith, who once more attributed the occurrence of the name Kṛṣṇa Devakīputra in the Upaniṣad to a euhemerism.[5] In a later review Keith again asserted his views on this issue:

> In the Chāndogya Upaniṣad (3.17.6) we hear of a pupil, Kṛṣṇa Devakīputra, of Ghora Āṅgirasa who is credited with certain doctrines. We are asked to believe that this is an historical reference to the Kṛṣṇa of the epic. It is a much more credible hypothesis on the theory of the Kṛṣṇas that we have in this Kṛṣṇa a euhemerism, a reduction to human rank of a tribal god, and it is the only hypothesis which does not raise serious difficulties

1. mahakṣatrapasa rājūvulasa putrasa svāmī (sya mahākṣatrapasya śoḍāsasya saṃvatsare)....bhagavatāṃ vṛṣṇiṇāṃ paṃcavīrāṇāṃ pratimāḥ śaila-devagṛ (he sthāpitāḥ)....yastoṣ (ā) yāḥ śailaṃ śrīmadgṛhamatulamudadhasamadhāra (?).... ārcādeśāṃ (?). śailaṃ paṃca jvalat iva parama-vapuṣā..) (D.C. Sircar, *Select Inscriptions*, v.1, p. 122.) The second part of the text is not clear.

2. ..vasunā bhagava (to vāsude-) vasya mahāsthāna.... (śai)laṃ toraṇaṃ ve(dikā ca prati)ṣṭhāpito prito bha(gavan vāsu) devaḥ svāmi(sya) (mahākṣatra)pasya śoḍā(sa) (sya) saṃvartayatāṃ. K. G. Goswami, *A Study of Vaiṣṇavism*, p. 11. A seal found at Kumrahar, South of Patna, bears the legend 'gopālasa' (gopālasya). It has been dated first century B.C., but if the name Gopāla is related to Kṛṣṇa is not certain. See *ASIAR*, 1912-13, p.82 f.

1. H. T. Colebrooke, *Miscellaneous Essays*, 2 vol., London 1837, v.2, p. 177n; rep. as *Essays on the Religion and Philosophy of the Hindus*, 1 v., Williams and Norgate, London 1858, p.284.

2. Albrecht Weber, *The History of Indian Literature*, 1st German Ed. 1852; English tr. from the 2nd German Ed., Chowkhamba Sanskrit Series Studies, v.8, Varanasi, 6th rep. 1961, p. 71.

3. Auguste Barth, *Les Religions*....p. 152.

4. Edward Washburn Hopkins, *The Religions*.., p. 465; Max Müller, *The Upanishads*, 1889, SBE, v.1, rep. Dover, New York 1968, p. 52n; Richard Garbe, *Die Bhagavadgita*, H. Haessel, Leipzig 1905, p. 20; Moritz Winternitz, *A History of Indian Literature*, 1905, English tr. 1926, rep. Russell & Russell, New York 1971, p. 457; George Grierson, 'The Nārāyaṇīya and the Bhāgavatas', in *The Indian Antiquary*, v. 37, 1908, p.253, and 'Bhakti Marga', in *ERE*, v.2, 1909, p. 540; Hermann Jacobi, 'Incarnation (Indian)', in *ERE*, v.7, 1914, p. 195.

5. A. A. Macdonell and A. B. Keith, *Vedic Index*, p. 184,

as to the date of the divinity of Kṛṣṇa and his appearance in the epic.[1]

However, except for a short discussion by Hopkins,[2] the scholars who supported the theory of the identity of the two Kṛṣṇas did not substantiate their views. It was only with the publication of Raychaudhuri's *Materials* that the reasons for this identification were explained in more detail.[3]

The arguments of Raychaudhuri are given in refutation of those of Keith just quoted and are summed up in four points: (1) the similarity of names and above all of matronymics; (2) the Āṅgirasas and the Bhojas, the clan to which Kṛṣṇa belonged, were closely related from the times of the *Ṛg Veda* (*RV* 3.53.7); (3) the teaching in the Upaniṣad and the teaching of Kṛṣṇa in the Epic are both related to the sun cult; and (4) the teaching in the Upaniṣad is essentially the same teaching as that of the *Bhagavad Gītā*. In a short review of Raychaudhuri's book F.E. Pargiter[4] again attacks the identification which, according to him, is based on the identity of names only, because 'Kṛṣṇa was a very common name, and Devaka (and so the feminine Devakī) an ordinary name.'

In a rejoinder to that review H.C. Ray belittles Pargiter's objection and once again states Raychaudhuri's views.[5] About the same time L.D. Barnett in England was sustaining the same theory of the identification of the two Kṛṣṇas for much the same reasons as Raychaudhuri, although he was more specific on the similarities in the teachings of Ghora Āṅgirasa and those of the *Bhagavad Gītā*:

> Ghora compares the functions of life to the ceremonies of the *dīkshā*: and this is at bottom the same idea as the doctrine of *karma-yoga* preached again and again in the *Bhagavad-gītā*. "Whatever be thy work, thine eating, thy sacrifice, thy gift, thy mortification, make of it an offering to me", says Krishna (BG 9.27); all life should be regarded as a sacrifice freely offered ... Ghora in his list of moral virtues enumerates "mortification, charity, uprightness, harmlessness, truthfulness"; exactly the same attributes, with a few more, are said in the *Bhagavad-gītā* to characterise the man who is born to the gods' estate (BG 16.1-3). Ghora's exhortation to think of the nature of the Supreme in the hour of death is balanced by Krishna's words: "He who at his last hour, when he casts off the body, goes hence remembering me, goes assuredly into my being" (BG 8.5; cf. 10).[1]

Barnett admitted that 'these parallels are indeed not very close; but collectively they are significant.'[2] Later, in a review of 1929, he came to the conclusion that the Gītā's 'dominant idea, expressed in many keys and variations, is a reaffirmation of the old text of the Chāndogya Upaniṣad in an ennobled form'[3] and in another review of the same year he stressed that:

> Ghora's sermon is exactly what we should expect a *summula theologiae* of the early Bhāgavatas to be, expressed of course in the language of an Aupaniṣada-worship of the Sun-god as blessed universal spirit, to whom the souls of the faithful pass on death, and a primitive form of *Karma-yoga*. In the Gītā all this reappears, with more or less modification, and fortified by much additional matter from other sources.[4]

In the same place he explains that the identity of names is indeed a strong reason to believe in the identity of the personages:

1. A.B. Keith, review of George Foot Moore's 'History of Religions', v.1, 1913, in *JRAS*, 1915, p. 548. The use of the word euhemerism by Barth, Macdonell and Keith in this context seems a bit odd but is justified. The word means 'a historical interpretation of a myth' (*Concise Oxford Dictionary*) and refers to the philosopher Euhemerus who claimed that the gods were men originally; our authors seem to be saying here that an original god was later described as human.
2. E.W. Hopkins, *ibid.*, pp. 465-66.
3. H. C. Raychaudhuri, *Materials....*, pp. 51-61.
4. *JRAS*, 1923, pp. 140-41.
5. H. C. Ray, "Allusions to Kṛṣṇa Devakīputra in the Vedic Literature', *JRASB*, n.s., v.19, 1923 pp. 371-73.

1. L. D. Barnett, *Hindu Gods....*pp.82-83.
2. *Ibid.*, p. 83.
3. L. D. Barnett, Review of W. Douglas P. Hill's 'The Bhagavadgītā' 1928, *JRAS*, 1929, p. 129. Hill includes in the first seventeen pages of his introduction to his translation of the BG a very good summary of the evidence on the early history of Kṛṣṇa. However in dealing with the problem that we now review he states that (W.D.P. Hill, *The BG*, p. 6): 'Barth and Hopkins consider the Kṛṣṇa of the Upaniṣad to be one with the Kṛṣṇa of the Epic. Keith is less positive', but as we have seen above (pp. 24f) Barth and Keith denied very clearly this identity. Another instance of this kind of misinterpretation on the same issue is furnished by Raychaudhuri (*Materials....*, 2nd ed., p. 52) who asserts that: 'Max Müller denies and Macdonell and Keith doubt the identity of Kṛṣṇa Devakīputra of the epic and the Purāṇas with Kṛṣṇa Devakīputra of the *Upanishad*' when reading carefully one can see that Müller accepts and Macdonell and Keith clearly deny that identity. (M. Müller, *The Upanishads*, *SBE*, v.1, p. 52; Macdonell and Keith, *Vedic Index*, v.1, p. 184.
4. L. D. Barnett, Review of Etienne Lamotte's 'Notes sur la Bhagavadgītā', 1929. *BSOS*, v.5, 1928-30, p. 636.

I submit that his identification [the upanishadic Kṛṣṇa's] with Kṛṣṇa Vāsudeva is based on very strong probabilities indeed. The name Kṛṣṇa is common; but the name *Devakī* is so very rare that the only bearer of it in Epic, Puranic and Classical literature, as far as I know, is the mother of Kṛṣṇa Vāsudeva. Hence the combination of "Kṛṣṇa" with the practically unique "Devakī-Putra" on both sides of the equation is in itself enough to prove that Kṛṣṇa Devakī-Putra of the Chāndogya = Kṛṣṇa Vāsudeva.[1]

The theory of the identity of Epic and Upaniṣadic Kṛṣṇa thus put forward by L.D. Barnett came once more under attack by S.K. De in a short article where he tried to refute Barnett's and Raychaudhuri's opinions point by point.[2] There he raises a point not much stressed before: the fact that the traditional story of Kṛṣṇa does not mention Ghora as his teacher, but a certain Sāndīpani:

The identity of the Vedic Kṛṣṇa with the Epic Kṛṣṇa is not at all supported by the Purāṇic tradition. We have no description, either in the Epic or in the Purāṇa, of Kṛṣṇa as a seer of Vedic Mantras or as a pupil of an Upaniṣadic seer. In the Purāṇic tradition the name of Vāsudeva Kṛṣṇa's teacher is given as Kasya Sāndīpani of Avanti, and that of his initiator as Gārga.[3]

S.K. De then admits that the argument for the identification based on the similarity of names is a strong one, but, he says, 'this one circumstance alone cannot be taken as conclusively supplying the means of connexion between the two Kṛṣṇas.'[4] To supply this means, he argues, a 'somewhat doubtful similarity' between the teaching of the passage in the Upaniṣad and the message of the *Gītā* has been "industriously discovered".' De admits the parallels might look close, but he attributes the similarities to the fact that the *Gītā* draws admittedly from the main Upaniṣads and even quotes them *verbatim* in some instances. Besides, he continues, the teaching of the Āṅgirasa is not uncommon in the late Vedic period, so that possibly the *Gītā* may have borrowed its concept of sacrifice as symbolised in human life from some other Scripture. And the other similarities pointed out before, like the enumeration of a list of moral virtues in *Chāndogya Upaniṣad* 3.17.4., or the doctrine of the last thoughts (3.17.6) or the mention of the words *akṣara* and *acyuta*, amply used in the *Gītā*, are really only of minor importance and not all the cardinal doctrines of this latter text, 'even their omission in the *Gītā* would not materially affect the substance of the work.'[1]

Another argument points out that Ghora was a priest of the Sun and ends his teaching with some verses from a Vedic hymn to the Sun, and that Kṛṣṇa in the *Gītā* says that his teaching was first taught by him to Vivasvān and then handed down by him to other disciples.[2] This argument is put forward by De in another article[3] where he rejects Grierson's theories on the Solar origin of the Kṛṣṇa religion but does not specifically discard the similarity of the Upaniṣad and the *Gītā* on this point. Finally De fails to take note of Raychaudhuri's mention of the relation between the Bhojas and the Āṅgirasas from Vedic times. However, as we can see, he presented a fairly strong case against the identification of the Upaniṣadic Kṛṣṇa and the Epic Kṛṣṇa.

The problem has not been discussed in detail after De's article. A.D. Pusalker accepted his conclusions without reservations.[4] Suvira Jaiswal agrees with De's arguments although she thinks that 'it is probable that the notion of a preacher Kṛṣṇa was derived from the tales of a sage Kṛṣṇa mentioned in the Upaniṣad.'[5] However, a new interpretation of the *Chāndogya* passage was advanced in 1969 by Bimanbehari Majumdar. This novel view proposes that Kṛṣṇa is there already considered the Supreme being and that Ghora never taught him anything, but that in the said passage he is really extolling Kṛṣṇa. This, Majumdar proves by saying that Ghora's words: 'You are the indestructible; you are the unshaken; you are the very essence of life'[6] are addressed to Kṛṣṇa, and so taking the Upaniṣad's expression 'for he had become

1. L. D. Barnett, *ibid.*
2. S. K. De, 'The Vedic and the Epic Kṛṣṇa', in *IHQ*, v.18, 1942, pp. 297-301.
3. S. K. De, *ibid.*, p. 298.
4. *Ibid.*

1. *Ibid.*
2. *BG* 4.1-3.
3. S. K. De, 'Bhagavatism and Sunworship', in *BSOS*, v.6, 1931.
4. A. D. Pusalker, *Studies in the Epics and Purāṇas*, Bharatiya Vidya Bhavan, Bombay 1955, p. 31; Swami Svahananda, *The Chāndogya Upaniṣad*, Ramakrishna Mission, Madras 1956, p. 245, tries to connect the traditional longevity of Kṛṣṇa with the span of life gained through the teachings of Ghora Āṅgirasa.
5. Suvira Jaiswal, *The Origin....*, p. 71.
6. *Chānd. Up.*, 3.17.6.

free from desire'[1] as referring to Ghora himself. By this Majumdar claims to remove the difficulty for the identification of the *Chāndogya* Kṛṣṇa with the Epic-Purāṇic Kṛṣṇa caused by the difference of the name of Kṛṣṇa's teacher in both traditions, as well as the necessity to postulate the originally separate existence of Vāsudeva and Kṛṣṇa. This interpretation of the passage has not yet been either challenged or generally accepted by the specialists.[2]

Finally, Professor Dandekar contemplates the possibility of the identity of Kṛṣṇa of the *Chāndogya* and the Yādava Kṛṣṇa, but separates this latter from the original Vāsudeva:

> Perhaps a little later than Vāsudevism, another religious sect grew round the figure of Kṛṣṇa, who had originally been the tribal hero and religious leader of the Yādavas. This Yādava Kṛṣṇa may as well have been the same as Devakīputra Kṛṣṇa who is represented in the *Chāndogya Upaniṣad* 3.17.1, as a pupil of Ghora Āṅgirasa and who is said to have learnt from his teacher the doctrine that man's life is a kind of sacrifice. The chronological evidence does not go against such assumption; if at all, it supports it.[3]

We will discuss in the concluding part of this chapter all these opinions as well as our own in the summary and analysis of all evidence and studies of the historical evolution of the Kṛṣṇa figure.

We now review Pāṇini's mention of Vāsudeva (Pāṇ. 4.3.98), probably the most widely and hotly discussed item of all our evidence. Since this *sūtra* of Pāṇini has generally been studied together with Patañjali's commentary on it we will follow the same method but will discuss the rest of Patañjali's references to Kṛṣṇa in a separate section.

The main issue of discussion on Pāṇini's *sūtra* is that it appears in the explanation of the word *bhakti*. The *sūtras* 4.3.95 to 4.3.100 all refer to the word *bhakti* that, according to the context, can carry different meanings. The problem is that in later times this word obtained an exclusively religious connotation so that some scholars now think that 4.3.98 refers to worshippers of Kṛṣṇa and Arjuna and others are of the opinion that Pāṇini was not referring to religious worshippers but to simple followers. What makes this question more complicated is that Patañjali commented on this *sūtra* in his grammar and so we are now left with the task not only of interpreting Pāṇini but also Patañjali's interpretation of Pāṇini.

The five *sūtras* that concern us here read:

> (The following affixes are used with words denoting objects for which) *bhakti* (is entertained) /95
> With insentient objects not being the name of a country or time, *ṭhak* [is used] / 96
> With [the word] Mahārāja, *ṭhañ* / 97
> With [the names] Vāsudeva and Arjuna, *vun* / 98
> With the names of Gotras of Kṣatriyas *vuñ* is frequently used / 99[1]

The problem here is: is Vāsudeva of Pāṇini a god? The answer to this question depends on the interpretation of the word *bhakti* as well as on the meaning of the group of *sūtras*. Modern scholars do not agree on an interpretation of the passage. Some see in it the clear proof of the worship of Kṛṣṇa as well as of Arjuna.[2] This position might be stated in the words of L.D. Barnett:

> Pāṇini informs us (4.3.98) that from the names of Vāsudeva and Arjuna the derivative nouns Vāsudevaka and Arjunaka are formed to denote persons who worship respectively Vāsudeva and Arjuna. Plainly then Kṛṣṇa Vāsudeva and Arjuna were worshipped by some, probably in the same connection as is shown in the *Mahābhārata*.[3]

This opinion draws support from Patañjali, in the place already quoted. But the advocates of the other interpretation, the one that holds that bhakti in Pāṇini does not convey a religious meaning, try also to find support in Patañjali for their view. They argue that the words *tatra-bhavataḥ* do not perforce denote a divine being. So Kielhorn says 'the word indeed conveys an honorific sense but would be equally applicable to a human being.'[4] In fact, he continues, the word occurs fourteen times in the *Mahābhāṣya* and twelve of them refer to human beings; only once does it refer unmistakably to a

1. *Ibid.*
2. B. B. Majumdar, *Kṛṣṇa*. . . .,pp. 2-4.
3. R. N. Dandekar, 'The Beginnings of Vaiṣṇavism', in *Indologica Taurinensia*, v.3-4, Torino 1977.

1. Pāṇini, 4.3.95-99; bhaktiḥ / acittādadeśakālāṭṭhak / mahārājaṭṭhañ / vāsudevārjunābhyāṃ vun / gotrakṣatriyākhyebhyobahulaṃ vuñ /.
2. A. Barth, *Les Religions*. . . .,p. 155, n.4; R.G. Bhandarkar, *Vaiṣṇavism*. . . . ., p. 3; R. P. Chanda, 'Archaeology and Vaiṣṇava Tradition', in *ASIAR*, 1919, pp. 153-54.
3. L. D. Barnett, *Hindu Gods*, p. 87.
4. F. Kielhorn, 'Bhagavat, Tatrabhavat, and Devānāṃpriya' in *JRAS*, 1908, p. 503.

god in the case of Prajāpati (Patañjali on Pāṇini 4.2.25) and the other is the case of Vāsudeva.

To this argument R.G. Bhandarkar replies that the epithet *tatrabhavat*, when it appears qualifying a substantive, refers to it only, but when it stands alone it means 'the eminently worshipful one', i.e. a god. In Patañjali it appears in the first sense in eleven of the instances referred to by Kielhorn and in the other three, including our case, it takes the second meaning.[1]

However, those who oppose this view argue, we still have to account for the meaning of bhakti. If Vāsudeva is a god then bhakti can be rendered as adoration; and then Arjuna, and the Mahārāja, the Gotras and famous kṣatriyas and even insentient objects would be adored in a religious sense in the *Aṣṭādhyāyī*. If we are ready to accept this, then, and only then, can Vāsudeva be a divinity in Patañjali. This is the argument of U.C. Bhattacharjee:

> There is nothing to show that *bhakti* as applied to rule 98 is different from what it means in rule 96, or 99, or 100. So, if we speak of worshippers of Vāsudeva or Arjuna under rule 98, we ought to be prepared to think of other objects, too, under the other rules,.... If, however, we are not prepared to infer the existence of these other worshippers, are we justified in inferring Arjuna-worship, or even Vāsudeva-worship from rule 98?[2]

This article of Bhattacharjee was quickly followed by an answer by K.G. Subrahmanyam, and initiated a controversy that was to last through several numbers of the *Indian Historical Quarterly*. Subrahmanyam defended his position that Patañjali refers to Vāsudeva as a divine being by quoting the *Mahābhāṣya* again, where it says that either we have here a case of *pūrvanipātaṃ* or in this instance Vāsudeva is not just the name of a famous kṣatriya but it refers to the worshippable one (*tatrabhavataḥ*). But arguing that bhakti in the *sūtras* can be taken both in a religious and in a profane sense[3] failed to convince Bhattacharjee, and after three more articles the polemic was ended without his arguments being answered.

A different solution to the problem had been given before by K.B. Pathak. His position, that has since been supported by others, is that Patañjali means that in fact there were two different Vāsudevas: the kṣatriya Vāsudeva, and the *tatrabhavat*, i.e. god. This makes the bhakti in Pāṇini's *sūtras* an authentic religious worship, but leaves the problem raised by the word being applicable to other contexts without an answer. Pathak uses the authority of later traditional Sanskrit commentaries to sustain his position, starting with the famous *Kāśikā Vṛtti* of the Buddhist Jayāditya (seventh century) and followed by the commentary on the same *Kāśikā* by Jinendrabuddhi (eighth century), and by the rest of the illustrious line of commentators on Patañjali: Kaiyaṭa (twelfth century), Haradatta (thirteenth century), and the well known Bhaṭṭojī Dīkṣita (seventeenth century) down to Jñānendrasarasvatī (seventeenth century) and Nāgojī Bhaṭṭa of the early eighteenth century. All these commentators recognise in Patañjali's *tatrabhavat* a divinity.[1]

Bhandarkar and Subrahmanyam accepted that *tatrabhavat* means a divine being but did not deem it necessary to split Vāsudeva's personality into two different people, the kṣatriya Vāsudeva and the divine Vāsudeva. The latest research on the theme follows, however, the opinion of K.B. Pathak who, as we have seen, takes Patañjali's words as implying that difference. Such is the case with R.C. Hazra who, in a lengthy and thorough article published not long ago at the University of Calcutta, reaches the same conclusion as Pathak.[2] Hazra reviews again the traditional commentaries on Patañjali as well as using evidence from the Buddhist Jātakas, the *Mahābhārata* and the Purāṇas, in addition to some other sources, to substantiate his conclusion that Patañjali did acknowledge the separate identity of the kṣatriya Vāsudeva and the divine Vāsudeva. He is not very clear, however, in his own statements, seemingly contradicting himself at the end of his article. So he conclusively says that it is 'evident that Pāṇini was quite familiar with kṣatriya Vāsudeva's being the *bhakti* of some people',[3] and three pages after this he also says: 'it is evident that by *Vāsudeva* Pāṇini means that Vāsudeva (the Supreme Being) Who is not a kṣatriya'.[4] Possibly he is trying

1. R. G. Bhandarkar, 'Vāsudeva of Pāṇini 4.3.98' in *JRAS*, 1910, p. 169.
2. U. C. Bhattacharjee, 'The Evidence of Pāṇini on Vāsudeva-Worship', in *IHQ*, v.1, 1925, p. 485.
3. K. G. Subrahmanyam, 'A Note on the Evidence of Pāṇini on Vāsudeva-Worship', in *IHQ*, v. 2, 1926, p. 188.

1. K. B. Pathak, 'The Divine Vāsudeva different from the Kṣatriya Vāsudeva in Patañjali's opinion', in *JDBRAS*, v. 123, 1909-14, pp. 96-103.
2. R. C. Hazra. 'Vāsudeva Worship as known to Pāṇini', in *Our Heritage*, v.18, 1970, pp.1-45; 97-123, p.122.
3. Hazra, *ibid.*, p. 119.
4. *Ibid.*, p.122.

to say that Pāṇini includes the kṣatriya Vāsudeva among the famous kṣatriyas of *sūtra* 4.3.99 and in *kṛṣṇārjunābhyāṃ vun* he refers to the divine Vāsudeva. However he recognises the difficulty of this theory as residing in the fact that Pāṇini mentions Vāsudeva and Arjuna together, and these are the famous pair of the *Mahābhārata*, i.e. famous kṣatriyas. He tries to relate Arjuna with Indra and with Nara of Nara and Nārāyaṇa as well as with the arjuna-tree, but he accepts that 'still we fail to understand what Pāṇini actually means by the word *arjuna* in the said compound.'[1]

This problem is not considered a great difficulty by R.N. Dandekar, the last scholar to review this question. Professor Dandekar, in a recent article,[2] follows the opinion of Pathak (without referring to him) and accepts the consequence of having to take Arjuna in Pāṇini as a god, with the reservation, however, of explaining bhakti as taking different meanings in each *sūtra*.[3] To quote his own words:

> We have ... to assume that *tatrabhavān* Vāsudeva (mentioned in P. 4.3.98) is a god and is to be distinguished from a kṣatriya whose name might be Vāsudeva and who could then be covered by P. 4.3.99. It may be, incidentally, added that Vāsudeva, when coupled with Arjuna, usually denotes a god.[4]

And also: 'We have to acquiesce in the fact that, in Pāṇini's time, there did prevail two independent religious cults, namely, the Vāsudeva-cult and the Arjuna-cult.'[5] But he not only assumes the existence of a separate Arjuna-cult, he also proposes another separation, one between a deified Vṛṣṇi prince Vāsudeva and a deified tribal hero and religious leader of the Yādavas, namely Kṛṣṇa,[6] as we have seen above.

After looking into the interpretations of the Pāṇini-Patañjali Vāsudeva by all these scholars we can really appreciate the difficulty of the problem posed by the sūtras and their commentaries in relation to the whole question of the history of the Kṛṣṇa legends. This last question is best answered by the evidence shown in the testimonial of Megasthenes.

1. *Ibid.*; see also P. Banerjee, *Early Indian Religions*, Vikas, Delhi 1973, pp. 62-67.
2. R. N. Dandekar, 'The Beginnings of Vaiṣṇavism'.
3. Dandekar, *ibid.*, pp. 170-71.
4. *Ibid.*, p. 173.
5. *Ibid.*, p. 177.
6. *Ibid.*, p. 179.

As we pointed out above, the *Indika*, the book of Megasthenes, has not reached our day; all that we have are references to it in later authors. The most complete of these accounts of the contents of the original book is that given by Arrian, a Hellenistic Greek of the first-second century A.D., famous for his *Anabasis* (*Expedition*) *of Alexander*. He also wrote a book called *Indika*, following Megasthenes. The Greek ambassador to Candragupta Maurya of Pāṭaliputra is also referred to or quoted as an authority on Indian subjects by many other classical writers, among them Pliny, Diodorus Siculus and Strabo.

Most modern scholars have agreed that Megasthenes' reference to the Indian Heracles points to Kṛṣṇa. This identification was, however, challenged not long ago by a Swedish clerical scholar, Allan Dahlquist,[1] who tries at all costs to disprove that Kṛṣṇa could have been referred to by Megasthenes. Before him only three scholars had identified Megasthenes' Heracles with a god other than Kṛṣṇa. Cunningham identifies him with Śiva[2] and so does Kennedy.[3] The latter was one of the most active participants in the controversy on the Christian influence on Kṛṣṇa bhakti started fifty years before by Weber's famous article.[4] The Christian missionaries, who had still at that time great hopes of converting vast numbers of Indians, were concerned when it was pointed out that the bhakti religion had many tenets similar to those professed by Christianity. So from many Christian sects attempts began to be made to prove that every ethically or doctrinally acceptable point of Kṛṣṇaism was in fact derived from Christianity. These claims were met immediately with replies to the effect that there were in fact textual and archaeological evidences that showed the existence of the Kṛṣṇa cult in the centuries before the Christian Era, and among these evidences Megasthenes' account was mentioned. So Kennedy was committed to disproving all these evidences and leaving the way open for the possibility of Christian influence on the Kṛṣṇa religion. Fifty years after

1. A. Dahlquist, *Megasthenes and Indian Religion*, Uppsala 1962, 2nd rep. Delhi 1977.
2. A. Cunningham, *Coins of Ancient India*, London 1891, pp. vii-viii.
3. J. Kennedy, 'The Child Kṛṣṇa, Christianity, and the Gujars', in *JRAS*, 1907, pp. 964-68.
4. A. Weber, 'On the kṛṣṇajanmāṣṭamī, or Kṛṣṇa's Birth Festival', in *IA*, 1874 and 1877; first read in the Royal Academy of Sciences, Berlin 1867.

him (a hundred after Weber), there were evidently some Christians who still felt a need to keep this possibility open, since Dr. Dahlquist set himself again to the task of invalidating those evidences, especially that of Megasthenes whose statements 'form the decisive arguments in the great discussion which, until some fifty years ago, raged among Indologists on the possibility of a relationship between Christianity and Kṛṣṇaism'.[1] The work of Dahlquist was examined by Professor Kuiper, who, in a review of his book,[2] wonders 'if the considerable labour and time that must have gone into its composition could not have been turned to better advantage.' Kuiper has very clearly expressed the basic trend of the book: 'Dahlquist apparently was so profoundly convinced of the correctness of his new identification "Herakles = Indra" that he continued, in the face of all indications to the contrary, to heap theory upon theory in an effort to defend his thesis.'[3]

We do not intend to write another review of Dahlquist's book, since Professor Kuiper has already shown its weakness. We only have to point out that, despite all the painstaking labour put up by Dahlquist in gathering all the material and analysing it minutely point by point, he fails to disprove the identity of Kṛṣṇa with Heracles. Despite all his efforts to minimise and distort the evidence, the fact still remains that the mention in Megasthenes and his followers of Mathurā, the river Yamunā and the Śūrasenas in connection with Heracles, very definitely favours an identification with Kṛṣṇa. Later on we will review the points of similarity between the Kṛṣṇa story and the legends of Heracles. Dahlquist mentions that before him only L. von Schroeder had 'by sheer chance stumbled upon the correct result, despite the superficiality of his method'.[4] After Dahlquist only one other scholar has advocated the identification of Heracles with Indra, without, however, mentioning Megasthenes, and therefore his work is not relevant to our present theme.[5]

1. Dahlquist, *Megasthenes....*, p.9.
2. F.B.J. Kuiper, 'Review of Dahlquist's *Megasthenes....*', in *IIJ*, v.11, 1969, pp. 142-46.
3. Kuiper, *ibid.*, p. 142.
4. Dahlquist, *Megasthenes....*, p. 89. In fact Indra, as an example of the traditional hero, is very logically comparable to Heracles, and that is why von Schroeder and Dumézil compare them, but this is not what Dahlquist alleges, he is out to deny that Megasthenes referred to Kṛṣṇa as Heracles and to this purpose he infructuously dedicates his pen.
5. Georges Dumézil, *Heur et malheur du guerrier*, Presses Universitaires de France, 1969.

We now review the rest of the evidence found in Patañjali's *Mahābhāṣya*, listed previously. Patañjali mentions the killing of Kaṃsa by Kṛṣṇa as represented in tales and theatrical representations of a certain kind.[1] He also says that the events told in the story were thought of as occurring long ago. It is also mentioned in another passage that Kṛṣṇa was at enmity with his maternal uncle, i.e. Kaṃsa.[2] In another place it is again said that Kaṃsa is killed, but the name of his vanquisher is given there as Vāsudeva, and not as Kṛṣṇa as in the previous passage.[3] In his commentary to sūtra 4.3.64 Patañjali mentions one more personage in the story of Kṛṣṇa when he speaks of followers of Akrūra and followers of Vāsudeva. On 2.2.34 he quotes a line referring to a temple apparently dedicated to Kubera, Balarāma and Kṛṣṇa. In another place he includes a quotation that reads: 'May the power of Kṛṣṇa, assisted by Saṃkarṣaṇa, increase',[4] where he refers to the same pair of brothers as before. Finally he mentions also one epithet of Kṛṣṇa at the same time that probably points to one of the theological tenets of his cult when he gives the example 'Janārdana with himself as the fourth'.[5]

All these passages were collected first by R.G. Bhandarkar,[6] who arrived at the conclusion that they clearly indicate that the stories of Kṛṣṇa 'were current and popular in the second century before Christ', and therefore 'some such works as the *Harivaṃśa* and the Purāṇas must have existed then'.[7] Bhandarkar, however, nearly forty years after, revised his opinion and conceded: 'There is no allusion to the cowherd Kṛṣṇa in the authorities we have hitherto quoted. The inscriptions, the work of Patañjali and even the Nārāyaṇīya itself indicate no knowledge of the existence of such a god'[8] and he further argues: 'The story of the Vṛṣṇi prince Vāsudeva having been brought up in a cow-settlement is incongruous with his later career as depicted in the *Mahābhārata*. Nor does any part of it require the presupposition of such boyhood as has been ascribed to him.'[9] What Bhandarkar started in 1874 as a

1. On Pāṇini 3.1.26.
2. On Pāṇini 2.3.36.
3. On Pāṇini 3.2.111.
4. On Pāṇini 2.2.24.
5. On Pāṇini 6.3.6.
6. R. G. Bhandarkar, 'Allusions to Kṛṣṇa in Patañjali's Mahābhāṣya', in *IA*, v.3, 1874, pp. 14-16.
7. *Ibid.*, p. 16.
8. R. G. Bhandarkar, *Vaiṣṇavism....*p.35.
9. *Ibid.*

rejoinder to those European scholars who 'find in Christ a prototype of Kṛṣṇa, and in the Bible the original of the *Bhagavad Gītā*, and who believe our Puranic literature to be merely a later growth',[1] he ended by agreeing with these same scholars in thinking that the tribe of the Ābhīras brought the figure of Christ to India:

> They must have migrated into the country in the first century. They probably brought with them the worship of the boy-god and the story of his humble birth, his reputed father's knowledge that he was not his son, and the massacre of the innocents ... the stories of Kṛṣṇa's boyhood such as that of killing Dhenuka, a demon in the form of a wild ass, were brought by Ābhīras, and others were developed after they came to India. It is possible that they brought with them the name Christ also, and this name probably led to the identification of the boy-god with Vāsudeva-Kṛṣṇa.[2]

Other scholars however did not agree with Bhandarkar and as Raychaudhuri noted: 'there is no inherent improbability in Kṛṣṇa's being a shepherd as well as a warrior teacher. Moses and Mahomed furnish good parallels. It is, however, possible that the tales about the pastoral Kṛṣṇa really arose from the Vedic legend of Viṣṇu Gopa.'[3] This notwithstanding, he concedes in a later paragraph: 'But though the idea of a pastoral Kṛṣṇa may have been borrowed from the Vedas its development was clearly due to some such tribe as the Ābhīras who were closely connected with the Pāṇḍu migration to the South.'[4] So Raychaudhuri accepts the connection of the Ābhīras with the development of the Kṛṣṇa story although he does not at all explain what this 'Pāṇḍu migration to the South' may be. Only later he refers for this to the book *Tamils Eighteen Hundred Years Ago*, of V. Kanakasabhai, that 'says that the Ayar (Ābhīras) had a tradition that they came into the Tamil land along with the founder of the Pāṇḍyan family, i.e. several centuries before Christ.'[5] So he recognises the Ābhīra influence but puts it earlier than Bhandarkar. Raychaudhuri draws

1. Bhandarkar, *IA*, v.3, p.16.
2. Bhandarkar, *Vaiṣṇavism*....,pp. 37-38.
3. H. C. Raychaudhuri, *Early History*...., 2nd ed., p. 55.
4. Raychaudhuri, *ibid.*, p. 74.
5. *Ibid.*, p. 152. Professor Basham thinks that the relation of the people called *Āy* in the Tamil anthologies to the Ābhīras is extremely doubtful.

support not only from the said book but also from Patañjali himself, who mentioned the Ābhīras in his commentary to Kātyāyana's *vārtika* on Pāṇini 1.2.72 (*vārtika* 6)[1] where he mentions them together with the Śūdras as two distinct peoples. The evidence in Patañjali has been dealt with by Raychaudhuri also in connection with the problem of theatrical representations of the Kṛṣṇa story and in making a criticism of A.B. Keith's opinion on this problem. Keith follows in his interpretation of the Patañjali passage the ritualistic theories of the school of Sir J. G. Frazer, and finds in it evidence of the ritual representation of the battle of 'the genius of summer who overcomes the darkness of the winter'.[2] The problem had been discussed, however, long before Keith, and was still being debated at the time when he wrote. The problem involved the interpretation of the key words *śobhanika*, *citra*, and *granthika* and the manner of narrative techniques they implied. Everybody agreed on seeing in the passage in question reference to recited narration in the word *granthika*, to pictorial representation in the word *citra*, and to theatrical dramatisation in the word *śobhanika*.[3] The passage, however, presented other peculiar problems like the mention of facial coloration and the reference to Vāsudevabhaktas and Kaṃsabhaktas that links it also with the problem raised by Pāṇini's sūtra 4.3.95 (*bhaktiḥ*).

We are not concerned here with the history of the Indian theatre and so we do not attempt to review the particulars of the lengthy controversies that arose over such questions as the colouring of the faces during the act presented by the *granthikas* and the exact nature of the means employed by the *śobhanikas* to represent the story of Kṛṣṇa. Norvin Hein[4] has already reviewed those polemics for us. On the other hand, we have to account for the use of the word *bhakta* in the passage. This problem has also been discussed many times without coming to any certain conclusion. Some suggest that it indicates the existence of a real cult of Kaṃsa. Others believe that in the audience itself parties supporting Kṛṣṇa and Kaṃsa respectively separated during

1. Kielhorn's ed. of *Mahābhāṣya*, 3rd ed. v.1, p. 252.
2. A. B. Keith, *The Sanskrit Drama*, Oxford University Press, Oxford, 1924.
3. A. Weber, *Indische Studien*, v. 13, 1873, pp. 354 f. and 487 f; R. G. Bhandarkar, 'Allusions...', *IA*, v.3, 1874, pp. 14-16; Sylvain Levi, *Le Théatre Indien* (1890), Collège de France, Paris, 1963, pp. 314 f.
4. N. Hein, *The Miracle Plays*...., pp. 240-51.

the narration, owing to the identification and fixed attention that the public gave to the enactment of the story. Some of the historians of drama are of the opinion that the separation between supporters of Kṛṣṇa and supporters of Kaṃsa took place on the stage itself and not among the public, arguing that it is difficult to believe that the Indian popular audience could have any sympathy with the wicked Kaṃsa. The latest research however favours the view that:

> the story of the enmity between Kaṃsa and Kṛṣṇa ... may have a deeper significance; and it seems to symbolise a struggle getween the mother-right represented by the maternal uncle Kaṃsa and the father-right by the sister's son Kṛṣṇa, in which the latter, a representative of the younger generation, emerges victorious. Patañjali refers to the dramatic presentations of the killing of Kaṃsa by Vāsudeva-Kṛṣṇa. Probably these were ritual-dramas, at least in origin, commemorating the victory of the patriarchal way of life.[1]

So accepting the possibility that 'there were people whose sympathies lay with Kaṃsa',[2] and adhering at the same time to the ritual school on the origin of myth started by Frazer and followed as we have seen by scholars like A.B. Keith.

Professor Dandekar in his last article on the subject[3] is of the opinion that the *granthikas*

> through their remarkable narrative skill ... make the episode of Kaṃsa-vadha live before their large audiences. By means of suitable modulation of voice, often accompanied by corresponding gesticulation, they succeed in rousing the dormant emotions of their hearers, some of whom subconsciously sympathise with Kaṃsa and some with Vāsudeva, and these their emotions then become manifest on their faces.[4]

Here Professor Dandekar points to the subconscious character of the sympathies felt for Kaṃsa. In fact he uses this term 'subconscious sympathies' as a synonym of bhakti in this passage from Patañjali.[5] He cannot accept that the audience could in any way feel real sympathy for Kaṃsa. He adds to the meanings of bhakti given in Pāṇini also 'subconscious sympathies'. This argument implies however that in Patañjali the Vāsudeva *bhaktas* are not religious followers of Kṛṣṇa; this is of course in disagreement with the contemporary evidence provided by the Besnagar column that declares Vāsudeva 'god of gods'. Dandekar clearly states that 'the words *kaṃsabhaktaḥ* and *vāsudevabhaktaḥ* do not denote two different religious cults — *bhakta* here simply means "having sympathy for".'[1] This on the other hand contradicts what he himself said previously,[2] accepting that in Pāṇini we have evidence of two religious cults, the Arjuna-cult and the Vāsudeva-cult. Or is he implying that the *vāsudevakas* (those who entertain bhakti for Vāsudeva) are different from the *vāsudevabhaktas*?

Professor Dandekar refers also to all the rest of the evidence found in the Grammar of Patañjali. He points out that the mention in 4.1.114 of Vāsudeva and Baladeva as instances of Vṛṣṇi names proves that Vāsudeva is not a patronymically derived form but an original name due to the Pāṇinian rules of grammar[3] where the termination *aṇ* appended to Vṛṣṇi names such as Vāsudeva produces the form Vāsudeva. And from the fact that this name appears in connection with the Vṛṣṇis and Balarāma Professor Dandekar concludes that Vāsudeva 'was a Vṛṣṇi prince who was later deified', since Balarāma, who is traditionally his brother, was also a Vṛṣṇi prince who was later deified.[4] Dandekar makes an important point in correcting the view that was generally held on Patañjali 2.2.34 that two quarter-verses quoted there, one reading 'in the assemblies they severally sound drums, conchs and flutes', the other: 'in the temple of Dhanapati, Rāma and Keśava' form one line and belong 'to one and the same context, namely, the playing of musical instruments in festivals celebrated in the temple of Dhanapati-Rāma-Keśava'. In Dandekar's opinion this is not correct, since the first verse is in the *pramāṇikā* metre and the second in the *praharṣiṇī* metre 'the words *saṃsadi* and *prāsāde* clearly indicate two different contexts; so too perhaps do the two different metres.'[5] And even more, he adds: 'archaeologists have so far not come across any temple dedicated jointly to Kubera, Balarāma, and Kṛṣṇa.'

The point raised by Patañjali in 3.1.26 mentioning

1. Suvira Jaiswal, *The Origin*...., p. 66.
2. *Ibid.*
3. *Indologica Taurinensia*, v. 3-4.
4. Dandekar, *ibid.*, p. 181.
5. *Ibid.*, p. 182.

1. *Ibid.*, p. 183.
2. See above, p. 29.
3. vṛṣṇyaṇo'vakāśaḥ, vāsudevaḥ bāladevaḥ, ṇyasya sa eva.
4. *Ibid.*, p. 174.
5. *Ibid.*, pp. 184-85.

kaṃsa-bhaktas and *vāsudeva-bhaktas* leads us to another suggested reference to followers of both Kaṃsa and Kṛṣṇa in the religious sense rather than the historical, since we can obviously expect that Kaṃsa would have had his followers as tyrant of Mathurā. The reference to this appears in the chronologically debatable *Arthaśāstra* attributed to Kauṭilya, first minister of Candragupta Maurya (fourth century B.C.). There in 14.3.44, in a list of magic spells, appears the formula *vande kṛṣṇa-kaṃsa-upacāram* that has been taken as meaning 'I bow to the followers of Kṛṣṇa' (ignoring the presence of Kaṃsa altogether),[1] or 'I bow to the service of Kṛṣṇa and Kaṃsa'.[2] Suvira Jaiswal[3] uses the invocation to point out that 'even in the fourth century B.C. both Kaṃsa and Kṛṣṇa were regarded as pastoral deities, as Kauṭilya prescribes their invocation for those engaged in collecting medicinal herbs.' We fail to see, however, how Dr. Jaiswal can ascertain that they were 'pastoral deities', or where she can find any reference to 'those engaged in collecting medicinal herbs' in the text of the *Arthaśāstra* that we are now dealing with. Chapter three of book fourteen of the *Arthaśāstra* is entitled 'the application of drugs and spells in deception' (*pralambhane bhaiṣajyamantraprayogaḥ*) and consists of recipes for seeing in the darkness, recipes for making oneself and other objects invisible, charms to make sleep, charms to open doors, charms to cause harm, and charms to obtain wealth. As we see, it is a section dealing with black magic for the uses of statecraft. The invocation that concerns us here appears in the fourth and last of the incantations to cause sleep. We quote Kangle's translation :

> I bow to Bali, the son of Virocana and to Śambara of the hundred guiles, to Nikumbha, to Naraka, to Kumbha, to Tantukaccha, the great Asura;
>
> [I bow] to Armālava, to Pramila, to Maṇḍolūka, to Ghaṭodbala, and to the service of Kṛṣṇa and Kaṃsa, and to Paulomī, the successful.
>
> ... May the dogs sleep happily, and those who, in the village are curious. May those who have achieved their object—the object which we seek—sleep happily till the rising [of the sun] after its setting, till the object is mine as the fruit.[4]

This incantation was probably prescribed for the spies of the king to enter an enemy city or encampment unnoticed. We can hardly imagine how Dr. Jaiswal arrived at her interpretation. The words *vande kṛṣṇakaṃsopacāram* do not indicate that they were 'pastoral deities' as they do not mean 'the followers of Kṛṣṇa' or 'the service of Kṛṣṇa and Kaṃsa', although Kangle came closer to the mark in his rendering. The word *upacāra* has in this passage the meaning of 'treatment',[1] medical or magical as here, as the word *bhaiṣajya* in the title of the chapter indicates. And the invocation then reads 'I bow to the treatment of Kaṃsa by Kṛṣṇa' or 'to the treatment [given] to Kaṃsa by Kṛṣṇa'. The fact that this particular magical operation is performed to cause sleep suggests immediately the story told of Kṛṣṇa and Kaṃsa in this context that on the night Kṛṣṇa was born Kaṃsa and all of his people in Mathurā and Gokula were put fast asleep under the influence of Yoganidrā, the personified goddess of the 'yoga of sleep', sent by Kṛṣṇa, so permitting Vasudeva to take the new-born child out of the prison and exchange him for the daughter of the unconscious Yaśodā.[2]

This invocation in the treatise on statecraft attributed to Kauṭilya shows a knowledge of the Purāṇic story of the birth of Kṛṣṇa. Besides this, we find in the *Arthaśāstra* other references to the life of Kṛṣṇa. His brother and fast companion in his early career, Balarāma, is mentioned in 13.3.54 and associated with intoxicating drink just as he is in the Purāṇas. And in 1.6.10 an example is given that points very definitely to the legend of the death of Kṛṣṇa and the destruction of his clan. The passage refers to kings and warriors who met with destruction through their infatuation and lack of restraint, mainly in their dealings with brāhmaṇas. The final example given in this connection is that of the fate of the Vṛṣṇis, Kṛṣṇa's family, who were destroyed because of their conflict with Dvaipāyana, i.e. Vyāsa. The story is told in the *Mausala Parvan* of the *Mahābhārata* and the *Ghaṭa Jātaka*. The reference is quite clear. Although the name of the sage or sages in question is not the same in the *Mahābhārata* and Purāṇas as in the *Arthaśāstra*, it occurs in the otherwise similar Buddhist version appearing in the Jātaka collection. This coincidence in the mention of the

1. Samasastry, *Kauṭilya's*...p. 463.
2. R. P. Kangle, *The Kauṭilīya Arthaśāstra*, 1963, pt. II, p. 58.
3. *Origin and Development*... p. 65.
4. Kangle, *ibid.*, pp. 586-87.

1. We thank Dr. V. N. Shukla, of Aligarh, for his help in the reading of the passage.
2. *VP* 5.3.20; *BhP* 10.3.48; *DBP* 4.3.25.

name of Vyāsa is remarkable and suggests that this is the oldest tradition. The *Mahābhārata* and Purāṇas could not have used Vyāsa in this episode, since he is supposed to have been the author of these texts and he dies in this version of the story. So they had to use some other sages for the occasion, the Buddhists and Kauṭilya on the other hand did not feel this need, since they were writing before the full *Mahābhārata* legend took its present shape.

Further evidence of the antiquity of the Kṛṣṇa story is provided in the fifth century B.C., *Nirukta*, the etymological treatise of Yāska. As M.A. Mehendale has shown,[1] in presenting the etymology of *daṇḍa* Yāska uses as an example a reference to the story of the Syamantaka jewel. Drawing evidence from this episode as it appears in the *Harivaṃśa* and the Purāṇas, Mehendale was able to clarify the meaning of the verb *dad* in the example given in the *Nirukta*. The rendering 'Akrūra holds in trust the jewel' is clearly justified by the Purāṇic story and so the meaning 'to wear' given by the scholiasts Skandasvāmin and Maheśvara has to be discarded.

We now turn to our archaeological evidences. These have not been as extensively commented upon by earlier scholars as the literary references and therefore will not require a great deal of criticism and reviewing.

The first and most important of them is the Besnagar column of Heliodorus. This has been discussed by several scholars who have shown very interesting features about it. We are concerned here, however, only with the origins and evolution of the Kṛṣṇa story, and for that purpose the Besnagar column, as well as the other inscriptions mentioned before, provide but little evidence. The Heliodorus inscription shows that Kṛṣṇa-Vāsudeva was adored as supreme god around 100 B.C., that his followers were called Bhāgavatas and that he was associated with Viṣṇu, since Garuḍa is the emblem and vehicle of that god.

We need not discuss here the very interesting fact that the column was dedicated by a Greek ambassador, but we must report on the opinions given on the second part of the inscription: 'Three immortal steps when practised lead to heaven: charity, self-control and vigilance' (*dama*, *tyāga* and *apramāda*). L.D. Barnett first suggested that the mention of three steps was a reference to Viṣṇu and his three steps.[1] H.C. Raychaudhuri[2] suggested that a comparison could be made with the words *devam devatrā* applied to Sūrya in *RV* 1.50.10, a hymn from which Ghora Āṅgirasa quoted when instructing Kṛṣṇa Devakīputra,[3] and in an article of 1922[4] Raychaudhuri points to the occurrence of all three virtues of the second part of the inscription in *Mahābhārata* 11.7.23,[5] where they are mentioned in the same order.[6] He also mentions in the same article the fact that Heliodorus came from Taxila and that 'it was at that city that Janamejaya heard from Vaiśampāyana the famous story of the Kurus and the Pāṇḍus.'[7] He then goes on to suggest that 'Heliodorus of Taxila actually heard and utilized the teaching of the Great Epic', since we know from Pāṇini that the Epic was 'well known to the people of Gandhāra' long before the Greek ambassador.[8]

The next in the list of our archaeological evidences is the famous Ghosūṇḍī Inscription with its duplicate found at Hathibāḍā. The text of this inscription presents certain problems that have been discussed by various scholars. Several suggestions as to the date and the king mentioned in the dedication have been offered. D.R. Bhandarkar[9] dated it in between the fourth and third centuries B.C., K.P. Jayaswal[10] attributes it to the second or first centuries B.C., and J.C. Ghosh[11] proposes the later half of the first century B.C. as the more correct dating. His reckoning is followed by D.C. Sircar who, however, does not follow Ghosh's other conclusion, that the King of the inscription was one of the Kāṇvad ynasty; he prefers to believe that this could have been a local ruler.[12]

1. 'Yāska's Etymology of *daṇḍa*', *JAOS*, v.80, 1960, pp. 112-14; see also R. C. Hazra, 'Vāsudeva Worship...', *Our Heritage*, v.18, pp. 41-42.

1. *Hindu Gods...*, p. 89.
2. *Materials...*, 2nd ed., p. 100.
3. *Chāndogya*, 3.17.7.
4. H. C. Raychaudhuri, 'The *Mahābhārata* and the Besnagar Inscription', *JRASB*, v.18, p. 269.
5. Crit. ed., 11. 7.19.
6. M. C. Choudhury ('Besnagar Garuḍa Pillar Inscription of Heliodorus—An Assessement', *Visv. Indol. Journal*, 1964, p. 343) drew attention to an occurrence in the *Mahābhārata* 5.43.14; in a list of virtues that occurs in *BG* (16.1-2) appear *tyāga* and *dayā* that Raychaudhuri tries to connect with the Heliodorus' inscription.
7. Raychaudhuri, *JRASB*, 1922, p. 270; *Mbh.* 18.5.34; Crit. ed. 18.5.29.
8. *Ibid.*, p. 271.
9. *MASI* no. 4, 1920.
10. *EI*, v.16, 1915-16, p. 25.
11. 'Notes on the Ghosūṇḍī stone inscription', *IHQ*, 1933, p. 799.
12. D. C. Sircar, *Select Inscriptions*...v.1, p. 91 nl.

One other suggestion of J.C. Ghosh is more relevant to our subject. He contends that the interpretation of the compound *pūjāśilāprākāra* should not be 'the stone enclosure (*śilāprākāra*) for worship (*pūjā*)', but 'a rampart for the stone object of worship' and wants this stone object of worship to be interpreted as a *śālagrāma* stone of the type that even to this day is worshipped as a manifestation of Viṣṇu-Kṛṣṇa.[1] His interpretation sounds reasonable and attractive, but cannot be corroborated. On the other hand this need not worry us in the pursuit of our theme, as we need be concerned only with the fact that Kṛṣṇa and Balarāma are mentioned together as Vāsudeva and Saṃkarṣaṇa, that they are called *bhagavān*, that the king is referred to as *bhāgavata* and that they were considered as *sarveśvara* 'Lords of all' and were worshipped in a sacred compound dedicated to Nārāyaṇa.

Next we have another inscription from a column found at Besnagar, two inscriptions from Mathurā and finally an inscription from the Western Deccan. From these four, dating from the first century B.C. to the early first century A.D., we can gather that the epithets *bhagavān* and *bhāgavata* were in widespread use, that big and very important temples were erected to Vāsudeva (*prāsādottama* and *mahāsthāna*), that Saṃkarṣaṇa and Vāsudeva were invoked first in a list of salutations to protective deities that included Candra, Sūrya and the four guardians of the quarters, so indicating their pre-eminence, and lastly the very significant mention of images of 'the five heroes of the Vṛṣṇis' (*bhagavatāṃ vṛṣṇināṃ paṃcavīrāṇām pratimāḥ*). Lüders identified these five heroes as: Baladeva, Akrūra, Anādhṛṣṭi, Saraṇa, and Viduratha[2] of the Jaina tradition. It is however easier and more obvious to identify them with Saṃkarṣaṇa, Vāsudeva, Pradyumna, Śāmba and Aniruddha, as J.N. Banerjea did, basing himself on the *Vāyu Purāṇa* 97.1-4,[3] and relating them to the Pañcarātra sect.[4]

1. J. N. Banerjea, *Development of Hindu Iconography*, University of Calcutta, 1941, p. 101, is also of the same opinion.

2. *EI*, v.24, pp. 194f.

3. J. N. Banerjea, *Evolution of Indian Iconography*, 1956 (2nd ed.), p. 94.

4. J. N. Banerjea published an article on the subject in 1941 that unfortunately we are unable to procure ('The Holy Pañcavīras of the Vṛishṇis', *JISOA*, 1941). His results were however summarised by himself in one book published more recently (*Paurāṇic and Tāntric Religion*, 1966, pp. 29-31).

R.P. Chanda[1] following a modified version of J.Ph. Vogel's reading,[2] reads the inscription as *bhagavato vṛṣṇeḥ paṃcavīrāṇāṃ pratimā* 'images of Bhagavān of the Vṛṣṇis and of the five heroes', i.e. the five Pāṇḍavas, so adhering to Vogel's view that the five brothers of the *Mahābhārata* were to be understood here.[3] If this is correct we shall have to presuppose a cult of the Pāṇḍavas, as their images were installed in the temples along with that of Kṛṣṇa-Vāsudeva.

iii. SUMMARY

We now propose our own suggestions in the matters that have been discussed in this chapter. We do not intend—or pretend—to give definitive answers on the multiple problems raised by the scanty evidence. We will only try to let a little more light enter into the obscurities of the maze by putting some order in the arrangement of the materials.[4] Then, using this new light, we will try to give a picture, hopefully a little more complete than those of earlier students of the subject, of what for us is to remain necessarily a very incomplete image of the formation and evolution of the Kṛṣṇa story.

The evidence gathered out of fourteen sources—eight literary and six archaeological—consists of eight different names of Kṛṣṇa, two of Balarāma, one title, five names of other personages in the Kṛṣṇa story, two geographical names, six names of tribes and tribal units, one name of a sect and, finally, four references to episodes in the life of Kṛṣṇa. This is in bare numbers the material on which we have to build an image of the early stages in the development of the Kṛṣṇa cycle. In terms of the so-called 'sober history' that these data can provide, this evidence is at best very tenuous. An analysis of its correspondences yields very meagre results. We can however, following the reflections of the critics and dealing only with the Kṛṣṇa story as the subject of our enquiry, give a view of the diffusion of that saga or of certain motifs in it during the period previous

1. 'Archaeology and Vaiṣṇava Tradition', *ASIAR*, 1920, pp. 166-67.

2. J. Ph. Vogel, *Catalogue of the Archaeological Museum at Mathura*, Allahabad 1919, p. 184.

3. J. Ph. Vogel, *ASIAR*, 1911-12, pt. 2, p. 127. Professor Basham notes that literally it seems to mean 'an image of the five heroes of the Lord Vṛṣṇi'.

4. We have presented a scheme of all the materials and the evidences found in them in table form. See table 1.

to the composition and compilation of the Purāṇas as we have them.

To start with, as we have already seen, the name or nickname Kṛṣṇa is at least as old as the *Ṛg Veda*, but the connection of the several Kṛṣṇas in the *Ṛg Veda* with the hero of the legends that we are dealing with is however, to say the least, very unlikely. A better claim to be our first true mention of that hero has the *Chāndogya Upaniṣad*. Despite the doubts cast on this identification by some scholars, as mentioned before,[1] we feel that the evidence favours a connection. Certainly we cannot accept the view that Kṛṣṇa appears in the *Ṛg Veda*, but nevertheless we have to reckon with the mention of the Yādavas and the Bhojas in the hymns and it is quite probable that these tribes and families traditionally associated with Kṛṣṇa had already a tradition of a certain hero of this name.

That stories about Kṛṣṇa were current not long after the accepted dates of the Upaniṣad we can gather from the *Nirukta*, where Akrūra, one of the influential people in the Vṛṣṇi branch of the Yādavas and sometime pretender to the hand of Satyabhāmā—one of Kṛṣṇa's wives—is mentioned in a context that presupposes the presence of Kṛṣṇa. Not long after the *Nirukta* we have the evidence furnished by Pāṇini's Grammar, where not only is Kṛṣṇa mentioned but he is also connected with Arjuna, his fast companion of the Epic tradition, and with bhakti, a word which could by then well have acquired a religious meaning. In Pāṇini we also have, as we have already seen, references to the Andhaka-Vṛṣṇis, the family of Kṛṣṇa, to the Epic history,[2] and to Yudhiṣṭhira, Arjuna's brother, one of the most prominent personages in the *Mahābhārata*.[3] All this points also to the existence in pre-Alexandrian times of legends where Kṛṣṇa played an important role.

One further evidence in this direction is the testimony of Megasthenes. In spite of Dahlquist's futile attempts to dismiss his evidence, Megasthenes' account as preserved in the works of other writers is still one of the most valuable pieces of information pointing to the state of the legends centering around Kṛṣṇa during the fourth century B.C. Dahlquist started with an unsound premise, i.e. that Megasthenes' description of the Indian Heracles does not completely agree with what we know about Kṛṣṇa. However, to get the real importance of what Megasthenes said it is not only necessary to compare his account with the Kṛṣṇa legend but, even more essential, to compare to it the legends about Heracles such as the Greeks knew them. This we propose to do in the following chapter.

Two brāhmaṇical texts, the *Taittirīya* and the *Baudhāyana Dharma Sūtra*, provide us with four names referring to Kṛṣṇa, these are: Vāsudeva, Govinda, Dāmodara and Keśava. This may help us to trace some episodes in the biography of Kṛṣṇa, especially the last two names, on which there are passages in the Purāṇas explaining them in the light of Purāṇic tradition. The name Govinda, although very important for establishing the date of the cowherd legends, is explained otherwise in the *Mahābhārata* as referring to Varāha, who found the Earth (*gāṃ vindata*).[1]

Patañjali in the second century B.C. provides the bulk of our information on the story of Kṛṣṇa in pre-Christian times. As Professor Basham once wrote, 'it is a sad comment on the inadequacy of the sources for many periods of early Indian history that a grammatical text has achieved the status of a major historical record.'[2] That is however our situation and we have to cope with it. The *Mahābhāṣya* furnishes us with invaluable information on the existence of stories about Kṛṣṇa; its mention of theatrical representations of the killing of Kaṃsa is a proof that the legends of Kṛṣṇa were widely circulated at the time.

The *Arthaśāstra*, parts of which may be as early as the fourth century B.C., mentions two more episodes of Kṛṣṇa's biography, his birth and his death. And finally the inscriptions found at Besnagar, Ghosūṇḍī and Mathurā give proof of the divinisation and cult of Kṛṣṇa.

What we can gather from all this is that it is certain that there was a Kṛṣṇa story even from the time of the *Nirukta* and perhaps even from the time of the *Chāndogya Upaniṣad*. The mention of many personal names and family names is a certain indication that there was a tradition of a certain Kṛṣṇa, a hero of the Vṛṣṇis of the Yādava tribe. Since the Yādavas and the Bhojas are mentioned as early as the *Ṛg Veda*, we can very well suppose that this tradition may go as far back as the Vedic period. The form of those primitive tales is however out of our reach. The name of Kṛṣṇa's mother mentioned in the

1. See above pp. 24-27 *passim*.
2. Pāṇini 6.2.38.
3. Pāṇini 8.3.95.

1. *Mbh* 1.21.12; 12.209.7.
2. A. L. Basham, 'Review of B. N. Puri's "India in the Time of Patañjali"', *BSOAS*, v.22, 1959, p. 595.

Chāndogya Upaniṣad and the Syamantaka episode mentioned in the *Nirukta* are only parts of the story as we know it from the Purāṇas and cannot tell us about the rest of the legend. The same thing happens with all the rest of our evidence; they are fragmentary bits of information. Put together, however, they give us a fairly clear picture of the existence of a cycle of legends having Kṛṣṇa as its main hero. Altogether we have specific mentions of four episodes in the cycle: the birth of Kṛṣṇa, the killing of Kaṃsa, the Syamantaka episode, and the death of Kṛṣṇa. Each one of these episodes presupposes other parts of the story that can give us an approximate idea of the form that the whole cycle had.

We do not want to speculate about the possibility of a separation of personalities as others have done. In view of the reduced materials on which we have to build, all such speculations are condemned to remain unproved. So are all other speculations on a historical basis for Kṛṣṇa's legends. We can, however, give a chronological outline of the apparent data about Kṛṣṇa, gathered from all those sources, in what has to be a very tentative reconstruction as follows :

Already in the sixth century B.C. or earlier, some Upaniṣadic compilers felt the need to include Kṛṣṇa-Devakīputra among those who learnt and, most probably, taught a doctrine of self-control and selfless activity as a substitute for sacrifice and ritual observance. Even at that time stories of the exploits of Kṛṣṇa, like the Syamantaka episode, were known and current and his reputation, till then only that of a hero, spread on two fronts: heroic and religious. His figure was also incorporated into the cycle of legend surrounding the Pāṇḍava-Kaurava war.

Fourth century B.C. By this time Kṛṣṇa was widely worshipped as a god, especially in and around Mathurā.

Third century B.C. or later. An unknown genius combines in a marvellous philosophical poem all three aspects of the Kṛṣṇa figure: Kṛṣṇa the preacher of selfless action, Kṛṣṇa the god, and Kṛṣṇa the hero. The *Bhagavad Gītā* comes to form a pivotal part of the *Mahābhārata*.

100 B.C. By this time the doctrine of Kṛṣṇa's divinity is widely accepted in Northern India and the Deccan. His exploits are subjects of drama and song and even some of the Greeks worship him.

Throughout all this period there existed a unified account of the life of Kṛṣṇa, as we will try to show in the next chapter. However, some features in the legend were later given special significance and gained widespread popularity in preference to other traits of the hero. Such features as the mischievous child full of vitality and pranks but nevertheless adorable, or as the young, irresistible, lover of the gopīs, came in certain circles to overshadow all other aspects of Kṛṣṇa the hero. Perhaps this fact was due to the assimilation into the Kṛṣṇa hero-figure of another popular, perhaps tribal, god in which these features were especially important.

In our next chapter we shall review the legend of Kṛṣṇa and try to find out its fundamental themes and motifs as well as the connections of some of these motifs with others in the legends of comparable heroes in and outside India.

TABLE 1. EARLY HISTORICAL EVIDENCE

	Ṛg Veda	*Atharva*	*Brāhmaṇas*	*Chāndogya*	*Nirukta*	Pāṇini	Buddhists	Jains	Megasthenes	*Taitt. Āraṇ.*	*Baudh. Dh. S.*	*Artha Śāstra*	Patañjali	Besnagar Cols.	Ghosūndī Insc.	Mathurā Insc.	
Kṛṣṇa	*			*				*				*	*				The one in *ṚV* is different from our subject Patañjali uses both K. and Vāsudeva.
Vāsudeva						*	*			*			*	*	+	*	It is the most widely used name.
Govinda											*						Mentioned together with Dāmodara and Keśava in a list of 12 names of V (in *Mbh*= Varāha).
Gopa	*																In *ṚV* used for Viṣṇu.
Dāmodara											*						Mentioned together with Govinda and Keśava (see 3).
Janārdana													*				Name of K.
Keśava											*		*				(see 3).
Bhagavān														*	*	*	Used for K., Balarāma and other gods too.
Devakī				*													Mother of K. in the very first source and in the full tradition (Purāṇic).
Baladeva							*						*				The brother of K. Not sure if he ever was an independent deity.
Saṃkarṣaṇa												*	*		+		Mentioned sometimes before K. in dual compounds.
Arjuna						*											The fast companion of K. mentioned as early as Pāṇini and very prominently in *Mbh.*
Akrūra					*								*				Apparently an important part in the K. story, in the long episode of the stolen magical jewel.
Ugrasena													*				Father of Kaṃsa—not clear if grandfather of K. on his mother's side.
Kaṃsa												*	*				The principal enemy of K : the reason for K.'s descent was killing him according to some sources. The central episode.
Mathurā									*								Birthplace of K. and the capital of the Vṛṣṇis.
Yamunā									*								The river on the banks of which K. played (*līlā*) as a young cowherd.
Śūrasenas									*								Said by Megasthenes to worship Heracles.
Sātvatas			*														Branch of the Yādavas
Yādavas	*																One of the five tribes of the lunar race.
Andhakas						*							*				Mentioned together with the Vṛṣṇis.
Vṛṣṇis			*			*						*	*			*	Not always in conjunction with the Andhakas.
Āṅgirasas	*			*													Mentioned in connection with the Bhojas and with K-Devakīputra.
Ābhīras													*				They are not mentioned in connection with K.
Bhāgavatas														+	*	*	Mentioned in ALL archaeological sources but not in the literary.
Bhojas	*																Mentioned in *ṚV* in connection with the Āṅgirasas.
Birth of K.												*					
Killing of Kaṃsa													*				Public representations of this episode were performed through various means.
Syamantaka jewel			*														
Death of K.												*					

Both in Besnagar and Ghosūndī we refer to two separate inscriptions.
+means that the name appears in both of them.

CHAPTER THREE

Kṛṣṇa as a Traditional Hero

i. SOME METHODOLOGICAL CONCEPTS AND THE SOURCES FOR THE INVESTIGATION

The legend of Kṛṣṇa presents a great array of themes and motifs similar, and very probably related, to themes and motifs in the folklore and myth of other parts of Asia and even some parts of Europe. It is not possible to deny that many traits in the figure of Kṛṣṇa can be found in Indra, Viṣṇu and Nārāyaṇa from Vedic times, and that other motifs in the story appear also in connection with other figures in the stock of India's folklore. This would point to the view that motifs, long current in Indian folklore, were used in the Kṛṣṇa cycle. That is perhaps the reason why we find the same motifs in other lands, since they also derive from an Indo-European stock of folklore and mythology. Can it be that all the story of Kṛṣṇa is drawn from that same ancient Indo-European stock, through earlier examples of the same motifs found in India's previous literature and folklore? It is difficult to give an answer to this question owing to the scarcity of historical material. We can, however, examine the problem from the point of view of comparative folkloristics and trace the presence of themes and motifs of the Kṛṣṇa cycle in a series of somewhat similar stories in the Mediterranean area and the Middle East as well as in Ancient India, many centuries before the legends of Kṛṣṇa as we know them were compiled.

To come to a better understanding of these problems and of the Kṛṣṇa story itself, we must analyse the literary motifs and themes, the different versions and variants in the legends of the cycle and their correspondence with other legends in other cycles. For this purpose the methods of content analysis as used by modern folklorists will be of great value. Hitherto we have spoken indiscriminately of Kṛṣṇa myths, Kṛṣṇa stories and Kṛṣṇa legends. The last two terms are equivalent, but not the first, which carries the implications of a very old dispute that still emerges from time to time. Since we do not wish to get involved in terminological discussions we will try to avoid as far as practicable the word 'myth', without committing ourselves to a ritual interpretation of the term or to a cosmogonical one.[1] It is obvious that there are in the legends of Kṛṣṇa mythical elements, both ritual and cosmogonic, but we are concerned here with the stories themselves and their elements and not with their supposed meaning. The interpretation of myths is a very difficult and dangerous task that we are in no position to undertake. It is far more practicable, and, to our mind, useful simply to present the themes and motifs found in the legends and to analyse them in order to discover the narrative patterns peculiar to the Kṛṣṇa saga. This method will give us a clearer idea

1. G. J. Larson, 'The Study of Mythology and Comparative Mythology', introduction to : *Myth in Indo-European Antiquity*, ed. by G. J. Larson, University of California Press, 1974; pp. 3-9 gives at least seven different conceptions of what myth is.

of the image of Kṛṣṇa as popular hero-god. The Kṛṣṇa saga presents such great variety of half motifs that it is almost impossible to render it in a clear and simple form, without the help of comparative literary folklore analysis.

In our pursuit of the Kṛṣṇa cycle we shall be well advised to use some of the categories arranged by Professor Fontenrose in his study of the legends of the killing of the dragon.[1] Fontenrose gives us a clear picture of the character of the materials to be dealt with by the student of folk stories of the same class as the Kṛṣṇa story.

> Any narrative that we find is the version known to one man at one time. A myth or folktale, moving from place to place, passing from one person to another, from generation to generation, is constantly undergoing change; new versions are formed in every region and age. A new version appears when details are changed - when a theme or episode is given a somewhat different expression, when something is added or subtracted, when the sequence of episodes is shifted - but the personal and place names remain unchanged. When a particular version in its progress from place to place acquires new names for its persons and places, then a new variant has been formed.[2]

In the Kṛṣṇa cycle we find examples, numerous indeed, of each one of these accidents which might affect a story. Our sources for the stories of Kṛṣṇa themselves provide several examples of the transformations referred to by Fontenrose. As we have already explained and examined in detail, the literary sources on the Kṛṣṇa biography earlier than the beginning of the Christian Era are minimal and negligible. It is however just around that time that, in a, for us, sudden manner, there appears a large mass of literature dealing with the subject. Within a period of four or five centuries we encounter our major sources of information, all in different versions. The *Mahābhārata*, the *Harivaṃśa*, the *Viṣṇu Purāṇa*, the *Ghaṭa Jātaka* and the *Bāla Carita* all appear between the first and the fifth centuries A.D. and each one of them represents a tradition of a Kṛṣṇa cycle different from the others. Besides these accounts of the life of Kṛṣṇa we find also several variants of certain themes and motifs in other legends referring to different personages. And finally we also find story-types similar to the Kṛṣṇa one in the earliest Indian literature, the Vedic. According to Fontenrose a type

> is a traditional plot which appears in several variants. It is a series of episodes, a constellation of themes, that remains fairly well fixed among the variants. There may be changes in sequence; less essential episodes or themes may drop out; new features may be added. But there must be a durable core; observable in all variants, if we are to speak of a type.[1]

And we can certainly recognise a type in the fragmentary accounts of the legends and myths of Indra, a type in which we have also to include Kṛṣṇa. Another problem is, as we have said, to find if the Kṛṣṇa story is just a transformation of this primitive type or if its different versions have been collected from a more ample breadth of variants of that type, variants that also probably come not only from India but from other geographical areas. Fontenrose has found that when one of these type-stories comes to a new country it is usually ascribed to the traditional heroes of that place. The names of the personages usually change, but their general character remains akin. So that our study will have to deal more with plots and themes than with the actual identity of the persons in the story. Names are not of much significance. We want however to arrive at an image, as complete as possible, of Kṛṣṇa, the traditional hero. But to this end it is best to look separately at each thread of the story, to disentangle the warp and woof of the weaving, to be able to identify each colour and each shade and their total relationship in the picture. And these threads and knots are nothing but themes. Fontenrose defines a theme as 'a recurrent feature or episode of traditional stories. It is an integral part of the story in which it is found; but it is separable in the sense that it may occur in other story types too. Some themes are essential to a type; some may appear in one variant and be absent from another.'[2] In other words the theme of Fontenrose is very much the same as what Stith-Thompson calls a 'motif'.

> A motif is the smallest element in a tale which has the power to persist in tradition. In order to have this power it must have something unusual and striking about it. Most motifs fall into three

1. Joseph Fontenrose, *Python : A Study of Delphic Myth and its Origins*, 2nd ed., Biblo and Tannen, New York, 1974 (1st ed., 1959).
2. Fontenrose, *Python*, p. 6.

1. *Ibid.*
2. *Ibid.*, pp. 6-7.

classes. First are the actors in a tale—gods, or unusual animals, or marvelous creatures like witches, ogres, or fairies, or even conventionalized human characters like the favorite youngest child or the cruel stepmother. Second comes certain items in the background of the action—magic objects, unusual customs, strange beliefs, and the like. In the third place there are single incidents—and these comprise the great majority of motifs. It is this last class that can have an independent existence and that may therefore serve as true tale-types. By far the largest number of traditional types consist of these single motifs.[1]

But, leaving aside questions of terminology, we must turn now to the actual methodology to be used in our analysis of the Kṛṣṇa saga. We have said that we will try to find the basic narrative elements in the story, but what will our criteria have to be to define these? Following Robert Plant Armstrong[2] we find that the narrative elements or units are isolated for the purpose of helping in the analysis of the contents of a story. But the contents, according to Armstrong's methodology, may be scrutinised looking for their substance, or their structure, or their condition, and the manner in which we array our constituent units depends on which of these three we are looking for. It is clear that we shall be concerned mainly with the substance of the Kṛṣṇa story, that is with its plain primal message, without any interpretations. We will review some of the interpretations of the stories that have been advanced but, in a sincere scientific spirit, we will try not to commit ourselves to any one of them, so that our analysis should not be biassed. We shall also have to deal in certain cases with the structure and the conditions of the stories, as Armstrong defines these two aspects of analysis.

The structure of the content designates its shape, its physical array of elements, determined by means of establishing and describing the parts, however defined, together with their distributions and relationships. These two terms, elements and array, represent two different kinds of analysis, the first corresponding to a morphemic analysis of language, while the second is more nearly similar to the determination of syntax. Structure, in a sense, may be said to designate the physical dimensions of the communication. Finally, the condition of the content refers to such notions as the truth, emotional and aesthetic values of the segments of the communication.[1]

The elementary units for analysis of the substance of the text as described by Armstrong are in many respects equivalent to these same categories, although, according to himself, they differ from what Thompson called motifs, and what Fontenrose called themes. According to him:

The defining characteristics for appropriate units will be found in those modes proper to the substance, for example in nouns; or in the assertion patterns of the language, as for example in some carefully established actor-action phase, or in whatever segment of an utterance flow might be said to constitute a sentence. The principle may, further more, be found in the fictive properties or dramatic movements of the text, or, if it is nonfictive discourse, or poetry, then in features of rhetoric, prosody, sense or device peculiar to treatment of substance in these types. Finally, such units may be established upon the basis of the manifestation of psychological mechanisms, upon economic, political, or religious attitudes.[2]

As we can see, these characteristics apply both to the motifs of the folk-tale as arranged by Thompson, and to the themes extracted by Fontenrose in his analysis of the myths of the dragon slayer. And following the same methods we will examine the Kṛṣṇa cycle. As Armstrong points out: 'Such procedures in defining content analysis units ensure the delineation of a grid adequate to the subtlety and variety of the cases which will be encountered in the texts. In addition, they will permit generalization at either the individual or cultural level.'[3] Along these lines we can also include the methodological observations of Vladimir Propp:

Quelles sont les méthodes qui permettent de'effectuer une description exacte des contes ? Comparons entre eux les cas suivants: 1. Le roi donne un aigle à un brave. L'aigle emporte le brave dans un autre royaume. 2. Le grandpère donne un cheval à Soutchenko. Le cheval emporte Soutchenko dans un autre royaume. 3. Un magicien donne une barque à Ivan. La barque emporte

1. Stith-Thompson, *The Folktale*, New York, 1946.
2. Robert Plant Armstrong, *Content Analysis in Folkloristics* (1959), rep. in *Mythology*, ed. by P. Maranda, Penguin Modern Sociology Readers, Harmondsworth, 1972.

1. Armstrong, *Content Analysis in Folkloristics*, p. 153.
2. *Ibid.*, pp. 155-56.
3. *Ibid.*, p. 156.

Ivan dans au autre royaume. 4. La reine donne un anneau à Ivan. De vigoureux gaillards sortis de l'ammeau emportent Ivan dans un autre royaume. etc. On trouve dans les cas cités des valeurs variables. Ce qui change, ce sont les noms (et en même temps les attributes) des personnages; ce qui ne change pas, ce sont leurs actions, ou leurs *fonctions*. On peut en conclure que le conte prête souvent les mêmes actions a des personnages differents. C'est ce qui nous permet d'étudier les contes *a partir des fonctions des personnages*.[1]

The functions of the characters, as Propp defines them, are again nothing else than themes or motifs. If we set the examples given by Propp in abstract terms our motif would be something like: 'one character of superior standing gives the hero the means of locomotion that carry him into another kingdom'. The changes in every case are due to adaptations to individual necessities, and the individual tales are suited to the places where they are told. National customs have to be observed, chronological and geographical considerations have to be made, when equating different versions of the same themes. An eagle may be necessary to escape from a mountain kingdom, a boat from an island, a horse from the steppe or the desert. Fontenrose has given a list of six kinds of variation that are often encountered: 1. Mutations of role; 2. Mutations in action; 3. Reduction of features; 4. Transference of deeds or traits; 5. Combination and fusion of themes and roles; 6. Expansion or doubling of themes, persons, or episodes.[2] The mutations in role and in action are very well represented by Propp's examples. The reduction of features refers to that transformation where an action is reduced in its effects but not in its significance: aggression is aggression whether the result is death or beating. The transference of traits may occur between the characters in the tale, the combination and the expansion of themes, roles or episodes is also very likely to occur in any given variant of a story.

In our pursuance of the study of the Kṛṣṇa cycle we shall encounter instances of each one of these kinds of transformation. Through their classification here we shall be able to identify in a much easier way the parallel themes occurring in the Kṛṣṇa story and in the stories of other heroes in India and elsewhere.

Once we have defined the scope of our methodology we can pass on to the problems of the analysis itself. The sources from which we draw our information all present a unified account of the story of Kṛṣṇa but differ widely among themselves in several details and, more importantly, in their general character and attitude towards Kṛṣṇa.

First and foremost is the *Harivaṃśa*, that gives us the largest number of episodes in Kṛṣṇa's biography, and on which the accounts of the *Viṣṇu Purāṇa* and the *Bhāgavata Purāṇa* are based. Differently from these two, however, the *Harivaṃśa* presents a down-to-earth relation of Kṛṣṇa's activities. The later texts are preoccupied with making Kṛṣṇa an all-powerful and fully fledged divinity, nothing less than the Supreme Brahman in the flesh, while the *Harivaṃśa*, keeping more within the epic tradition, shows Kṛṣṇa as a folk-hero, a divine hero it is true, but still very much based on the image of the hero of popular tales and not a theologian's creation like the Kṛṣṇa of the *Viṣṇu Purāṇa* and the *Bhāgavata Purāṇa*. These tell the story, admittedly, but Kṛṣṇa in their account is always a god, knowing that he is god and acting accordingly. Kṛṣṇa in the *Harivaṃśa*, on the other hand, handles the tasks and perils that come his way with superhuman strength and ease, yet still fulfils his role of simple hero in the manner of the epic narrative. As Professor D.H.H. Ingalls puts it: 'The motives of the individual adventures are always simpler in the Harivaṃśa, always closer to a true folklore.'[1] The other Purāṇas elaborated, and at the same time on occasions abridged and modified, the stories of the *Harivaṃśa*.

Our other sources are not taken from the Purāṇic literature; one, the *Ghaṭa Jātaka*, is from the famous Buddhist collection of folk-tales, and the other, the *Bālacarita*, is a play by the dramatist Bhāsa. Both are of extreme value for our purpose, since they present a view differing from the official religious attitude towards the legends. In the Jātaka, the only work in prose among our sources, we have a condensed account of the story that leaves out many episodes but, at the same time, keeps enough of it for us to recognise the gist of the saga and therefore to isolate subsidiary elements. The play of Bhāsa, on its part, is a charming little piece dealing only with the first part of the legend, up to the death of Kaṃsa, and this also provides us with new insights that are lacking in the Purāṇas.

1. V. Propp, *Morphologie du conte* (1928), Editions du Seuil, Paris 1970, pp. 28-29.

2. Fontenrose, *Python*, pp. 7-8.

1. D. H. H. Ingalls, 'The Harivaṃśa as a Mahākāvya', *Mélanges d'Indianisme à la Mémoire de Louis Renou*, Boccard, Paris 1968.

Lastly we will also use another version of the story, that is given in the *Devī Bhāgavata Purāṇa.* This account is important for two reasons, first because it has never been studied in comparison with the other versions, and second because it also gives us polemic view of the saga. The *Devī Bhāgavata Purāṇa* is a Śākta text of approximately the same date as the more famous *Bhāgavata Purāṇa* and is intended to present Indian religion as known to its authors from the Śākta point of view. It therefore takes the Kṛṣṇa legends and retells them without all their Vaiṣṇava theological garb, giving us an opportunity to look at them again as merely stories and also bringing new variants that greatly illuminate the old motifs.

As we can see with these sources we have enough material to provide us with the variety that our analysis will require. This analysis we base on the techniques of modern folkloristic studies, and arrange around the following folk-type stories: 1. The Birth of the Hero; 2. The Miraculous Child; 3. The Strong Man; and 4. The Killing of the Dragon.

ii. THE BASIC PATTERN OF HERO STORIES

Kṛṣṇa is one of many heroes in the *Mahābhārata.* Besides being the All-God, a character that keeps revealing itself at crucial points in the Epic—and that is a later accretion according to some scholars—Kṛṣṇa is the warrior, the prince who belongs to and represents a chivalric tradition. With Arjuna and Karṇa, Bhīṣma and Yudhiṣṭhira and all the rest he stands for the *Kṣatriyadharma,* the heroic tradition of the Aryan Epic.

As a prince and a hero it is just and right that he should fight and conquer and excel in all martial activities, for after all that is what heroes are supposed to do. It is also normal that on asking about his birth and childhood we should be told of marvellous adventures, portents and prodigies, for heroes usually start their careers early. Kṛṣṇa is thus a full fledged hero, and his life follows that of other heroes—to what extent, however, is a question that we will now analyse, and what we find will permit us to see and appreciate better the elements conducive to the formation of the Kṛṣṇa figure and the Kṛṣṇa saga.

It is convenient at this point to sketch the Kṛṣṇa story in its main points, so that we may compare it with other stories and find if indeed there are common elements. The tale, as we have it in the several versions that we are to use, begins with a cruel king to whom a prophecy is told that a child soon to be born will kill him and seize his kingdom. This child will be born from the king's own sister (cousin in some versions, daughter in others) and therefore the king puts her in prison with the intention of killing any offspring that she may have. Since she is married (or gets married when in prison) she eventually has a child that is killed by the tyrant, and this happens five more times, but the seventh and eighth children are saved miraculously. Kṛṣṇa, the eighth, is smuggled out of prison on the night of his birth and taken across the river Yamunā to a cowherd's settlement, where he is replaced by another baby and where he is brought up by the cowherds. The child grows up to be exceedingly strong and kills several monsters that have been sent by the king to destroy him. After several unsuccessful attempts to kill him the king brings him back to the city for a final trial. The boy overcomes the forces of the tyrant and kills him. He frees his parents and installs his grandfather on the throne. A little afterwards he moves away with his tribe and founds a city by the sea, wins a princess and fights and defeats other kings. After a long reign he dies a mysterious death, when shot in the heel accidentally following a great hecatomb in which all his tribe is destroyed and his city sinks in the ocean.

This is in its bare essentials the story of Kṛṣṇa, which can be compared to the biographies of a number of other heroes and found to have certain similar characteristics. As far back as 1871, one folklore scholar elaborated a list of fifteen heroes that fitted into a scheme that he devised to analyse stories of this type. J.G. von Hahn summarised what he called 'The Aryan Expulsion and Return Formula' (*Arische Aussetzung-und-Rückkehr-Formel*) in tabular form in his *Sagwissenschaftliche Studien.*[1] The scheme has sixteen points arranged in four headings: Birth; Youth; Return, and Subordinate figures. The points that summarise the basic hero story according to Hahn are:

> 1) The principal hero is illegitimate, 2) the mother is the daughter of a native prince, 3) the father is a god or a stranger. 4) There is an omen to a parent; 5) and the hero is, in consequence, exposed. 6) He is suckled by brutes, 7) and reared by childless herdfolk. 8) Arrogance of the youth

1. Jena, 1871-76. I use Henry Wilson's translation of this chart included by him in his edition of John Dunlop's *History of Prose Fiction,* George Bell and Sons, London 1888, 2 vols; chart no. 2 after p. 504, vol.1.

and 9) service abroad. 10) Triumphal home-coming and return abroad. 11) Fall of the persecutor; acquisition of sovereignty and liberation of the mother. 12) He founds a city. 13) He has an extraordinary death. 14) is slandered as incestuous and has an early death. 15) Vengeance of an injured servant, and 16) murder of the younger brother.[1]

Fifteen heroes follow this pattern, two Indians among them, according to Hahn. They are: Perseus, Herakles, Oedipus, Amphion and Zethus (twins), Leucastus and Parrhasius (twins), and Theseus from Greece; Romulus and Remus (twins) from Rome; Dietrich, Siegfried and Wolfdietrich from the Germanic world; Cyrus and Kei Khosrov (Khusrau) from Persia; and Karṇa and Kṛṣṇa from India. Hahn finds significant resemblances in the legends of all these. Everyone of them follows the general scheme in several points, some of them in more, some in less, but always in sufficient number to rule out a fortuitous coincidence. Out of Hahn's thirteen points the heroes that score least are Oedipus and Herakles, who get six and seven points respectively. Of the other thirteen heroes five get eight points, five get nine points, one gets ten and two get eleven. Kṛṣṇa scores nine points and Hahn overlooked another four that, if taken into account, would give a full score of thirteen points. Hahn did not know the story of Kṛṣṇa very well, since he could have easily given him point number six: 'the hero was suckled by brutes', on the strength of the Pūtanā episode. In the same manner Kṛṣṇa could have scored on points eight, nine and ten: 'the arrogance of the youth, the service abroad and the triumphal return and new departure', on the strength of the Govardhanadhara episode and that Kṛṣṇa, as foster-son of Nanda, a servant of Kaṃsa, was in fact in servitude to Kaṃsa.[2] Kṛṣṇa's father, Vasudeva, was also a tributary of Kaṃsa,[3] and the return to Mathurā and short departure to Dvārakā covers Hahn's tenth point. He also overlooked in point number thirteen: 'extraordinary death', to mention that the hunter Jarā was also a brother of Kṛṣṇa,[4] a fact that would fit very well in his point number sixteen: 'Murder of the younger brother'. But we leave these details until later; here it is enough to say that Hahn took the first great step towards a classification of hero stories and that he rightly included Kṛṣṇa among the typical examples of heroic biography. Most later scholars, who are few in number, have virtually ignored Hahn's classification, and have not considered Kṛṣṇa in the context of their studies of hero legends. Hahn himself did not follow this line of his research and was satisfied with having opened a new field for further investigation. He did not try to give an explanation of the similarities found in the stories, other than calling his scheme 'the Aryan formula' and he did not follow up in detail any of the particular instances of close coincidence, like the presence of several pairs of twins among his examples. In this too he overlooked obvious instances, like the case of Herakles who was also born a twin, and of the same Kṛṣṇa who in many ways can be also considered an example, with Balarāma, of the twin birth of the hero.

Ten years after its publication there appeared what seems to be the only recognition of Hahn's work. Alfred Nutt in England used his 'formula' to analyse Irish Hero stories.[1] Nutt improved upon Hahn's scheme by adding two new points and by amending three of the original points. The two new points he inserted between nine and ten of Hahn's list and numbered them IXA and IXB. IXA says: 'He attacks and slays monsters', and IXB: 'He acquires supernatural knowledge through eating a magic fish.'[2] Of these only IXA applies specifically to Kṛṣṇa, IXB apparently not having parallels outside Europe. Nutt gave a new table of the episodes in the story-pattern that, both for its improvements upon Hahn's and for its giving a different translation of Hahn's terms, we present here for comparison:

1) Hero born: A. Out of wedlock; B. Posthumously; C. Supernaturally ; D. One of twins. 2) Mother: princess residing in her own country. 3) Father: God or Hero from afar. 4) Tokens and warnings of hero's future greatness. 5) He is in consequence driven forth from home. 6) Is suckled by wild beasts. 7) Is brought up by childless (shepherd) couple, or widow. 8) Is of passionate and violent disposition. 9) Seeks service in foreign lands. 9A) Attacks and slays monsters. 9B) Acquires supernatural knowledge through eating

1. J. G. von Hahn, in Dunlop, *ibid.*
2. *HV* 65.34.
3. *HV* 45.35
4. *HV* 98.23.

1. Alfred Nutt, 'The Aryan Expulsion-and-Return-Formula in the Folk and Hero tales of the Celts', *Folk-Lore Journal*, vol. 4, 1886.
2. Alfred Nutt, *ibid.*, p. 2.

a magic fish (or other animal). 10) Returns to his own country, retreats, and again returns. 11) Overcomes his enemies, frees his mother, and seats himself on the throne. 12) Founds cities. 13) The manner of his death is extraordinary. 14) He is accused of incest. Dies young. 15) He injures an inferior who takes revenge upon him or upon his children. 16) He slays his younger brother.[1]

This pattern is followed in fourteen stories of Celtic folklore, according to Nutt. These are four versions of the story of Fionn, the Gaelic hero; two versions of the story of Cuchulain; the stories of Labhraid Maen, Conall and the Great fool; two versions of the story of Perceval; and the stories of Arthur, Merlin and Taliesin—nine heroes in all, although Nutt accepts that Arthur and Merlin do not completely follow the pattern except in the first three points. Finally Nutt mentions another hero who, although not included in his table, follows Hahn's formula; this is Havelock the Dane.[2]

More than forty years after Hahn's publication Otto Rank published a study dealing with the same theme of the similarities in traditional hero biographies, without surprisingly, mentioning Hahn's pioneering attempt, although Rank used as his examples seven of the heroes already studied by Hahn and mentioned another two of them in the course of his discussion (i.e. out of fifteen examples quoted by him nearly half had been previously used by Hahn) and, what really interests us here, he added eight new names to the list. We must note that among those eight new names Rank included those of Sargon and Gilgamesh from Mesopotamia and Moses and Jesus from the Jewish tradition, taking the pattern beyond the Aryan (i.e. Indo-European) world in which Hahn had circumscribed it, and bringing it also into the Semitic world. The other four names added by Rank were two from the Classical tradition, Bellerophon and Telephus, and two from the Germanic world, Tristan and Lohengrin. We also have to note that Rank did not include Kṛṣṇa in his list.[3]

But more important than the examples chosen to illustrate his scheme of the basic pattern is this scheme itself. Rank did not give numbers to the different points, but we can do it for him to make easier the task of comparing it. In the words of Rank:

The standard saga itself may be formulated according to the following outline: 1) The hero is the child of most distinguished parents, usually the son of a king. 2) His origin is preceded by difficulties, such as continence, or prolonged barrenness, or secret intercourse of the parents due to external prohibition or obstacles. 3) During or before the pregnancy, there is a prophecy, in the form of a dream or oracle, cautioning against his birth, and usually threatening danger to the father (or his representative). 4) As a rule, he is surrendered to the water, in a box. 5) He is then saved by animals, or by lowly people (shepherds), and is suckled by a female animal or by an humble woman. 6) After he has grown up, he finds his distinguished parents, in a highly versatile fashion. 7) He takes his revenge on the one hand, 8) and is acknowledged on the other. 9) Finally he achieves rank and honours.[1]

This outline is shorter than that of Hahn and does not include events in the later life of the hero, stopping at his return and revenge. It is also orientated to suit Freud's psychoanalytical theories. Words like 'most distinguished parents', 'secret intercourse of the parents due to external prohibition', and 'threatening danger to the father (or his representative)', are full of implications and are used to great advantage in the interpretation of the particular cases. Rank has grasped the main elements of the story, but his therapeutical orientation has made him, in its narrowness, reduce and simplify the facts and thus to lose a clearer and wider perspective of the problem. He is not concerned about historical relations between the different versions, but is more worried about trying to give a psychological explanation of the recurrence of motifs. He finds this explanation in children's fantasies about their own birth and family. Rank's inferences and elucidation read very well, but are rather simplistic and facile. In his interpretation he applies the methods used to analyse the psychology of neuroses.[2]

For the young child, the parents are, in the first place, the sole authority and the source of all faith. To resemble them, i.e., the progenitor of the same sex ... is the most intense and portentous wish of the child's early years. Progressive intellectual development naturally brings it about that the child gradually becomes acquainted with the cate-

1. Nutt, *ibid.*, table between pp. 42 and 43.
2. Nutt, *ibid.*, p. 43.
3. For a detailed comparison of the two lists, see table 2.

1. Otto Rank, *The Myth of the Birth of the Hero* (1914), Vintage Books, New York, 1964, p. 65.
2. Rank, *ibid.*, p. 67.

gory to which the parents belong. Other parents become known to the child, who compares these with his own, and thereby becomes justified in doubting the incomparability and uniqueness with which he had invested them. Trifling occurrences in the life of the child, which induce a mood of dissatisfaction, lead up to criticism of the parents; and the gathering conviction that other parents are preferable in certain ways is utilized for this attitude of the child toward the parents.[1]

From this, Rank goes on to explain that these sentiments of dissatisfaction, together with sexual drives of the type called by Freud 'Oedipus complex', lead the child to invent what he calls the 'family romance of neurotics', where the child pretends not to be the son of his actual parents, who are only foster-parents, but of kings, queens or other very rich and distinguished people, and 'these consciously remembered psychic emotions of the years of childhood supply the factor which permits the interpretation of the myth.'[2] Every scene in the story is made to fit this interpretation and it all joins very well, but even Rank has to admit that these real and recorded modern fantasies may in fact be derived from the myth itself, since the childrens' fantasies are contemplated 'usually under the influence of storybooks'.[3] That tales should be used by children in the building of fantasies is far from strange, but to make these fantasies the origin of the tales in the first place is unwarranted. Myths can be very well used to interpret the psychology of neurotic processes and modes of thought but it is surely unjustified to reverse directions and try to interpret myths in the light of psycho-pathological cases, in that way confounding and misrepresenting cultural and historical traits. Rank does this when he attributes much of the child's fantasising to the concealment by the parents of the sexual facts of human birth and the subsequent discovery by the child of these facts: 'the concealment of these processes is presumably the root of the childish revolt against the parents. The exposure in the box and in the water asexualizes the birth process, as it were, in a childlike fashion.'[4] Here he extrapolates his own moralistic prejudices into other cultures. There is no evidence to suggest that the sexual origin of birth was concealed from children in ancient Greece or Egypt, Mesopotamia, Ireland or India.[1]

1. Rank, *ibid.*, p. 68.
2. Rank, *ibid.*, p. 69.
3. Rank, *ibid.*, p. 68.
4. Rank, *ibid.*, p. 91.

But, in spite of this, the work of Rank provides great help in the analysis of several aspects of the myth. He misses, however, the very important episodes of the youth of the hero, when it is discovered that he is endowed with superhuman strength. This part is very important in Kṛṣṇa story, not used by Rank, as well as in most of the other stories. Rank does not make a numerical division of his scheme and does not give an exact account of the number of traits shared in each story. It is easy, however, to see that the number of common characteristics is enough to suppose a relationship between the different versions. What sort of relationship, is hard to say.

Lord Raglan confronted the problem in 1934 and added some new names to the list of heroes that follow the story-pattern, as well as proposing a new and more complete outline of that same pattern. Raglan did not acknowledge the previous contributions of Hahn and Rank just as Rank did not acknowledge Hahn's. It is strange that people working on the same problem within easy access of each other did not realise the other's labours and achievements. It is curious in the first instance that they found the same problem and attacked it in the same way, although their results were vastly different. Raglan's outline of the basic tale has twenty-two points arranged in the following order:

(1) His mother is a royal virgin. (2) His father is a king, and (3) Often a near relative of his mother, but (4) The circumstances of his conception are unusual, and (5) He is also reputed to be the son of a god. (6) At birth an attempt is made, often by his father, to kill him, but (7) He is spirited away, and (8) Reared by fosterparents in a far country. (9) We are told nothing of his childhood but (10) On reaching manhood he returns or goes to his future kingdom. (11) After a victory over the king and/or a giant, dragon or wild beast, (12) He marries a princess, often the daughter of his predecessor, and (13) Becomes king. (14) For a time he reigns uneventfully, and (15) Prescribes laws, but (16) Later he loses favour with the

1. Professor Basham draws our attention to the famous Greek story of Daphnis and Chloe, who, when they fell in love in early puberty, had not the least idea of the facts of life. But this looks to us a romantic literary device, since surely shepherd boys and girls raised up in the country would have firsthand knowledge of their animals' sexual behaviour.

gods and/or his subjects, and (17) Is driven from the throne and city. (18) He meets with a mysterious death, (19) Often at the top of a hill. (20) His children, if any, do not succeed him. (21) His body is not buried, but nevertheless (22) He has one or more holy sepulchres.[1]

This outline, like Rank's, is highly subjective. Raglan has emphasised certain traits to better suit his own theory of the causes of the tale's unity and distribution. He also tries to make the scheme more inclusive by bringing in more motifs, but this dilutes the story, and if more heroes can be fitted in, the number of traits shared by them, out of the total in the outline, is reduced. Something very important to note is that Raglan left out the motif of the prophecy, an essential part of the story and one without which his point number six, 'attempt by the king to kill the child' does not make any sense. Another weak spot in Raglan's scheme is his point number nine, an *argumentum ad silentium*. That 'we are told nothing of his childhood' does not mean that this omission is necessary or significant. Rank also missed this point, that Hahn called 'arrogance of the youth', but 'the wonderful child' motif is a fundamental part in the story of the hero, as we shall see later. All in all, one feels that by enlarging the number of traits Raglan greatly impaired the effectiveness of the argument for an original hero story. It is very unlikely that points like 'death at the top of a hill; his body is not buried and he has one or more holy sepulchres' were part of a primitive basic story.

The examples presented by Raglan include seven names already given by his predecessors; these are those of Theseus, Moses, Oedipus, Perseus, Romulus and Remus, Herakles and Siegfried. To these he added another fourteen names to make a total of twenty-one examples to illustrate his theory. These other heroes are Jason, Paris, Pelops, Asclepius, Dionysus, Apollo, Zeus, Joseph, Elijah, Arthur, Nykang, Watu Gunung, Llew Llawgyffes and Robin Hood.[2] He did not include Kṛṣṇa and, in leaving out Karṇa, used by both Hahn and Rank, he eliminated altogether the Indian examples. Another very important omission in Raglan's list is that of Cyrus, perhaps the only truly historical name among all those legendary heroes. Out of the fourteen new names presented by Raglan he included seven from the Classical tradition, two from the Bible, one from Indonesia, one from Africa and three from the British Isles. All of them follow the basic pattern more or less closely, although, as we have said before, by augmenting the number of points the individual examples are more loosely fitted in the scheme. Again like Rank, Raglan manages, even if sometimes forcedly, to make most of the points in his outline tally with the several heroes, all in the interest of his theory. For some reason he left out Jesus—included by Rank who had no such scruples —but his inclusion of Joseph and Elijah show very well how far he was prepared to go to prove his point. These two are given twelve and nine points respectively on very slender grounds.[1]

Raglan's interpretation of the undeniable correspondences between the different stories is that the similarities are due to all the stories being derived from ritual. 'The story of the hero of tradition is the story, not of real incidents in the life of a real man, but of ritual incidents in the career of a ritual personage.'[2] Again, as in the case of Rank, this interpretation at first seems very attractive, and one would wish to be convinced; but somehow the reasoning given is too facile and sketchy. It is difficult to accept that 'the attribution of divine descent to a hero has nothing to do with his heroism, but is associated with the ritual union of a princess to her own husband, disguised as a god.'[3] And all of Raglan's argumentation follows those lines. We do not accept his ritual theory, but his treatment of the problem offers several new insights as well as providing further evidences of the existence of one common pattern, and it presented new and important examples such as Zeus, Apollo and Dionysus.

More names have been added to the list of those that follow a typical hero story. A.D. Rees took Lord Raglan's scheme and modified it to suit the lives of Irish Saints.[4] He had to change points like the hero being the son of a god, logically not applicable to a Christian saint, and his marriage with a

1. Lord Raglan, 'The Hero of Tradition', *Folk-lore*, v.45, 1934, pp. 212-13.

2. In the first version of his paper (Raglan, *ibid.*), he only gave eighteen names in total, but in a second version (Lord Raglan, *The hero*, Methuen, London 1936, chapters 16 and 17, pp. 178-99), he added the names of Watu Gunung, Llew Llawgyffes and Robin Hood. No other significant alterations were made in this second version.

1. Raglan, *Folk-lore*, v.45, pp. 218-19.

2. Raglan, *ibid.*, p. 220.

3. Raglan, *ibid.*, p. 222.

4. Alwyn D. Rees, 'The Divine Hero in Celtic Hagiology', *Folk-lore*, v.47, 1936, pp. 30-41.

princess, equally unsuitable to an ascetic. Rees mentions several Irish saints whose stories agree with the outline of the story in one or more points, but he particularly brings out three that substantially follow the modified Raglan scheme[1]; these are St. David, St. Cadoc and St. Patrick. It is not strange that the Irish hagiographers attributed a traditional heroic story to their subjects, since their task was to gain admiration and fame for them, but it is indeed remarkable that we find heroes in the other extreme of the Eurasian continent following the same traditional pattern in their stories.

Dr. Ken Gardiner has brought to our attention two Korean traditional heroes that partially follow Raglan's version of the typical pattern. In a recent publication[2] he has shown that T'an-shih-huai and Tung-ming score seven points each in Raglan's scheme. In T'an-shih-huai's life we can see illustrated points 4) 'The circumstances of his conception are unusual', 6) 'At birth an attempt is made, often by his father, to kill him, but' 7) 'He is spirited away, and' 8) 'Reared by foster-parents in a far country' 11) 'After a victory over the king and/or a giant, dragon or wild beast,' 13) 'Becomes king' and 15) 'Prescribes laws'. In the story of Tung-ming on the other hand we have further illustrated points 2) 'His father is a king' and 10) 'On reaching manhood he returns or goes to his future kingdom', although he misses points 8) and 15) scored by the other Korean hero. Dr. Gardiner also pointed out to us a paper dealing further with the patterns of Korean hero stories;[3] in it we find one scheme more on the lines of those reviewed but adapted to the Korean peculiarities. The scheme has eight points:

1) The hero's parents are of the nobility but their intercourse occurs in a most unusual and mysterious manner. 2) His birth is fraught with difficulties, or comes only after long childlessness and a tortuous course of events. 3) The circumstances of his birth are extraordinary and mysterious. 4) He is either abandoned, exiled or persecuted. 5) He is protected either by animals or by an old woman. 6) He performs miracles. 7) He makes a name for himself and builds a capital city or founds a clan or establishes a sect. 8) Usually, he dies a mysterious death and is deified after death.[1]

1. See table 3.
2. K. Gardiner and R. de Crespigny, 'T'an-shih-huai and the Hsien-pi Tribes of the 2nd cent. AD', *Papers on Far Eastern History*, 15, ANU 1977.
3. Kim Yol-Gyu, 'Traditional Oral Literature and Folklore of Korea: With emphasis on the types of Biographical patterns', unpublished paper.

The points, as we can see, are kept very vague and general, but still we can easily recognise the very same pattern found by Hahn and analysed by Rank and Raglan, a pattern in which Kṛṣṇa can be easily fitted. The author gives a list of eight Korean heroes that follow the pattern at least partially. These are: Tongmyong,[2] Yongpumri, Chinhwon, T'arhae, Pongu, Hyokkose, Alchi and Pari, among whom the ones that score more points are Tongmyong, T'arhae and Pari.

To return to the general problem, we may, by combining all five lists and the four examples given by Rees and Gardiner, find fifty-eight different heroes who are said to follow a general pattern, some less closely and some on a larger scale. To these fifty-eight names we can add those of two figures not considered before, Horus from Egypt and Indra from India, which gives us a grand total of sixty names. Of these sixty examples fifty appear only once in the different lists, six appear twice and the other five thrice. Those that appear twice are: Theseus, Arthur, Moses, Karṇa, Tung-ming, and Cyrus. Those that appear thrice are: Oedipus, Perseus, Romulus and Remus, Herakles and Siegfried (where Romulus and Remus count as one unit). Kṛṣṇa appears only once.

The general outline of the story shows also a basic consensus, but Raglan misses two very important points: the prophecy and the childhood of the hero, and Rank also misses the latter. Both of these points are very important to the Kṛṣṇa story. In 1964 Archer Taylor presented a good summary of the findings of Hahn, Nutt, Rank and Raglan[3] but overlooked the work of Rees and was not aware of the existence of the Korean material. Taylor included in his article a review of the work of Joseph Campbell and Vladimir Propp but these scholars did not really produce a scheme of the traditional hero story. Campbell's formula: 'a separation from the world, a penetration to some source of power, and a life-enhancing return'[4] and Propp's outline of

1. Kim Yol-Gyu, *ibid.*, p. 12.
2. The same Tung-ming mentioned by Gardiner and de Crespigny in their article.
3. Archer Taylor, 'The Biographical Pattern in Traditional Narrative', *Journal of the Folklore Institute*, Indiana University, v.1, 1964, pp. 114-29.
4. Joseph Campbell, *The Hero with a Thousand Faces* (1949), Bollingen Series vol. xvii, Princeton 1968; A. Taylor, *ibid.*, p. 120.

Russian fairy tales do not bear comparison with the schemes of Hahn, Rank and Raglan.[1]

Kṛṣṇa follows very closely the basic pattern as enunciated by all those scholars; in fact Kṛṣṇa is one of the heroes who scores more points than the average in all the different versions of the general scheme. However, as we have expressed our misgivings about each one of those versions, we present a further outline that, to our mind, expresses better the fundamental traits of the Kṛṣṇa story and at the same time, this being typical of all hero stories, of other heroic sagas.

Our own version of a general outline would be like this: 1) A king (a tyrant and a usurper). 2) A princess (wife/daughter/sister/cousin of the king). 3) A prophecy (the princess will bear a child that will kill the king). 4) The king puts the girl in prison. 5) The hero is born supernaturally. 6) Is exposed (generally cast into water). 7) Reared by cowherds. 8) Grows up to be exceedingly strong and kills monsters. 9) Comes back to the capital and kills the king. 10) Frees his parents. 11) Becomes a king (or instals a new king). 12) Founds a city. 13) Wins a princess. 14) Defeats other kings. 15) After a long life dies in strange circumstances.

This basic pattern follows *a grosso modo* the story of Kṛṣṇa as outlined at the beginning of this section. The Kṛṣṇa legend suits almost point by point all three schemes presented by Hahn, Rank and Raglan, but these schemes are, as mentioned before, not completely satisfactory. The thirteen points of Hahn's outline—up to the death of the hero, the nine points of Rank and the twenty-one of Raglan, do not allow for the best representation of the Kṛṣṇa story. Of the three, Hahn's is the most accurate, although in point 4 he does not make clear what sort of omen is given and in point 11 he does not identify the persecutor. Rank moreover does not specify about the prophecy and Raglan misses the point completely. All this ambiguity was necessary to the authors, understandably, to permit them to include the largest possible number of examples. We feel that the wide number of coincidences following a general pattern having been amply demonstrated, these ambiguities can be dispensed with and a more prceise outline, such as ours in fifteen points, can be given. This outline is a precis of the Kṛṣṇa story, divided into points for purposes of classification, that does not make concessions for easy comparison with other stories; it still, however, bears a strong resemblance to all the other stories mentioned before. We should not be merely speculating if we said that the Kṛṣṇa legend is a very typical example of the hero story as we find it spread all over the Eurasian continent. We do not have the necessary evidence to say where the story originated and how it came to appear in such different epochs and places, nor are we concerned with such problems. It is enough for our purpose to show the close relationship between Kṛṣṇa and other traditional heroes. That will lead us to consider the legends of Kṛṣṇa from a wholly new perspective, not just as an isolated Indian phenomenon but as a cycle akin to many others and open therefore to close comparative analysis of its constituent elements. We cannot, within the scope of this research, carry out this comparative analysis with each one of the sixty recorded versions of the basic story, mainly because the Kṛṣṇa cycle itself is of such length that to make a detailed study even of this alone, in all its Indian versions, would reach gigantic proportions. What we propose to do is to take some of the most characteristic episodes in the cycle of Kṛṣṇa and arrange them into themes according to the folkloristic classifications mentioned before. At the same time we will compare these episodes with similar ones in the stories of two heroes that follow the general pattern already discussed. We will take one of these heroes from India and the other from another tradition.

We will compare Kṛṣṇa with Indra because Indra was the principal hero of the Indo-Aryans, because the legend of Indra follows to a certain extent the basic scheme of the hero stories, and because a relationship between him and Kṛṣṇa has already been established. By comparing Kṛṣṇa with Indra we may find whether the agreement of the story of Kṛṣṇa with the traditional heroic stories is due only to Kṛṣṇa's dependence on the Indra legends or if Kṛṣṇa is a folk-hero in his own right and not just a derived figure. The choice of a hero outside India best suited for comparison with Kṛṣṇa is not a difficult one. One name comes immediately to our mind, that of Hercules, the Herakles of the Greeks. In fact that comparison was, in all probability, made already by Megasthenes in the fourth century B.C. (see above p. 21). Hercules is the only hero among all the sixty

1. Besides the omission of Rees' article, Taylor also forgot to mention the first version of Raglan's paper (*Folk-lore Journal*, vol.45, 1934) and, a graver mistake, Raglan did not include Quetzalcoatl, Horus and Attis among the names of the heroes that follow his scheme but mentioned them as examples of a different pattern (Raglan, *The Hero*, pp. 204-6; Archer, *ibid.*, p. 118).

listed that approximates to Kṛṣṇa in his overall cultural importance. In India only Rāma is comparable to Kṛṣṇa as a heroic-religious popular figure. No other character is comparable to Hercules. Not even Dionysus, Apollo or Zeus among the gods, or Theseus, Jason or Perseus among the heroes, come close to his overwhelming presence as a hero in the Greek and Roman worlds, to his enormous popularity as the strong man by antonomasia. The comparison of Hercules with Kṛṣṇa is quite a natural one, and we shall find that in looking at them closer the similarities grow amazingly. It is not merely the fact that both belong to the group of traditional heroes, or that both fulfil all the fifteen points of our own scheme or almost all of the points of the schemes of Hahn, Rank, Raglan, etc. We shall find that the closeness of the legends of Kṛṣṇa and Hercules gives good reason to believe that a very close contact actually occurred between them.

iii. THE THEMES OF THE BIRTH OF KṚṢṆA

Once we have stated the similarities between the Kṛṣṇa cycle and other hero stories, we can discuss in greater detail particular themes within the cycle and at the same time, as we said before, compare the treatment of these themes in the Kṛṣṇa legends with the same themes in the legends of Indra and Heracles. By this comparison we may illuminate further, general characteristics in the story of Kṛṣṇa, contrasting it with the two others and finding the points of agreement that will show their membership of one family.

If we look again at our outline of the general pattern of the story we shall see that it includes six points: (1) a king; (2) a princess; (3) a prophecy; (4) the king puts the girl in prison; (5) the hero is born supernaturally; (6) is exposed. The question is, does the legend of Indra follow this pattern? It is very difficult to answer this question with certainty since we do not have a unified tale of the life of Indra. Only scattered references are available to us on this matter; from these references, however, it is possible to gather some allusions to incidents in the legends of Indra. And these incidents closely follow incidents in the Kṛṣṇa pattern. The connecting passages are lost but the remaining details are highly significant and strongly suggest a similar narrative development.

Indra's parents are in later tradition said to be Aditi and Kaśyapa[1] but in the *Ṛg Veda* they are

1. *Mbh* a.60.33-35.

Heaven and Earth, according to W. Norman Brown[1], even though the goddess Earth (Pṛthivī) is not specifically mentioned as his mother. In fact the name of Indra's mother is not given in the *Ṛg Veda*, although she is referred to as a cow[2] and Indra as a calf. Indra's father is said to be Dyaus, Heaven, in one verse,[3] but in other passages he is alluded to as Tvaṣṭṛ.[4] Independently of the names of his parents we find evidence of a troublesome birth. In the words of Professor Brown: 'We may, at least, take it as certain that danger threatened him at birth.'[5] His mother abandoned him soon after birth,[6] and cast him away apparently in the waters; but he was saved and survived to become very strong.[7] It is likely that the peril to the baby came from his own father, from whom the child was to steal the soma[8] and whom he was finally to kill, dragging him by the foot.[9] In the same manner Agni, Indra's twin brother,[10] was concealed from his father by his mother.[11]

Indra was born to be very powerful and strong[12] in order to destroy demons.[13] Even as a child he defeated his enemies,[14] one of whom was a four-footed demon called Araru.[15]

From these disparate elements we can still follow a certain narrative sequence with the help of our scheme. It is in fact very easy to see how these Indra episodes fit the general pattern. It seems that as soon as he was born Indra had to be concealed by his mother. He was cast away in the waters but miraculously survived. Apparently the mother spirited away her child on account of the enmity of the father towards him. Why would the father feel such hatred against his son? This is not said, but the

1. 'The Creation Myth of the Ṛig Veda', *JAOS*, v.62, 1942, pp. 85-98.
2. *RV* 4.18.10.
3. *RV* 4.17.4; suvīras te janitā manyata dyaur.
4. *RV* 1.52.7; 2.17.6; 3.48.2-4; 4.18.3 & 11; see Bergaigne, *La Réligion Vedique*, v.3, pp. 58-62.
5. Brown, *ibid.*, p. 94, also W. N. Brown, 'Indra's Infancy According to *Ṛg Veda* 4.18', *Siddha Bharati*, *Siddheshwar Varma Presentation Volume*, VVRI, Hoshiarpur 1950, v.1, pp. 131-36.
6. *RV* 4.18.3 & 5. parāyatīm mātaram anvacaṣṭa.
7. *RV* 14.18.8.
8. *RV* 3.48.2-4; 4.18.3; 3.36.8.
9. *RV* 4.18.12.
10. *RV* 6.59.2.
11. *RV* 5.2.1-2.
12. *RV* 6.38.5; 7.28.3; 10.108.3.
13. *RV* 1.51.6.
14. *RV* 3.36.8; 5.30.4; 8.45.4; 8.66.1; 8.85.16; 10.73.1; 10.99.10; 10.120.1.
15. *RV* 10.99.10.

TABLE 2 — THE SCHEMES

HAHN	RANK	RAGLAN
1. Hero, illegitimate		
2. Mother, daughter of native prince		1. The hero's mother, a royal virgin
3. Father, a god or stranger	1. Hero, son of a king	2. His father is a king, and
		3. often a near relative of his mother.
4. Omen to a parent	2:3. Difficult conception; A prophecy	4. Circumstances of conception unusual.
		5. Reputed to be the son of a god
		6. Attempt by king (father) to kill him at birth
5. Exposed	4. Exposed	7. Exposed
6:7. Suckled by brutes; reared by herdsmen	5. Suckled by animals, saved by lowly people	8. Reared by foster-parents in far country
8. Arrogance of the youth		9. We are told nothing of his childhood
9. Service abroad		
10. Triumphant home-coming and return	6. Finds his parents when grown-up	10. On reaching manhood returns or goes to his kingdom
11. Fall of the persecutor	7. Takes revenge	11. After victory over king and/or monster
		12. marries a princess, often daughter of predecessor
. Acquisition of sovereignty	8. Is acknowledged	13. and becomes king
. Liberation of mother	9. Achieves rank	14. For a time reigns uneventfully, and
12. Foundation of a city		15. prescribes laws
		16. Later loses favour with gods and/or subjects
		17. Is driven from throne and city
13. Extraordinary death		18. Meets a mysterious death
		19. at the top of a hill
		20. His children, if any, do not succeed him
		21. His body is not buried
		22. but has one or more sepulchres.

TABLE 3 — THE EXAMPLES

a. HAHN	b. NUTT	c. RANK	d. RAGLAN	e. KIM	f. OTHERS
+Theseus	Fionn	Sargon	+Theseus	+Tongmyong	+Tungming
Amphion &	Cuchulain	+Moses	+Moses	Yongpumri	Indra
Zethus	Labhraid Maen	+Karṇa	Jason	Chinhwon	
+Karṇa	Conall	*Oedipus	*Oedipus	T'arhae	
*Oedipus	The Great Fool	Bellerophon	Paris	Pongu	
Pelias & Neleus	Perceval	Telephus	Pelops	Hyokkose	
Leucastus &	+Arthur	*Perseus	*Perseus	Alchi	
*Parrhasius	Merlin	Gilgamesh	Asclepius	Pari	
Dietrich	Taliesin	+Cyrus	Dionysus		
+Cyrus	Havelock the	Tristan	Apollo		
Wolfdietrich	Dane	*Romulus & Re-	*Romulus & Remus		
*Romulus & Remus		mus	*Heracles		
*Heracles		*Heracles	Zeus		
Kei Khosrav		Jesus	*Siegfried		
*Siegfried		*Siegfried	Joseph		
Kṛṣṇa		Lohengrin	Elijah		
			+Arthur		
			Nykang		
			Watu Gunung		
			Llew Llawgyffes		
			Robin Hood		

List a, 15 names; list b, 10 names; list c, 15 names; list d, 21 names; list e, 8 names; and two other names. Names marked * appear thrice; names marked + appear twice; names unmarked appear once.

60 names in all.

TABLE 4—THE DIVINE HERO IN CELTIC HAGIOLOGY[1]

1. The birth is foretold by an angel, an omen, or a miracle.
2. His mother is of royal descent.
3. His father is invariably a king or noble.
4. He or one of his ancestors is born of incest.
5. The circumstances of his conception are unusual.
6. The divine nature of the child is often represented symbolically.
7. A miracle occurs at the time of the birth.
8. An attempt is made on the life of the infant.
9. Is reared far from the birth place.
10. On reaching manhood performs a miracle.
11. Immediately sets out in his missionary career.
12. Gains a victory over a chieftain, a wizard and/or a dragon.
13. After this victory becomes the supreme power in the land.
14. For the remainder of his life he founds churches and looks after the spiritual needs of the people.
15. He knows the time of his death beforehand.
16. Welsh and Irish saints have a calm death; Cornish ones suffer martyrdom.
17. Death is accompanied by angelic visitations and a great brilliance of supernatural light.
18. The body retains a miraculous element after death.
19. The saint has one or more holy sepulchres that become centres of pilgrimage.

1. From Alwyn D. Rees, 'The Divine Hero in Celtic Hagiology', *Folk-lore*, v. 47, 1936, pp. 30-31.

TABLE 5— A HYPOTHESISED BIOGRAPHICAL PATTERN FOR KOREAN FOLKTALES

1. The hero's parents are of nobility but their intercourse occurs in a most unusual and mysterious manner.
2. His birth is fraught with difficulties or comes only after long childlessness and tortuous course of events.
3. The circumstances of his birth are extraordinary and mysterious.
4. He is either abandoned, exiled or persecuted.
5. He is protected either by animals or an old woman.
6. He performs miracles.
7. He makes a name for himself and builds a capital city or founds a clan or establishes a sect.
8. Usually, he dies a mysterious death and is deified after death.

from Kim Yol-Gyu, 'The Traditional Oral Literature and Folklore of Korea : With Emphasis on the Types of Biographical Patterns'.

prophecy motif seems a very viable and logical explanation. We know that Indra eventually killed his father and also that he stole the soma from him; it is therefore not unreasonable to suggest that the father must have known beforehand about the risks he ran were his son to live. The whole episode strongly resembles the story of the birth of Zeus. Cronos had heard a prophecy that one of his children was to kill him and seize the throne of heaven, so he decided to devour his children as soon as they were born. In this manner he disposed of several of them, but his wife and sister, Rhea, decided to save Zeus and concealed him. Zeus was suckled by the goat Amaltheia and grew up among shepherds. Later on he was to kill Cronos as prophesied.

One motif hinted at in these Indra verses is specially significant because of its relation to others in the Kṛṣṇa story; this is the casting in the waters. We have seen that Indra's mother apparently throws him into the water.

When the girl had abandoned you,
When Kuṣavā had swallowed you,
Then the waters were gracious to the child,
Then Indra became powerful.[1]

This is the very common 'finding of Moses' motif, one of the stock episodes in the hero stories as mentioned before.[2] We are not going to enter here into the problem of the symbolic meaning of 'the child floating in the waters' motif. We have already mentioned Rank's Freudian interpretation.[1] And a very deep and learned discussion of the subject will be found in Erich Neumann's *The Origins and History of Consciousness*.[2] We can, however, mention the similarity of this motif to the description of Hiraṇyagarbha in the *Ṛg Veda*[3] and the floating baby of Mārkaṇḍeya's vision[4] who is none other than Nārāyaṇa-Kṛṣṇa.

But does this motif of the floating child appear in the story of Kṛṣṇa's birth? It appears in fact, although in a slightly modified form, as an example of what Professor Fontenrose calls 'reduction' as a variation form in folkloristics.[5] We will remember that on the night of Kṛṣṇa's birth a terrible storm was raging, and Vasudeva, the father of Kṛṣṇa, having to take the baby to Gokula to hide him from the demonic Kaṃsa, was dejected to find that the river Yamunā was flooded and was impossible to cross. A miracle occurred, however. The river became calm in spite of the furious storm, and permitted Vasudeva to ford it with ease. The rain kept pouring, but Śeṣa, the divine *nāga*, came and covered the child with its hoods to protect him.[6] The image here is just as that in the 'floating child' motif, that of a helpless baby, apparently lost in a deluge, and as in the stock motif again, delivered safe and sound. As Indra's mother puts it, 'the waters had pity on the baby.' It is true that in Kṛṣṇa's case he is not all alone, but in the arms of his father. The position, however, is the same. The baby is in extreme peril, almost certain to be drowned, but finally mysteriously protected. In the Purāṇic account we are told, as in the Vedic version, that the waters have pity on the child, show him favour; this is indicated by the fact that the *nāga*, a symbol of the water and the river, comes by himself and covers the baby with his hoods in order to protect him. By introducing

1. mamac cana tvā yuvatiḥ parāsa mamac cana tvā kuṣavā jagāra / mamac cid āpaḥ śiśave mamṛḍyur mamac cid indraḥ sahasod atiṣṭhat //. Renou translates the first line as 'ce n'est pas de mon fait si la jeune femme t'a exposé, demon fait si Kuṣavā t'a avalé.' (Louis Renou, *Anthologie Sanscrite*, Paris 1961). Geldner surprisingly renders 'Um meinetwillen hat dich die junge Frau nicht beseitigt, noch hat dich um meinetwillen die Kuṣavā verschlungen.' where 'nicht beseitigt' is unwarranted. We prefer to give to mamac cana-mamac cid its traditional value as correlatives (cf. Bötlingk-Roth, Monier-Williams, Grassman W.R.V.). Kuṣavā is most probably the name of a river and not that of a demoness as Sāyaṇa supposes.

2. Fifteen heroes among those listed already have this motif in their biographies. They are: Perseus, Oedipus, Telephus, Romulus, Moses, Sargon, Darab, Siegfried, Lohengrin, Taliesin, Saint Cennydd, Karṇa, Bhīṣma, and Tongmyong and Tarhae from Korea, in whose story the motif appears as the crossing of a river. Bhīṣma was not mentioned before but, as we shall see, the story of his birth has very important parallels to that of Kṛṣṇa. The legend of Osiris-Horus in Egypt has also a resemblance to this motif. One very important variant of the motif we have in the Jaina *Vasudevahiṇḍi* where it is Kaṃsa, the uncle of Kṛṣṇa, who is cast away in the river because of an omen: 'Thinking that the child which was growing in the womb would certainly cause the destruction of the family, he was put into a large bronze casket after birth and floated down the river Jamuṇā.' Jagdishchandra Jain, *The Vasudevahiṇḍi*, L. D. Institute of Indology, Ahmedabad, 1977, pp. 551-52.

1. See above, p. 45.
2. London, Routledge and Kegan Paul, 1954.
3. See above, p. 9.
4. *Mbh* 3.186-187.
5. See above, p. 42.
6. *VP* 5.3.17-18: varṣatāṃ jaladānāṃ ca toyamatyulbaṇaṃ niśi / saṃvṛtyānuyayau śeṣaḥ phaṇairānakadundubhim // yamunāṃ cātigambhīrāṃ nānāvarttaśatākulām / vasudevo vahanviṣṇuṃ jānumātravahāṃ yayau //. *BhP* 10.3.49: tāḥ kṛṣṇavahe vasudeva āgate svayaṃ vyavaryanta yathā tamo raveḥ / vavarṣa parjanya upāṃśugarjitaḥ śeṣo'nvagād vāri nivārayan phaṇaiḥ //.

this narrative device the anonymous bard is trying to impress on the minds of the listeners the actual identity of the child with the eternal Nārāyaṇa, the cosmic giant floating in the universal ocean couched on the serpent Śeṣa at the beginning and the end of the aeons.

The *Viṣṇu Purāṇa* says that the river, in allowing Vasudeva to cross it, reached only up to his knees, but this detail is not given in the *Bhāgavata Purāṇa*, and the *Devī Bhāgavata* says that the water reached up to his hip (*kaṭidaghnī*),[1] and this is the way the scene is represented in modern iconography.[2] The popularity of the motif is attested, by the frequent representation of the scene in modern calendars and popular religious prints —a man carrying a beautiful blue boy over his head, while standing with water up to his waist in the middle of a horrific black storm and an enormous serpent covering the baby with his various hoods—this picture can be seen today, in almost any tea-stall or sweet shop in the bazaars of India. The *Bālacarita* of Bhāsa also refers to the episode, without mentioning how deep in the water Vasudeva went. It only says that Vasudeva was astonished to see how the water of the river was divided in two, still and quiet where he was to cross and swift and agitated everywhere else.[3] This all goes to show that the floating child motif is present conspicuously, although in a modified form, in the Kṛṣṇa cycle.

Coming now to the prophecy motif, we find it present both in the Kṛṣṇa and the Heracles stories. Although differing in details it is still essentially the same motif. The prophecy does not occur specifically in the Indra myths, as we saw, but its narrative probability, if not necessity, is easily discernible in them. This motif is an essential element in the hero story, since it provides a cause for the persecution suffered by the child, and his eventual hiding and rearing up among cowherds or other rustic people. It is therefore the initial incident that starts that chain of events that will take the hero through a series of adventures that ineluctably bring him to glory and his enemy to death.

The account of the prophecy differs but little in our texts. The Purāṇas present a unified version, except for the *Harivaṃśa* that omits a scene. The *Bālacarita* starts only from the actual birth of Kṛṣṇa and therefore does not include the prophecy. The *Ghaṭa Jātaka* presents a variant of the motif. The Purāṇic version tells how on the wedding day of Devakī and Vasudeva, among much merriment and gaiety, Kaṃsa himself offered to drive the bridal cart in order to oblige his cousin Devakī (the *Harivaṃśa* says his aunt, the *Prem Sāgar* his sister). And it was while the three of them were in the cart that a voice resounded, warning Kaṃsa, 'Fool, the eighth child of that one that you now convey will take your life.'[1]

At this Kaṃsa took hold of Devakī's hair and pulling her down drew out his sword to slay her. According to the *Viṣṇu Purāṇa* and the *Bhāgavata Purāṇa* Vasudeva's attitude in view of this unseemly treatment of his bride was very meek and submissive, begging Kaṃsa to spare her and finally promising to hand over to him all his future children to be killed. This was an unfatherly promise exacted under

1. *DBP* 4.23.30.

2. I have found only a few representations of the motif in Rājput painting. Surely there are more. Examples are illustrated in M. S. Randhawa's *Kangra Paintings of the Bhāgavata Purāṇa*, National Museum of India, Delhi 1960, fig. 2, belonging to the collection of the Indian Museum, Calcutta, and in W. Spink's *Kṛṣṇa Maṇḍala*, University of Michigan, Ann Arbor 1971, figs. 12 and 13.

3. hanta dvidhā chinnaṃ jalam, itaḥ sthitam, itaḥ pradhāvati. The *Prem Sāgar* puts the episode in a more dramatic form; it says that Vasudeva 'fixing his thoughts upon Bhagwan [*sic*]... went into the Jumna; and the depth of the river increased as he advanced. When the water came up to his nose, he was agitated, Sri Krishna extending his foot, uttered the mystical sound, 'hun', and in consequence of the stretching out of his foot, the Jumna became fordable', *The Prem Sagar in English*, Ram Narain Lal Beni Prasad, Allahabad, n.d., p. 20 (this is in fact Captain W. Hollings' translation, 1848, but it is not acknowledged by the publisher). To show how deeply impressed in the popular mind is this episode we reproduce here a note from Growse's *Mathura*. 'This incident is popularly commemorated by a native toy called "Vasudeva Katora", of which great numbers are manufactured at Mathura. It is a brass cup with the figure of a man in it carrying a child at his side, and is so contrived that when water is poured into it it cannot rise above the child's foot, but is then carried off by a hidden duct and runs out at the bottom till the cup is empty', F. S. Growse, *Mathura, a District Memoir*, 1874, 2nd ed., 1880, p. 52, n.3. In Prambanam, Jaya, we find a relief where we can actually see the child coming out of the water safe and sound; his experience in the water has not scared him in the least and he plays with a fish he has caught (see plate 57). In it no sign of Vasudeva is seen and it looks as if the child was in the water alone. The carrying of Kṛṣṇa across the river is highly reminiscent of the legend of St. Christopher in Christianity.

1. *VP* 5.1.8: yāmetāṃ vahase mūḍha saha bhartrā rathe sthitām / asyāstavāṣṭamo garbhaḥ prāṇānapahariṣyati. *BhP* 10.1.34: pathi pragrahiṇaṃ kaṃsamābhaṣyāhāśarīravāk / asyāstvāmaṣṭamo garbho hantā yāṃ vahase'budha. *DBP* 4.20.64: kaṃsa kaṃsa mahābhāga devakīgarbhasaṃbhavaḥ / aṣṭamastu sutaḥ śrīmāṃstava haṃtā bhaviṣyati.

Vasudeva Crossing the Yamunā

The Vision of Mārkaṇḍeya

duress that no one would expect him to keep, but in fact he did keep it. Indeed the figure of Vasudeva in the legend of Kṛṣṇa is a very obscure and secondary one, contrasting with the strong personality of Kaṃsa. After this promise of Vasudeva, Devakī and he are, nevertheless, imprisoned by Kaṃsa.

The *Devī Bhāgavata Purāṇa* presents the father of Kṛṣṇa in a more favourable way. There he seems to be a sort of chieftain in his own right since he has armed men under him who fight with Kaṃsa's men to defend Devakī.[1] He, however, gives of his own will the fateful promise to yield his children to the wicked tyrant. After this Devakī and he are free to go to their own house and, as a free man and not as a prisoner, Vasudeva surrenders Devakī's issue. Kaṃsa puts them in prison only when the eighth child is about to come.[2] In fact Kaṃsa's intentions were to spare all first seven children. He does specifically say this and returns to Vasudeva the first born,[3] but he is later convinced by Nārada not to run any risks and kills them all.[4] A curious passage in the *Bhāgavata Purāṇa*[5] makes Kaṃsa beg forgiveness of Devakī and Vasudeva after the killing of the eighth child (the goddess Yogamāyā) and, forgiving him sincerely, they are set free.

As we mentioned before, the *Harivaṃśa* completely omits this episode, but the account of the *Ghaṭa Jātaka* is extremely interesting. In it, we find Kaṃsa is given a double in the form of a brother—and even a triplet in the form of the father—that Devakī is his real sister and that the marriage only comes after the prophecy, here delivered by priests and not by a voice from heaven. All these are minor variants that do not alter the significance of the story. The tale goes that:

> In Uttarāpatha, in the city of Asitañjana of the Kaṃsa Kingdom, there was a king called Mahākaṃsa. This king had two sons, called Kaṃsa and Upakaṃsa, and one daughter, called Devagabbhā. On the day of her birth the soothsayer brāhmaṇas foretold: "a son born of this girl will destroy the kingdom and the line of Kaṃsa." The king loved his daughter too much to destroy her, and thinking: "the brothers will know [what to do] on this matter", lived on to the end of his life span. At his death Kaṃsa became King and Upakaṃsa viceroy. And they thought: "if we kill our own sister we will be blameworthy, [so] we will look after her without giving her to anyone and keep her without a husband. And they built a palace upon a single pillar and made her live there.[1]

1. vasudevānugā vīrā yuddhāyodyatakārmukāḥ, *DBP* 4.20.72.
2. *DBP* 4.23.67.
3. *DBP* 4.21.39-44.
4. *DBP* 4.51.54.
5. *BhP* 10.4.14-28.

In this version the prophecy is given at the time of the birth of the girl, long before any husband or possible suitor might appear, and there is no attempt on the girl's life. The *Ghaṭa Jātaka* follows closely other variants of the motif in imprisoning the princess to avoid her meeting a man and conceiving a son. One example of this variant is found in the Perseus story where king Acrisius imprisons his daughter Danae in a dungeon with brazen doors to prevent the birth of any son from her, because of a prophecy that Acrisius' grandson would kill him. In the *Jātaka* Kaṃsa and Upakaṃsa incarcerate their sister Devagabbhā in a palace built upon a single pillar where ineluctably Upasāgara will come to seduce her and beget the feared son. To our mind the *Ghaṭa Jātaka* is just using a stock variant of this stock theme and not inventing circumstances to deride Kṛṣṇa's parents and the rest of the characters in the story, as R.C. Hazra believes.[2] It is probable that the *Jātaka* does contain some of this intentional slandering but this instance does not seem to be part of it.

Coming now to the birth itself, we have again a unified Purāṇic account and a variant, this time a significant one, in the *Ghaṭa Jātaka*. The Purāṇas make Devakī give birth in prison consecutively to six sons who are all killed by Kaṃsa.[3] These chil-

1. Uttarāpathe Kaṃsabhoge Asitañjananagare Mahākaṃsonāma rājjam kāresi. Tassa Kaṃso ca Upakaṃso ca'ti dve puttā ahesuṃ, Devagabbhā nāma ekā dhītā. Tassā jātadivase nemittikabrāhmaṇā "etissā kucchiyaṃ nibbataputto Kaṃsabhogaṃ Kaṃsavaṃsaṃ nāsessatīti" vyākariṃsu. Rājā bālasinehena dhītaraṃ nāsetuṃ nāsakkhi, "bhātaro jānissantīti" yāvatāyukaṃ ṭhatvā kālam akāsi. Tasmiṃ kālakate Kaṃso rājā ahosi Upakaṃso uparājā, te cintayiṃsu: "sace mayaṃ bhaginiṃ nāsessāma gārayhā bhavissāma, etaṃ kassacī adatvā nissāmikaṃ katvā paṭijaggissāmā" 'ti te ekathūṇakaṃ pāsadaṃ kāretvā taṃ tattha vasāpesuṃ. *Ghaṭa Jātaka*, Faussboll ed., p. 79.
2. R. C. Hazra, 'Vāsudeva Worship...', *Our Heritage*, v.18, p. 20; '...The union of a dissolute and treacherous prince with a princess who allowed herself to be enjoyed by her lover even before marriage...'.
3. *VP* 5.1.72; 5.2.1; *BhP* 10.1.66; *DBP* 4.22.22; H. H. Wilson, *The Viṣṇu Purāṇa*, p. 401, n.1, erroneously says that *Bhāgavata Purāṇa* 'makes Kaṃsa spare them, and restore them

dren, it is explained, were the sons of the demon Kālanemi, reborn as Kaṃsa, and grandsons of Hiraṇyakaśipu, the old enemy of Viṣṇu, who cursed them to be reborn from Devakī to be killed by Kaṃsa because they propitiated Brahmā.[1] The *Viṣṇu Purāṇa* does not explain at all the motive for which they had to be killed, and the *Bhāgavata Purāṇa* gives a different account of the curse. According to this text the *ṣaḍgarbha* were originally the sons of Marīci and Ūrṇā, who once laughed at Brahmā when he was about to make love to his own daughter. Because of this they were cursed to be reborn as sons of Hiraṇyakaśipu and then to be killed by Kaṃsa when reborn once again from Devakī.[2] The *Devī Bhāgavata* combines both accounts. In fact it uses the same words of the *Bhāgavata Purāṇa* to describe how the six sons of Marīci laughed at Brahmā;[3] then it relates how they were cursed to be reborn as sons of Kālanemi and then as sons of Hiraṇyakaśipu who again cursed them after they propitiated Brahmā, to be reborn from Devakī and killed by Kaṃsa, their father of a previous birth. It is very interesting that these accounts stress the fact that Kaṃsa was actually the father of the six first children of Devakī, even if he did not beget them this time directly. In a separate section we will examine the importance of the birth of these first six brothers of Kṛṣṇa to complete the symbolic number eight.

After the killing of their first six children, Vasudeva and Devakī begot a seventh one, who was an incarnation of Viṣṇu-Nārāyaṇa. According to the *Viṣṇu Purāṇa*[4] the god plucked off two hairs, one white and one black, and promised that through these hairs he would be incarnated to destroy the demons that were overburdening the earth. The *Bhāgavata Purāṇa* and *Devī Bhāgavata Purāṇa* say that it was Ananta-Śeṣa, the gigantic *nāga* on which Viṣṇu-Nārāyaṇa reclines, that was incarnated as the seventh son of Devakī.[5] As we have said, our other source, the *Bālacarita*, does not mention all this, starting the action only later at the moment of the birth of Kṛṣṇa. All three Purāṇas and the *Harivaṃśa* agree in that this seventh issue of Devakī was transferred by Yoganidrā from her womb into Rohiṇī's, another wife of Vasudeva, and that is why this child was called Saṃkarṣaṇa.[1] The eighth child, of course, is Kṛṣṇa. The *Harivaṃśa* gives a very interesting account of the antecedents to the incarnation of Viṣṇu as Balarāma-Kṛṣṇa. In it is told how Brahmā requested Viṣṇu to be born on earth to rid her of innumerable kings who by their weight were making her sink.[2] According to the *Harivaṃśa* Viṣṇu accepts the request of Brahmā and then, strangely enough, asks him to tell 'in what country, in what conditions of birth, by which occupation [to earn a living] or in what house, I will kill them in battle, that tell to me O Grandfather'.[3] Brahmā then proceeds to relate how once upon a time Kaśyapa, the main Prajāpati or progenitor of the human race, stole Varuṇa's cows and, at the instigation of his two wives Aditi and Surabhi, refused to give them back. Varuṇa therefore complained to Brahmā and the latter cursed Kaśyapa to be born on earth with his two wives among the cows as a cowherd in Govardhana mountain as a tributary of Kaṃsa.[4] There Viṣṇu would have to be born as a child with the marks of a cowherd (made) upon him, and there he would have to grow as of yore did Trivikrama.[5] The *Harivaṃśa* ends this chapter with a remarkable passage where it says that Viṣṇu left his old body in a cave in mount Meru and himself proceeded to the house of Vasudeva.[6]

The Purāṇas agree in describing portentous happenings just before and at the time of Kṛṣṇa's birth.[7] The *Devī Bhāgavata Purāṇa*, as a Śākta work written with the purpose of extolling the religion of the

to their parents.' An absolute mistake, Wilson is perhaps referring to *Devī Bhāgavata Purāṇa* (4.21.39-44).

1. *HV* 47.12-22.
2. āsan marīceḥ ṣaṭ putrā ūrṇāyāṃ prathame'ntare /devāḥ kaṃ jahasurvīkṣya sutāṃ yabhitumudyatam // tenāsurīmagan yonimadhunāvadyakarmaṇā / hiraṇyakaśiporjātā nītāste yogamāyayā // devakyā udare jātā rājan kaṃsavihiṃsitāḥ / *BhP* 10.85.47-49 a.
3. brahmāṇam jahasurvīkṣya sutāṃ yabhitumudyatam // *DBP* 4.22.9b.
4. 5.1.59-60; the *DBP* 4.23.50-51; follows *VP* in this.
5. saptamo vaiṣṇavaṃ dhāma yamanantaṃ pracakṣate / garbho babhūva devakyā harṣaśokavivardhanaḥ // *BhP* 10.2.5.

1. karṣaṇenāsya garbhasya svagarbhe cāhitasya vai / saṃkarṣaṇo nāma śubhe tava putro bhaviṣyati // *HV* 48.6.
2. rājñāṃ balairbalavatāṃ pīḍyate vasudhātalam // seyaṃ bhārapariśrāntā pīḍyamānā narādhipaiḥ / pṛthivī samanuprāptā naurivāsannaviplavā // *HV* 42.17 b-18.
3. yatra deśe yathā jāto yena veṣeṇa vā vasan / tānahaṃ samare hanyāṃ tanme brūhi pitāmaha // *HV* 45.16.
4. tābhyāṃ saha sa gopatve kaśyapo bhuvi raṃsyate // tad asya kaśyapasyāṃśastejasā kaśyapopamaḥ / vasudeva iti khyāto goṣu tiṣṭhati bhūtale // girigovardhano nāma mathurāyāstvadūrataḥ / tatrāsau goṣu nirataḥ kaṃsasya karadāyakaḥ / *HV* 45.33-35.
5. tatra tvaṃ śiśurevādau gopālakṛtalakṣaṇaḥ / vardhayasva mahābāho purā traivikramo yathā // *HV* 45.39.
6. purāṇam tatra vinyasya dehaṃ harirudāradhiḥ / ātmānaṃ yojayāmāsa vasudevagṛhe prabhuḥ // *HV* 45.49.
7. *VP* 5.3.3-7; *HV* 48.14-17; *BhP* 10.3.2-7.

Goddess, often tries to belittle and disparage the stories of other gods. Hence it presents a new account of the causes that prompt Viṣṇu to take birth on earth. It mentions the gods' deputation to Viṣṇu to beg him to incarnate himself and relieve the earth of her burden,[1] but it adds that Viṣṇu had to be born on earth numerous times owing to the curse of Bhṛgu.[2] This sage had cursed the god because when helping the devas against the daityas he, together with Indra, killed his wife, mother of Śukra, guru of the demons, who was protecting the enemies of the gods.[3] The *Bālacarita* also describes the miraculous events of that night in similar terms to the Purāṇas.[4]

The *Harivaṃśa*, as said before, does not elaborate on the description of the exchange of babies. The other Purāṇas tell how everybody in the palace fell fast asleep and how Vasudeva took the baby Kṛṣṇa, crossed the Yamunā by a miracle and proceeded to Vraja, Nanda's hamlet, where everybody was also asleep, and there exchanged his own son for the newborn daughter of Yaśodā and Nanda; then he returned to the palace, deposited the girl by Devakī's side, and put himself back in chains.[5] The *Devī Bhāgavata* again takes the opportunity to enhance the glory of the goddess and tells how, previous to the birth of the babies, Yaśodā offered Devakī to exchange them once they were born. This is in agreement with the *Ghaṭa Jātaka*, as we shall see.[6] Then, on the night of the delivery, the goddess herself handed Vasudeva the girl.[7]

The *Bālacarita* relates the whole episode in a more dramatic form, quite in agreement with its character as a play. It refers to how, after crossing the Yamunā, Vasudeva met Nanda at dead of night. The latter, who was angry with Vasudeva because he had flogged and fettered him at the instance of Kaṃsa,[8] was carrying his baby daughter who had been born and had died that same night.[9] Vasudeva, who called him friend (*vayasya*), persuaded him to exchanging the dead girl for the baby Kṛṣṇa. Nanda, who called Vasudeva lord (*bhaṭṭa*) and himself a slave (*dāsa*), handed Vasudeva his own dead daughter and promised to take care of Kṛṣṇa.[1]

1. *DBP* 4.22.50.
2. *DBP* 4.10.30.
3. *DBP* 4.10.33—12.9.
4. *BC* 1.14-20.
5. *VP* 5.3.20-23; *BhP* 10.3.51-52.
6. *DBP* 4.23.16-17.
7. *DBP* 4.23.32-35.
8 sa khalu mayā kaṃsājñayā nigaḍitaḥ kaśābhihataśca; *BC* 1.19.
9. jādamatta evva aoggadappāṇā; *BC ibid.*

The *Ghaṭa Jātaka*, that, as we said, makes Devakī (Devagabbhā) a prisoner before her marriage, tells how Upasāgara, the Viceroy of Uttaramdhura, was hiding in the kingdom of Kaṃsa, because he had offended his brother the king by violating the royal harem. He came to know of the princess Devagabbhā and, bribing her attendant Nandagopā, gained access to her and visited her frequently. Eventually the girl conceived and her brothers found out what had been happening. Instead of killing the offenders they married them and a few months later the princess delivered a baby girl who was kept with the knowledge of her brothers, who were only afraid of her bearing a son. After some time she again conceived and this time was delivered of a son who was exchanged for a girl born at the same time of Nandagopā. In the same way Devagabbhā had nine more sons and Nandagopā nine more daughters and all of them were exchanged without anybody knowing the truth. Thus the *Ghaṭa Jātaka* varies the story, making all the sons of Devakī and even the girl survive.

All our sources, except for the *Ghaṭa Jātaka*, agree in the account of the killing of Yaśodā's daughter by Kaṃsa. In spite of Devakī's pleadings, the wicked tyrant took the defenceless child and dashed her against a stone but, at that moment, an astonishing transformation took place. The girl rose in the sky and, assuming the terrifying shape of the goddess Kātyāyanī, she announced to Kaṃsa the futility of his attempt to save himself, since his real killer was already born and safe.[2] The *Harivaṃśa*, as usual, gives the more realistic description. According to it the baby was still afflicted by the delivery (*sā garbhaśayane kliṣṭā*) and her hair was still wet from the womb (*garbhāmbuklinnamūrdhajā*). This realism is also appreciated in the words of the goddess to the terrified Kaṃsa. 'Therefore at the time of your death, of your dragging by your enemy, I, having torn your body apart with my own hands [or nails in a variant], will look at your warm blood [or the blood of your heart in another version]'.[3] Contrasting with these words of the *Harivaṃśa*, the goddess in the *Devī Bhāgavata Purāṇa* speaks 'sweetly' (*mṛdusvanā*).[4] As

1. *BC, ibid.*
2. *HV* 48.25; *VP* 5.3.24-29; *BP* 10.4.7-13; *DBP* 4.23.44-47.
3. tasmāttavāntakāle'haṃ kṛṣyamāṇasya śatruṇā / pāṭayitvā karairdehamuṣṇaṃ pāṣyāmi śoṇitam. *HV* 48.35.
4. *DBP* 4.23.46.

we have noticed, the *Ghaṭa Jātaka* dispenses with all these gory details and killing and makes all the children survive.

After this scene Kaṃsa, now aware that his plot has failed and that his future killer is already born and safe, starts plotting again to kill the child and, summoning his demonic allies, he orders them to destroy the boy at all costs. The first of these demons to attempt to kill Kṛṣṇa is Pūtanā.

The Pūtanā episode would seem to fall better in our discussion of the themes of the Miraculous Child, i.e. the episodes of the youth of Kṛṣṇa when he defeats many monsters, themes and motifs that are also connected with the themes of the Strong Man and the killing of the Dragon. However, the Pūtanā episode, although perhaps the first in those series, enters more easily within the themes of the Birth of the Hero, and we shall present it as the last motif in that series. Later we will give our reasons for doing so.

This episode, as well as all the rest in the next series, is lacking in the *Ghaṭa Jātaka* and the *Devī Bhāgavata Purāṇa*, both of them polemic works not interested in promoting a too favourable image of Kṛṣṇa. It is present in all our other sources, that differ but little in their account of it. According to these works Pūtanā, a demoness, went to the cowherds' encampment and, approaching the baby Kṛṣṇa, tried to suckle him at her poisonous breast; but the child, taking firm hold of her, sucked with such force that he killed her then and there. The *Harivaṃśa* puts this episode after the overturning of the cart (*śakaṭabhaṅga*) but all the other versions have it as the first in the series of monster-killings. The *Viṣṇu Purāṇa* does not mention anything about the appearance of the monster, but only says that she came by night and when Kṛṣṇa was asleep she gave him her breast.[1] The *Harivaṃśa* speaks specifically of a bird, or bird-like monster. Since she had breasts, she was horrible and caused those who saw her to fear for their lives; her name was Pūtanā and she came in the middle of the night flapping her wings in anger.[2] She perched on the axle of the cart where the baby was lying and while everybody else was sleeping she gave him her breast full of milk.[3]

1. *VP* 5.5.7; suptam kṛṣṇamupādāya rātrau tasmai stanaṃ dadau.

2. *HV* cr. ed. 636*; pūtanā nāma śakunī ghorā prāṇabhayaṃkarī / ājagāmārdharātre vai pakṣau krodhādvidhunvatī.

3. *HV* 50.21-22; nililye śakaṭākṣe sā prasnavotpīḍavarṣiṇī // dadau stanaṃ ca Kṛṣṇāya tatra suptajane niśi.

The *Bālacarita* mentions that the child was ten days old (*daṣarattappaṣude* = *daśarātraprasūte*), and is the first to mention that Pūtanā, whom it calls a *dānavī*, took the form of a woman to approach the child, in this case, remarkably, the shape not of any woman but that of Yaśodā herself.[1] Another variant in the *Bālacarita* is that it is not Kṛṣṇa, as in the *Viṣṇu Purāṇa*, or the people, as in the *Harivaṃśa*, who are asleep, but Pūtanā is killed when she falls asleep.[2] The text does not explain clearly how Pūtanā was killed, it only says how after death she recovered her form as a demoness (*dāṇavī bhavia tato evvamudā* = *dānavī bhūtvā tata eva mṛtā*).

Finally, the *Bhāgavata Purāṇa* gives a much embellished account of the incident. It seems to refer again to Pūtanā coming in the form of a bird, but it does not say so clearly, it prefers to use the circumlocution *khecarī*, 'one that moves in the air', that can be applied both to a bird and almost to any kind of fantastic being said to be able to fly.[3] This Purāṇa also mentions the transformation of Pūtanā into a woman, this time 'a very desirable or beautiful woman'[4] and not just the foster-mother of Kṛṣṇa as in the *Bālacarita*. So disguised the demoness is able to penetrate the village in full view of everybody, differently from the other versions where she comes in the middle of the night. Another significant difference in the *Bhāgavata Purāṇa* version is that it refers to the house of Nanda (*nandagṛhe*) where the child was staying and not to a wagon or cart, although at the beginning of the scene it mentions cow-settlements or cow-stations among the places visited by the demoness in her wanderings to kill children.[5] Pūtanā entered the house and taking the baby Kṛṣṇa suckled him with her poisonous breast, and then 'the Lord, having pressed strongly with his hands, full of anger, drank that [poison] together with her

1. ṇandagovīe rūvaṃ gahṇia āadā = nandagopyā rūpaṃ gṛhītvā gatā.

2. tado taṃ vijāṇia ṣuvidā pāḍidā = tatastāṃ vijñāya suptā pātitā.

3. Actually the word *śakunī* used in the *Harivaṃśa* in the corresponding passage can also be interpreted both as a bird and as a flying monster. That this passage refers to a bird, however, is borne out by iconographic evidence. This episode is also mentioned in *Mbh* 2.38.7 (see plate 43); the presence of a bird in these reliefs has not been explained before, as is the case with so many other points in Kṛṣṇa iconography.

4. yoṣitvā māyayā 'tmānaṃ prāviśat kāmacāriṇī. *BhP* 10.6.4.

5. *BhP* 10.6.2; śiśūṃścacāra nighnantī puragrāmavrajādiṣu

life'.[1] The demoness fell to the ground shaking her arms and legs, yelling so horribly that the whole earth trembled. She recovered her original form and her gigantic body smashed all the trees within an area of more than three *gavyūtis*.[2] A significant comparison is made with the most outstanding of Indra's battles; Pūtanā fell down dead just as Vṛtra, killed by the *vajra* of Indra.[3]

This whole episode can be interpreted as having traces of reality, as has been done by some scholars[4] who believe Pūtanā represents an infantile disease in personified form. Monier-Williams gives a similar description: 'Name of female demon (said to cause a particular disease) in children, ...; ... a kind of disease in a child (ascribed to the demon Pūtanā).[5] Now this interpretation may be supported by the description of the fiend in the *Viṣṇu Purāṇa* and the *Bhāgavata Purāṇa* as a 'child-killer'[6] and by a verse included in the *Viṣṇu Purāṇa*: 'That [child] to whom Pūtanā gives her breast in the night, of that child the body is killed in an instant'.[7] This indicates that Pūtanā was in the habit of killing children in general and that Kṛṣṇa was just another victim in her career.[8] Thus perhaps the episode expresses the general fear of the people, and of mothers particularly, that their children might die, infantile mortality being widespread. The baby Kṛṣṇa killing the demoness embodied their hopes that their own children could survive just as Kṛṣṇa did.

This interpretation can apply to other variants of the hero story that include the same motif, but we shall not follow these lines. We can analyse the motif in more general terms simply as 'the suckling of an enemy', as such, the motif is widely prevalent in the traditional hero legends. Hahn called it 'the suckling by brutes or wild beasts'. It seems to represent in various degrees the utter helplessness of a baby abandoned by his mother, his certain death in the wilderness, and the astonishing miracle of a savage beast, the natural enemy of the child, taking pity on him and actually feeding him of her milk. The contrast is between the real mother that casts away her child and the natural enemy of the baby that suckles him, a reversal of roles that seems to be at the bottom of the motif. In the Kṛṣṇa story the motif suffers various transformations. We have in the first place a mutation of role and a mutation of action. Pūtanā is the enemy of Kṛṣṇa just as the she-wolf was the natural enemy of the abandoned children Romulus and Remus, or the she-bear the natural enemy of the baby Paris. All of them suckled the children i.e. took the place of the mother,[1] but whereas the two beasts are in fact saving the life of the castaway babies, Pūtanā is trying to kill Kṛṣṇa, and, although Kṛṣṇa is also a castaway, she comes to his own cradle, where he is supposed to be safe. Then we have a reduction of features and another mutation of role in that the wild beasts, of horrible and menacing appearance, turn out to be beneficent and instead of killing the babies give them life. Pūtanā on her part, a fearful demoness, assumes the aspect of a beautiful girl who pretends to suckle the child, but intends to kill him. The results of the action are equally contrasting: in one the terrible wild beast adopts the defenceless child as if she was his mother, in the other the little baby kills the pretended mother who is in fact a monster.

The parallels and contrasts are indeed striking. As we said, this motif is common in hero sagas and we find at least twenty-four examples of it, without

1. *BhP* 10.6.10; gāḍhaṃ karābhyāṃ bhagavān prapīḍya tat prāṇaiḥ samaṃ roṣasamanvito'pibat.

2. *BhP* 10.6.14; patamāno'pi taddehastrigavyūtyantaradrumān. Three *gavyūtis* are approximately twenty-one kilometres.

3. *BhP* 10.6.13; vajrāhato vṛtra ivāpatan.

4. A. D. Pusalker, *Studies in the Epics and Purāṇas*, Bharatiya Vidya Bhavan, Bombay, 1955, p. 100.

5. Monier-Williams, *SED*, p. 641, col. 2.

6. bālaghātinī, *VP* 5.5.7; *BhP* 10.6.2.

7. *VP* 5.5.8; yasmai yasmai stanam rātrau pūtanā samprayacchati / tasya tasya kṣaṇenāṅgaṃ bālakasyopahanyate.

8. This is also indicated by the medical texts. Belief in Pūtanā as a destroyer of small children must have been widespread. Pūtanā occurs as the name of some of the nine *grahas* causing diseases in infants: skanda grahas tu prathamaḥ, skanda apasmāra eva ca / śakunī revatī caiva pūtanā cāndhapūtanā// pūtanā śītanāmā (referred to later as śītapūtanā) ca tathaiva mukhamaṇḍikā / navamo naigameṣaśca yaḥ pitṛgrahasaṃjñitaḥ. *Suśruta* (*Uttaratantra*) 6.27.4-5. Note that one of these *grahas* is called Śakunī (bird); *Su.* 6.27.12, describes the infant afflicted by Pūtanā : srastāṅgaḥ svapiti sukhaṃ divā na rātrau viḍ bhimnaṃ sṛjati ca kākatulyagandhiḥ / chardyārto (vomiting?) hṛṣitatanuruhaḥ kumārastṛṣṇālurbhavati ca pūtanāgṛhītaḥ. *Su.* 6.32.9-11, gives instructions for the treatment of children affected by Pūtanā, including incantations and offerings: pūjyā ca pūtanā devī balibhiḥ sopahārakaiḥ // malināmbarasaṃvītā malinā rūkṣamūrdhajā / śūnyāgārāśritā devī dārakaṃ pātu pūtanā // durdarśanā sudurgandhā karālā meghakālikā / bhinnāgārāśriyā devī dārakaṃ pātu pūtanā.

1. The frequency of these accounts could actually make us believe that such cases did happen in some instances. Even in this century reports have appeared of jungle-children rescued after having survived in the wilderness through their adoption by wild animals. The famous character of Kipling, Mowgli, in *The Jungle Book*, was inspired by some of these reports.

counting Kṛṣṇa. The motif presents several variations in those different examples but the essential trait persists so that we may recognise it easily. In various cases the compassion of the beast has, by a reduction of features, transformed the beast itself from a dangerous carnivorous one into a more amiable animal like a doe (as in the case of Siegfried), a goat (as in the case of Zeus), or a cow (as in the case of Feridun). The wolf is still, however, one of the most favoured animals for this motif (with three instances) followed by the bitch, the doe and the goat (with three examples each). In the case of Kṛṣṇa, as we have seen, the enemy is a demoness in human form, and humans[1] are also present in two other examples of the motif. These occur in the stories of Moses and Heracles. The motif is only faintly hinted at in the Moses legend as his being rescued from the river and reared by the Pharaoh's daughter, his enemy, being himself a Jewish baby persecuted by her father. But in the legend of Heracles the motif is present in a form astoundingly close to its counterpart in the Kṛṣṇa story.

The presence of this episode in the cycle of Heracles' legends first called our attention to the close similarities in the stories of Kṛṣṇa and Heracles, similarities that until then we thought few and of a much more general character. As we looked closer into the matter we found that the parallels were indeed many and very specific. We found also that many other heroes shared a basic biographical pattern, as we have seen already, but the Heracles and Kṛṣṇa stories were much more closely related than any of the others, and that the number of their parallels went far beyond the number of parallel episodes in the general basic heroic legend. Let us see how the story of Heracles lends itself to interpretation according to our outline.

The Heracles version of the theme presents several variations of varying degrees of importance. To follow the sequence of the story we start with Electryon, king of Mycenae, grandfather of Heracles, who had been wronged by some relatives of his who stole his cattle and killed his sons when these opposed the rustlers. In the words of Apollodorus:

> Wishing to avenge his sons' death, Electryon purposed to make war on the Teleboans, but first he committed the kingdom to Amphitryon along with his daughter Alcmene, binding him by oath to keep her a virgin until his return. However, as he was receiving the cows back, one of them charged, and Amphitryon threw at her the club which he had in his hands. But the club rebounded from the cow's horns and striking Electryon's head killed him.[1]

After that Amphitryon was banned from the country and had to take refuge with his bride Alcmene in Thebes. But Alcmene refused to consummate the marriage until Amphitryon had exacted revenge on her brothers' assassins. So Amphitryon had to go back to fight the Teleboans and after some adventures he finally succeeded in vanquishing them. He started to return home to tell his bride the news and finally cohabited with her, but, to quote Apollodorus again:

> ... before Amphitryon reached Thebes, Zeus came by night and prolonging the one night threefold he assumed the likeness of Amphitryon and bedded with Alcmene and related what had happened concerning the Teleboans. But when Amphitryon arrived and saw that he was not welcomed by his wife, he inquired the cause; and when she told him that he had come the night before and slept with her, he learned from Tiresias how Zeus had enjoyed her. And Alcmene bore two sons, to wit, Hercules, whom she had by Zeus and who was the elder by one night, and Iphicles, whom she had by Amphitryon.[2]

Before Heracles was born, Zeus announced in Olympus that the descendant of Perseus who was soon to be born would be the king of Mycenae. Hera, Zeus' wife, was enraged at this, knowing the child to be a son of her husband and a mortal, and made up her mind to eliminate the baby. First she ordered Eileithya the goddess of child-birth to impede the birth of Heracles and speed up that of Eurystheus, another issue of the family of Perseus, who eventually was born—after only seven months in the womb—before Heracles, and had to be recognised by Zeus as the king of Mycenae. Zeus, reluctantly, admitted his wife's triumph but extracted from her the promise that Heracles could be elevated to immortality if he served Eurystheus on earth and accomplished the twelve tasks that the latter would impose on him. Hera, however, resolved to kill Alcmene's son before that could happen. And, to follow the story in the words of Diodorus Siculus:

1. Or supernatural beings with human shape.

1. Apollodorus, *Bibliotheke* 2.4.6.; Sir J. G. Frazer, *The Library of Apollodorus*, Heinemann, London, 1921, v.1, p.169.
2. *Apo*., 2.4,9; Sir J. G. Frazer, *ibid*., pp. 173-75.

After Alcmene had brought forth the babe, fearful of Hera's jealousy she exposed it at a place which to this time is called after him the Field of Heracles. Now at this very time Athena, approaching the spot in the company of Hera and being amazed at the natural vigour of the child, persuaded Hera to offer it the breast. But when the boy tugged upon her breast with greater violence than would be expected at his age, Hera was unable to endure the pain and cast the babe from her.[1]

The correspondence with the Pūtanā episode in the Kṛṣṇa story is amazing, but before looking into it let us review the themes of the birth of Heracles following our scheme of the traditional hero's story. In the first place we have a king, Electryon, then a princess, Alcmene, then a prophecy, made by Zeus, that the child to be born would be king, then we have obstacles and perils to the birth of the child and, finally, his supernatural birth, his exposure and suckling by an enemy. All the points of the general pattern are there but with several variations.

In the first place the prophecy says that the child will get the kingdom but not that he will be a real danger to his grandfather; this part, however, is present in a mutation of role by which the father of the princess, the king, is killed not by her son but by her husband. Another mutation of role is that the enemy of the child is not the king but the child's stepmother, the wife of his real father. It is she who conspires to prevent his birth and to kill him. One motif that recurs constantly in the hero stories, and that here presents very close parallels to the Kṛṣṇa legend, is the twin birth. Alcmene gives birth to two sons of different fathers, while Vasudeva begets two sons of different mothers. In one case only one of the children is divine, in the other both children are divine but the divinity of the one is much more strongly marked than that of the other. Throughout all these motifs we can notice the parallels and correspondences between the Kṛṣṇa and the Heracles stories, but when we come to the Pūtanā episode we see an even closer link between the Indian and the Greek heroes.

As we said before, the 'suckling by an enemy motif' in the Kṛṣṇa and the Heracles legends distinguishes them from the rest of the examples of the motifs in other stories, in that here the enemy takes human form. But our two heroes' examples are even more distinct from the rest, and correspondingly closer among themselves, in that here the presumptive threat to the child, his mortal enemy, is quite unexpectedly punished by this same apparently inoffensive baby. Both Hera and Pūtanā cried for help when the child they were going to suckle pressed their breasts so strongly and sucked their milk with such force that they suffered unbearable pain. A reduction of features is found in that Pūtanā is actually killed by Kṛṣṇa, and Hera, being an immortal, escapes with nothing worse than pain and cries. Another variation is that Pūtanā went with all evil intent to kill the baby, whereas Hera, although his mortal enemy, did not know that the child she was suckling was Heracles. There is ample room here for Freudian interpretation and Rank gives some of it in his essay on the myth of the birth of the hero.[1] but we will not indulge in this kind of speculation, but will only quote the words of Diodorus Siculus at the end of his relation of the episode, words that sum up the reflections on this theme that we have already made: 'And anyone may well be surprised at the unexpected turn of the affair; for the mother whose duty it was to love her own offspring was trying to destroy it, while she who cherished towards it a stepmother's hatred, in ignorance saved the life of one who was her natural enemy.'[2]

We end our account of this episode and of the themes of the birth of Kṛṣṇa, by pointing to the version of the *Harivaṃśa* quoted before, when Pūtanā is represented as a bird. This particular variation in the story of Kṛṣṇa is actually also represented in other variants from different countries, but with the same mutation of action, however, that we noted before, that the animal protected the child and was not, as in the story of Kṛṣṇa, trying to kill him. Thus we have the story of Gilgamesh as related by Claudius Aelianus, who tells how Gilgamesh when a baby was thrown over a cliff by orders of his grandfather who feared him because of a prophecy, and how an eagle picked up the child before touching ground and took him to a safe place. The same author mentions the story of Ptolemy I, who was also exposed as a child and protected by an eagle 'with his wings against the sunshine, the rains, and birds of prey'.[3] We have also the story of Semiramis as told by Diodorus Siculus, 'that her mother the goddess Derceto, being ashamed of her, exposed the child in a barren

1. Diodorus of Sicily, *The Library of History*, 4.9.6; tr. by C. H. Oldfather, Harvard University Press, 1961, v.2, p. 371.

1. Rank, *The Myth*...., pp. 90-91.
2. Dio. 4.9.7 *ibid.* p. 371.
3. Rank, *The Myth*..., pp. 26-27 and n.8.

and rocky land, where she was fed by doves and found by shepherds, who gave the infant to the overseer of the royal flocks'.[1]

Unfortunately birds are not mammals and so are not very well suited to nurture a child. This perhaps accounts for the rarity of the examples using these animals in the motif. On the other hand we may suppose that the occurrence of birds as the saving beasts in this motif is due to the fact that, being flying animals, birds represent divine intervention and divine protection for the child better than any other kind of animal. In the *Harivaṃśa* version we are told, however, with the mutation of action, that the bird does not protect the child but tries to kill him. On the other hand, a trace of the original meaning of the motif remains in that the way of killing the child is still by feeding him, a symbol for protection, and so we arrive at the bizarre notion of the breasted bird.

Representations of this episode are extant, but have never been discussed; we shall deal with them in the last chapter.

iv. KṚṢṆA AS THE EIGHTH CHILD

The story of the birth of Kṛṣṇa has, in common with an older Indian tradition, an episode that keeps it apart from the general pattern of the birth of the Hero as outlined by Hahn, Rank, Raglan and others.

This episode refers to the account of Kṛṣṇa as the eighth child and the killing of previous brothers. This episode in the story of Kṛṣṇa shares with the myth of the birth of Mārtāṇḍa, in the *Ṛg Veda* with the story of the birth of the Maruts, and with the story of the birth of Bhīṣma.

The birth of Mārtāṇḍa is only passingly referred to in the *Ṛg Veda*. Verses eight and nine of 10.72, a hymn dedicated to the gods in general, say:

> Of Aditi's eight sons, born from her body, she came to the gods with seven and cast away Mārtāṇḍa. With seven sons Aditi came to the previous era. After that she bore Mārtāṇḍa for birth and death.[2]

These words are apparently unintelligible, but, examining them in the light of the stories mentioned, as well as in the light of commentaries and variants in other texts, we can get a clearer view of the passage.

1. *Ibid.*, p. 93 n.1.
2. *RV* 10.72.8-9; aṣṭau putrāso aditer ye jātās tanvas pari / devān upa pra ait saptabhiḥ parā mārtāṇḍam āsyat // 8 // saptabhiḥ putrair aditiḥ upa prait pūrvyaṃ yugam / prajāyai mṛtyave tvat punar mārtāṇḍam ābharat // 9 //

In *Atharva Veda* 8.9.21 it is mentioned that Aditi had eight sons and eight wombs[1] and in *Taittirīya Āraṇyaka* 1.13.1 the earth had eight wombs, eight sons and eight husbands.[2] In *Śatapatha Brāhmaṇa* 3.1.3-4 another version of the myth is found:

> Now Aditi had eight sons. But those who are called 'the gods, sons of Aditi' were only seven, for the eighth, Mārtāṇḍa, she brought forth unformed: it was a mere lump of bodily matter as broad as it was high. Some however, say that he was of the size of a man.—The gods, sons of Aditi, then spake, 'that which was born after us must not be lost: come let us fashion it.' They accordingly fashioned it as this man is fashioned. The flesh which was cut off him, and thrown down in a lump, became an elephant: hence they say that one must not accept an elephant [as a gift], since the elephant has sprung from man. Now he whom they thus fashioned was Vivasvat, the Āditya [or the sun]; and of him [came] these creatures.[3]

This version does not, as the one in *Ṛg Veda*, stress the fact that Mārtāṇḍa was cast away; it does, however, following the words 'she bore Mārtāṇḍa for birth and death', identify Mārtāṇḍa as the ancestor of the human race: 'They accordingly fashioned it as this man is fashioned...and of him [came] these creatures.' This seems to be the original purpose of the myth, tracing the ancestry of the human race to the gods, to whom man is brother but, having been cast away by his own mother, different, since he is subject to birth and death.

A later version of the myth of Mārtāṇḍa (*Mārkaṇḍeya Purāṇa* 105) stresses the solar aspect of the god and makes him incarnate in order to help the gods against the *asuras*, a theme that also appears in the Kṛṣṇa story. In this version Aditi does not cast away the child in the real sense, but rather delivers the foetus prematurely. The story goes that at the beginning of time, just after creation, the demons defeated the gods and obtained sovereignty over the

1. aṣṭayonir aditir aṣṭaputrā.
2. aṣṭayonīm aṣṭaputrām aṣṭapatnīm imāṃ mahīm.
3. aṣṭau ha vai putrā aditeḥ / yāṃstvetad devāḥ ādityāḥ ity ācakṣate sapta haiva te'vikṛtaṃ hāṣṭaṃ janayāṃ 'cakāra mārtāṇḍaṃ / sandegho haivāsa yāvān evordhvas tāvāṃs tiryaṅ puruṣammita ityu haika'āhuḥ / ta'haita' ūcuḥ devāḥ ādityā yad asmān anvajanimā tad amuyeva bhūddhante mam vikaravameti taṃ vicakrur yathāyam puruṣo vikṛtas tasya yāni māṃsāni saṃkṛtya sannyāsus tato hastī samabhavat tasmād āhur nahastinam pratigṛhṇīyāt puruṣājāno hi hastīti / yam u ha tad vicakruḥ sa vivasvān ādityas imāḥ prajāḥ. Eggeling tr.

three worlds. Aditi, the mother of the gods, seeing this, engaged in severe austerities to propitiate the sun. After a long time of this *tapasyā* the sun appeared to her and granted her a boon. Aditi prayed for the sun to be incarnated in her womb for the deliverance of the universe. In a remarkable passage she addresses him as 'Lord of the cows',[1] an epithet that immediately recalls Kṛṣṇa. The sun therefore entered Aditi's womb and started growing there as an embryo. Aditi then commenced a severe fast to purify herself. Realising her state and seeing her fast Kaśyapa, her husband, told her angrily that she would destroy that embryo. Much annoyed at Kaśyapa's words, she retorted that the embryo was not being destroyed but was growing for the destruction of the demons, and then and there she delivered a shining egg from which came out the sun. And that is why this son of Aditi was called Mārtāṇḍa 'the dead embryo', according to the words of Kaśyapa.

This version fails to mention the number of Aditi's other sons, therefore leaving out the important detail of Mārtāṇḍa being the eighth. It does however introduce, as we noted, the messianic aspect, as well as emphasising the solar character of the god. It also specifically mentions an embryo (*garbha*) that justifies the name Mārtāṇḍa. The *Śatapatha Brāhmaṇa* on the other hand, does not accentuate these aspects but lays stress on Mārtāṇḍa being the originator of humanity. Together both these versions provide a better viewpoint from which to consider the two obscure *Ṛg Vedic* verses. We cannot yet however explain the words 'she came to the gods with seven' and 'with seven sons Aditi came to the previous era'. These words can be interpreted best, we suggest, with the help of another variant of the myth, that of the birth of Bhīṣma found in the *Mahābhārata*. The story of the birth of Bhīṣma[2] is a very close parallel to the myth of Mārtāṇḍa, as well as to the legend of Kṛṣṇa's birth. It has however been overlooked as a key link and as a key that would prove helpful in analysing the meaning of the eighth child motif. The myth of Mārtāṇḍa agrees with the Kṛṣṇa one, both in the number eight and in the casting away of the last child. It does not agree with it in the killing of the rest. The Epic narrative of the birth of Bhīṣma agrees with the Kṛṣṇa story in the killing of the other brothers, but not in the casting away of the eighth.

The tale begins when on one occasion all the gods and *ṛṣis* as well as a certain King Mahābhiṣa, who had attained to heaven, were worshipping Brahmā. To that assembly came also the goddess Gaṅgā and it happened that a breeze blew her garment, revealing her body to the eyes of all present. All the gods and *ṛṣis* cast down their eyes, all but Mahābhiṣa, who looked at her intently. Brahmā, angry at this lack of respect, cursed the king to be born again on earth. But the goddess of the river herself was not completely dissatisfied at the audacity of the king, since she promised the eight Vasus, who had on their part been cursed too to take birth among mortals, to be their mother on earth, and for this purpose to join king Mahābhiṣa's next incarnation. The Vasus, who dreaded very much to live as mortals, begged of Gaṅgā to be spared that fate and to be killed as soon as they were born. She agreed, but asked that one of them should be permitted to live so that her union with king Mahābhiṣa should bear fruit.

So, eventually, all of them appeared on earth. Mahābhiṣa was born as Śāntanu, the grandfather of the Pāṇḍavas, a king of great virtue and truthfulness. Once when this king was out hunting he met a marvellously beautiful girl, with whom he fell passionately in love. This girl was, of course, the goddess Gaṅgā, and she agreed to his advances on condition that he would never question any of her actions. The king accepted whatever she asked and in that manner won her and enjoyed her for a long time. They begot seven children, but each time one of them was born the mother would throw him into the river. King Śāntanu, remembering his promise, never questioned her actions, but when an eighth child was born and the lady was about to throw him too into the river, the king could not stand it any more and spoke out to her, venting his long-suppressed grievance. The goddess then explained to him the circumstances of the curse, took the child with her and left.

This story can be used to interpret those obscure words in *RV* 10.72.89. If we take into account the belief that there is a heavenly as well as a terrestrial world and that to heavenly beings birth on earth is like death, then we have the elements to solve the riddle of: 'she came to the gods with seven; with seven sons Aditi came to the previous era'. While in the *Ṛg Veda* Aditi cast away the eighth son, in

1. *MarP.* 105.5a, tannimittaprasādaṃ tvaṃ kuruṣva mama gopate /

2. *Mbh.* 1.91-93.

the *Mahābhārata* Gaṅgā spares the eighth. Sparing him, however, means excluding him from the celestial realm, the previous era or condition to which his brothers attained. Bhīṣma is not a saviour as Mārtāṇḍa is, but the tale of his birth brings us a step closer to the story of the birth of Kṛṣṇa. Another feature in Bhīṣma's story also suggests connections with Kṛṣṇa. This is the account in the *Mahābhārata* of the cause for the curse placed on the Vasus and principally on Dyaus, the one that was born as Bhīṣma. They were cursed by Vasiṣṭha because once, instigated by Dyaus and his wife, they stole the sage's wonderful cows. Cattle rustling is also attributed to Kṛṣṇa, and on this subject we shall have more to say later. We can also refer to the *Harivaṃśa* account of the incarnation of Kaśyapa and Aditi as Vasudeva and Devakī, Kṛṣṇa's parents, because they stole Varuṇa's cows.[1]

In *Maitrāyaṇī Saṃhitā*[2] we have another version of the birth of Mārtāṇḍa within an account of the birth of Indra. This later account also resembles the legends of the birth of Kṛṣṇa and of his brothers.

> Wishing for children Aditi cooked a pap. She ate what was left over. Dhātṛ and Aryaman were born to her. She cooked another. She ate what was left over. Mitra and Varuṇa were born to her. She cooked another. She ate what was left over. Aṃśa and Bhaga were born to her. She cooked another. She thought: Each time I eat what is left over, two sons are born to me. Probably I shall get something still better when I eat beforehand. After she had eaten beforehand she served the pap. Her two next sons spoke even as children in the womb: "We both shall be as much as all the sons of Aditi". The sons of Aditi searched for someone to procure their abortion. Aṃśa and Bhaga procured the abortion of those two. Therefore no oblation is made to them at the sacrifice. Instead Aṃśa's portion is the stake in betting. Bhaga ('Fortune') went abroad. Therefore people say: "Go abroad, you meet fortune there!" Due to his vital energy Indra rose up. The other foetus fell down dead. This, forsooth, was Mārtāṇḍa of whom men are the descendants. Now Aditi turned to her sons saying: "This should be mine, this ought not to perish uselessly." They said: "He should then call himself one of us, he should not look down on us." This, verily, was Aditi's son Vivasvat, the father of Manu Vaivasvata and Yama. Manu dwelled in this, Yama in yonder world.[1]

In this version the brothers want to kill the eighth child (seventh and eighth here), whereas we have other versions that make Indra, the first brother, kill his seven brothers. According to the Purāṇic accounts Kaśyapa, Indra's father, promised his wife Diti, Aditi's sister, that she would have a son who would rule the gods. Knowing Diti's son, Indra by deception managed to come close to Diti and then penetrated into her womb where he cut the embryo in seven parts with his thunderbolt. His brother cried out with pain and Indra, telling him to be quiet, cut again each part in seven. So the forty-nine Maruts were born.[2] The number forty-nine here is obviously just a substitution for the more common number seven, and Indra, being contrasted to his brothers, is here again the eighth.[3]

Reviewing all the variants, we have here accounts of the birth of the eight Ādityas from Aditi, the eight Vasus from Gaṅgā, and the forty-nine Maruts (seven squared) plus Indra from Diti and Aditi. Kṛṣṇa was, as is well known also the eighth son, in this case of Devakī, who, according to the *Harivaṃśa* and the *Devī Bhāgavata Purāṇa*,[4] was also an incarnation of Aditi. Kṛṣṇa's first six brothers were destroyed and the seventh, Balarāma, was transferred to another womb, so that he was, in a certain sense, a miscarriage. Kṛṣṇa himself had to be taken to Gokula, far from the royal palace, that is he was cast away. It is highly probable that Kṛṣṇa's story was modelled upon those older versions. In fact in the one from the *Maitrāyaṇī Saṃhitā* the first six sons are separated from the last two, the seventh was an abortion and the eighth survived, just as in the legend of Kṛṣṇa's birth.

The view that the account of the birth of Kṛṣṇa as the eighth child may be taken from the myth of the eight Vasus and that of the eight Ādityas can be better assessed if we examine the meaning of the number eight in this context and the names and functions of those eight gods. The Indian mind is very fond of classifications and Indian mythology is no exception to this. Gods and other mythical beings are frequently mentioned in groups, and are arrayed

1. See above, p. 54.
2. 1.6.12.

1. Wilhelm Rau tr. in 'Twenty Indra Legends', *German Scholars on India*, v.1, p. 202, Delhi, 1973.
2. See *VP* 1.21; *HV* 1.3.23 ff; and *DBP* 4.3.21-55.
3. See *RV* 8.85.16; 10.99.2; Bergaigne, *La Réligion*.., v. 3, p. 108.
4. *DBP* 4.20.62; *HV* 45.33-36.

together according to various criteria. Thus we find the Rudras, the Maruts, the Vasus, the Ādityas and several others. Not only is Kṛṣṇa the supreme and ultimate divinity, but he also belongs to several of these groupings and it is as a member of one of them that he has to be born as the eighth.

Kṛṣṇa is also one of a divine pair. He is not only coupled with Balarāma, his brother and fast companion in the Purāṇic legends, but also with Arjuna. With this latter he keeps a close friendship that goes back to the pair Nara and Nārāyaṇa, of whom they are incarnations according to the *Mahābhārata*, and also to the pair Indra-Viṣṇu of the *Ṛg Veda*, since Indra commends Arjuna to Kṛṣṇa's care, Arjuna being Indra's son, i.e. like himself, and Kṛṣṇa being Indra's younger brother. Kṛṣṇa is also one of a triad, together with his brother Balarāma and their sister Subhadrā, a group that is worshipped to this very day in the great temple at Puri, Orissa. Again Kṛṣṇa is one of a group of four, the famous four Vyūhas of the Pañcarātras: Vāsudeva, Saṃkarṣaṇa, Pradyumna and Aniruddha, these last two his son and grandson respectively.

Another group, this with five members, is compounded around Kṛṣṇa; these are the *pañcavīras*, the five heroes of the Vṛṣṇi tribe that have been identified as Kṛṣṇa, Baladeva, Pradyumna, Śāmba and Aniruddha.[1] And finally we are told that Kṛṣṇa is the eighth child of Devakī and therefore a member of a group of eight. As we said before, the variant of the *Maitrāyaṇī Saṃhitā* agrees more closely than the others with the Purāṇic account of Kṛṣṇa's birth, in that two of the brothers are contrasted to the other six and it is not a case of one brother alone being separated from seven others. The version of the *Harivaṃśa* and *Viṣṇu Purāṇa* is that when Viṣṇu decided to incarnate as Kṛṣṇa to save the earth once more, he ordered the goddess of delusion to fetch from hell the six sons of the demon Hiraṇyakaśipu, who were lying there as embryos, due to a curse from their father. These demons were successively born from Devakī and killed by Kaṃsa.[2] In the *Bhāgavata Purāṇa* 10.85, Kṛṣṇa and Balarāma recover these children from the abode of death and bring them back to Devakī, who is pining for them.

We believe that, besides these versions, there formerly existed another one in which Kṛṣṇa was the principal member of a group of eight modelled on that of the eight Vasus. That this version was not clearly recorded in the Purāṇas is due to their preference for the divine pair Kṛṣṇa-Balarāma. As this left six members of the eight without a role to play, they were disposed of by converting them into demons and casting them down to hell. That numbers were not always kept the same has been shown by Bergaigne, who believes that there was originally one Āditya by antonomasia: Varuṇa to whom Mitra was later added, and later still Aryaman, in turn, to form a triad. *RV* 9.114.3 mentions seven Ādityas and, as we know, Mārtāṇḍa was the eighth. These Ādityas are also called Vasus in *RV* 2.27.11; 7.52.1-2 and 8.27.20.

> Les confusions qui s'opèrent entre ces groupes, et surtout leur indetermination, suggèrent naturellement l'idée qu'ils s'equivalent ... comme designant les dieux en general, sans distinctions de personnes.[1]

Bergaigne recognised that ultimately the Ādityas had a cosmic significance, referring to a division of the universe into several parts which they would severally govern or preside over. *RV* 10.65.9 in fact says that the Ādityas are distributed over the earth, the waters and heaven, the three parts of the world.

> C'est a elle que se rattachent sans doute les différentes notions d'un couple, d'une triade et d'une heptade d'Adityas. Ce couple, cette triade et cette heptade correspondraient aux differents systèmes de division de L'univers en deux, trois et sept mondes.[2]

This notion we find again in the group of the eight Vasus, here even more clearly drawn. The Vasus have traditionally been considered as representing the five elements plus the sun, the moon and an eighth that is either light or the stars. The five elements in the Indian system are earth, water, air, fire and *ākāśa*, and in the lists of the eight Vasus they are sometimes given different names but are always recognisable by their functions and position. The *Śatapatha Brāhmaṇa* gives their names as: Pṛthivī, Agni, Vāyu, Antarikṣa, Āditya, Dyaus, Candramas and Nakṣatras,[3] and the *Harivaṃśa* lists them as: Āpa, Dhruva, Soma, Dhara, Anila, Anala, Pratyuṣa and Prabhāsa,[4] where earth

1. See above, pp. 35.
2. *HV* 47; *VP* 5.1.

1. Abel Bergaigne, *La Religion*.., v.3, p. 101.
2. *Ibid.*, p. 102.
3. *SB* 11.6.3.6; katame vasava iti / agniśca pṛthivī ca vāyuścāntarikṣaṃ cādityaśca dyauśca candramāśca nakṣatrāṇi caite vasavaḥ.
4. *HV* 3.32; āpo dhruvaśca somaśca dharaścaivānilo'nalaḥ/ pratyusaśca prabhāsaśca vasavo nāmabhiḥ śrutāḥ.

is Dhara, water is Āpa, air is Anila, fire is Anala and space is Pratyuṣa, Soma stands for the moon, Dhruva is given here instead of the sun, and the eighth is Prabhāsa or light.[1] These eight Vasus correspond to some extent with other groups of eight, particularly with the eight *lokapālas*, the deities ascribed to the different points of the compass.

The *lokapālas* are given in the *Mānava Dharma Śāstra* as: Indra, Agni, Yama, Sūrya, Varuṇa, Vāyu, Kubera and Candra.[2] These, following the scheme of the five elements, can be arranged as follows: earth-Kubera, water-Varuṇa, air-Vāyu, fire-Agni, space-Yama, moon-Candra, sun-Sūrya, and the eighth as Indra. As we can see, this cosmic scheme was generally acknowledged and we find it again in the list of the eight Prakṛtis given by Kṛṣṇa in the *Bhagavad Gītā* 7.4[3] where *ahaṃkāra* occupies the eighth place, bringing the scheme, following the Sāṃkhya system, from a cosmic to a psychological level. This correspondence of the cosmic to the human level is again mentioned in *Mahābhārata* 14.20. The Pañcarātras called the scheme the eight *akṣaras*.[4]

As mentioned before, in the Purāṇic account of the life of Kṛṣṇa this aspect of him, as the last and best in a group of eight gods, has been only partially preserved. We have, however, other sources that could point to this tradition having been at one time current within the cycle of Kṛṣṇa legends. The *Ghaṭa Jātaka*, the Buddhist version of the Kṛṣṇa saga, forgets about the killing by Kaṃsa of Devakī's children and instead makes the exchange of Kṛṣṇa for the daughter of the cowherds occur ten times, one for each time that Devakī gives birth, in this version ten. The ten brothers exchanged for the ten girls are, according to the Jātaka: Vāsudeva, Baladeva, Candadeva, Sūriyadeva, Aggideva, Varuṇadeva, Ajjuna, Pajjuna, Aṃkura and Ghaṭa Paṇḍita, among whom we recognise four of the Vasus and *lokapālas*, and even five if we count either Vāsudeva or Arjuna as Indra. We also have the two heroes with whom Kṛṣṇa forms a pair: Baladeva and Arjuna; and three of the four Vyūhas are there too: Vāsudeva, Baladeva and Pradyumna. We can also identify four of the five heroes of the Vṛṣṇis; if we follow the opinion of Lüders who counted Akrūra among their number[1] these *pañcavīras* would be Vāsudeva, Baladeva, Pradyumna and Akrūra, with Aniruddha missing.

It is obvious that the Buddhists confused a number of stories and traditions, but the inclusion of five out of eight names in their list is significant enough. Another very important point of evidence in the same direction is the list of names in the Nānāghat Cave Inscription of Queen Nāganikā[2] where Kṛṣṇa and Balarāma are mentioned together with: Candra, Sūrya, Yama, Varuṇa, Kubera and Vāsava, i.e. Indra, and where these last four are called *lokapālas*. This, together with the *Ghaṭa Jātaka*, shows that Kṛṣṇa was not only considered the eighth of a number of divinities and that the account of his birth was probably inspired by the myths of Mārtāṇḍa and the Vasus, but also that the names and functions of the rest of the group of eight divinities were preserved to a certain extent in connection with him.

One last piece of evidence is furnished by the discoveries made by M.D. Khare at Besnagar, in the place where the famous column of Heliodorus still stands. The excavations carried out in 1965 served to find the technique used to erect the Garuḍa column and they also found:

> Seven more pits, with similar material like alternating layers of laterite, black earth, occasionally mixed with brick-bats and small pebbles, and a number of steel and stone wedges placed on the basal slabs, show that there were eight pillars in front of the Vāsudeva temple of the second century B.C.[3]

Were these pillars dedicated to the eight Vasus, or the eight *lokapālas*, or a similar group allied with Kṛṣṇa? In view of the evidence presented we tend to believe so.

To end this account of the different variants of the birth of the hero as the eighth child, we should mention three variants found in European folklore. In these variants the cosmological element is missing, but the numerical element—which indicates the probable presence of a cosmological symbolism—survives. It also survives the narrative device that makes the children be killed and only one of them be saved.

1. Other lists are given in *Mbh.* 1.60.17-18; *VP* 1.15.111.
2. *Manu* 5.96; somāgnyarkānilendrāṇāṃ vittāppatyoryamasya ca aṣṭānāṃ lokapālānāṃ vapurdhārayate nṛpaḥ ; see also 7.4.
3. *BG* 7.4; bhūmir āpo'nalo vāyuḥ khaṃ mano buddhir eva ca / ahaṃkāra itīyaṃ me bhinnā prakṛtir aṣṭadhā.
4. F. Otto Schrader, *Introduction to the Pāñcarātra and the Ahirbudhnya Saṃhitā* (1916), Adyar, 2nd ed., 1973 p. 119, n. 6.

1. See above, p. 35.
2. See above, p. 23.
3. M. D. Khare, Comments on 'The Heliodorus Pillar at Besnagar', *Puratattwa*, no. 8, p. 178.

The first of these variants is also the most important, since it concerns the birth of Achilles, a hero closely related to Kṛṣṇa by the legend of his death. Now we shall review how, at least in some versions, the legend of the birth of Achilles equally resembles the legend of the birth of Kṛṣṇa. This account is given by Sir James George Frazer in his edition of Apollodorus's *Bibliotheka*:

> According to another legend, Thetis bore seven sons, of whom Achilles was the seventh; she destroyed the first six by throwing them into the fire or into a kettle of boiling water to see whether they were mortal or to make them immortal by consuming the merely mortal portion of their frame; and the seventh son, Achilles, would have perished in like manner, if his father Peleus had not snatched him from the fire at the moment when as yet only his ankle-bone was burnt.[1]

Here we can see an astonishing similarity to the story of the birth of Bhīṣma given in the *Mahābhārata*, that we have already reviewed. It is the mother who throws the children to their death 'to make them immortal', and it is only the last one that is saved by the intervention of the father. A later European version of this theme, this time without the pretext of giving immortality to the children, but in a more crude manner, we have in the *Historia Longobardorum* of Paulus Diaconus, a text of the eighth century.

> It was in Agelmund's day that a certain prostitute gave birth to seven male children at one and the same time and crueller than any beast, threw them into a pond to drown. ... Now king Agelmund chanced to pass by the very pond in which the babies were lying and, reining in his horse, he stared at the wretched children, turning them over with his spear. One of them stretched out his hand and seized the spear. Touched with pity and indeed greatly surprised, the king predicted a great future for this child, and at once ordered it to be taken out of the pond and given to a nurse, to be brought up with all possible care. Since the boy was brought out of a pond, which in the Langobard tongue was called 'Lama', the king gave him the name 'Lamissio'.[1]

This is the story of the birth of a famous King and probably his anonymous first biographers, before Paulus, tried to connect him to the legends of the traditional hero. By that time, however, the exact details of the motif of the eighth or seventh surviving child had been lost or greatly changed, and in this version the mother becomes a prostitute without relation, at least explicitly, to the king who saves the seventh child and rears him up as his son. The final version of the motif that we will review connects it with the more common theme of the exposure of the baby because of persecution:

> The saga of the Knight with the swan, as related in the Flemish *People's Book* contains in the beginning the history of the birth of seven children, borne by Beatrix, the wife of king Oriant of Flanders. Matabruna, the wicked mother of the absent King, orders that the children be killed and the Queen be given seven puppy dogs in their stead. But the servant contents himself with the exposure of the children, who are found by a hermit named Helias, and are nourished by a goat until they are grown.[2]

Here we see once more the old story of the boy grown up in exile and suckled by a beast, this time multiplied by seven, since all the children survive. We can also find here another typical motif in these stories: the substitution of the child. This motif reminds one of the famous fairy tale of Snow White and the seven dwarfs, where the number seven is also important. All these Western versions of our theme show that a very old motif, probably Indo-Aryan, and probably with an original cosmological meaning, survived in many different versions, losing through its transmission from one country to the other and one generation to the other this cosmological symbolism and changing several traits that, however, may reappear now and again in later versions.

1. Sir J. G. Frazer, *The Library of Apollodorus*, v.2, p. 69, n. 4.

1. K. Gardiner and I. de Rachewiltz, *The History of the Langobards of Paul the Deacon*, unpublished.
2. O. Rank, *The Myth of the Birth*. .p. 62.

CHAPTER FOUR

Some Basic Themes in the Legends of Kṛṣṇa

i. THE THEMES OF THE MIRACULOUS CHILD

As we have already seen, the child aspect is extremely important in the story of Kṛṣṇa. It dominates the greater part of his legends, and it has proven the aspect that attracts the biggest number of followers. In fact the biography of Kṛṣṇa may be divided into two parts: first his childhood and early youth until the killing of Kaṃsa, in what may be described as 'Kṛṣṇa the cowherd', shorter in time span but longer in the number of episodes and adventures, and second from the killing of Kaṃsa until Kṛṣṇa's own death, which can be called 'Kṛṣṇa the prince', longer in years than the first but with fewer episodes and much less popularity.

However, out of the many episodes of the first part of Kṛṣṇa's life, only a few can be considered as fully illustrating the themes of the Miraculous Child. Most of his killing of monsters takes place when he is a mere child, but this fact is not very much emphasised. Were it not for the occasional mention of his worrying his foster parents, or of the other boys who were playmates of Kṛṣṇa, these episodes would not suggest the deeds of a child. We will, therefore, consider them rather under the themes of the Strongman, since they fit in a more natural way into that category. The child and youth aspect is still very much present, but the overall picture is more that of an athlete, a strong man showing his endurance and force, a champion protecting the innocent and the weak. This is reflected in the iconography, where only four episodes of Kṛṣṇa's life are represented portraying him as a child. These are the Pūtanāvadha already discussed, the Śakaṭabhaṅga, the Yamalārjuna and the Dugdhaharaṇa. These episodes of the narrative of necessity portray Kṛṣṇa as a young child, but all other *gopāla* episodes represent Kṛṣṇa as of adult stature. According to the Purāṇas he was just a boy, but the earlier sculptures portray him as a man. He was perhaps thought of only as an adolescent, but from his deeds it is clear that he was visualised as a powerful man. This can be seen in every plastic representation, but it is most easily discernible in the Mahābalipuram panel of Govardhanadhara.[1]

The episodes, however, where Kṛṣṇa's childhood is evident and necessary from the narrative are unmistakable examples of the Miraculous Child motif. Instances of this theme are not generally common in the Traditional Hero stories, and this led Lord Raglan to propose as point 9 of his basic pattern of the Biography of the Hero that 'we are told nothing of his childhood'.[2] But, as we shall see, this is not true of Kṛṣṇa, as it is not true of Indra and Heracles. The episodes of the childhood of Kṛṣṇa with which we will deal here can be divided into two groups: those that tell simply of the boy's extraordinary and super-human energy, and those that reflect a religious attitude by presenting Kṛṣṇa as the incarnation of a Supreme God.

As examples of the first kind we have the Śakaṭa-

1. See plate 36.
2. See above, p. 44.

bhaṅga and the Yamalārjuna episodes. The *Ghaṭa Jātaka* does not mention either of these episodes and only the *Viṣṇu Purāṇa*, the *Harivaṃśa* and the *Bhāgavata Purāṇa* describe the Śakaṭabhaṅga episode in detail. The *Bālacarita* mentions this episode in the general account of Kṛṣṇa's deeds in Gokula, and so does the *Mahābhārata* in the deriding discourse of Śiśupāla. The *Devī Bhāgavata*, although giving a list of the demons killed by Kṛṣṇa, does not mention the Śakaṭabhaṅga episode.

Let us first look at the shorter versions of the *Bālacarita* and the *Mahābhārata*, and then we will deal with the more detailed accounts of the episode. The words of Śiśupāla in the *Sabhāparvan* are very significant; he refers there very clearly to the cart as an object 'deprived of consciousness' (*cetanārahitam*) or 'inanimate', as van Buitenen puts it.[1] The *Bālacarita* on the other hand is very specific in identifying the cart as a demon, and it is the first text to mention this fact: 'then, when the son of Nandagopa was a month old, a demon called Śakaṭa came, taking the form of a cart; having discovered him he [the demon] was pulverized with one single kick and, he became [again] a demon and then died.'[2] This distinction between the cart as an insentient object and the cart as a disguised demon is important as revealing two different attitudes towards the stories of Kṛṣṇa. In the first one we have perhaps the original version of the legend, which tells only of the amazing strength of Kṛṣṇa, who even as a small child smashed a big cart with a kick of his little foot. The second one tries to make the episode still more marvellous, anticipating perhaps comments such as that of Śiśupāla, and adds that, after all, it was not merely a simple cart but a dangerous demon that was destroyed by the baby Kṛṣṇa.

These two different approaches to the episode are also evident in the three longer versions. The *Harivaṃśa* does not speak of any supernatural being involved in the episode, the *Viṣṇu Purāṇa* follows it in this but brings out an element of religiosity, and, finally, the *Bhāgavata Purāṇa* again tells the same story as the *Viṣṇu Purāṇa* including the supernatural element. Although not clearly stating that a demon was involved, the passages in these last two texts hint at something of the sort. The story, as related in those works, goes that once Yaśodā left the baby Kṛṣṇa sleeping under a cart when she went over to the river, according to the *Harivaṃśa*,[1] or when she was busy attending to the guests who had come to celebrate the ceremony on Kṛṣṇa's first turning over in his cradle, according to the *Bhāgavata Purāṇa*.[2]

At that time, feeling hungry and wanting to suck his mother's breast, the child started crying, raising his arms and kicking, and with one of those kicks he reached the cart and overturned it,[3] breaking with it all the pots and pans that were there. The *Viṣṇu Purāṇa* does not mention where Yaśodā had gone, but only says that Kṛṣṇa was sleeping under the cart and that when the cowherds and their woman became alarmed at the noise they were informed by some boys of what had happened.[4] The *Harivaṃśa* and the *Bhāgavata* repeat this same account, and the *Harivaṃśa* finishes its version of the episode there, but the *Viṣṇu Purāṇa* and the *Bhāgavata* add a final detail that brings to mind the account of the *Bālacarita*, where the cart was a demon in disguise. The two Purāṇas mention that a prophlyactic ceremony was performed immediately after the incident, homage being paid by Yaśodā to the broken pieces of the cart and the utensils, according to the *Viṣṇu Purāṇa*,[5] or by brahmins, who were close at hand, to the rebuilt cart, according to the *Bhāgavata*.[6] This last text specifically mentions that Yaśodā 'suspected an evil spirit' (*grahaśaṅkitā*) had been the cause of the incident. But only the later *Prem Sāgar*, a vernacular work purporting to be a translation of the tenth book of the Bhāgavata Purāṇa, again brings out clearly the version of the *Bālacarita* that a demon was trying to kill the baby Kṛṣṇa.

1. J. A. B. van Buitenen, *The Mahābhārata*, University of Chicago, 1975, vol. 2, p. 98; the text says : cetanārahitaṃ kāṣṭhaṃ yadyanena nipātitam / pādena śakaṭaṃ bhīṣma tatra kiṃ kṛtamadbhutam // *Mbh* 2.38.8.

2. *BC* 3; tado māṣamate ṇandagovavutteṣaaḍo ṇāmadāṇavo ṣaaḍaveṣaṃ gahṇia āado / taṃ pi jāṇia ekapādappahāreṇa cuṇṇikido ṣo vi dāṇavo bhavia tatto evva mudo = tato māsamātre nandagopaputre śakaṭo nāma dānavaḥ śakaṭaveṣaṃ gṛhītvāgataḥ / tamapi jñātvaikapādaprahāreṇa cūrṇīkṛtaḥ so'pi dānavo bhūtvā tata eva mṛtaḥ.

1. *HV* 50.4; śakaṭasya tvadhaḥ suptaṃ kadācitputragṛddhinī / yaśodā taṃ samutsṛjya jagāma yamunāṃ nadīm

2. *BhP* 10.7.6; autthānikautsukyamanā manasvinī samāgatān pūjayati vrajaikasaḥ.

3. *HV* 50.5-6; śiśulīlāṃ tataḥ kurvansvahastacaraṇau kṣipan / ruroda madhuraṃ kṛṣṇaḥ pādāvūrdhvaṃ prasārayan // sa tatraikena pādena śakaṭam paryavartayat / nyubjaṃ payodharākāṅkṣī cakāra ca ruroda ca.

4. *VP* 5.6.4-5; gopāḥ keneti kenedaṃ śakaṭaṃ parivartitam/ tatraiva bālakāḥ procurbālenānena pātitam // rudatā dṛṣṭamasmābhiḥ pādavikṣepapātitam / śakaṭaṃ parivṛttaṃ vai naitadanyasya ceṣṭitam.

5. yaśodā śakaṭārūḍhabhagnabhāṇḍakapālikāḥ / śakaṭaṃ cārcayāmāsa dadhipuṣpaphalākṣataiḥ, *VP* 5.6.7.

6. viprā hutvārcayāñcakrurdadhyakṣatakuśāmbubhiḥ; *BhP* 10.7.12.

We can see a similar evolution in the version of the second episode of Kṛṣṇa's childhood that we will deal with. The accounts of the Yamalārjuna incident all agree in their description of Kṛṣṇa's pranks that led Yaśodā to tie him a mortar, and they also agree in their account of how Kṛṣṇa uprooted two enormous trees by pulling the mortar in between them; they do not agree, however, in describing the nature of those two trees. The difference between an account of the extraordinary strength of a child and that of the marvels achieved by a young god is drawn by the description of the trees either as ordinary trees or as supernatural beings. The first version we consider is that of the *Bālacarita*:

> Then, when he was one month old, the son of Nandagopa, having gone into one house, would drink the milk, and going into another house he would eat the curds, and going to other he would swallow the fresh grain, and going into still another house he would look at the pot of butter-milk. Then [this] was told to Nanda's wife by the young angered cowherdesses, and Nanda's wife, taking in anger a rope, having tied him by the middle, tied the end to a wooden mortar. Then, having seen that the mortar moved, he threw it at two demons called Yamala and Arjuna, and then the two became one. Going in between them Nandagopa's son destroyed the trees down with roots, and ground those two demons to powder, and they died. And then, when dead, they became again demons. Then it was said by the cowherds: as from today let his name be Lord Dāmodara, because of his great strength and prowess.[1]

Here we can see both imageries, that of the naughty little boy, so dear to the Indian public, and that of the childhood of the strong-man. At the same time the child's feat is given a supernatural, religious tinge by incorporating the two demons. The whole episode is told with an aetiological purpose: to explain the origin of Kṛṣṇa's name Dāmodara. This aetiological sense is repeated in all versions of the incident, but the demons or other supernatural beings do not occur in every one. The *Viṣṇu Purāṇa* repeats the account on the same lines as the *Bālacarita*, but its version of the pranks of the baby Kṛṣṇa is different. Here Kṛṣṇa is accompanied by his brother Balarāma and they do not steal foodstuffs but their actions are more in keeping with their character of strong, tough boys. They go to the enclosures and pull the tails of cows and new born calves[1] without their mother's being able to prevent it. The description of the scene found by the cowherds when they arrived, attracted by the noise, is full of tenderness and charm, and illustrates very well the tone of devotion inspired by the little child-god: 'In coming, the people of Vraja saw the two big trees fallen and the child, smiling with the little white buds of his newly cut teeth, in between them bound tight by a rope on his belly.'[2]

The *Harivaṃśa* repeats this account with slight variations. There again the two boys are described as going into cowpens to have fun, and as molesting the neighbours. Their strength and toughness is emphasised in pictures like: Moving everywhere, their arms like serpent hoods, they appeared like two proud young elephants, their limbs smeared with dust.'[3] Descriptions like these and others give to the incident a character of profound devotion for childhood as represented by Kṛṣṇa and Balarāma. The poet relishes his depiction of the charming naughty boys and fills it with lovely little details such as 'their sight was disturbed by their locks falling over their eyes'.[4] Narratively this version follows the other two: Yaśodā ties Kṛṣṇa to a mortar, angered at his pranks,

1. *BC* 3; tađo māṣaparivutte ṇanđagovavutte ekaṣṣiṃ gehe gacchia khīraṃ pibai aṇṇaṣṣiṃ gehe gacchia đađhiṃ bhakkhai ekaṣṣiṃ gehe gacchia ṇavaṇīđaṃ gilađi, aṇṇaṣṣiṃ gehe gacchia pāasaṃ bhuñjai aparaṣṣiṃ gehe gacchia takkaghaṭaṃ paloađi / tađo luṭṭhāhi govajuvađīhi ṇanđagovīe uttam / tado luṭṭhāe ṇanđagovīe đāmaṃ gahṇia taṣṣa majjhe banđhia ṣeṣaṃ ulūhale bajjham / tađo taṃ pi ulūhalaṃ aāghattaantaṃ pekkhia jamalajjuṇe ṇāma đāṇave ṇikkhitaṃ / tađo đuve ekkībhuđe teṣaṃ antaleṇa gacchanteṇa ṇanđagovavutteṇa āghaṭṭaanteṇa ṣamūlaviḍavaṃ cuṇṇīkiđe te vi đāṇave bhavia tatto evva muđe / tađo govajaṇehi uttaṃ mahābala palakkamo ajjappahuđi bhaṭṭiđāmođalo ṇāma hođu tti=tatomāsaparivṛtto nanđagopaputra ekasmin gṛhe gatvā kṣīraṃ pibati, anyasmin gṛhe gatvā đađhi bhakṣayati, ekasmin gṛhe gatvā navanītaṃ girati, anyasmin gṛhe gatvā pāyasam bhuñjate, aparasmin gṛhe gatvā takraghaṭam pralokate tato ruṣṭābhir gopayuvatibhirnanđagopyai uktam / tato ruṣṭayā nanđagopyā đāma gṛhītvā tasya mađhye bađđhvā śeṣamulūkhale bađđham / tatastađapyulūkhalamāghaṭṭayat prekṣya yamalārjunayornāma đānavayornikṣiptam / tato đvāvekībhūtau / tayorantareṇa gacchatā nanđagopaputreṇāghaṭṭayatā samūlaviṭapam cūrṇīkṛtau tāvapi đānavau bhūtvā tata eva mṛtau / tato gopajanair uktam mahābala parākramo'đyaprabhṛti bhartṛđāmođaro nāma bhavatu iti.

1. tađaharjātagovatsapucchākarṣaṇatatparau; *VP* 5.6.12.

2. *VP* 5.6.18b-19; ājagāma vrajajano đađarśa ca mahāđrumau // navođgatālpađantāṃśusitahāsañca bālakam / tayormađhyagataṃ đāmnā bađđhaṃ gāḍhaṃ tathođare.

3. *HV* 51.7; visarpantau tu sarvatra sarpabhogabhujāvubhau / rejatuḥ pāṃśuđigđhāṅgau đṛptau kalabhakāviva.

4. *HV* 51.11; mūrđhajavyākulekṣaṇau.

and the child crawls dragging the mortar behind him until it gets stuck between two big trees. The little boy then starts pulling with force, trying to go on his way, and he pulls so strongly that he uproots the trees. The *Harivaṃśa* adds that he did this to show the cowherds that this occurred by his own divine force and that the rope became strong because of his superhuman strength.[1] This shows that the divinity of Kṛṣṇa was never lost sight of even in the *Harivaṃśa*, a text notable for passages full of realism.

The *Harivaṃśa* does not, like the *Bālacarita*, depict the trees uprooted by Kṛṣṇa as demons, but does not either, like the *Viṣṇu Purāṇa*, leave them as ordinary trees. A point of transition between those two alternatives seems to be reached in the *Harivaṃśa's* apparent description of the trees as a sort of *vṛkṣa-devatā*, tree-godlings, since they were being solicited or begged, presumably for gifts or benefits.[2] Here the trees are not demons whom Kṛṣṇa destroys, but apparently they are divine beings. The *Harivaṃśa* also includes the aetiological explanation of the name Dāmodara.

The *Bhāgavata Purāṇa* is the last of our texts to present a version of the Yamalārjuna incident, and as usual its account is much embellished and very ornate. Moreover, differently from the *Harivaṃśa*, it clearly states the two Arjuna trees to be supernatural beings in disguise, and openly proclaims Kṛṣṇa's divinity. The *Bhāgavata* version echoes in its general outline the other versions that we have seen already. Kṛṣṇa, as usual, and this time he alone, has been behaving naughtily, and Yaśodā decides to tie him to the mortar as a punishment. The child remains quiet for a little while and then notices two trees growing near-by. Being god, he knows that those trees are in fact the sons of Kubera, god of riches, converted into trees because of a curse of Nārada. The story of these two Guhyakas is then given. It happened that they were once intoxicated with the *Vāruṇī* liquor, and went about the lovely forest of Mount Kailāśa sporting with a number of damsels. They all came upon the sacred river Gaṅgā and decided to have a dip and sport in the water. They were engaged in this dalliance and merriment when the sage Nārada passed by and saw them drunk and stark naked. And then 'having seen him the naked nymphs were ashamed and, fearful of a curse, quickly put on their clothes. Not so the two naked

1. nidarśanārthaṃ gopānāṃ divyaṃ svabalamāsthitaḥ / taddāma tasya bālasya prabhāvādabhavaddṛḍham; *HV* 51.19.
2. yau tāvarjunavṛkṣau tu vraje satyopayācitau; *HV* 51.22.

Guhyakas.'[1] Reflecting on this impropriety, Nārada decided to curse them for their own benefit (*tayoranugrahārthāya*), and told them that because of their conduct, the product of the pride of wealth, they would have to be born as trees and remain in that condition until Viṣṇu, in his incarnation as Kṛṣṇa, would touch them and free them both from their pride and from their vegetal condition.[2]

So the *Bhāgavata Purāṇa* uses this episode as a pretext to extol Kṛṣṇa. The incident itself gets but little space compared with the account of the cursing of Kubera's sons and the hymn of praise that these intone upon their liberation. That the episode is the reason for the name Dāmodara is not repeated in the *Bhāgavata*; instead we are told that Nārada's curse is the cause of the episode. Very undramatically the baby Kṛṣṇa is made to say: 'The Devarṣi (Nārada) is most beloved of mine; then, I will cause that which was prophesied by the Mahātmā to those two sons of Kubera to be accomplished.'[3] And then, not by chance as in the other versions but intentionally, he goes to the two trees, gets the mortar in the middle of them and pulls them down. This causes the two divine beings to appear, free and ever thankful. They express their gratitude, singing Kṛṣṇa's praises, and the little boy accepts this graciously and dismisses them.[4]

Attracted by the noise the cowherds then come and wonder what has happened when they see the baby tied to the big mortar and the felled trees. Some boys who had been playing around told the *gopas* that the mortar was being dragged by the child when it got stuck between the trees, and that they also could see two men.[5] But these words were not believed by everybody. Some thought it was impossible for a baby to achieve a feat like the uprooting of the trees, but others were not so sure.

Thus the *Bhāgavata Purāṇa* again brings into the story the supernatural element of the animated trees, first presented by the *Bālacarita*, overlooked by the *Viṣṇu Purāṇa* and hinted at by the *Harivaṃśa*. This element gives a religious and moral colouring to what otherwise would be merely an account of the prodigi-

1. *BhP* 10.10.6; taṃ dṛṣṭvā vrīḍitā devyo vivastrāḥ śāpaśaṅkitāḥ / vāsāṃsi paryadhuḥ śīghraṃ vivastrau naiva guhyakau.
2. *BhP* 10.10.2-22.
3. *BhP* 10.10.25; devarṣirme priyatamo yadimau dhanadātmajau / tattathā sādhayiṣyāmi yad gītaṃ tanmahātmanā.
4. *BhP* 10.10.29-42.
5. bālā ūcuraneneti tiryaggatamulūkhalam / vikarṣatā madhyagena puruṣāvapyacakṣmahi; *BhP* 10.11.4.

ous force of the young hero. The *Bhāgavata* gives one more episode in this series. This episode, as well as several others, is peculiar to this Purāṇa and is ignored in the other versions of the Kṛṣṇa story. We are speaking about the killing of Tṛṇāvarta, another demon sent by Kaṃsa to kill the dreaded child. The episode occurs in the *Bhāgavata Purāṇa* in the same chapter as the Śakaṭabhaṅga incident and, in fact, the chapter takes the name of 'The liberation of Tṛṇāvarta' (*tṛṇāvartamokṣa*) and not that of 'the overturning of the cart'. There must be some reason for the inclusion of this episode in the *Bhāgavata* and we think we can explain it.

The Tṛṇāvartāsuravadha resembles very closely the episode of the killing of Pralamba by Balarāma. In both incidents a demon comes in disguise, takes a child on his shoulders, and flies away with the evident purpose of killing him. On both occasions the demon is surprised to find the extraordinary force of the child he thought an easy victim, and is killed by him while soaring through the air. The Tṛṇāvarta episode as related in the *Bhāgavata Purāṇa* closely follows in its imagery the Pralamba episode as it appears in the *Viṣṇu Purāṇa*. The *Bhāgavata* says that once the demon Tṛṇāvarta came to Gokula, sent by Kaṃsa, and, taking the form of a whirlwind, snatched away the baby Kṛṣṇa.[1]

Yaśodā and all the other *gopīs* were crying when they realised that the boy had disappeared, and in the air the demon was also suffering when he found that he could no longer sustain the terrible weight of the small child that was crushing him. Tṛṇāvarta was unable to dislodge Kṛṣṇa from his back as the child had caught him by the throat. His eyes burst out of their sockets and, finally, the demon fell down to earth together with the child.[2] The *asura* was, of course, dead, and Kṛṣṇa obviously survived without suffering any harm, as his delighted parents found out.

The Pralambāsuravadha is told in all our sources, and the *Bālacarita* presents the only variations in the episode. It tells how once the demon Pralamba came, when the two brothers could already run and hop, and, taking the form of Nanda, their foster-father, took Balarāma on his shoulders and ran away with him. But when the boy discovered that this was a demon, he struck him on the head with his fist and made his eyeballs burst out, killing him.[1] Our other three texts, the *Harivaṃśa*, the *Viṣṇu Purāṇa* and the *Bhāgavata Purāṇa*, do not mention that the demon disguised himself as Nanda, but just as another cowherd. All these texts tell how Pralamba approached Kṛṣṇa and Balarāma when they were playing with all the other boys of Vraja. The demon joined them in their games with a view to killing them, and passed unnoticed. The boys then started a new game called 'game of the deer',[2] and Pralamba had to compete in jumping with Balarāma. Balarāma won and, as the winners had to be carried on the backs of the losers, he mounted on the shoulders of the false *gopa*, who immediately took flight, carrying him away. At first Balarāma was frightened, but he came back to his senses when Kṛṣṇa reminded him of his divine nature in a *stotra* that has as its model, evidently, the Puruṣa Hymn of the *Ṛg Veda* (10.90).[3] Hearing those words and similar ones, Balarāma took heart and smote down the demon with his fist.

The similarity of this story to the Tṛṇāvarta episode of the *Bhāgavata Purāṇa* is indeed close, and this resemblance was made more evident by the use of the same images. Tṛṇāvarta appears as a whirlwind, Pralamba as a cowherd. The cowherd, however, is able to fly and resembles a cloud. This cloud image is used three times in the account of the incident in the *Harivaṃśa*,[4] and is also used in the *Viṣṇu Purāṇa*. In this last text it is also said that the demon could not bear the enormous weight of the child, just as in the Tṛṇāvarta episode, and that his body grew as a cloud in the summer: 'Unable to bear the weight of Rauhiṇeya, the best of demons expanded his great body as

1. đaityo nāmnā tṛṇāvartaḥ kaṃsabhṛtyaḥ praṇođitaḥ / cakravātasvarūpeṇa jahārāsīnamarbhakam; *BhP* 10.7.20.

2. tamaśmānaṃ manyamāna ātmano gurumattayā / gale gṛhīta utsraṣṭuṃ nāśaknođađbhutārbhakam // galagrahaṇaniśceṣṭo đaityo nirgatalocanaḥ / avyaktạrāvọ nyapatat sahabālo vyasurvraje; *BhP* 10.7.27-28.

1. tađo āhāvaṇappahāvaṇamatte ṇanđāgovavutte palaṃbo ṇāma đāṇavo ṇanđagovaveṣaṃ gahṇia āađo / tađo ṣaṅkaliṣaṇaṃ kaṇṭhe ṇikkhivia gacchantaṃ taṃ vijāṇia bhaṭṭiṇā ṣaṅkaliṣaṇena taṣṣa đāṇavaṣṣa ṣīṣe muṭṭhippahāro kiđo / teṇa ppahāreṇa ukkhittacaksūṣo vi đāṇavo bhavia tatto evva muđo= tata āđhāvanaprađhāvanamātre nanđagopaputre pralambo nāma đānavo nanđagopaveṣam gṛhītvā gataḥ / tataḥ saṃkarṣaṇaṃ kaṇṭhe nikṣipya gacchantaṃ taṃ vijñāya bhartrā saṃkarṣaṇena tasya đānavasya śīrṣe muṣṭiprahāraḥ kṛtaḥ / tena prahāreṇotkṣiptacakṣuḥ so'pi đānavo bhūtvā tata eva mṛtaḥ; *BC* 3.

2. hariṇākrīḍanaṃ nāma:; *VP* 5.9.12.

3. śiraḥ khaṃ te jalaṃ mūrtiḥ kṣamā bhūrđahano mukham/ vāyurlokāyurucchvāso manaḥsraṣṭā manustava // sahasrāsyaḥ sahasrāṅgaḥ sahasracaraṇekṣaṇaḥ / sahasrapatranābhastvaṃ sahasrāṃśuđharo'rihā; *HV* 58.38-39.

4. iva toyađaḥ; *HV* 58.23; ivāmbuđaḥ; *HV* 58-24; ivāmbuđaḥ; *HV* 58.28.

a summer cloud'.[1] Another recurrent image, also taken by the authors of the *Bhāgavata*, is the horrible description of the demon's eyes coming out of their sockets from the terrible impact of Balarāma's fist. We have seen already this description in the *Bālacarita*, and the *Viṣṇu Purāṇa* repeats it in other words, telling how Balarāma beat the demon on the head, and how from those blows and Balarāma's tight hold on his neck his two eyes were driven out.[2] Tṛṇāvarta died in the same way.

One may easily see that the Tṛṇāvarta episode in the *Bhāgavata Purāṇa* was modelled upon the Pralamba episode of earlier Purāṇas. But why should the authors of the *Bhāgavata* again tell a story that is already part of the full saga and is included by themselves in their own Purāṇa? It is quite probable that this was done with a view to add to Kṛṣṇa's lustre by attributing to him feats and prowesses equal to those of his strong elder brother. From early epigraphical records we can gather that Balarāma was initially a divinity in his own right and that he even had his followers.[3] Sculptural representations of him alone, not accompanied by Kṛṣṇa, are extant, and are much older than any statues of Kṛṣṇa alone.[4] In the Purāṇas he is not much referred to, but it is always acknowledged that he is the other half of Viṣṇu's dual incarnation,[5] and discourses like the one addressed to him by Kṛṣṇa, that we have just quoted, show that his divinity was fully recognised. Balarāma, in spite of Kṛṣṇa's much wider popularity, kept in all the Purāṇas two episodes of childhood where he was the hero and not Kṛṣṇa. These are the Pralambāsuravadha, already mentioned, and the Dhenukavadha. These two episodes are presented consecutively in the *Harivaṃśa* and the *Viṣṇu Purāṇa*,[6] as if to separate them from the rest of the Kṛṣṇa story, and these same two episodes were copied by the authors of the *Bhāgavata* and attributed to Kṛṣṇa.

The incident of the killing of the demon Dhenuka is the other marvellous feat for which Balarāma is celebrated. Together with the Pralamba episode, it is represented in a number of sculptures as part of the Kṛṣṇa story.[1] The main point of these iconographical depictions as well as of the Purāṇic story is to show the incredible strength of Balarāma who, even as a boy, could take a big donkey by the hind legs, hurl it around and throw it to the top of a tree, from where it would fall dead together with the tree's fruits.[2] This episode was also copied in the *Bhāgavata Purāṇa*, and is the last in our list of examples of Kṛṣṇa's prowess as 'the marvellous strong child'. It tells how once, when the boys were grazing the calves—being too young to take the bigger animals—a demon came to kill them disguised as a calf, but Kṛṣṇa, having detected him, took him by the hind legs, hurled him around and threw him already dead to the top of a Kapittha tree, from where he fell along with the fruit of the tree.[3] This episode is called Vatsāsuravadha, and together with another incident not recorded anywhere else—that of Bakāsura, the demon in crane form—it forms a whole chapter of the *Bhāgavatat Purāṇa*. Its modelling upon the Dhenukavadha by Balarāma is quite evident and is an example of that process by which the Kṛṣṇa saga was formed, borrowing themes and motifs from different sources. In the *Bālacarita* the killing of Dhenuka is altogether attributed to Kṛṣṇa, contrary to all other sources,[4] showing that the process is not exclusive to the *Bhāgavata Purāṇa*, and that it started much earlier. What we learn from these stories acknowledging that the *Bhāgavata* copied the Balarāma episodes, is that twin divinities tend to separate, with one of the pair gradually assuming more and more importance. This is understandable since, from the point of view of narration, it is very difficult to keep the public's atten-

1. *VP* 5.9.17; asahanrauhiṇeyasya sa bhāraṃ dānavottamaḥ / vavṛdhe sa mahākāyaḥ prāvṛṣīva balāhakaḥ.

2. muṣṭinā so'hananmūrdhni kopasaṃraktalocanaḥ / tena cāsya prahāreṇa bahiryāte vilocane, *VP* 5.9.35.

3. See above, p. 20; consider also the Umācal Rock Inscription of Surendravarman that records the carving of a cave-temple dedicated to Lord Balabhadra (Balarāma) and proves the popularity of this god as late as the fifth century A.D. According to M. Sharma 'this is the earliest of all the inscriptions issued or inscribed by the kings of ancient Assam'. (M. M. Sharma, *Inscriptions of Ancient Assam*, Gauhati University, 1978.)

4. Like the one in the Lucknow Museum from the first century B.C.; see pl. 3.

5. *VP* 5.1.59-60; *BhP* 10.43.23.

6. *HV* 57-58; *VP* 5.8-9.

1. See plates 8, 21-3, 49, and 60.

2. tābhyāmeva sa jagrāha padbhyāṃ taṃ daityagardabham/ āvarjitamukhaskandhaṃ prairayattālamūrdhani // sa bhagnorukaṭigrīvo bhagnapṛṣṭho durākṛtiḥ / kharastālaphalaiḥ sārdhaṃ papāta dharaṇītale; *HV* 57.19-20.

3. gṛhītvāparapādabhyāṃ sahalāṅgūlamacyutaḥ / bhramayitvā kapitthāgre prāhiṇod gatajīvitam / sa kapitthair mahākāyaḥ pātyamānaiḥ papāta ha; *BhP* 10.11.43.

4. govajaṇehi parivudo tālahalāṇi gahṇiduṃ tālavaṇaṃ gado / tahiṃ tālavaṇe dheṇvo ṇāma dāṇavo gaddabhavesaṃ gahṇia āado / tado taṃ pi jāṇia bhaṭṭidāmodaleṇa taṣṣa vāmapādaṃ gahṇia ukkhivia pādidāṇi tālaphalāṇi=gopajanaiḥ parivṛttas tālaphalāni grahītuṃ tālavanaṃ gataḥ / tatra tālavane dhenuko nāma dānavo gardabhaveṣam gṛhītvāgataḥ / tatas tamapi jñātvā bhartṛdāmodareṇa tasya vāmapādaṃ gṛhītvotkṣipya pātitāni tālaphalāni; *BC* 3.

tion and sympathies on two main heroes at once. Naturally one of them gets more popularity, especially if religion is also an issue, and the heroes, besides their epic adventures, have a cult. Theism tends to be very exclusive, and a faithful devotee of any god looks on him as the supreme god who does not bear comparison even with his closest associates. This has happened not only between gods mythologically related as brothers but even between husband and wife, as in the case of Śiva and Durgā, where each has a different group of followers. Other twin heroes followed the same process, Romulus even killed Remus, his twin brother, and gained the cult of the Romans alone; Iphicles is scarcely ever mentioned, but Heracles, his twin brother, is universally recognised. Balarāma had better luck, with his prowesses being copied in favour of his brother.

The themes of 'the miraculous child' in the Kṛṣṇa saga do not end with the Vatsāsuravadha episode. As we mentioned at the beginning of this section, these themes may be divided into two groups, one consisting of those dealing with the miraculous force and strength of the little boy, which we have just reviewed, and the second with the divinity of the child, accounts of miracles that represent the hero not just as a strong man in miniature but as the supreme and universal god in baby form. We have, in other heroes, parallels to the first set of themes, but the second set is exclusive to Kṛṣṇa and is not found in the general heroic biographies.

We have already mentioned[1] that Indra is said in several places to have vanquished various enemies while still a child. He is even mentioned as having defeated a four-footed demon called Araru,[2] in Vedic parlance a 'fourfooted' being either a cow or a horse. Not much is known of Heracles' childhood, but at least one story is told that approximates closely to the Kṛṣṇa stories we have seen. This is his killing of two serpents sent by his enemy to kill him, just as Kaṃsa sent monsters to kill Kṛṣṇa. The episode is related by most biographers of Heracles, and Pindar and Theocritus in the fifth and third centuries B.C. respectively gave especially beautiful versions of it. We can quote the short account of Apollodorus:

> When the child was eight months old, Hera desired the destruction of the babe and sent two huge serpents to the bed. Alcmene called Amphytrion to her help, but Hercules arose and killed the serpents by strangling them with both his hands.[1]

1. See above, p. 50.
2. ayaṃ kanīna ṛtupā avedy amimītārarum yaś catuṣpāt; *RV* 10.99.10b.

The scene is represented in a beautiful Hellenistic bronze in the Capitoline Museum, Rome.[2] These two heroes, then, present the same themes of 'the miraculous child', as Kṛṣṇa does, perhaps not in such abundance and detail as Kṛṣṇa, for which the Kṛṣṇa saga is unique, but still they present the theme as a regular part of the story of the hero, as the normal evolution of a person, who, if he was supernaturally strong in adulthood, must also have been so since the cradle. The theme is a logical appendage to the life of the hero.

But the strong child is not necessarily the divine child, and the biographers of Kṛṣṇa needed to make this point clear. They added therefore some episodes to show the absolute divinity of the baby Kṛṣṇa and in this they distinguished him from the 'ordinary' hero of legend. These episodes we will review now.

ii. THE COSMIC CHILD

Six episodes are related in the Kṛṣṇa childhood stories that present the theme of 'the Miraculous Child' as 'the Cosmic Child'. These episodes are peculiar to Kṛṣṇa and form a basic trait of his personality, one that links him to the Cosmic deities of the Veda, as we described them at the end of the first chapter. Five of these episodes appear in the *Bhāgavata Purāṇa*, and one would think that the theme is characteristic of this text only. There is, however, one incident related in the *Harivaṃśa* and in no other text, that presents 'the Cosmic Child' in a manner that permits a new light to be shed on the analysis of the theme. That incident occupies a whole chapter in the *Harivaṃśa*, and we suspect that it was not included in the other Purāṇas because of its violent character that does not give a favourable image of Kṛṣṇa as a naughty but lovable child.

The episode in question is called the Vṛkadarśana, or 'Vision of the Wolves'[3] and it occurs after the Yamalārjuna episode. In fact it occurs after the infancy of Kṛṣṇa, since the Yamalārjuna incident happened when the two boys were just crawling,[4] and

1. Apollodorus, *The Library*, 2.4.8, tr. by Sir J. G. Frazer, vol. 1, p. 175.
2. G. K. Galinsky, *The Herakles Theme*, Blackwell, London 1972, I 11.16.
3. *Harivaṃśa*, Crit. Ed. by P. L. Vaidya, B.O.R.I., 1969, v.1, p. 354, col .1.
4. kṛṣṇasaṃkarṣaṇau cobhau riṅgiṇau samapadyatām; *HV* 51.1.

the Vṛkadarśana occurs when their infancy has passed and they are already seven years old.[1] The chapter starts with a very idyllic description of the games and amusements enjoyed by the boys in the forests of Vraja. They spent there many a happy hour playing all sorts of games with the cowherd boys. They adorned themselves with paint and feathers[2] in what could be tribal costumes. They played music With drums and flutes[3] and were as happy as strong and healthy boys can be. But one day they realised that things had been changing around them.

By the long occupancy of the cowherds the formerly wild forests of Vraja had been greatly disturbed and the boys could no longer enjoy them as they used to. The passage that describes the changes caused in the forest by human habitation reflects very clearly and objectively the aspirations of the nomadic cowherds for a free life. We have seen indications of the kind of life led by the tribe of gopas, in two previous episodes. In the Pūtanāvadha and the Śakaṭabhaṅga incidents, mention is made of the wagons in which the cowherds lived, but in this passage it is specifically stated that the cowherds should not stay permanently in any one place. The yearning for a nomadic life prompts Kṛṣṇa to look for a new place to establish the encampment, and he finds it in Vṛndāvana.

First, Kṛṣṇa describes to his brother the inconvenience of settled life, both for the people and for the forest: 'Then Dāmodara said to Saṃkarṣaṇa, O Noble one, "it is not possible to play with the cowherds in this forest [any more]".'[4] He explains that this is caused by the cowherds having destroyed the trees[5] and 'through the forest-produced wood and vegetables which are sold, this settlement, with its abundant grass destroyed, looks like a city'.[6]

The life of a city, of any permanent settlement, seems unwholesome to the wandering cowherds. Kṛṣṇa makes it clear that by long occupation even the health of the animals and the people is endangered, since the refuse matter of the village impregnates with its poisons the soil and grass and then the cows

1. evaṃ tau bālyamuttīrṇau kṛṣṇasaṃkarṣaṇāvubhau / tasminnevavrajasthāne saptavarṣau babhūvatuḥ; *HV* 52.2.

2. pītaśvetānulepanau; kākapakṣadharāvubhau; *HV* 52.2.

3. parṇa; *HV* 52.3; gopaveṇu; *HV* 52.5.

4. *HV* 52. 8; atha dāmodaraḥ śrīmānsaṃkarṣaṇamuvāca ha / ārya nāsminvane śakyaṃ gopālaiḥ saha krīḍitum //

5. gopairmathitapādapam; *HV* 52.9.

6. *HV* 52.15; vikrīyamāṇaiḥ kāṣṭhaiśca śākaiśca vanasaṃbhavaiḥ / utsannnasaṃcayatṛṇo ghoṣo'yaṃ nagarāyate //

do not want to eat that grass and the milk produced is not good.[1] Everybody knows that cowherds have to be always moving and never stay permanently anywhere, 'they do not have doors, ties or locks, neither houses or fields; cowherd stations are famous in the world for being like Cakracārin birds [or for always going in circles]'.[2] Therefore the cowherds should move their encampment once more and go to a more suitable place, and Kṛṣṇa knows just such a place. Vṛndāvana, by the side of the Yamunā river and the Govardhana mountain, is where Kṛṣṇa wants to go. He praises highly the virtues of the new forest: 'I have heard of a delectable forest with a full cover of grass; it is called by the name of Vṛndāvana and has sweet fruits and water.'[3] But will the cowherd tribe want to move only for the whim of some noisy children? The following passage is remarkable for its uniqueness among the Kṛṣṇa stories. In it we find the 'Cosmic Child' motif expressed in a peculiar manner, the divinity being at the same time playful and terrible. Kṛṣṇa has decided that they have to go, and they will move at any cost:

> Therefore, let this cow-station remain [here]. Let this forest without qualities be abandoned. We will make [the cowherds] move, if it pleases you, by creating some motive [to go]. // When Vāsudeva had said this, there appeared hundreds of wolves feeding on flesh, fat and blood. // As he thought thus, fierce and terrible wolves in hundreds were produced everywhere from his own body-hair. // When they saw these wolves produced at his will, there was great terror in the settlement among the cows and calves, men and herdwomen. // ... they issued out of his own body, marked with the Śrīvatsa, with Kṛṣṇa's black complexion, augmenting the fear of the cowherds. // Eating the calves and causing terror in the cowpens, taking the children in the night, the cowherd camp was destroyed by the wolves.[4]

1. śakṛnmūtreṣu teṣveva jātaṃ kṣararasāyanam / na tṛṇaṃ bhuñjate gāvo nāpi tatpayaso hitam; *HV* 52.19.

2. *HV* 52.18; nadvārabandhāvaraṇā na gṛhakṣetriṇastathā/ praśastā vai vrajā loke yathā vai cakracāriṇaḥ //

3. *HV* 52.21; śrūyate hi vanaṃ ramyaṃ paryāptatṛṇasaṃstaram / nāmnā vṛndāvanaṃ nāma svāduvṛkṣaphalodakam //

4. *HV* 52.28-31; 33-34; tatrāyaṃ vasatāṃ ghoṣastyajyatāṃ nirguṇaṃ vanam / saṃvāhayāma bhadraṃ te kiṃcidutpādya kāraṇaṃ // evaṃ kathayatastasya vāsudevasya dhīmataḥ / prādurbabhūvuḥ śataśo raktamāṃsavasāśanāḥ// ghorāścintayatastasya svatanūruhajāstadā / viniṣpeturbhayakarāḥ sarvataḥ śataśo vṛkāḥ // vṛkān niṣpatitāndṛṣṭvā goṣu vatseṣvatho nṛṣu / gopiṣu ca yathākāma vraje traso'bhavanmahān //. . . .niścerus-

This sudden brutality comes in the text as a surprise. Certainly we had previous scenes of violence and gory horror, but these were either caused by some villain, like Kaṃsa's dashing the little girl, 'still wet from the womb', on the stone,[1] or were deserved punishment inflicted upon a monster, like the baby Kṛṣṇa beating out the eyes of Tṛṇāvarta. But here his beloved gopas and animals are preyed upon by fierce wolves which appeared out of his own body. Those wolves were marked with the mystic Śrīvatsa sign and black as Kṛṣṇa himself. To the Western mind it is just monstrous that this child could have done such an unbelievable thing as causing the death of his own people merely to make them move their camp to a better place. In the Indian tradition, however, there is a justification for this. The Hindu supreme deity is a cosmic deity; the whole universe and the cosmic order are but his manifestations. All creative as well as destructive forces come from God and are divine. Kṛṣṇa does not generally manifest himself in his cosmic destructive form; he is ideally the god of love and happiness, play, song and dance. There are however three instances in his life when his terrible aspect is made apparent. Two of them appear in the *Mahābhārata* and the other is the one that we are now dealing with. In the Mausala parvan is related the horrible end of Kṛṣṇa's life. There we see that fearful aspect of the divinity once again. The other instance occurs in the *Bhagavad-Gītā*, and that we quote now to illustrate that side of Kṛṣṇa's character of which the Vṛkadarśana is the third example.

Chapter Eleven of the *Bhagavad-Gītā* is called *Viśvarūpadarśana*, 'Vision of the Universal form', and deals with the manifestation of that universal form to Arjuna at his own request. Arjuna is granted his petition to contemplate the true and eternal form of Kṛṣṇa, the Viśvarūpa, and even he, the great warrior, is frightened at what he sees: 'Then did the son of Pāṇḍu see the whole [wide] universe in One converged, there in the body of the God of gods, yet divided out in multiplicity.'[2] His vision is essentially the same as that of Mārkaṇḍeya and Yaśodā, terrifying just for its immensity, but its images are also connected with the horror of death and destruction. Arjuna describes what he sees:

> 24. Ablaze with many-coloured [flames] you touch the sky, your mouths wide open, [gaping] your eyes distended, blazing: so do I see You and my inmost self is shaken: I cannot bear it, I find no peace, O Viṣṇu. 25. I see your mouths with jagged, ghastly tusks reminding [me] of time's [devouring] fire: I cannot find my bearings, I cannot find a refuge; have mercy, God of gods, home of the universe. 26. Lo, all these sons of Dhṛtarāṣṭra accompanied by hosts of kings,—Bhīṣma, Droṇa and [Karṇa] son of the charioteer, and those foremost in battle of our party too, 27. rush [blindly] into your [gaping] mouths that with their horrid tusks strike [them] with terror. Some stick in the gaps between your teeth,—see them—their heads to powder ground—28. As many swelling, seething streams rush headlong into the [one] great sea, so do these heroes of the world of men enter into your blazing mouths. 29. As moths in bursting, hurtling haste rush into a lighted blaze to [their own] destruction, so do the worlds, well-trained in hasty violence, pour into your mouths to [their own] undoing. 30. On every side you lick, lick up—devouring—worlds, universes, everything,—with burning mouths. Viṣṇu your dreadful rays of light fill the whole universe with flames-of-glory, scorching [everywhere].[1]

This terrible vision of Arjuna is the climax of the *Bhagavad-Gītā*. In it the cosmic grandeur and horror are displayed in all intensity. The Vṛkadarśana does not have that grandeur and majesty; it is, however, horrible in a different way. In the episode of the

tasya gātrāddhi śrīvatsakṛtalakṣaṇaḥ / kṛṣṇasya kṛṣṇavadanā gopānāṃ bhayavardhanāḥ // bhakṣayadbhiśca tairvatsāṃstrāsayadbhiśca govrajān / niśi bālānharadbhiśca vṛkair utsādyate vrajaḥ //

1. See above, p. 55.

2. *BG* 11.13; Zaehner tr.; tatraikasthaṃ jagat kṛtsnaṃ pravibhaktam anekadhā / apaśyad devadevasya śarīre pāṇḍavas tadā //

1. *BG* 11.24-30; Zaehner tr; nabhaḥspṛśaṃ dīptam anekavarṇam vyattānanaṃ dīptaviśālanetram / dṛṣṭvā hi tvāṃ pravyathitāntarātmā dhṛtiṃ na vindāmi śamaṃ ca viṣṇo // daṃṣṭrākarālāni ca te mukhāni dṛṣṭvaiva kālānalasaṃnibhāni / diśo na jāne na labhe ca śarma prasīda deveśa jagannivāsa // amī ca tvāṃ dhṛtarāṣṭrasya putrāḥ sarve sahaivāvanipālasaṅghaiḥ / bhīṣmo droṇaḥ sūtaputrasthathāsau sahā'smadiyairapi yodhamukhyaiḥ // vaktrāṇi te tvaramāṇā viśanti daṃṣṭrākarālāni bhayānakāni / kecid vilagnā daśanāntareṣu saṃdṛśyante cūrṇitair uttamāṅgaiḥ // yathā nadīnāṃ bahavo'mbuvegāḥ samudram evābhimukhā dravanti / ytathā tavāmī naralokavīrā viśanti vaktrāṇyabhijvalanti / yathāpradīptaṃjvalanaṃ pataṅgā viśanti nāśāya samṛddhavegāḥ / tathaiva nāśāya viśanti lokās tavāpi vaktrāṇi saṃṛddhavegāḥ // lelihyase grasamānaḥ samantāllokān samagrān vadanairjvaladbhiḥ / tejobhir āpūrya jagat samagraṃ bhāsas tavogrāḥ pratapanti viṣṇo // ākhyāhi me ko bhavān ugrarūpo namo'stu te devavara prasīda / vijñātum icchāmi bhavantam ādyaṃ na hi prajānāmi tava pravṛttim //

Harivaṃśa the cosmic level is present as the amazing apparition of hundreds upon hundreds of wolves out of the hairs of the body of the boy Kṛṣṇa. This is in itself dazzling but not horrific, nor is the fact that ferocious animals are produced. What is so shocking about the episode is that it happens in the middle of normal everyday life. Arjuna's vision fits very well as a preliminary to the Kurukṣetra battle. There, in the presence of that carnage, the battlefield of hundreds of thousands of warriors, the manifestation of the Viśvarūpa has its logic. But in the Vraja of Nanda that cosmic occurrence is uncanny and, by its total outlandishness, almost grotesque. The bloody beasts issue from the body of the lovable boy, and maul and destroy, rip and devour the pacific and charming inhabitants of the cow station. The lesson is for the reader and listener of the story: 'Do not forget that the charming little boy that plays around in the Vraja is God Almighty: And the power and majesty of God are, of course, frightening to simple creatures.'[1] As we have said, the Vṛkadarśana episode is not the only incident where the Cosmic Child motif appears. It is, however, the only one where this element of terror and destruction is present. In the *Bhāgavata Purāṇa* we find five different passages where the Cosmic Child motif is displayed. In these, as in all cosmic manifestations, human nature is amazed and astonished, but the terror of death is not there. The fact that we have so many examples of the motif in a single text means that the religious element was already all-important at this stage in the evolution of the legend. Contrary to the Viśvarūpadarśana of the *Gītā* and to the Vṛkadarśana of the *Harivaṃśa*, there is nothing tremendously spectacular or eventful in these cosmic manifestations of the *Bhāgavata Purāṇa*. They are all told in a few short verses, they all happen in common, habitual surroundings, while Yaśodā and the baby follow their daily routine, and after they occur life continues on its normal course, without any major change due to the marvellous sight of the divine presence and power. Unlike the incident in the *Harivaṃśa*, that occurs when Kṛṣṇa was already seven years old, the *Bhāgavata Purāṇa* ones happen when he is just a baby who can barely walk and talk.

1. In the minds of the myth-makers the idea may also be present that even natural disasters are sent by God and may be for man's good in the long run. It tries in mythological terms to deal with the problem of evil, which is one of the persistent problems of theology.

The first of these episodes is related immediately before the Tṛṇāvarta incident and is connected with it because of the way in which the child's divinity is manifested. In this first example of the Cosmic Child motif in the *Bhāgavata Purāṇa*, it appears very discreetly, and on first sight one would not think it had any special importance. It is only when we compare it with other examples that we realise it is the same motif: the universal, cosmic divinity present in the lovely child. Our Purāṇa says very straightforwardly that once Kṛṣṇa was being playfully fondled by Yaśodā, when she realised that the baby has become enormously heavy, as heavy as a mountain peak. Unable to support the tremendous weight, the lady put the child on the ground and, looking at him astonished for a while, went on with her daily duties.[1] Here the universal form of the deity can be discerned in that Kṛṣṇa becomes 'heavy as a mountain peak' and in that in the second verse he is called Mahāpuruṣa, the name of the cosmic giant of the *Ṛg Veda*.[2]

The next two incidents are exact replicas, one of the other. That this is so proves the importance of the motif in the Purāṇa. The authors wanted so much to show the Universal divinity of the baby Kṛṣṇa that they repeated without any variations the same incident in two subsequent chapters. In them we can see again this clear reminiscence of the primeval Puruṣa of *RV* 10.90. The first example appears in the same chapter as the Tṛṇāvarta episode, just as our last example. It tells that once Yaśodā was suckling the baby and by chance looked at the inside of his mouth when he happened to yawn, and there she saw: 'The space, heaven and earth, the stars, the hosts of the quarters, the sun, the moon, the fire, the air and the oceans, the continents, their daughters [i.e. rivers] and forests, and all the beings that move and move not.'[3] Having seen the whole universe within the mouth of her child, Yaśodā was terribly frightened and trembling, and without being able to understand it she closed her eyes tightly.

1. ekadā'rohamārūḍhaṃ lālayantī sutaṃ satī / garimāṇaṃ śiśorvoḍhum na sehe girikūṭavat // bhūmau nidhāya taṃ gopī vismitā bhārapīḍitā / mahāpuruṣamādadhyau jagatāmāsa karmasu // *BhP* 10.7.18-19.

2. In *Bālacarita* the same image is also present when Vasudeva holds the baby Kṛṣṇa to take him to the other side of the Yamunā, and then when Nanda receives him. On both occasions it is said that the baby is as heavy as a mountain. *BC* 1.11; 1.14; 1.20.

3. *BhP* 10.7.36; khaṃ rodasī jyotiranīkamāśāḥ sūryendu-vahniśvasanāmbudhīṃśca / dvīpān nagāṃstadduhitṛrvanānī bhūtāni yāni sthirajaṅgamāni //.

In the next chapter the scene is repeated. This time Yaśodā is scolding the child after one of his customary pranks. The boy has eaten mud and his friends have told his mother. Yaśodā asks him angrily to open his mouth when he denies that he ate mud, and there she contemplates again the infinite cosmos and all the beings in it.[1] The description of what she sees is quite similar to the one in the previous chapter and, indeed, similar to most descriptions of a vision of this nature, since they are all derived, as we said before, from the Puruṣa hymn of the *Ṛg Veda*. Yaśodā contemplates again the space, the stars, sun and moon, etc., as well as more philosophical categories that, likewise, form part of the traditional description of the universe, such as the mind, the senses, the objects of the senses and the three *guṇas* etc.[2] The Viśvarūpa is once again manifested, and this time Yaśodā does not just close her eyes, but expresses her deep sentiments in a hymn-like utterance of praise and devotion.[3] Here in two consecutive chapters we see repeated an image that is like the archetypal symbol of the deity, a symbol that represents what the Kṛṣṇa image essentially is: an image of divine humanity, of the infinite and eternal incarnated in a human frame. This divinity in human form is even more dramatically expressed when the human form is that of a mere baby, for then the symbol is still more potent.

The giant Puruṣa is also the dwarf Vāmana and an even more innocuous figure: the baby Kṛṣṇa. The symbol is tremendously attractive and that must be the reason why the *Bhāgavata* emphasises it in the visions of Yaśodā, and the other Purāṇas also give to it the utmost importance in the form of the childhood adventures of Kṛṣṇa.

Two other incidents in the *Bhāgavata Purāṇa* reflect this attitude towards Kṛṣṇa. The Cosmic Child motif appears again in the chapter following the one we last mentioned. The text, as we can see, insists in reiterating the image of universal manifestation in the baby Kṛṣṇa. Here, in the introductory scene to the Śakaṭabhaṅga episode, we are told that when Yaśodā first tried to tie Kṛṣṇa with the rope, she was

1. *BhP* 10.8.36-39.

2. sa tatra dadṛśe viśvaṃ jagat sthāsnu ca khaṃ diśaḥ/ sādridvīpābdhibhūgolaṃ savāyvagnindutārakam // jyotiścakraṃ jalaṃ tejo nabhasvān viyadeva ca / vaikārikāṇīndriyāṇi mano mātrā guṇāstrayaḥ // etad vicitraṃ saha jīvakālasvabhāvakarmāśayaliṅgabhedam / sūnostanau vīkṣya vidāritāsye vrajaṃ sahātmānamavāpa śaṅkām // *BhP* 10.8.37-39.

3. *BhP* 10.8.40-42.

unable to do so, since the rope was short by two fingers' breadth. She then got another rope, tied it to the first, and tried again, but it was still short by two fingers. She tried again, tying yet another rope to the others, and still she could not encompass the child's body, and this happened many times until there was no more rope in the house.[1] She was astonished (*vismitābhavat*) and Kṛṣṇa seeing her tired bound himself as a favour to her.[2] Here the situation is different, and the image apparently changes, but the meaning is the same; the child is the infinite god. In the vision of Yaśodā she contemplates the whole universe within the body of her baby; here the outside of that apparently little body cannot be encompassed by any length of rope, in other words cannot be measured. The cosmic character of the scene is implied in a verse describing Kṛṣṇa: 'Of whom there is no inside nor outside, before nor behind: He who is the world is before and behind, outside and inside the world'.[3]

The last incident including the Cosmic Child motif is a very short one and does not refer to a vision of totality but rather to an image of the cosmic power of god in transforming and creating things. As in the Vṛkadarśana, where wolves appear out of the hairs of Kṛṣṇa's body, in this incident also a transformation occurs. The *Bhāgavata* relates how once Kṛṣṇa heard a fruit-seller announcing her merchandise. The little boy ran in haste to buy some fruit but, not having any money, paid the woman with grain. The fruit-seller did not mind this, although the child dropped even the grain with which he intended to pay her, and gave him much fruit. Then the basket of the fruit-seller was miraculously filled, not with fruit, but with gems.[4] Here the image of the Cosmic Child returns all the way from the terrifying Vṛkadarśana to the adorable baby. The scene is full of charm and brings a feeling of tenderness to the reader or listener as he imagines the little boy, barely able to walk and

1. tad dāma badhyamānasya svārbhakasya kṛtāgasaḥ / dvyaṅgulonamabhūt tena saṃdadhe'nyacca gopikā // yadā'sīt tadapi nyūnaṃ tenānyadapi saṃdadhe / tadapi dvyaṅgulam nyūnaṃ yad yadādatta bandhanam // evaṃ svagehadāmāni yaśodā saṃdadhatyapi / *BhP* 10.9.15-17a.

2. dṛṣṭvā pariśramaṃ kṛṣṇaḥ kṛpayā'sīt svabandhane; *BhP* 10.9.18b.

3. *BhP* 10.9.13; na cāntarna bahiryasya na pūrvaṃ nāpi cāparam / pūrvāparam bahiścāntarjagato yo jagacca yaḥ.

4. krīṇīhi bhoḥ phalāniti śrutvā satvaramacyutaḥ / phalārthī dhānyamādāya yayau sarvaphalapradaḥ // phalavikrayiṇī tasya cyutadhānyaṃ karadvayam / phalairapūrayad ratnaiḥ phalabhāṇḍamapūri ca // *BhP* 10.11.10-11.

ignorant of the value of money, trying to buy the sweet fruit he craves for with grain. The fruit-seller gives him the fruit, as almost anybody would do for such a lovely little child, and her kindness is recompensed by her fruits being turned into gems. The image is given in short in the description of Kṛṣṇa as *phalārthin* and *sarvaphalapradaḥ*. The force of the image resides in the fact that the dispenser of fruits of desire is here depicted as a baby asking for real fruit. It also has the practical moral, that the worship of God, or gifts to Him, will bring practical and material rewards.

This is the last example of the Cosmic Child motif and the last in the themes of the miraculous child, a series that includes some of the most, if not the most, representative and typical of the Kṛṣṇa stories. The story of Kṛṣṇa's childhood does not end here by any means, but continues in our next set of themes which we deal with under the general headings of the Strong Man and the Dragon Slayer.

iii. THEMES OF THE HERO AS STRONG-MAN, THE WRESTLER

In our survey of the Kṛṣṇa figure we have characterised it as a Hero figure. We have shown how numerous traits in the story of Kṛṣṇa, in fact most of it, follow a definite pattern common to many other heroes in other stories. We are not saying that there is no originality in the story of Kṛṣṇa; Kṛṣṇa is a fully developed character in his own right and his stories have a definite Indian flavour. The Kṛṣṇa figure, as a hero and as a god, is thoroughly unique. We have only pointed out the existence of that pattern upon which the Indian people and their bards have in a masterly manner built the saga of Kṛṣṇa and the other heroes of his family. To this we have to add that Kṛṣṇa, besides being a hero, is also God, and this very fact gives the whole story of his life a totally new gamut of meanings and symbolism that can be, and often are, interpreted in many ways. The Kṛṣṇa legend has that quality common to true and great works of art, of always suggesting new meanings and new sentiments. By analysing it in detail we intend to show some of the basic themes and motifs that make the Kṛṣṇa saga the kind of literary masterpiece that it is, with universal appeal. We have already surveyed the themes of the birth and infancy of the Hero, that in the case of Kṛṣṇa have particular importance. We now proceed to review a motif that has not been much studied in relation to Kṛṣṇa: the Strong-Man.

Kṛṣṇa is God, his devotees will say, but in his legends and stories he is foremost a Hero, a Protector, a Deliverer, a Saviour. As such he has to be also a champion and what a champion essentially is: a strong-man. The themes of the strong-man are found all through the life of Kṛṣṇa, and in the first section of this chapter we have already reviewed some episodes dealing with the strong-man as a child. Indeed this is the first characteristic of the strong-man: that he was prodigiously strong from his earliest days. We saw how Kṛṣṇa destroyed a heavy cart with a single kick and how he uprooted two enormous trees. We saw Herakles strangling two huge serpents in his own cradle, and Indra defeating several enemies when only a young child. The hero had to be tough in order to survive, since, as we have seen, he was a castaway. He grew up among animals, generally with cowherds as did both Kṛṣṇa and Herakles,[1] and there he played and fought with those animals. Kṛṣṇa and Balarāma used to grab the calves by the tails and let themselves be dragged around by them, to the admiration and laughter of the young *gopīs*.[2] When they were older Kṛṣṇa used to make the bulls fight in the roads of Vraja, and he also organised fights among the cowherds. Moreover, he engaged in more dangerous sports, like surprising the cows and holding them as a crocodile would do.[3] This led to the general reputation of the hero as a strong man and as a fighter, not just one who fights when the occasion presents itself or when he has to defend himself or others, but even as an amateur or semi-professional wrestler. This side of his personality has not been studied before, even though we can see from the Purāṇas that it is a rather important aspect of the figure of Kṛṣṇa.

Wrestling is not looked on now-a-days as a very honourable sport, and perhaps even in ancient India a gentleman or a prince would not engage gladly or often in an open wrestling bout, archery being considered as a more becoming activity to prove one's

1. 'Amphytryon sent him to the cattle farm; and there he was nurtured and outdid all in stature and strength', Apollodorus, *The Library*, 2.4.9; Frazer tr., v.1, p. 177.

2. yarhyaṅganādarśaniyakumāralīlāvantarvraje tadabalāḥ pragṛhītapucchaiḥ/ vatsairitastata ubhāvanukṛṣyamāṇau prekṣantya ujjhitagṛhā jahṛṣurhasantyaḥ; *BhP* 10.8.24.

3. sa karīṣāṅgarāgāsu vrajarathyasu vīryavān / vṛṣāṇāṃ jātarāgāṇāṃ yudhāni samayojayat // gopālāṃśca balodagrānyodhayāmāsa vīryavān / vane sa vīro gāscaiva jagrāha grāhavadvibhuḥ; *HV* 63.16-17.

martial skill. Wrestling was, however, very popular as a spectacle and 'nobles quite often hired athletes themselves, and made them fight in public.'[1] In fact, although perhaps not regarded as very refined, kings and princes had to know this art, and in the *Mahābhārata* we have the description of the long and strenuous match between Bhīma and Jarāsaṃdha, king of Magadha, that ended with the death of the latter.[2] It is curious to note that this match was also prompted by Kṛṣṇa in the same way as he used to make the cowherds wrestle for amusement. That Kṛṣṇa was an expert in the art of wrestling is shown in that same episode in the *Mahābhārata* where he advises Bhīma on the exact moment to finish Jarāsaṃdha.[3] A relief of the Gupta period showing this scene is extant and kept at the Lucknow Museum.[4]

As we said, Kṛṣṇa's reputation as an able and strong fighter had spread widely and came even to the ears of Kaṃsa. That he and Balarāma were so fond of wrestling was what decided Kaṃsa to set a trap for them in the form of a wrestling contest that would lure them into coming to Mathurā. The *Ghaṭa Jātaka* and the *Harivaṃśa* make this point very clear: 'I have heard that these two are forceful and strong, hard and enduring, two skilful fighters that know how to wrestle in the arena',[5] and 'O Deva, they are wrestlers, having organised a fight in the city, then, when they have come into the arena, having apprehended them we will kill them.'[6] Even the wrestler Cāṇūra mentions this to Kṛṣṇa and Balarāma before engaging in the fight, saying that the brothers are well known as valiant, and that, hearing that they were expert in wrestling, the king sent for them and wanted to see them. Cāṇūra also says that the cowherds divert themselves with wrestling matches while grazing the cows in the forests.[7] The description of the wrestling match is full of action and gusto, and presents Kṛṣṇa and Balarāma as consummate and expert wrestlers. S.N. Tadapatrikar notes that the Purāṇic account is based on the description of the fight of Bhīma and Jīmūta in the *Mahābhārata*,[1] and we can quote that passage here to compare both accounts.

In the fourth month there took place in Matsya a very grand festival of Brahmā, richly celebrated, which the people held in great esteem. Wrestlers gathered there by the thousands from all countries, O King, gigantic and powerful men like Kālakhañja Asuras. Glorying in their might, and of surpassing strength, with the shoulders, hips, and necks of lions, quite clean and in fine spirits, they all were welcomed by the king; many a time had they won their bouts before that prince in his arena. There was one big man among them who challenged all the wrestlers; and not a single one dared approach him as he pranced about the ring.

When all the wrestlers had lost heart and spirit, the king of the Matsyas ordered his cook to grapple with the wrestler. At his urging, Bhīma made up his mind with difficulty, for he could not publicly defy the king. Then the tiger-like man with the loose step of a tiger entered the great ring and brought happiness to Virāṭa. The Kaunteya, to the delight of the people, fastened his girdle, and thereupon Bhīma challenged the wrestler, who was the like of Vṛtra. They both had extraordinary staying power, both had ruthless strength and stood as large as two rutting sixty-year-old elephants. Enemy-killer Bhīma plucked at the bellowing wrestler and pulled him with his arms, roaring himself, as a tiger attacks an elephant. The big-armed strong-man lifted him up and spun him around, to the astonishment of the wrestlers and the Matsyas. Strong-armed Wolf-Belly swung the wrestler around a hundred times, till he lost nerve and wits, and then trampled him on the ground.[2]

Here we can see the popularity of wrestling at the time, in that special festivals were organised, nominally for a religious purpose, where wrestling matches were the principal attraction. To these festivals many wrestlers came from all over the country. In the same way Kaṃsa celebrates a festival to Śiva, called the

1. Jeannine Auboyer, *Daily Life in Ancient India*, Asia Publishing House, London 1967, p. 252 and illustration 27, a representation of a wrestling match in the Ashmolean Museum, Oxford.

2. *Mbh* 2.21-22.

3. *Mbh* 2.21.20-23.

4. Kalpana Desai, *Iconography of Viṣṇu*, Abhinav, Delhi, 1973, Fig. 95.

5. *HV* 65.86; etau yuddhavidau raṅge kālanirmāṇayodhinau / dṛḍhapratikṛtī caiva śṛṇomi vyāyatodyamau.

6. ete deva mallayuddhakā, nagare yuddhaṃ kāretvā tattha ne yuddhamaṇḍalaṃ āgate gāhapetvā māressāmā; *GJ*, Faussboll ed., p. 81, lines 18-20.

7. he nandasūno he rāma bhavantau vīrasammatau / niyuddhakuśalau śrutvā rājñā'hūtau didṛkṣuṇā // *BhP* 10.43.32, and nityaṃ pramuditā gopā vatsapālā yathā sphuṭam / vaneṣu mallayuddhena krīḍantaścārayanti gāḥ // *BhP* 10.43.34.

1. S. N. Tadapatrikar, 'The Kṛṣṇa Problem', *ABORI*, v. 10, 1929, p. 304.

2. *Mbh* 4.12.12-24; tr. van Buitenen, *The Mahābhārata*, v.3, p. 43.

Bow Festival, where competitors are given a trial of strength consisting of trying to string a mighty bow, and at which the final and biggest celebration is a wrestling match.[1] To this festival of Kaṃsa there came also wrestlers from different regions, of which at least two are mentioned, the wrestler Andhra, who obviously came from that region,[2] and Cāṇūra, who came from Karūṣa,[3] a region south of Banaras.[4] Bhīma is reluctant to fight against Jīmūta and finally does so only because he cannot defy the order of the King without jeopardising his disguise and that of his brothers, and he does not want to fight, not for fear but because it is below his dignity as a prince to fight a professional wrestler in a public spectacle. He was not impeded in that way when he fought Jarāsaṃdha, a Kṣatriya, in a private fight. Kṛṣṇa, being ostensibly a low caste cowherd, does not have such scruples and goes gladly into the arena to meet the professional wrestlers. Kṛṣṇa's love of wrestling persisted throughout his life. Many years after the wrestling match where Kaṃsa was destroyed, Kṛṣṇa offered his friends a great party after his defeat of the demon Nikumbha. At this party Kṛṣṇa, 'who loved wrestling', made wrestlers fight for the entertainment of the guests, and gave them different prizes.[5] On that occasion, however, Kṛṣṇa did not himself participate in the matches, perhaps because being then already known as a prince it would be unbecoming for him, his family and his guests that he should fight with a low-caste *malla*.

Tadapatrikar's suggestion that the Kṛṣṇa wrestling episode is derived from the Bhīma-Jīmūta match in the *Mahābhārata* is, however, prompted by the fact that Bhīma lifts the wrestler over his head, hurls him around many times, and then kills him by throwing him on the ground. This is the same method used by Kṛṣṇa to dispose of Cāṇūra.[6] Even so, we cannot agree with Tadapatrikar that the account is derived from the *Mahābhārata* for three different reasons: first because the Bhīma-Jīmūta fight is only a minor incident in the *Mahābhārata* and even in the life of Bhīma, who had much more momentous battles, such as that against Duryodhana, Jarāsaṃdha and Kīcaka, and it is not very likely that the Purāṇic bards would take a secondary event in the Epic as their model for their hero's main battle. Second, because not all the Kṛṣṇa sources agree in the way that Cāṇūra is killed. The *Harivaṃśa*, perhaps the main source of Kṛṣṇa stories, ignores the hurling in the air completely and instead refers to Kṛṣṇa keeping Cāṇūra down by pressing with his knees on his chest, and pounding the wrestler's head with his fists until his eyes burst out of their sockets and hung down, moving about like golden bells.[1] And third, because the hurling in the air was, and still is, one of the most, if not the most, accomplished feats of strength of a wrestler. The composers of the *Viṣṇu Purāṇa* and the *Bhāgavata Purāṇa* (as did the composers of the episode of the *Virāṭa Parvan*) chose this method of disposing of Kṛṣṇa's adversary because of this fact and not because Bhīma killed Jīmūta in the same way. That the hurling around of a defeated enemy was a favourite way of disposing of him is shown in two episodes that we have mentioned before: the Vatsāsuravadha by Kṛṣṇa and the Dhenukavadha by Balarāma, where the boys hurl these demons and throw them to the top of a tree.[2]

We come now to the main episode in Kṛṣṇa's life, the death of Kaṃsa. It shows the image that people had of Kṛṣṇa as a strong-man and as a wrestler, that they chose to represent this central event in the career of the hero as framed by the pomp and pageantry, the thrill and the excitement, the theatrical and circus atmosphere of a wrestling tournament, where they knew well the qualities of the hero, his cunning and ability, his force and endurance, his excellence in the arena, would show to the utmost and demonstrate clearly and with the maximum of effect Kṛṣṇa's supreme command of the art of a strong-man: wrestling. Hero-stories often culminate in a public spectacle where the hero crowns himself with glory, defeating the villains in front of the crowd and at the same time

1. bhavadbhyāmiha samprāptau hanyetāṃ mallalīlayā / mañcāḥ kriyantāṃ vividhā mallaraṅgapariśritāḥ / paurā jānapadāḥ sarve paśyantu svairasaṃyugam // ārabhyatāṃ dhanuryāgaścaturdaśyāṃ yathāvidhi / viśasantu paśūn medhyān bhūtarājāya mīḍhuṣe // *BhP* 10.36.24 and 26.

2. *HV* 75.17.

3. *HV* 75.22.

4. F. E. Pargiter, *The Mārkaṇḍeya Purāṇa*; *Translated with Notes* (1904), rep. Indological Book House, Varanasi 1969, p. 341.

5. niyuddhakuśalānmallāndevo mallapriyastadā / yodhayitvā dadau bhūri vittam vastrāṇi cātmavān // *HV* cr. ed., App. 1, 29B, lines 465-66.

6. *VP* 5.20. 74-76; *BhP* 10.44.22-23.

1. dorbhyāmānamya kṛṣṇastu cāṇūraṃ pūrṇajīvitam / prāharanmuṣṭinā mūrdhni vakṣasyāhatya jānunā // niḥsṛte sāśrurudhire tasya netre sabandhane / tāpanīye yathā ghaṇṭe kakṣyopari vilambite // *HV* 75. 42-43.

2. In *HV* 76.3-4, Kṛṣṇa kills Tosala by hurling him around, and in *Mbh* 1.142, Bhīma also Killed Hiḍimba in exactly the same manner.

demonstrating that he is the champion in some manly skill. Tellers and writers of hero-stories have used this narrative device innumerable times, from the archery contest in Robin Hood and the tournament in Ivanhoe, to the gun duels in Western movies. Arjuna and Robin Hood, the best archers, hit the mark in front of a public assembly to show their unexcelled dexterity, Ulysses strings the bow in front of the people to show he is the master of Penelope and the kingdom because he is the strongest. Kṛṣṇa breaks the bow at the festival and then defeats all wrestlers and kills his enemy in the arena surrounded by thousands of people, thus making evident who is the strongest and the best wrestler.

Kṛṣṇa's conduct while in the arena is thoroughly that of a professional wrestler. He claps his hands and slaps his arm and thigh muscles in the wrestler's signs of defiance.[1] This wrestler's behaviour he also displays when meeting other enemies, like the bull Ariṣṭa.[2] He expressly pledges to follow closely the rules of wrestling and not to infringe them, so that a stain may not be cast upon the fame of wrestlers. He also knows very well the practices of wrestlers, such as rubbing dried cowdung, water and other ointments on their bodies. He places the utmost importance on certain virtues of wrestlers, such as endurance, firmness, courage, skill and strength.[3] These rules are outlined previously by the Yādavas, the kinsmen of Kṛṣṇa, assembled for the occasion. They speak of the ancient rules of wrestling, where a judge is required and no weapons are allowed but the ability and the force of the participants. The exhausted athletes should be removed from the ring by the time-keepers and rubbed with dried cow-dung. The judges should see that every man fights with another in his same condition, a fallen one with a fallen one, a standing one with a standing one. If a boy or a man or an old man, or a strong man or a weak man stands in the arena, it should be known by others equal to them. And finally they stress that knowers of the art of wrestling, strong and skilful, should not continue to fight when they are victorious and the others are utterly defeated.[1]

All these details on the rules of wrestling show that the sport was widely popular and that Kṛṣṇa was closely associated with its practice, representing one of the all-time heroes and champions of the arena.

The *Viṣṇu Purāṇa* gives a thoroughly technical account of the fight between Kṛṣṇa and Cāṇūra: *sannipātāvadhūtaistu cāṇūreṇa samaṃ hariḥ / prakṣepaṇairmuṣṭibhiśca kīlavajranipātanaiḥ / / pādoddhūtaiḥ pramṛṣṭaiśca tayoryuddhamabhūnmahat / /*.[2] This is so specialised that Wilson had to add this note to his translation:

> The terms here used are technical, and refer to the established modes of wrestling amongst Hindu athletae. 1. Sannipāta, is described as mutual laying hold of. 2. Avadhūta, "letting go of the adversary". 3. Kṣepaṇa, "pulling to, and casting back". 4. Muṣṭinipāta, "striking with fists". 5. Kīlanipāta, "striking with the elbow". 6. Vajranipāta, striking with the fore-arm. 7. Jānunirghāta, "pressing or striking with the knees". 8. Bāhusighaṭṭana, "interlacing the arms". 9. Pādodhūta, "kicking". 10. Pramṛṣṭa, "intertwining of the whole body". In some copies another term occurs, Aśmanirghāta, "striking with stones", or "striking blows as hard as with stones"; for stones could scarcely be used in a contest specified as "one without weapons" (*aśastram yuddhaṃ*).[3]

That Kṛṣṇa was looked on not just as a very strong boy but also as a very able and expert wrestler there can be hardly any doubt. Besides Cāṇūra he also dispatched another professional wrestler called Tosala (Tośalaka in the *Viṣṇu Purāṇa* and in the *Bhāgavata*),[4] and even a third one called Śala according to the *Bhāgavata Purāṇa*. Tosala he hurled around a hundred times and then crushed him on the ground, according

1. *HV* 74.21; 75.1.
2. *HV* 64.12.
3. yuddhaṃ mama sahānena rocate bāhuśālinā // yuddhavyatikramaḥ kaścinna bhaviṣyati matkṛtaḥ / na hyahaṃ bāhuyodhānāṃ dūṣayiṣyāmi yanmatam // yo'yaṃ karīṣadharmaśca toyadharmaśca raṅgajaḥ / kaṣāyasya ca saṃsargaḥ samayo hyeṣa kalpitaḥ // saṃyamaḥ sthiratā śauryam vyāyāmaḥ satkriyā balam / raṅge ca niyatā siddhiretadyuddhamukhe vratam; *HV* 75.17b-20.

1. bāhuyuddhamidaṃ raṅge saprāśnikamakātaram / kriyābalasamājñātamaśastraṃ nirmitaṃ purā // adbhiścāpi śramo nityaṃ vineyaḥ kāladarśibhiḥ / karīṣena ca mallasya satataṃ prakriyā smṛtā // sthito bhūmigataścaiva yo yathāmārgataḥ sthitaḥ / niyudhyataśca paryāyaḥ prāśnikaiḥ samudāhṛtaḥ // bālo vā yadivā madhyaḥ sthaviro vā kṛśo'pi vā / balastho vā sthito raṅge jñeyaḥ kakṣyāntareṇa vai // balataśca kriyātaśca bāhuyuddhavidhiryudhi / nirghātānantaraṃ kiṃcinna kartavyaṃ vijānatā; *HV* 75.10-14.
2. *VP* 5.20. 66-67.
3. H. H. Wilson, *The Vishnu Purana* (1840), rep. Punthi Pustak, Calcutta 1972, p. 443, n.5.
4. Jīvānanda Vidyāsāgara edition of 1882 reads (*VP* 5.20.60) Tosalaka; Wilson's translation has Tomalaka.

to the *Harivaṃśa*.[1] According to *Viṣṇu Purāṇa* Kṛṣṇa killed him with a blow of his left hand.[2] According to the *Bhāgavata* Kṛṣṇa broke him in two, and Śala he kicked on the head, killing both of them.[3] Balarāma on his part also killed several wrestlers. They were Muṣṭika and Andhra according to the *Harivaṃśa*,[4] Muṣṭika and Sumālin according to the *Viṣṇu Purāṇa*,[5] Muṣṭika, Kūṭa and not just Sumālin but eight younger brothers of Kaṃsa according to the *Bhāgavata*.[6] All of them were defeated and killed by the two cowherd boys. The tyrant Kaṃsa did not get the honour of being killed in open battle or being pierced through with arrows, but died while being dragged by the hair. He was thus excluded from the path of the heroes.[7]

This great duel, this central episode in the great drama of Kṛṣṇa's life, served to put him right in the middle of the political arena where he was to remain till the end of his days. Coming to Mathurā as a simple cowherd boy, despised by the upper classes, he emerges after the wrestling match as a prince and the master of the city. His force and prowess in the ring impress and captivate everybody's heart: not the least among them, but indeed the most fervent admirers of this rustic champion, are the women. The *Harivaṃśa* makes, for once, a concession to chastity and mentions only public women as those enamoured of Kṛṣṇa when he first appears in Mathurā as a wrestling champion: 'all the courtesans stared fixedly at Kṛṣṇa, as if their eyes were bees going to drink of his lotus-like face.'[8] The *Bhāgavata Purāṇa* does not stop at public women, but makes all the women in Mathurā, young and old, married and unmarried, fall in love with the strong cowherd, come to participate in the wrestling match and defying the great champions. When they hear the news of his coming they rush to their windows and roofs without any care as to the state they are in. Leaving meals and children, they only care to see that charming young man of whom they have heard so often before.[1] Obviously Kṛṣṇa's fame as a strong man had preceded him and gained for him the admiration of the weaker sex usually bestowed on public heroes. The *Viṣṇu Purāṇa* is more restrained in its account of this sexual attraction produced by the young champion, and refers only to the two brothers being contemplated with pleasure both by men and women.[2] What has to be remarked is that all this excitement in town was caused mainly because of the festival to be celebrated and its principal and culminating attraction, the wrestling match. Kṛṣṇa was sought after by everybody, and women in particular, as the strong man of the cowherds, about whose force many stories were told, come to challenge as a champion wrestler other famous champions in the royal arena. The reader of the Purāṇas knows that Kṛṣṇa is god, but to the people living in Mathurā at the time, and even to the cowherds, he was just a strong man and a champion wrestler, not a little thing if we consider the fame and admiration that even in our day a hero-athlete or a movie star commands among the masses.

Of Indra we know that he was a strong man, but we do not know if he was considered a wrestler. He defeated many enemies, but it is generally said that he used his *vajra* to accomplish those deeds of prowess. Heracles on his part was not only a strong man but also a wrestler. Like Kṛṣṇa, his fame preceded him wherever he went and he was challenged on various occasions to wrestle against other strong men. When he was returning from the country of the amazons, where he went to get the girdle of Hyppolite, their queen, he stopped at Torone 'and there, being challenged to wrestle by Polygonus and Telegonus, sons of Proteus, son of Poseidon, he killed them in the wrestling match'.[3] In fact Heracles had also as an alternative name, that of Palaemon, that is, 'Wrestler'.[4]

1. kṛṣṇastosalamudyamya giriśṛṅgopamaṃ balī bhrāmayitvā śataguṇaṃ niṣpipeṣa mahītale; *HV* 76.3.
2. kṛṣṇastośalakaṃ bhūyo mallarājaṃ mahābalam / vāmamuṣṭiprahāreṇa pātayāmāsa bhūtale; *VP* 5.20.79.
3. tarhyeva hi śalaḥ kṛṣṇapadāpahataśīrṣakaḥ / dvidhā vidīrṇastośalaka ubhāvapi nipetatuḥ; *BhP* 10.44.27.
4. saṃkarṣaṇastu suciraṃ yodhayitvā mahābalaḥ / andhramallaṃ mahāmallo maṇḍalāni vidarśayan // muṣṭinaikena tejasvī sāśanistanayitnunā / śirasyabhyahanadvīro vajreṇeva mahāgirim; *HV* 76.5-6.
5. kaṃse gṛhīte kṛṣṇena tadbhrātā'bhyāgato ruṣā / sumālī balabhadreṇa līlayaiva nipātitaḥ; *VP* 5.20.90.
6. tataḥ kūṭamanuprāptaṃ rāmaḥ praharatāṃ varaḥ / avadhīllīlayā rājan sāvajñaṃ vāmamuṣṭinā // and, tasyānujā bhrātaro'ṣṭau kaṅkanyagrodhakādayaḥ / abhyadhāvannabhikruddhā bhrāturnirveśakāriṇaḥ; *BhP* 10.44.26 and 40.
7. asaṃgrāme hataḥ kaṃsaḥ sa bāṇairaparikṣataḥ / kaṇṭhagrāhānnirastāsurvīramārgānnirākṛtaḥ; *HV* 76.40.
8. vāramukhyāśca tāḥ sarvāḥ kṛṣṇasya mukhapaṅkajam / papurhi netrabhramarairnimeṣāntaragāmibhiḥ; *HV* 76.13.

1. muhuḥ śruta; *BhP* 10.41.24-29.
2. strībhirnaraiśca sānandam locanairabhivīkṣitau; *VP* 5.19.13a.
3. Apollodorus, *The Library*, 2.5.9; tr. J.G. Frazer, v.1, p. 209.
4. Fontenrose, *Python*, p. 352; R. Graves, *The Greek Myths*, Pelican, Harmondsworth 1960, v.2, p. 101d, refers to Apollo-

Heracles not only accepted challenges but he also came out and challenged other famous wrestlers. Such was the case with Antaeus, king of Libya, in the words of Diodorus of Sicily:

> ... he challenged to a fight Antaeus, whose fame was noised abroad because of his strength of body and his skill in wrestling, and because he was wont to put to death all strangers whom he had defeated in wrestling, and grappling with him Heracles slew the giant.[1]

This fight of Heracles versus Antaeus has remarkable parallels to that of Bhīma and Jarāsaṃdha prompted by Kṛṣṇa. Kṛṣṇa does not kill Jarāsaṃdha personally, but we know that the expedition against this king was organised by Kṛṣṇa and only at his instance. Kṛṣṇa had a personal grudge against Jarāsaṃdha, that the Pāṇḍavas did not have. Jarāsaṃdha was the father-in-law of Kaṃsa and after the death of this latter he attacked Mathurā several times, finally causing Kṛṣṇa and the Yādavas to move to Dvārakā.[2] The killing of Jarāsaṃdha is thus very much the deed of Kṛṣṇa and we have seen[3] how even the definitive blow was struck at his command. Antaeus, like Jarāsaṃdha, had defeated many adversaries. Jarāsaṃdha wanted to sacrifice them to the god Śiva; Antaeus used their skulls to roof the god Poseidon's Temple.[4] Both Antaeus and Jarāsaṃdha were killed by being lifted in the air and broken.[5] In a common wrestling technique, 'being forced to wrestle with him, Hercules hugged him, lifted him aloft, broke and killed him'.[6]

One other challenge to wrestle received by Heracles came from Eryx, a son of Poseidon, according to Apollodorus, or of Aphrodite, according to Diodorus Siculus. At the time, Heracles was returning home from the expedition against Geryon, and driving the cattle he had taken from him. If we follow the account of Apollodorus, the trouble arose when one of the bulls of Heracles straggled from the herd and was taken by Eryx.

> So Hercules entrusted the Kine to Hephaestus and hurried away in search of the bull. He found it in the herds of Eryx, and when the king refused to surrender it unless Hercules should beat him in a wrestling bout, Hercules beat him thrice, killed him in the wrestling, and taking the bull drove it with the rest of the herd to the Ionian sea.[1]

The bull incident is not mentioned by Diodorus Siculus, who only refers to the challenge to a wrestling match, and to a wager made that if Heracles lost he was to surrender the herd, while if Eryx was defeated he would surrender his land.[2] This episode is very important for us since, besides the wrestling part that has parallels in the Kṛṣṇa stories, it presents Heracles as driving a herd of cattle, tending it and protecting it, that is, a cowherd, here perhaps rather like a cattle rustler, but still in charge of the kine and protecting them. We have mentioned before (see above page 78) that Heracles was a cowherd, since as a boy he was sent by his father to the cow station and there he grew up.[3] From that time onwards he protected the cows, and once he killed a lion that used to prey on the herds.[4] The Eryx incident is also very important from the point of view of a comparison of the longer episode of Geryon's cows with which we shall deal in more detail later.

Many more examples of Heracles' wrestling can be found, but these are enough to establish the point of the importance of this activity in the career of the hero. Like Kṛṣṇa he too was a famous strong man and wrestling was a natural field for such heroes to develop and demonstrate their abilities.

iv. KṚṢṆA AS STRONG MAN: THE GREAT LOVER AND THE GREAT EATER

The feats of Kṛṣṇa, as those of Heracles, have a definite flavour of prowess of strength. Not only in their killing of monsters or in their wrestling bouts but in other ways too both proved their character of strong-men, of invincible heroes and paradigms of force. We shall deal now with two of these aspects that have not been dealt with before in the context of the deeds of a strong-man in the Kṛṣṇa legend. These two common traits of strong-men are: their enormous appetite that permits them to devour big amounts of food, and their powerful virility, mani-

dorus 2.4.12 and Diodorus 4.10.11 for this name, but we are unable to find it there; perhaps he had other sources.

1. Diodorus Siculus, *The Library of History* 4.17.4; tr. C. H. Oldfather, v.2, p. 399.
2. *HV* 79-82; *VP* 5.22-23; *BhP* 10.50.
3. Above, p. 79
4. *Mbh* 2.20.8-9; Fontenrose, *Python*, p. 330.
5. Apollodorus 2.5.11; *Mbh* 2.22.5-7.
6. Apollodorus, *ibid.*

1. Apollodorus, *The Library*, 2.5.10; tr. Frazer, v.1, p.217.
2. Diodorus Siculus, *The Library of History*, 4.23.2; tr. Oldfather, v.2, p. 417.
3. Apollodorus 2.4.9.
4. *Ibid.* 2.4.10.

fested in great sexual potency, that allows them to enjoy numerous women within a short time. Let us consider first this latter trait that in the Kṛṣṇa saga acquires new significance.

The relationship between Kṛṣṇa and the *gopīs* has been generally glossed over by Indian commentators as innocent playfulness and dance, or as unconsummated love, or as purely spiritual symbolism.[1] There are, however, numerous hints and references in the Purāṇas to show the carnal nature of the cowgirls' love for Kṛṣṇa and the sexuality involved in the *rāsa* dance. This dance called *Hallīsaka* in the colophon to the corresponding chapter of the *Harivaṃśa* and also in the *Bālacarita*, is described as the dance of one male with several females (Monier-Williams), and is interpreted by Nīlakaṇṭha the commentator on the *Mahābhārata* thus: 'The sporting of one man with several women is called *rāsa* sport'.[2] Probably, Kakati was not very far off the mark in considering the *rāsa* dance to be connected to an ancient fertility festival such as those performed in many societies.[3] It is hard to tell if Kṛṣṇa was originally associated with the deity of these festivals, but it is not improbable, in view of the explanation of his own name given by Kṛṣṇa in the *Mahābhārata*: 'I plough the earth, O Pārtha, having become a big ploughshare, and since my colour is black, I am, therefore, [called] Kṛṣṇa'.[4] Also if we take into account the description of the dance presented by Nīlakaṇṭha:

> Driving a stout, round and smooth spike of the measure of a *vitasti* [the length between the thumb and the small finger of the extended palm] into the earth, and then moving towards one another with the feet and rotating with the hands—this is the rāsa gathering.[5]

The interest of this verse is in its mention of that round and smooth spike driven into the earth, which is in all likelihood a phallic symbol, and around which the dancers perform their circular movements. In the Purāṇic accounts the *gopīs* dance around Kṛṣṇa, giving him the place of the original phallic symbol.

There is no doubt, however, about the sentiments of the cowherdesses who are deeply in love with the strong and valiant boy living in their village. They love him and admire him, and he has won that admiration through his prowess and feats of strength. The *gopīs* sing his adventures and imitate his deeds, they strike their own arms, as if they had big muscles, mimicking the wrestling attitudes of Kṛṣṇa.[1] When they sing of him they specifically mention him as a wrestler,[2] and it is very obvious that they are in love with the hero figure whom they idolise.

In spite of what they would like to do, the texts cannot gloss over the fact that the *gopīs* wanted to play and dally as much as Kṛṣṇa, to sing, dance and frolic together at night in the forest. The erotic nature of the games and the occasion is always understood. In the *Viṣṇu Purāṇa*, Kṛṣṇa considers the beauty of the full moon night and wants to sport with the *gopīs*,[3] the word here used being *rati* i.e. sexual love. Later in the chapter again this vocabulary is used, proving the nature of those nocturnal games of Kṛṣṇa and the *gopīs*: 'The cowherdesses, fond of [sexual] pleasure, enjoy Kṛṣṇa in the night'.[4] The *Harivaṃśa* equally expresses all the eroticism of those autumn nights when Kṛṣṇa and the *gopīs* gave themselves up to amorous pastimes. It repeats in almost the same words as the *Viṣṇu Purāṇa* that Kṛṣṇa, contemplating the new moon and the beautiful night of autumn, had set his mind on games of love.[5] It also describes in specific terms how they 'afflicted him with their erect breasts'[6] and again echoes the *Viṣṇu Purāṇa*, changing only one word in this line: 'cowherdesses, fond of pleasure, seek for Kṛṣṇa in the night'.[7] The *Harivaṃśa* ends its des-

1. S. K. De, *Early History of the Vaisnava Faith and Movement in Bengal*, K. L. Mukhopadhyay, Calcutta 1961, pp. 348-51; S. C. Chakravarti, *Philosophical Foundation of Bengal Vaisnavism*, Academic, Calcutta 1969, pp. 366-75.
2. ekasya puṃso bahubhiḥ strībhiḥ krīḍanam saiva rāsakrīḍā; in Banikanta Kakati, *Viṣṇuite Myths and Legends*, Tarini Das, Gauhati 1952, p. 41.
3. Kakati, *ibid.*, pp. 47-52 and 76-77.
4. kṛṣāmi medinīm pārtha bhūtvā kārṣṇāyaso mahān / kṛṣṇo varṇaśca me yasmāt tasmāt kṛṣṇo'hamarjuna; *Mbh* 12.330.14
5. pṛthuṃ suvṛttaṃ masṛṇaṃ vitastimātronnataṃ kau vinikhanya śaṅkum / ākramya padbhyāmitaretarantu hastairbhramo'yaṃ khalu rāsagoṣṭhī; in Kakati, *ibid*, p. 41.

1. kṛṣṇalīlānukāriṇyaḥ; *HV* 63-26; vaneṣu tālahastāgraiḥ kuṭṭayantyastathāparāḥ / cerurvai caritaṃ tasya kṛṣṇasya vrajayoṣitāḥ; *HV* 63.27.
2. barhiṇastabakadhātupalāśairbaddhamallaparibarhavidambaḥ / karhicit sabala āli sa gopairgāḥ samāhvayati yatra mukundaḥ; *BhP* 10.35.6.
3. vilokya saha gopībhirmanaścakre ratiṃ prati; *VP* 5.13.25.
4. kṛṣṇaṃ gopāṅganā rātrau ramayanti ratipriyāḥ; *VP* 5.13.59.
5. kṛṣṇastuyauvanāṃ dṛṣṭvā niśi candramaso navam / śāradīnāṃ niśānāṃ ca manaścakre ratiṃ prati; *HV* 63.15.
6. tāstam payodharottānairurobhiḥ samapīḍayan; *HV* 63.23a.
7. kṛṣṇaṃ gopāṅganā rātrau mṛgayanti ratipriyāḥ; *HV* 63.24b.

cription of the rāsa dance episode with this memorable verse: 'Their limbs covered with dust and dry cow-dung, they surround Kṛṣṇa sporting with him, as young female elephants delighted with a male'.[1] These images leave no doubt as to the carnality of the whole episode. As in the biblical *Song of Songs*, we do not deny that the erotic imagery may have, or definitely has, a spiritual and mystic symbolism. That this is so, in the later Kṛṣṇa cult, is out of the question. The words, however, are there, and they have a profane meaning also, a meaning more immediate and evident, and since we are dealing with the stories as such, and not as mystical allegories, this is the meaning narratively pertinent.

The eroticism keeps appearing in the *Bhāgavata Purāṇa*, if possible in clearer terms, although at the same time the religious symbolism is also stressed more and more. It states that the *gopīs* looked upon Kṛṣṇa 'only as a lover'.[2] Also, that 'they considered Kṛṣṇa as their dearest lover, and not as Brahman, O Muni'.[3] When Kṛṣṇa is pretending to want to dissuade them from their assignation he refers to it as *aupapatyam* i.e. 'adultery or intercourse with a paramour',[4] and the *gopīs*, for their part, acknowledge that they are going astray, but they argue: 'What woman in the three worlds would not swerve from pure conduct, as long as she is deluded by your soft melody?'[5] and later: 'The Lord of the lords of yoga, having heard their lamenting, smiling compassionately, though delighting [only] in [his own divine] self, gave intense delight to the *gopīs*'.[6]

Finally, the *Bhāgavata* describes, in more specific terms than any used until then, the dalliance of the hero and the cowgirls:

> By stretching his arms and embracing them, by caressing their hands and hair, their thighs, waists and breasts, by pleasing them with strokes of his fingernails, by his games, glances and smiles, Kṛṣṇa aroused the lust of the beauties of Vraja and made love to them.[7]

1. *HV* 63.30; karīṣapāṃsudigdhāṅgyastāḥ kṛṣṇamanuvavrire / ramayantyo yathā nāgaṃ sapramodāḥ kareṇavaḥ //
2. jārabuddhyāpi; *BhP* 10.29.11.
3. *BhP* 10.29.12. Kṛṣṇaṃ viduḥ paraṃ kāntaṃ na tu brahmatayā mune.
4. *BhP* 10.29.26.
5. kā stryaṅga te kalapadāyatamūrcchitena saṃmohitāryacaritānna calettrilokyām; *BhP* 10.29.40.
6. iti viklavitaṃ tāsāṃ śrutvā yogeśvareśvaraḥ / prahasya sadayam gopīrātmāramo'pyarīramat; *BhP* 10.29.42 (tr. A.L Basham).
7. *BhP* 10.29.46; bāhuprasāraparirambhakarālakorunīvīstanālabhananarmanakhāgrapātaiḥ / kṣvelyā'valokahasitairvrajasundarīṇāmuttambhayan ratipatiṃ ramayāṃcakāra //

The *Bhāgavata* does not reach the excesses of the *Brahmavaivarta Purāṇa*,[1] where Kṛṣṇa makes love to nine hundred thousand *gopīs*, using expertly all the arts of the Kāma Śāstra.[2]

All this goes to show that actually there is clear textual evidence on the amorous encounters of Kṛṣṇa and the cowherdesses. The stressing of this fact seems to be necessary in view of the numerous denials of it.[3] The point is not made, but it is clear that Kṛṣṇa, the hero, was able to sexually satisfy a great number of women in a short period, and this is one of the typical processes of the archetypal strong man. This we can show by quoting the accounts on the intercourse of Heracles and the daughters of Thespius, a king whose numerous cattle had been saved by Heracles from a lion:

> Now this Thespius was king of Thespiae, and Hercules went to him when he wished to catch the lion. The king entertained him for fifty days, and each night, as Hercules went forth to the hunt, Thespius bedded one of his daughters with him; ... for he was anxious that all of them should have children by Hercules. Thus Hercules, though he thought that his bed-fellow was always the same, had intercourse with them all.[4]

Diodorus Siculus brings the account closer to the Kṛṣṇa legend by stating that Heracles was at the time still a boy:

> When Heracles was still a boy, but already of extraordinary strength of body, the king strongly desired that his daughters should bear children by him. Consequently he invited Heracles to a sacrifice, and after entertaining him in brilliant fashion,

1. *BVP* 4.28.
2. The *Brahmavaivarta Purāṇa*, tr. R. N. Sen, SBH, v.24, Pāṇini Office, Allahabad 1922, v.2, pp. 229-35; "At the commencement of the sexual intercourse, in the middle and in the end, Lord Kṛṣṇa performed the incidental acts connected with the intercourse for the satisfaction of the girls in a manner better than that prescribed by the sexual science.' *Ibid.*, p. 233; nirūpitaṃ kāmaśāstre cakāreṣastato'dhikam / krīḍārambhe ca madhye ca viratau karma yoṣitām; *BVP* 4.28.113, ed. Jīvānanda Vidyasāgara, Calcutta 1888, v.2, p. 336.
3. Strangely enough for a trait so prominent in the Kṛṣṇa legend, there is not much iconographical evidence on the sports of Kṛṣṇa and the *gopīs* previous to the tenth century. In pl. 47 we present the only undisputable image of it. There is however one inscription of the 7th-8th centuries that refers to a 'maker of images of Kṛṣṇa and the Gopīs'. G. Bühler, 'Further Pabhosa Inscriptions', *EI*, v.2, p. 482.
4. Apollodorus, 2.4.10; tr. Frazer.

he sent his daughters one by one in to him; and Heracles lay with them all, brought them all with child, and so became the father of fifty sons.[1]

Other points of similarity can be found here. In the case of Kṛṣṇa, the episode occurs in a dance that is a sort of a festival, while in the case of Heracles, it happens at a sacrifice where he is entertained 'in brilliant fashion', most probably with songs and music. Contrasting points are that the *gopīs* are prohibited by their relatives from attending their tryst with Kṛṣṇa while the daughters of Thespius are prompted by their father to go and lie with the hero. But, like the rest of Heracles' prowess, this feat is related to show the extraordinary strength and endurance that he had. Oldfather gives a note that we can add here:

> This was done, according to some ancient writers, on fifty successive nights; according to others, on seven nights, when seven daughters lay with Heracles each night, one refusing and being sentenced by him to lifelong maidenhood. But some writers ... state that this deed was accomplished by Heracles in one night and counted as his thirteenth Labour.[2]

Besides this episode with the daughters of Thespius, one other side of Heracles may be brought here to show a parallel to the rāsa dance of Kṛṣṇa. Karl Galinsky in his admirable study, *The Herakles Theme*, studies a poem, attributed to Hesiod, called the shield of Heracles. Among other things Galinsky says: 'Wrestlers and boxers are represented, too, and Heracles was of course their patron. The athletes' endeavour is skilfully likened to Heracles.'[3] A little later, however, he adds that the poem: 'shows an early awareness of Heracles' softer and aesthetic side, which was to continue until it found its most striking expression in the figure of Hercules Musarum or Musagetes, Leader of the Muses, in Hellenistic and Roman times.' This informs us that Heracles was also in close relation to the nine Muses, the goddesses of the arts, who used to dance a circular dance around Apollo, and, in all probability, also around Heracles.

Kṛṣṇa's sexual prowess was not performed only for the benefit of the *gopīs*. Other women, and also divine beings, had the fortune to enjoy his incomparable charm and dexterity in amorous matters. The *Kūrma Purāṇa* relates how once Kṛṣṇa went to the Himālaya, to do penance in order to obtain a son from Jāmbavatī, one of his wives, and at her request. There, after meeting Śiva and Pārvatī and numerous speeches of mutual praise, he proceeded to Mount Kailāśa and:

> It so happened that once Kṛṣṇa, the increaser of Devakī's joy, resplendent with grace, moved about the caves in the hill for the purpose of sporting. Seeing him, the all-pervading one, the daughters of Gandharvas-Apsarases, the chiefs among the princesses of the Nāgas (serpent-Kings), and all the Siddhas, Yakṣas and Gandharvas, grew highly delighted and with eyes gazing with pleasure, they showered flowers over the head of that illustrious one. The Gandharva maidens, and the best of the celestial nymphs, with garments and ornaments slipping down from their bodies, felt a keen desire for Kṛṣṇa. One beautiful woman, proficient in music, began singing various songs of Devakī. Some other damsels took off the excellent ornaments from their own bodies and decorated the body of Kṛṣṇa, the ornament of the world with them. Others took off the ornaments from his body and decorated their own limbs with them while ornamenting Mādhava with their own ones. Some of them, fawn-eyed and infatuated with lust, approached Kṛṣṇa, and kissed the lotus-like lips of Hari. Some of them, being utterly lost in his enchantment, held Govinda by the hand and forcibly led him, the source of the world, to their dwelling abode. By assuming many forms sportingly, Lord Kṛṣṇa, the lotus-eyed one, fulfilled their desire. In this way, casting a spell on the world, Lord Hari, Nārāyaṇa, sported for a long time in the city of the god of gods.[1]

This description shows the image of Kṛṣṇa that, indeed, had come to be proverbial: the great lover, the supremely attractive man. That this is so is shown simply by the fact that this passage is included in the *Kūrma Purāṇa* without any narrative, mythological or religious justification, and evidently just to bring out a salient characteristic in the divine personality.

1. *Diodorus* 4.29.3; tr. Oldfather. A similar story is told about Samson, the strong-man of the Jews. The Talmud interprets this line of the book of Judges 'And he did grind in the prison house' (*Judges* 16.21) as : 'It teaches that everyone brought his wife to him to the prison that she might bear a child by him [who would be as strong as he was]'. *soṭah* 10.a, tr. A. Cohen, p. 45, in *The Babylonian Talmud*, ed. by I. Epstein, v.3, pt. 3, Soncino Press, London 1936.

2. C. H. Oldfather, Diodorus of Sicily, *The Library of History*, Harvard University Press, 1961, v.2, pp. 434-35.

3. Galinsky, *The Heracles Theme*, p. 18.

1. *Kūrma Purāṇa*, 1.25.6-17; tr. A. Bhattacharya, All-India Kashi Raj Trust, Varanasi, 1972, pp. 182-83.

That this aspect of Kṛṣṇa is chosen to characterise him, and not any of his other feats of strength, shows how deeply in the popular mind Kṛṣṇa had been identified with amorous sports with a number of women simultaneously. Differently from Heracles, however, and representing one of the big differences between the two heroes and their particular position in the mythology and religion of their respective countries, Kṛṣṇa does not, as a regular strong-man, take the women successively in a long, intense, bout of love, but, as the supreme god that he is, magically divides himself in many exact doubles, and in this way thoroughly satisfies all the ladies at the same time.[1] This trick takes from the episodes of Kṛṣṇa's loves much of that quality of prowess of strength, of monumental endurance, that the feat of Heracles possesses. On the other hand the erotic multiplication of Kṛṣṇa takes him from the level of a simple strong-man—a Bhīma for example—to that of the Cosmic and Universal god that he is in Indian Mythology. That is the difference between Kṛṣṇa and Heracles. Although the latter is the son of a god, and is finally divinised throughout his career, he is just a strong-man, a hero of superhuman strength, but no more than this. On the other hand, Kṛṣṇa is God, he takes human form and is also a strong-man and a hero, but, foremost, he is still God and keeps manifesting this fact throughout his life. In all the accounts of Kṛṣṇa's life there is this ambivalence in the depiction of the hero, a human strong-man that is probably the original figure, but also God himself. This ambivalence takes much of the force of a legend that otherwise could be the straightforward saga of a powerful hero, but, at the same time, gives to this saga a religious meaning that has converted it into one of the strongest of spiritual forces in India.

The multiplication of Kṛṣṇa for erotic purposes is just one more of his manifestations as the Cosmic deity some of which we have already reviewed.[2] It also appears in the accounts of the rāsa dance episode, where Kṛṣṇa actually multiplies himself in order to sport individually with each one of the *gopīs*. H.H. Wilson, in his translation of the *Viṣṇu Purāṇa*, furnishes the following note:

> Kṛṣṇa, it is said, in order to form the circle, takes each damsel by the hand, and leads her to her place: there he quits her; but the effect of the contact is such, that it deprives her of the power of perception, and she contentedly takes the hand of her female neighbour, thinking it to be Kṛṣṇa's. The *Bhāgavata* is bolder and asserts that Kṛṣṇa multiplied himself, and actually stood between each two damsels: *rāsotsavaḥ sampravṛtto gopīmaṇḍalamaṇḍitaḥ / yogeśvareṇa tāsāṃ madhye dvayordvayo praviṣṭena iti* // "the Rāsa dance, formed of a circle graced by the Gopīs, was then led by the Lord of magic, Kṛṣṇa having placed himself in the midst of every two of the nymphs." The *Harivaṃśa* intimates the same, though not very fully: *tāstu paṃktīkṛtāḥ sarvā ramayanti manoramaṃ gāyantyaḥ kṛṣṇacaritaṃ dvandvaśo gopakanyakāḥ* / "then all the nymphs of the cowherds, placing themselves in couples in a row, engaged in pleasant diversion, singing the deeds of Kṛṣṇa." The Paṃkti, or row is said by the commentator to mean here the Maṇḍala, or ring; and the "couples" to imply that Kṛṣṇa was between every two.[1]

From this note we can see that the magical multiplication was not originally a part of the episode and that it came later as part of the process that converted Kṛṣṇa from a folk-hero into the Supreme God. This process reaches its culminating point in the *Bhāgavata Purāṇa*, and there occurs an episode that is related to both the themes we are dealing with now, namely, the satisfaction of many women at once, and the magic multiplication of the hero. It is said that after the battle between Kṛṣṇa and the demon Naraka, our hero took with him the sixteen thousand women kept by that monster at his palace in Kāmarūpa.

Kṛṣṇa wedded all of these ladies and went to live with them in Dvārakā. He built for each one a beautiful palace so that there would be no jealousies and quarrelling in his household. But the sage Nārada was curious to know how Kṛṣṇa was faring and how he, with only one body, had married sixteen thousand women.[2] So he went to meet him in the company of Rukmiṇī, Kṛṣṇa's principal wife. After a short

1. bahūni kṛtvā rūpāṇi pūrayāmāsa līlayā; *KP* 1.25.16.
2. See above, pp. 73-78.

1. H. H. Wilson, *The Vishnu Purana*, p. 425, n.3; the verses quoted being respectively *BhP* 10.33.3, and *HV* 63.25; the mystical symbolism of the various versions is fairly clear. In the *VP* version each Gopī finds God in her human neighbour, whom she loves as God. In the *BhP* God is actually beside her in all his fullness. God, being infinite, can divide himself infinitely and every part is also infinite.

2. narakaṃ nihataṃ śrutvā tathodvāhaṃ ca yoṣitām / kṛṣṇenaikena bahvīnāṃ tad didṛkṣuḥ sma nāradaḥ // citraṃ bataitadekena vapuṣā yugapat pṛthak / gṛheṣu dvyaṣṭasāhasraṃ striya eka udāvahat; *BhP* 10.69.1-2.

complimentary conversation, Nārada proceeded to another of Kṛṣṇa's palaces, and there he saw him again with another of his wives. Astonished, Nārada went to another palace just to see Kṛṣṇa with yet another wife and engaged in a different occupation. In that manner Nārada visited many of the palaces and in each one he met Kṛṣṇa with a happy wife and dedicated to numerous activities, among them, notably, sporting amorously in the water with several courtesans.[1] The *Bhāgavata* here presents Kṛṣṇa as the divine prototype of the householder. If Śiva is the ascetic by antonomasia, Kṛṣṇa is the householder *par excellence* in this episode of the *Bhāgavata*.[2] As every householder he is naturally dedicated to the three aims of life: *Dharma*, *Artha* and *Kāma*.[3] This is the apparent purpose of this episode, to show Kṛṣṇa's married life, but at the same time the other two purposes of the tale are discernible: to show his Cosmic manifestation at work, and lastly, to show how the hero was capable of satisfying even sixteen thousand wives. We can see how this motif has been transformed in the Kṛṣṇa legend from a mere feat of endurance, to acquire religious and moral significance.

To come again to the 'strong-man' element, we may now consider the other trait of this stock character that we have referred to already: the enormous appetite of the athlete and the extraordinary amount of food and drink that he is capable of consuming. A voracious appetite is a characteristic attribute of strong-men everywhere. One of the epithets addressed to mighty heroes in Sanskrit is *vṛkodara*, i.e. 'wolf's belly', and Bhīma, the strong-man of the *Mahābhārata*, is constantly referred to by this adjective. He is, in fact, several times mentioned as eating excessive quantities of food. When the five Pāṇḍava brothers were in exile, Kuntī, their mother, would divide whatever food they had gathered during the day and give the larger part of this to Bhīma since he, as a strong man, needed it more than the rest.[4] In the Germanic Mythology also, heroes are remarkable for their ability to devour enormous amounts of food and drink even larger quantities of beer. For instance, we have the example of Loki and Thor who once went to the country of the giants and there entered into a contest with them:

> Loki first stepped forward. He boasted of his prowess in eating much and quickly. The king gave him the giant Logi for an opponent. The two contestants were served with vast quarters of meat on plates as big as vats. In a brief space of time Loki had eaten all his meat, leaving behind nothing but bones. But his adversary had, in the meantime, gulped down both meat and bones, and the plate as well ... At last it was Thor's turn to show his skill. No one, he declared with complete assurance, could drink as much or as quickly as he. Utgardloki then sent for the horn which the warriors of his establishment were accustomed to empty in one, or at the most, two draughts. Thor seized the drinking horn and once, twice, thrice took long, deep draughts. But when he put it down again, the level of the liquid was scarcely lower than when he had begun.[1]

Here, although the heroes lost the contest because of magic, it is shown that a great eating and drinking capacity was considered one of a strong-man's qualities. Similarly, Heracles was famous for his tremendous appetite; he was even called Buphagus, or 'Ox-eater'. This account is given by Graves:

> About this time, Heracles won his title of Buphagus, or 'Ox-eater'. It happened as follows. Lepreus ... had foolishly advised king Augeias to fetter Heracles when he asked to be paid for having cleansed the cattle-yards. Hearing that Heracles was on his way to the city, Astydameia persuaded Lepreus to receive him courteously and plead for forgiveness. This Heracles granted, but challenged Lepreus to a triple contest: of throwing the discus, drinking bucket after bucket of water, and eating an ox. Then though Heracles won the discus-throw and the drinking-match, Lepreus ate the ox in less time than he. Flushed with success, he challenged Heracles to a duel, and was at once clubbed to death.[2]

That Heracles actually challenged Lepreus to an eating and drinking contest shows how confident he was in these capacities. As early as Hesiod his enormous appetite was already well known and used as one of the main subjects in a poetical work by that bard:

> Being close to the people as he was, Hesiod also portrayed Heracles as the folksy, jolly good fellow.

1. jalakrīḍāratam kvāpi vāramukhyābalāvṛtam; *BhP* 10.69.27.
2. ityācarantaṃ saddharmān pāvanān gṛhamedhinām / tameva sarvageheṣu santamekaṃ dadarśa ha; *BhP* 10.69.41.
3. kvāpi dharmaṃ sevamānamarthakāmau ca kutracit; *BhP* 10.69.29.
4. *Mbh* 1.145.5.

1. E. Tonnelat, 'Teutonic Mythology', in *New Larousse Encyclopedia of Mythology*, Hamlyn, London 1974, pp. 264-65.
2. R. Graves, *The Greek Myths*, Penguin, Harmondsworth, 1974, v.2, pp. 177-78.

The few fragments that have been preserved of the Wedding of Ceyx give us some indication of this. One of the main subjects of the poem was the wedding-feast of Ceyx and Alcyone at which Heracles intervened. He crashed the party, justifying himself with jovial magnificence: "Of their own accord good men betake themselves to good men's feasts". This phrase became so proverbial that it was quoted, among others, by Plato in the *Symposium*. ... Much of the rest of the poem seems to have been concerned with Heracles' prodigious appetite, a theme on which the comic poets were to seize with so much glee.[1]

Galinsky dedicates a whole chapter of his book to 'The Comic Hero', and there he shows how that trait of the strong man, that is in other cultures treated seriously and just as one more among the qualities of the hero, was used in Greece by the satirical dramatists as a device to raise laughter. 'The multitude of pertinent fragments from the entire range of Greek comedy, Old, Middle and New, associate Heracles with seemingly endless gluttony.' And also: 'There are countless variations on the stock theme of Heracles the glutton.'[2] In the case of Kṛṣṇa the motif of the hero's great appetite is not so prominent but there is at least one instance that we can adduce to show this trait of the strong man present in his legends. Curiously, as it happened with Heracles, this fact led to disparagement and vituperation. In the *Mahābhārata*, when Śiśupāla is vilifying Kṛṣṇa in front of all the kings in the royal hall of Yudhiṣṭhira, he mentions that episode, which does not reflect Kṛṣṇa's best image: 'When we hear from you, Bhīṣma, that he ate a lot of food while playing on a mountain top, you astound us the more.'[3] Śiśupāla is, of course, referring to the Govardhana episode.

It is said in the *Harivaṃśa* and the Purāṇas that once when the cowherds were preparing themselves to celebrate a festival in honour of Indra, Kṛṣṇa dissuaded them from proceeding with it, and instead convinced them that they should worship Mount Govardhana.[4] In a discourse referring to the duties of the different orders of society he asserts that each profession should worship its own means of subsistence; since the cowherds wander in the forests and the cows are their wealth and living, they should consider the cows, the mountains and the forests as their deities.[1] The *gopas* agree to this and decide to start a new cult to the mountain. The chief feature of this worship of Govardhana was to be the presentation of great quantities of food, and the cowherds mention in detail what delicacies they would prepare to offer in the *giriyajña*,[2] showing the importance given to food in the cult implemented by Kṛṣṇa. But what Śiśupāla was referring to in his tirade against Kṛṣṇa, was the fact that it was finally Kṛṣṇa who ate all those viands presented by the cowherds. The *Ghaṭa Jātaka* and the *Bālacarita* do not include the Govardhana episode and the *Devī Bhāgavata Purāṇa* does not expatiate on it, but our other three sources all agree in the details of the incident. The *Viṣṇu Purāṇa* gives the shortest reference; it says that on the top of the mountain Kṛṣṇa said 'I am the mountain', and taking that form he ate the great quantities of food offered by the *gopas*, and at the same time in his own form as Kṛṣṇa he went with the cowherds to the summit of Govardhana and paid homage to his second self.[3] The *Harivaṃśa* says that at the end of the ceremony Kṛṣṇa, becoming the mountain by his *māyā*, ate all that food and the milk, curds and best of meats, and that having eaten his fill and drunk milk to his satisfaction, he said 'I am satisfied', and smiled with his divine form.[4] The *Bhāgavata*, being a later work, dispenses with any references to meat, and there Kṛṣṇa enjoins the cowherds to offer the mountain, i.e. to himself, an exclusively vegetarian feast.[5] Besides this difference, however, the *Bhāgavata* follows the other two texts in its account of how Kṛṣṇa transformed himself in the mountain taking a divine form, and how in that shape he ate all of the food offerings.[6]

1. G. K. Galinsky, *The Heracles Theme*, pp. 16-17.
2. Galinsky, *ibid.*, p. 91.
3. bhuktametena bahvannaṃ krīḍatā nagamūrdhani / iti te bhīṣma śṛṇvānāḥ paraṃ vismayamāgatāḥ; *Mbh* 2.38.10; tr. van Buitenen.
4. *HV* 59-60; *VP* 5.10; *BhP* 10.24.

1. vayaṃ vanacarā gopa gopā godhanajīvinaḥ / gāvo'smaddaivataṃ viddhi girayaśca vanāni ca; HV 59.20.
2. bhojanānyupakalpyantāṃ payasaḥ peśalāni ca / kumbhāśca viniveśyantāmudapāneṣu śobhanāḥ/lehyasya pāyasasyārthe droṇyaśca vipulāyatāḥ // bhakṣyaṃ bhojyaṃ ca peyaṃ ca tatsarvamupanīyatām / bhājanāni ca māṃsasya nyasyantāmodanasya ca; *HV* 60.11-12ab.
3. girimūrdhani kṛṣṇo'pi śailo'hamiti mūrtimān / bubhuje'nnam bahutaraṃ gopavaryāhṛtam dvija // svenaiva kṛṣṇo rupeṇa gopaissaha gireśśiraḥ / adhiruhyārcayāmāsa dvitīyāmātmanastanum; *VP* 5.10.47-48.
4. yajanānte tadannaṃ tu tatpayo dadhi cottamam / māṃsaṃ ca māyayā kṛṣṇo girirbhūtvā samaśnute //....bhuktvā cavabhṛthe kṛṣṇaḥ payaḥ pītvā ca kāmataḥ / saṃtṛpto'smīti divyena rūpeṇa prajahāsa vai; *HV* 60.18 and 20.
5. pacyantāṃ vividhāḥ pākāḥ sūpāntāḥ pāyasādayaḥ / saṃyāvāpūpasaṣkulyaḥ sarvadohaśca gṛhyatām; *BhP* 10.24-26.
6. kṛṣṇastvanyatamaṃ rūpaṃ gopaviśrambhaṇaṃ gataḥ /

The Govardhana festival is celebrated up to this day in North India by shaping a mass of cowdung mixed with milk into the figure of Kṛṣṇa as the mountain, and offering to this image big amounts of food that afterwards will be eaten by the people of the house.[1] We are not concerned here with the anthropological side of that festival; what we want is simply to emphasise the presence in the Kṛṣṇa cycle of a motif prevalent in legends of other hero figures characterised also as strong men. Perhaps not directly related, but still with some significance in this context, we can remember that Kṛṣṇa was from his very early days notorious for his appetite, that he used to satiate by stealing foodstuffs from his own house and those of the neighbours.[2] In the Govardhana episode it is said that he also drank a lot of milk, but drinking of intoxicating beverages was not one of Kṛṣṇa's outstanding traits, although during the last episode of his life, when he exterminates the race of the Yādavas, he is drunk. His brother Balarāma, on the other hand, being also a strong-man figure, was notable for his drinking capacities, reminding us in this of that first of Indian strong men, Indra, who was also a remarkable drinker.

With this we can leave this theme of the hero as a great eater and continue with his regular prowess as a strong man. We come now to Kṛṣṇa's supreme feat of strength, the one that comes from the incident we have just related: his lifting of Mount Govardhana. Kṛṣṇa, and the other strong men, realised many marvellous deeds of strength, but it is obvious that none of them can be compared as a paramount proof of might and power to the uprooting and lifting of a mountain. This must be the most outstanding deed of prowess of any strong man, and it is because of this that Kṛṣṇa's most popular image was precisely that as *Govardhanadhārī*.[3] This feat of tearing mountains apart and lifting them is not new in Indian mythology. In the *Ṛg Veda* Indra is said to have cleaved asunder a big rock,[4] and, in what is more reminiscent of Heracles, to have sustained the sky,[1] and to keep apart heaven and earth.[2]

Closer to Kṛṣṇa we have the account of the gods and demons uprooting Mount Mandara to use it as a churning rod in the search for the lost earth, and Viṣṇu lifting it up for them when they were crushed by its weight.[3] We have also the *Rāmāyaṇa* account of Hanumān uprooting one of the Himalayan peaks and transporting it all the way to Laṅkā,[4] and finally there is another monkey, one that seems to be the evil counterpart of Hanumān as a strong-man figure, Dvivida, who used to uproot mountains and crush villages with them[5] before being killed by Balarāma. As we can see there are antecedents to Kṛṣṇa's lifting Govardhana, and all of them appear as examples of the supernatural might and force of a hero or strong-man figure.

The story goes that after Kṛṣṇa had stopped the sacrifice to Indra and enjoyed the offerings that were to have been given to that god and were now given to the mountain, Indra, full of anger, decided to teach Kṛṣṇa and the cowherds a lesson, and show them that they could not slight him and go without punishment. So the chief of the gods sent torrential rains that poured down over the *gopas*' village. The dreadful storm raged interminably and men and animals alike suffered greatly. The cows especially were afflicted by the long and hard rain, and they implored Kṛṣṇa to save them.[6] It is curious to note that only after this plea of the cows did Kṛṣṇa decide to take action and uproot the mountain in order to cover with it the cows and the cowherds, thus protecting them from the rain.[7] 'Having thought thus, that Viṣṇu whose deeds of valour are true, to show the force of his arms on that occasion, Kṛṣṇa, like another mountain, uprooted the nearby mountain with his arms.'[8] Here we can see by that phrase 'to show the strength of his arms', *bāhvorbalaṃ darśayiṣyan*, that this prowess of lifting a mountain is a proof of strength, in fact, the supreme feat of strength for the mighty champion. The *Bhāgavata Purāṇa* adds to

śailo'smīti bruvan bhūri balimādad bṛhadvapuḥ; *BhP* 10.24.35. This follows the doctrine of the *Bhagavad Gītā*. Whatever god a man may worship, Kṛṣṇa receives his offerings and answers his prayers, because Kṛṣṇa IS the god worshipped. All gods whatever, are in fact Kṛṣṇa.

1. Ch. Vaudeville, 'The Govardhan Myth in North India', *IIJ*, v.22, 1980, pp.1-35, esp. 2-5; J. S. Hawley, 'Krishna's Cosmic Victories', *JAAR*, v.47, 1979, pp. 201-21.
2. See above, p. 69, and plates 7, 30, 46 and 53.
3. See plates 6, 7, 10, 15, 16, 17, 19, 22, 27, 33, 34, 36, 44, 49, 51 & 52.
4. *RV* 5.30.4.

1. *RV* 2.17.5.
2. *RV* 10.89.4.
3. *BhP* 8.6.33-39.
4. *Ram.* 6. 74.
5. *VP* 5.36.6; *BhP* 10.67.4.
6. trāhīti vadanairdīnaiḥ kṛṣṇamūcurivārtavat; *HV* 61.24.
7. ayaṃ dhṛto mayā śailo bhumīgṛhanibhopamaḥ / trāsyante savrajā gāvo madvaśyaśca bhaviṣyati; *HV* 61.28.
8. *HV* 61.29; evaṃ sa cintayitvā tu viṣṇuḥ satyaparākramaḥ/ bāhvorbalaṃ darśayiṣyansamīpaṃ taṃ mahīdharam / dorbhyāmutpāṭayāmāsa kṛṣṇo giririvāparaḥ //

this description of a marvellous deed, that Kṛṣṇa did it with one hand only and playfully, as a child holds up a small umbrella[1].

For seven days and nights Kṛṣṇa held the mountain aloft protecting the cows and the people from the rains sent by Indra to destroy them, and finally the latter realised that he could not harm them and ordered the rain to stop.[2] Several interpretations have been given of this episode, like the one that finds in it evidence of the supplanting of the Indra-cult by the Kṛṣṇa-cult,[3] or the one that sees in it a motif describing the establishment of order in the cosmos, a motif that can be interpreted psychoanalytically.[4] We are not concerned here with this kind of interpretation; probably they all have a certain amount of truth. What we are chiefly interested in is in the stories as such, in the narrative itself and in the themes and motifs that compound it. From that point of view the lifting of the mountain is extremely important, being one of the main motifs in the themes of the strong man, a series that has not been considered in relation to Kṛṣṇa and that can, as we see, account for most of the episodes in the life of the hero. That this episode forms a central image in the career of Kṛṣṇa is shown by the number of sculptural representations of it that we find even as far as South East Asia. It is common sense to think that what the general public saw in these images was not the supplanting of Indra's cult or the ordering of the cosmos but the feat of the strongest man in the world, a Hercules or a Samson.[5] Unlike the other episodes in the legend, this one was represented in larger size, reaching on occasions monumental proportions (see plates 16 and 36), this again demonstrating its importance.

1. ityuktvaikena hastena kṛtvā govardhanācalam / dadhāra līlayā kṛṣṇaschatrākamiva bālakaḥ; *BhP* 10.25.19.

2. saptarātraṃ mahāmeghā vavarṣurnandagokule / indreṇa coditā vipra gopānāṃ nāśakāriṇā // tato dhṛte mahāśaile paritrāte ca gokule / mithyāpratijño balabhidvārayamāsa tāṅghanān; *VP* 5.11.22-23.

3. O. C. Gangoly, 'Indra-Cult versus Kṛṣṇa Cult', *JGJRI*, v.7, 1949, pp. 1-27.

4. J. S. Hawley, 'Krishna's Cosmic Victory', *JAAR*, v.47, 1979; 'Indra, as captain of the gods who dwells in the regions above, shows that religion, insofar as it involves the world of projection and the imagination, can be just as dangerous if it is unmoored. In the Govardhana story Krishna stabilizes this realm, holding it at a proper distance but anchoring it to earth and making explicit the tie that binds humanity to the symbolic configuration it projects', p. 211; although it is hard to understand exactly what this passage means.

5. Although the supplanting is surely also reflected in the story.

As we have said already, this motif is not new in Indian mythology, and neither is it in other mythologies. We find similar feats performed by other strong men in other countries. Samson's destruction of the temple of Dagon, an image of the world mountain, is related to it, but, more important, we have the same theme in the legend of Heracles. There are three instances in the stories of Heracles that we can bring in relation to this motif. The first one is the erection of the Pillars of Heracles, the two rocks on each side of the Strait of Gibraltar, which, according to some authorities, he opened by his might to join the two oceans. Being in this case an example of the cleaving of the mountain as Indra did. According to others, however, what he did was to narrow the pass between the two oceans so that monsters would not enter the Mediterranean. In this latter case his feat forms an example of the lifting and transporting of the mountain.[1] The second example of the motif is in the episode of the fight with Antaeus that we have quoted already (see above p. 83). This giant was a son of the earth, i.e. a mountain, according to Lucan, that got his strength by contact with his mother, and so Heracles had to kill him when he was lifted in the air. Sir J.G. Frazer gives in his edition and translation of Apollodorus a note that provides a remarkable coincidence with the Govardhana episode:

> Antaeus is said to have reigned in Western Morocco, on the Atlantic coast. Here a hillock was pointed out as his tomb, and the natives believed that the removal of soil from the hillock would be immediately followed by rain, which would not cease till the earth was replaced.[2]

The third example of the motif in the Heracles legend is the sustaining of the vault of heaven, replacing Atlas for a moment while the latter went to fetch the apples of the Hesperides for Heracles.[3] This event, as in the case of Kṛṣṇa's supporting mount Govardhana, was one of the most popular episodes of the Heracles' stories, representing very clearly his formidable strength, and was often depicted in sculpture, as in the famous relief from the temple of Zeus at Olympia, dating from the fifth century B.C. There are other parallels here with Kṛṣṇa besides the obvi-

1. See Dio. 4.18.5; Frazer, *The Library of Apollodorus* v.1, p. 212, n. 1.

2. J. G. Frazer, *The Library of Apollodorus* , v.1, p. 223, n.2; see also Fontenrose, *Python*, p. 331, n. 15.

3. Apo. 2.5.11.

ous one of the lifting of the mountain in one case, of the sky in the other. In the cases of both Heracles and Kṛṣṇa, we have an opposition and confrontation of a new strong man coming to supplant the previous type-figure in his pre-eminence as strong man *par excellence*. In the case of Kṛṣṇa, Indra is explicitly irritated at Kṛṣṇa's taking away from him the offerings of the cowherds. In the case of Heracles we cannot see a conflict of cult since Heracles, unlike Kṛṣṇa, was normally looked on as an extraordinary hero and never attained the position of supreme god as did Kṛṣṇa. However, we can still see the confrontation of the new and the old type-figures of the strong man, in both cases represented by the supreme feat of strength. We can note here that Atlas is also considered as being a mountain. So, in this case we would see Heracles actually substituting or taking the place of the mountain which would bring us even closer to the Kṛṣṇa episode, where it is specifically stated that Kṛṣṇa took the shape of the mountain divinity.

We end this account of the lifting of the mountain motif by looking at another episode in the story of Kṛṣṇa that has some resemblance to it, and that at the same time will lead us to our next section: the slaying of the dragon. This is the episode of the killing of Aghāsura, related only in the *Bhāgavata Purāṇa*. The tale goes that once when the cow-boys were in the forest grazing the calves and having great fun with games and pranks, a demon sent by Kaṃsa came there to kill Kṛṣṇa and disguised himself to look like a mountain:

> Having made up his mind thus, the wicked demon assumed a gigantic body of a python one *yojana* in length and stout like a big mountain, and with a desire to swallow them all, he lay motionless on their path, with his terrifying cave-like mouth kept wide open.
>
> His lower lip lay on the earth, while the upper lip touched the clouds; the mouth between them appeared like a vale; his fangs were like summits of mountains, and the interior part of his mouth was full of darkness; his tongue was like a broad road; his breath was like a tempestuous blast, while his enraged red-hot eyes were like a forest conflagration.[1]

In that shape the cowboys saw the monster and took him for a mountain naturally resembling the form of a giant snake with open mouth. They thought those enormous gaping jaws to be just a cave and playfully they decided to enter into it. All the boys and the calves, among much merriment, marched in, only Kṛṣṇa staying outside, since he knew the true nature of the demon and was unable to prevent the children in time. At last he decided to enter also in order to rescue them, causing shouts of despair from the gods and of delight from the demons who were all observing the incident:

> Hearing those [cries and shouts of joy], the Imperishable glorious Lord Kṛṣṇa instantly increased himself in huge dimensions into the throat of that demon who desired to crush to powder Kṛṣṇa along with children and calves.
>
> All the passage of breath of that huge-bodied monster was choked, and his eyes shot out of their sockets. He was writhing on all sides. His breath being completely obstructed in his lungs, forced its way out through his head.
>
> When all the vital breaths of the demon passed out that way, Lord Kṛṣṇa revived to life with his nectarine look, all his friends and calves who were as good as dead, and came out of the mouth of the demon again, along with them.[1]

Here we have again that motif of the cleaving of the mountain found in the myths of Indra. Indra also tore asunder a big rock and rescued, presumably from inside, the cows (*aśmānaṃ cicchavasā didyuto vi vido gavām ūrvam usriyāṇām*; *RV* 5.30.4b). In an Epic version of the myth of the battle of Indra against Vṛtra we have a second parallel with the Aghāsuravadha. Sent by Tvaṣṭā to kill Indra, Vṛtra went to heaven and:

> Thereupon there occurred a most gruesome and protracted battle between the raging Vṛtra and Vāsava, O best of the Kurus. The heroic Vṛtra

1. *BhP* 10.12.16-17; iti vyavasyājagaraṃ bṛhad vapuḥ sayojanāyāmamahādripīvaram / dhṛtvādbhutaṃ vyāttaguhānanaṃ tadā pathi vyaśeta grasanāśayā khalaḥ // dharādharoṣṭho jaladottaroṣṭho daryānanānto giriśṛṅgadaṃṣṭraḥ / dhvāntāntarāsyo vitatādhvajihvaḥ paruṣānilaśvasadavekṣaṇoṣṇaḥ; tr. G. V. Tagare (we have slightly modified the translation).

1. *BhP* 10.12.30-32; tacchrutvā bhagavān kṛṣṇastvavyayaḥ sārbhavatsakam / cūrṇīcikīrṣorātmānaṃ tarasā vavṛdhe gale // tato'tikāyasya niruddhamārgiṇo hyudgīrṇadṛṣṭerbhramatastvitastataḥ / pūrṇo'ntaraṅge pavano niruddho mūrdhan viniṣpāṭya vinirgato bahiḥ // tenaiva sarveṣu bahirgateṣu prāṇeṣu vatsān suhṛdaḥ paretān / dṛṣṭyā svayotthāpya tadanvitaḥ punarvaktrānmukundo bhagavān viniryayau; tr. G. V. Tagare (we have modified his translation).

lay (*sic.*) hold of God Indra of the hundred Sacrifices and, filled with fury, opened his maw and swallowed him. But when Śakra had been swallowed by Vṛtra the mettlesome Gods, disturbed, created the Yawn to be Vṛtra's perdition; and when Vṛtra yawned, the Slayer of Vala gathered up his limbs and came out of the gaping maw. Ever since in these worlds the yawn has dwelled in breathing creatures.[1]

Here a different motif is present, that of the swallowing of the hero, that is also found in the Aghāsuravadha. This motif was considered characteristic of hero stories by Joseph Campbell who dedicates a whole section of his book on the Hero to it.[2] Jonah comes immediately to the mind, and we have to remember that also Heracles was swallowed by a monster.[3] In medieval times this episode became popular in miniature painting,[4] but the motif is present in Indian sculpture as an ornamental motif even before the Christian Era in Buddhist *stūpas* and from then on until medieval times also in Hindu temples.[5] In plate 39 we have a representation of Kṛṣṇa rescuing the cowherds from the monster jaws. It proceeds from Pāhārpur and could be as early as the seventh century, since the *Bhāgavata Purāṇa* is the only text that mentions the incident, this image could be used as an argument for an early date of this text.

With this we conclude this section on the lifting of the mountain and pass on to the series of themes of the Hero as monster killer or the Slaying of the Dragon.

v. THE SLAYING OF THE DRAGON OR THE MONSTER KILLER

We come finally to this most characteristic set of themes in the life of the hero, the monster killer, that is closely related to the slaying of the dragon motif. As we saw in Chapter Three, the destruction of monsters and/or wild beasts, is one of the regular activities of the traditional hero, and Kṛṣṇa follows in this the general pattern as closely as, or even more closely than, in the other points of it. The legends of Kṛṣṇa are full of his battles against these monsters and there is no other hero in India comparable to him in this. A detailed account of all these episodes in their different versions would take an entire volume. We have already reviewed some of these encounters and here it will be sufficient to mention only the most important and characteristic. We will deal first with the more conventional combats against wild beasts, and then we will analyse the slaying of the dragon motif.

Among the many enemies vanquished by Kṛṣṇa three in particular seem to have captivated the popular imagination more than the others. Of these three, one is conspicuous for its importance and popularity. This is the Kāliyadamana, the quelling of the serpent Kāliya; the other two are the Keśiniṣūdana and the Ariṣṭāsuravadha, the killing of the demon-horse Keśin and the killing of the bull Ariṣṭa. The killing of the serpent belongs among the themes of the slaying of the dragon, and we will deal with it under that heading. The other two we can briefly review now. Both the Ariṣṭāsuravadha and the Keśiniṣūdana are represented in the iconography numerous times, coming only after Govardhanadhāraṇa and Kāliyadamana in frequence of appearance.[1]

The episode of the death of the bull Ariṣṭa is given in *Bālacarita*, *Harivaṃśa*, *Viṣṇu Purāṇa* and *Bhāgavata Purāṇa.* All these texts present the same account without much variation in each version, and even with the repetition of certain phrases, which points to the existence of one unified story. Ariṣṭa's appearance is compared to a cloud and his eyes to the sun both in the *Viṣṇu Purāṇa* and the *Harivaṃśa* in almost identical words.[2] All four texts mention abortions caused by the beast, on cows only in the *Viṣṇu Purāṇa* and the *Harivaṃśa*,[3] on cows and women in the *Bālacarita* and the *Bhāgavata Purāṇa.*[4] The story goes that:

> One evening, whilst Kṛṣṇa and the gopīs were amusing themselves in the dance, the demon Ariṣṭa, disguised as a savage bull, came to the spot,

1. *Mbh* 5.9.46-48; tr. van Buitenen.
2. J. Campbell, *The Hero of a Thousand Faces*, 'The Belly of the Whale', pp. 79-83.
3. Frazer, *The Library of Apollodorus*, v. 1, pp. 207-8, n.2.
4. Spink, *Kṛṣṇa Maṇḍala*, figs 28-30.
5. O. Viennot, 'Typologie du Makāra et essai de Chronologie', *Arts Asiatiques*, v.1, 1954, pl. I-6, and pl. V-2 and 4; also H. Zimmer, *Art of Indian Asia*, v.2, fig. 105c.

1. See plates 9, 22, 25, 31, 32, 37, 43, 49, 55, 59, 60 and 70.
2. nirvāṇāṅgārameghābhastīkṣṇaśṛṅgo'rkalocanaḥ ; *HV* 64.2; satoyatoyadacchāyastīkṣṇaśṛṅgo'rkalocanaḥ; *VP* 5.14.2.
3. pātayāno gavāṃ garbhāndṛpto gacchatyanārtavam; *HV* 64.8; pātayansa gavāṃ garbhāndaityo vṛṣabharūpadhṛk; *VP* 5.14.5.
4. huṃkāraśabdena mameha ghoṣe sravanti garbhāḥ vanitājanasya; *BC* 3.6; patantyakālato garbhāḥ sravanti sma bhayena vai; *BhP* 10.36.4.

after having spread alarm through the station. His colour was that of a cloud charged with rain; he had vast horns, and his eyes were like two fiery suns: as he moved, he ploughed up the ground with his hoofs: his tongue was repeatedly licking his lips; his tail was erect; the sinews of his shoulders were firm, and between them rose a hump of enormous dimensions; his haunches were soiled with ordure, and he was a terror to the herds; his dewlap hung low, and his face was marked with scars from butting against the trees. ... the herdsmen and their women were exceedingly frightened, and called aloud on Kṛṣṇa, who came to their succour, shouting and slapping his arm in defiance. When the Daitya heard the noise, he turned upon his challenger, and, fixing his eyes and pointing his horns at the belly of Keśava, he ran furiously upon the youth. Kṛṣṇa stirred not from his post, but, smiling in sport and derision, awaited the near approach of the bull, when he seized him as an alligator would have done, and held him firmly by the horns, whilst he pressed his sides with his knees. Having thus humbled his pride, and held him captive by his horns, he wrung his throat, as if it had been a piece of wet cloth; and then, tearing off one of the horns, he beat the fierce demon with it until he died, vomiting blood from his mouth.[1]

In this account we see clearly the position of Kṛṣṇa among the cowherds. Just when he is sporting with the girls this horrid monster appears, creating havoc among the people and the herds. At this everybody cries aloud for help from the champion who, always ready, appears, clapping his arms in defiance as a professional wrestler does, and makes short work of the villain that is disturbing the peace of the hamlet. He confronts the bull singlehanded, plucks forcefully one of his horns and with it kills him. This detail of the horn is repeated in the *Harivaṃśa*, the *Viṣṇu* and the *Bhāgavata Purāṇas*,[2] whereas the twisting of Ariṣṭa's neck as if it were a piece of wet cloth appears in the *Viṣṇu* and *Bhāgavata Purāṇas*.[3]

Ariṣṭa was not the only bull killed by Kṛṣṇa. In a curious episode narrated only in the *Bhāgavata Purāṇa* from among our sources, he defeats seven bulls to gain the hand of a princess. A similar passage is found in the Tamil text *Śilappadikāram*, where it is also associated with Kṛṣṇa. The text seems to refer to an ancient custom of the Tamil country of winning brides through a test of strength in dominating a bull. The account in the *Śilappadikāram* is strangely mixed with the episode of the *rāsa* dance, and this makes us notice that in the narrations of the killing of Ariṣṭa the bull appears when Kṛṣṇa is engaged in that same dance and sporting. We quote here the passage of the Tamil work:

> This love-dance shows one of the games young Kṛṣṇa and Balarāma, his elder, had played on the dance-ground of the cowherds with the darling Pinnai, whose eyes looked like the points of lances.
>
> Mādari, pointing at one of the girls, announced: "This charming woman with the flower wreath shall give her heart to him who rides the huge black bull.
>
> "The lovely shoulders of the girl with gold rings are for the fortunate suitor who can master the bull with red marks on its head.
>
> "The girl whose lovely hair is crowned with jasmine shall be the wife of anyone who can ride this strong and petulant young bull."
> (It continues up to seven girls and seven bulls.)
>
> ... When the seven maidens had each taken from the herd the bull that she had brought up, Mādari placed the girls in line and gave each a role to play.[1]

In the *Bhāgavata Purāṇa* version there is only one maiden to be won, but there are still seven bulls to be dominated. As on so many occasions the authors of this Purāṇa are only too happy to introduce a miraculous element into the story. Not being satisfied with having in Kṛṣṇa just a hero and a champion, they do not miss an opportunity to show that he is God. We can compare the two descriptions of the fights, the one we quoted from the *Viṣṇu Purāṇa* where Kṛṣṇa seems to be really in danger meeting that formidable bull, and this one of the *Bhāgavata* where apparently without even a drop of sweat being spent he vanquishes all seven bulls in a wink. The episode occurs when Kṛṣṇa is already a prince of the Yādavas living in Dvārakā. He has heard that king Nagnajit of Kosala has a beautiful daughter called Satyā who will only be betrothed to him who subdues seven powerful bulls, and so he goes to Kosala to get the princess. There he is received with much

1. *VP* 5.14; tr. Wilson.
2. *HV* 64.21; *VP* 5.14.13; *BhP* 10.36.13.
3. *VP* 5.14.12; *BhP* 10.36.13.

1. *Śilappadikāram*, tr. A. Danielou, Allen and Unwin, London 1967, pp. 113-14.

honour and informed of the conditions on which the lady can be obtained and then pointed to the bulls:

> These are the seven bulls untamed and ungovernable, O warrior. A great many princes have been discomfited and got their limbs pierced and broken by them.
>
> [How strongly I wish it] if these [bulls] be tamed and controlled by you alone. O scion of the Yadu clan, your honour will be the desired-most suitor to my daughter, O Lord of the goddess Śrī.
>
> Hearing the nature of the convention, the Lord fastened his girdle tightly. He divided himself into seven persons and controlled the bulls easily as if in a sport.
>
> With their pride crushed and spirit broken, he tied them with ropes [after passing the cords through their noses] and he sportively drew them [after him] like unto a child drawing wooden toy-bulls.[1]

Here we have again that magic multiplication of the Cosmic deity that permits him to accomplish all sorts of marvellous activities otherwise impossible to perform even for a mighty hero. But leaving aside this we can say according to the evidence shown that the victory over a bull is one of Kṛṣṇa's most important feats. As we mentioned before,[2] Indra is said to have fought and defeated a quadruped, probably a bull or perhaps a horse. Heracles on his part defeated a bull in very similar circumstances to those met by Kṛṣṇa in our last two examples, i.e. fighting to obtain a woman, and, as in the battle against Ariṣṭa, Heracles broke one horn of his enemy, although it is not said that he killed him with it.

> And having come to Calydon, Hercules wooed Deianira, daughter of Oeneus. He wrestled for her hand with Achelous, who assumed the likeness of a bull; but Hercules broke off one of his horns. So Hercules married Deianira, but Achelous recovered the horn by giving the horn of Amalthea in its stead.[3]

Besides the killing of the bull another episode is much celebrated among the adventures of Kṛṣṇa against the demons that in many shapes came to kill the hero; this is the killing of Keśin the horse. The version of the *Viṣṇu Purāṇa* says that:

> Keśi, confiding in his prowess, having received the commands of Kaṃsa, set off to the woods of Vṛndāvana, with the intention of destroying Kṛṣṇa. He came in the shape of a steed, spurning the earth with his hoofs, scattering the clouds with his mane, and springing in his paces beyond the orbits of the sun and the moon .... Govinda went to encounter Keśi. The demon ran upon him, with his mouth opened wide; but Kṛṣṇa, enlarging the bulk of his arm, thrust it into his mouth, and wrenched out the teeth, which fell from his jaws like fragments of white clouds. Still the arm of Kṛṣṇa in the throat of the demon continued to enlarge, like a malady increasing from its commencement till it ends in dissolution. From his torn lips the demon vomited foam and blood; his eyes rolled in agony; his joints gave way; he beat the earth with his feet; his body was covered with perspiration; he became incapable of any effort. The formidable demon, having his mouth rent open by the arm of Kṛṣṇa, fell down, torn asunder like a tree struck by lightning.[1]

As in the case of the Ariṣṭāsuravadha, here also all the accounts agree closely in their description of the battle. The *Bhāgavata Purāṇa* adds a detail that is not included in the other texts. It says that Keśin tried to kick Kṛṣṇa, who took him by the hind legs, hurled him around and threw him to a distance of one hundred bows,[2] just as Balarāma hurled Dhenuka and the same Kṛṣṇa hurled Vatsāsura.[3] This Purāṇa omits the description of Keśin being split into two parts by Kṛṣṇa's arm, each part having one, one ear, etc.[4] The *Harivaṃśa* includes a detail that is very important for a comparison with the battle of Heracles against Diomedes' horses. Following the account of Diodorus Siculus we hear that:

> The next labour which Heracles undertook was the bringing back of the horses of Diomedes, the Thracian. The feeding-troughs of these horses were of brass because the steeds were so savage, and they were fastened by iron chains because of their

1. *BhP* 10.58.43-46; tr. G. V. Tagare.
2. See above, p. 50.
3. Apollodorus, 2.7.5; tr. Frazer, v.1, p. 257; besides Achelous, Heracles also vanquished another bull; this was the bull from Crete that he brought to king Eurystheus as his seventh labour.

1. *VP* 5.16.1-2 and 8-14; tr. Wilson.
2. tad vañcayitvā tamadhokṣajo ruṣā pragṛhya dorbhyāṃ parividhya pādayoḥ / sāvajñamutsṛjya dhanuḥśatāntare yathoragaṃ tārkṣyasuto vyavasthitaḥ; *BhP* 10.37.4.
3. See above, p. 72.
4. *HV* 67.42; *VP* 5.16.15.

strength, and the food they ate was not the natural produce of the soil but they tore apart the limbs of strangers and so got their food from the ill-lot of hapless men. Heracles, in order to control them, threw to them their master Diomedes, and when he had satisfied the hunger of the animals by means of the flesh of the man who had taught them to violate human law in this fashion, he had them under his control.[1]

Here we do not have a fight where Heracles vanquishes the horses by force, but rather he captures them by cunning, at the same time punishing the real villain. Now what matters here is not this but a curious fact stressed by the mythographer, that the horses fed on human flesh. This is a strange detail since everybody knows that horses are not carnivorous animals. But what is surprising is that this same detail should be repeated in the *Harivaṃśa* and also remarked upon. This text repeats this fact three times within a few verses. It first describes Keśin as 'furious and violent, feeding upon the flesh of men',[2] and then says that the forest where the evil Keśin dwelt was covered with human bones as a cremation ground,[3] and that the roads were blocked because he madly devoured human flesh in great abundance.[4] Now, this is the very fact that shocked the Greeks about Diomedes' horses; it was something that 'violates human law' that they ate human flesh. Since such behaviour on the part of horses is not common by any means, nor is it easy to invent as a literary motif, have we to suppose here a connection between the two accounts that goes further than their common participation in the international hero legend? This question is better left to be dealt with later.

Having briefly reviewed the two most typical examples of the killing of beasts in the story of Kṛṣṇa, we now have to address ourselves to that most heroic motif of all heroic themes: the slaying of the dragon. In order to review the abundant material on this motif it will be convenient for us to avail ourselves of the outline of themes of the slaying of the dragon compiled by J. Fontenrose. We include his full classification in Table 6, but in fact not all of these themes are found in the Kṛṣṇa stories, so we give here a selected list of those themes we use in our survey of the Kṛṣṇa legend. In Table 7 we give a correspondence of these selected themes with various episodes in the legends of Kṛṣṇa found by us to fit in Fontenrose's scheme, as well as Fontenrose's own correspondence to the Vṛtra episode in Indra's myth and the Geryon and Cacus episode in Heracles' legend. Fontenrose divided his themes under ten headings:

1. The Enemy was of divine origin.
2. The Enemy had a distinctive habitation.
3. The Enemy had extraordinary appearance and properties.
4. The Enemy was vicious and greedy.
5. The Enemy conspired against heaven.
6. A divine Champion appeared to face him.
7. The Champion fought the Enemy.
8. The Champion nearly lost the battle.
9. The Enemy was finally destroyed after being outwitted, deceived or bewitched.
10. The Champion disposed of the Enemy and celebrated his victory.[1]

These are called by Fontenrose 'Themes of the Combat Myth' and are subdivided in several subheadings, of which the following are pertinent to Kṛṣṇa's cycle:

1A. He was son of the primordial mother. 1B. He was son of a father god. 2B. He lived in a cave, hut or tree. 2D. He was guardian or spirit of a spring. 2E. He lived in sea, lake, or river. 3A. He was gigantic. 3B. He had non-human form. 3C. He had several heads, arms, legs, etc. 3D. He sent death by fire, glance, or breath. 3E. He could change his shape at will. 3F. He was a death spirit, evil demon, spectre, rising from the lower world. 4A. He plundered, robbed, murdered, made war. 4B. He was a despotic ruler or master who oppressed his subjects and imposed tribute. 4C. He carried off the young of man and beast. 4D. He was gluttonous, devouring whole herds, and a man-eater. 4E. He was a lecher and ravisher, demanding that maidens be offered to him. 4F. He commanded a road and killed travellers upon it, often in a contest that he forced upon them. 4G. He blockaded rivers or springs to keep men from water, or he drained rivers in his thirst. 5A. He wanted to rule the world. 6A. The weather god or sky god went forth to fight him. 6B. It was his first exploit: he was then a boy or youth. 7A. The

1. Diodorus, *The Library of History*, 4.15.3.

2. *HV* 67.5; mānuṣaṃ māṃsamaśnānaḥ kruddho duṣṭaparākramaḥ.

3. tadaraṇyaṃ śmaśānābhaṃ nṛṇāmasthibhirāvṛtam / yatrāste sa hi duṣṭātmā keśī turagadānavaḥ; *HV* 67.7.

4. niḥsampātaḥ kṛtaḥ panthāstena tadviṣayāśrayaḥ / madāccalitavṛttena nṛmāṃsānyaśnatā bhṛśam; *HV* 67.12.

1. J. Fontenrose, *Python*, pp. 9-11.

Champion, using his favourite weapons, fought and killed the Enemy. 7B. He had to use numerous missiles. 7C. The other gods were panic-stricken. 7E. The Champion was helped by another god or hero. 7F. The Enemy fled during the combat. 8A. He suffered temporary defeat or death. 8E. The dead Champion was lamented. 10B. He celebrated his victory with a banquet and other festivities; he was cheered by gods and men. 10C. He was purified of blood pollution.[1]

Fontenrose has devised this list to classify dozens of Dragon myths from Greece and Rome, Egypt, Mesopotamia and even India, therefore his themes have been given in as general terms as possible and we are not taking them as strict categories but allow a good deal of interpretation of them, for example, in point 6A we are not perforce admitting that Kṛṣṇa is a weather god or sky god, although he could in certain contexts, giving these titles a very loose meaning, be called so.

Just by glancing at this list of themes we can immediately recognise various items that apply to episodes already reviewed by us. So in 4D we could very well include Keśin, that was a man-eater, and in 3E we could accommodate Pūtanā, who could change shape at will, and in 6A and 6B we could include almost everyone of Kṛṣṇa's battles. By means of our Table 7 we can analyse fourteen episodes in the Kṛṣṇa cycle, following Fontenrose's classification, in order to try to find out if any of them can be branded as Dragon Slaying according to these categories, and also, and more importantly to try by the use of this classification to arrive at a clearer understanding of the several legends that by their number and intricacies of narration are almost unmanageable without a system like that devised by Fontenrose.

The episodes that we take for this survey are the battles against: Kāliya;[2] Aghāsura;[3] Śaṅkhacūḍa;[4] Jarāsaṃdha;[5] Śambara;[6] Bāṇa;[7] Naraka;[8] Vajranābha;[9] Pañcajana;[10] Nikumbha;[11] Keśin;[12] Pralamba;[13] Kaṃsa[1] and Ariṣṭa.[2] If we look at Table 7, we can see that Kāliya is the one that scores the largest number of points in Fontenrose's classification, followed closely by Aghāsura, Naraka, Kaṃsa and Nikumbha; these are therefore perhaps the episodes entitled to be classified as killing of dragons. But let us see one of these cases in some detail.

1. Fontenrose, *ibid.*
2. *HV* 55; *VP* 5.7; *BhP* 10.16.
3. *BhP* 10.12.
4. *BhP* 10.34.
5. *BhP* 10.70-72.
6. *HV* 99; *VP* 5.27; *BhP* 10.55.
7. *HV* 106-113; *VP* 5.32-33; *BhP* 10.62-63.
8. *HV* 92; *VP* 5.29; *BhP* 10.59.
9. *HV* App.1-29F. 613-842.
10. *HV* 79; *VP* 5.21; *BhP* 10.45.
11. *HV* App. 1-29E.
12. *HV* 67; *VP* 5.16; *BhP* 10.37.
13. *HV* 57; *VP* 5.9; *BhP* 10.18.

Kāliya, the nāga king, was one of Kṛṣṇa's most formidable adversaries. C.S. Hawley gives to this episode together with the Govardhanadhāraṇa the category of a Cosmic Victory,[3] and indeed, as we said before, if we judge from the iconography, this episode is only second to the lifting of the mountain in the number of occurrences. Perhaps it is not a Cosmic Victory, as Indra's against Vṛtra and as Hawley tries to interpret it, but the Kāliya combat can certainly be called a Dragon slaying. To follow Fontenrose's classification we can see that it fulfills both points 2D and 2E. Kāliya was a guardian of the pool in the Yamunā river where nobody could approach, and he lived there in the river. He also gets points 3B, 3C, and 3D: he had non-human form, he had several heads, and he sent death by his breath. He gets point 4G again because he blockaded the river, keeping men from the water. Kṛṣṇa was then just a boy and this gives to the episode point 6B. During the battle ominous portents appeared in the sky, indicating the fear of the gods, which fulfills point 7C, and 7E is gained by Balarāma, who cheered Kṛṣṇa on. Kṛṣṇa suffered temporary defeat by being immobilised under water, as in point 8A and he was lamented by all the cowherds who were expectantly waiting on the shore, as in 8E. Finally, after his victory, the champion was celebrated by gods and men. These are the points obtained by Kāliya. Equally in the other examples we can find their correspondences to the list just by looking at Table 7. So Aghāsura, Śambara, Bāṇa and Naraka were all gigantic, and Aghāsura, Pañcajana, Keśin, Pralamba and Ariṣṭa had non-human form. But this exercise may prove rather boring, and even futile, if we do not consider Fontenrose's conclusions.

The conclusion that Fontenrose draws from his monumental labour is that the battle of the Hero against the Dragon represents in the last instance an opposition at the ontological level, but in mythological garb, of Eros versus Thanatos, Life against Death, the forces of order and creation against the forces

1. No specific place.
2. *HV* 63; *VP* 5.14; *BhP* 10.36.
3. C. S. Hawley, *JAAR*, v.47, 1978, pp. 201-21.

of chaos and destruction. Of course this is no discovery at all; it is like showing and proclaiming what everybody can see and what everyone knows. Fontenrose's contribution to the study of these myths is not in this conclusion but in the analysis itself, in his dissection of the stories into their most elementary parts that can truly show us what the mechanism of the narrative is like. Fontenrose's general conclusion on Heracles is, however, very relevant to the meaning of the Kṛṣṇa image in many of the legends of his cycle:

> There is something distinctive about Herakles: he is specifically cast as the conqueror of death; it is Thanatos whom he meets again and again under many names and forms. And in saying this I mean something much more specific than the truism that a warrior faces death when engaged in mortal combat: I mean that the original and typical Herakles legend, reflected in every legend of the cycle, is the hero's combat with and victory over the death lord himself.[1]

We cannot say, as Fontenrose boldly affirms of Heracles, that we find this motif 'in every legend of the cycle' in the case of Kṛṣṇa. Kṛṣṇa is, as we have repeated many times, a very complex figure, a Universal god in true Indian fashion who includes within him every facet and aspect of human life. As we said before, he is an heir to Puruṣa, the Cosmic giant of the *Ṛg Veda*, from whose body the universe was shaped. If at all one formula can be used to describe Kṛṣṇa, this will be it: 'the Universal god in human flesh', thoroughly divine and thoroughly human. He is the baby, the child, the youth and the man; the low cowherd and the prince; the husband and the lover, the terrible fighter and the religious teacher, and also, as Fontenrose says of Heracles, the vanquisher of death. He is a saviour from death and from hell. He rescues the cowherd boys from the jaws of Aghāsura[2] and brings them back to life. He rescues Nanda, who had been taken by a demon to Varuṇa's submarine world.[3] He rescues the son of his teacher Sāṃdīpani who had died of drowning.[4] He rescues sixteen thousand women from the power of Naraka (Hell).[5] He rescues one hundred kings who were in the hands of Jarāsaṃdha to be sacrificed.[6]

1. Fontenrose, *Python*, p. 358.
2. *BhP* 10.12.
3. *BhP* 10.28.
4. *BhP* 10.45.
5. *HV* 91-92.
6. *BhP* 10.70-72.

He rescues his six elder brothers from the realm of death.[1] He rescues Nanda from the jaws of a serpent that was devouring him.[2] All these as explicit examples and many others as symbolic ones may be adduced to present this other image of Kṛṣṇa: the saviour from death. That is also the idea of Michael Grant, who calls the chapter on Heracles in his book on Classical myths: 'Heracles who conquers Death'.[3]

Kṛṣṇa is also, and very much so, a Dragon killer, as Heracles and Indra also are, and this means primarily: a hero that conquers death. But does this assertion and the application of Fontenrose's analysis to Kṛṣṇa's stories tell us more about that relationship of the stories of Kṛṣṇa and of Heracles that we have been showing in particular examples throughout our survey of different themes and motifs in the Kṛṣṇa saga? We find that, like the schemes in Chapter Three outlining the basic hero story, through the use of Fontenrose's categories we can see that both Heracles and Kṛṣṇa belong to one and the same class, with many others. They not only belong to the class of heroes, but also to the class of Dragon fighters; but we argue that this common membership of the same class does not account for all the similarities in the legends of the two. One last example will suffice to show this: in our Table 7 where we examine Kṛṣṇa episodes in the light of Fontenrose's analysis and compare them with three of Fontenrose's own examples taken from Indra and Heracles, we have in the second column Geryon and in the ninth Bāṇa, and we can see that they only correspond between themselves on five counts from thirty selected by us. Now if we compare the stories we can see that their resemblance goes much further than what their belonging to the life of the traditional hero or to the kind of Dragon slaying episodes can account for.

We see first what the points of agreement are within Fontenrose's classification of themes. They both score point 1B, the son of a god, Bāṇa being a *protégé* of Śiva and Geryon grandson of Oceanus. They get 3C, Geryon for his triple body and Bāṇa for his thousand arms. They also have 3F, both being evil demons and death spirits; 6A because the hero comes to attack them, and 7A because the hero fights with his favourite weapon. Not a very impressive set of coincidences, these similarities grow amazingly, how-

1. *BhP* 10.85.
2. *BhP* 10.34.
3. M. Grant, *Myths of the Greeks and Romans*, Mentor, London, 1962.

ever, if we look in more detail at the episodes themselves. We cannot quote directly the text because of its excessive length, but can give here an outline. All three texts, the *Harivaṃśa*, the *Viṣṇu Purāṇa* and the *Bhāgavata Purāṇa* agree in the basic account, although the *Harivaṃśa* version is much more detailed, and we will follow that. It tells how Bāṇa, a demon king who had propitiated Śiva, had a daughter who became enamoured of Aniruddha, Kṛṣṇa's grandson, in a dream. Through magic she managed to get the boy into her palace and there she enjoyed herself with him until they were discovered. Aniruddha fought valiantly but was finally defeated and bound with serpent fetters (a symbol of death). Coming to know of this, Kṛṣṇa went to the rescue and when he was about to depart one of his wives told him to bring also the wonderful cows of Bāṇa, that yielded *amṛta* instead of milk, from Śoṇitapura, the City of Blood (the realm of the dead), capital of Bāṇa. Now if we look into Heracles' Geryon episode we see that he also went to fetch some marvellous cows from that monster who lived at Erytheia, the Red Island (and the realm of the dead). Kṛṣṇa flew there on Garuḍa, that as everyone knows is a solar bird, and Heracles obtained from the Sun a magic goblet in which to cross the ocean. On the way Kṛṣṇa was attacked by Śiva and by Fire and defeated them; Heracles was attacked by Oceanus and also defeated him. When Kṛṣṇa arrived at Śoṇitapura he was met by Jvāra, fever personified, a monster with three feet, three heads and nine eyes, the equivalent of Geryon, who had three bodies, three heads and six arms. Kṛṣṇa defeated Jvāra by creating a double of himself. Heracles was also met by an enemy in the shape of the dog guarding the kine, a beast that attacked him and was killed by the hero (here we may note that as Erytheia is equivalent to the Island of the dead, i.e. Hades, this dog is the equivalent of Cerberus, the dog with three heads). Afterwards Kṛṣṇa again encounters Śiva who protected Bāṇa and who plays an important role throughout this episode, and Heracles encountered and killed the herdsman that guards Geryon's kine. One more Parallel can be drawn here: 'Śiva is Paśupati, the Lord of the beasts, *paśu* meaning especially kine, so that he is also in a sense a herdsman protecting both Bāṇa and his cows. We have also to note that throughout this episode Heracles kills his adversaries while Kṛṣṇa spares them. This is a consistent attitude that may be due to the fact that Kṛṣṇa is fighting—except for Bāṇa who has the protection of Śiva—divine beings. It is enough for him to defeat them to show his superiority, whereas Heracles is not impeded in that way. Only one of his enemies he does not kill, and this is the goddess Hera.

Following our account of the two episodes we have Kārttikeya, Śiva's son, also intervening in the battle against Kṛṣṇa, who defeats him, but spares him on the intervention of the Goddess, who also intervenes in defence of Bāṇa when Kṛṣṇa fights him. Kṛṣṇa also spares Bāṇa after this plea of the Goddess. Heracles on his part also meets a goddess protecting his enemy, but he kills the latter and wounds the goddess. After their victories both Kṛṣṇa and Heracles instal new kings in Śoṇitapura and Erytheia and leave, taking with them the daughter of the defeated monster, Kṛṣṇa marrying her to his grandson. Finally they take the famous cows also. On his way back, Heracles encounters two sons of the Ocean who try to steal the kine, and he kills them. Kṛṣṇa goes to fight Varuṇa, here god of the ocean, who kept Bāṇa's cows, and defeats him, but at his pleading Kṛṣṇa spares Varuṇa and leaves the cows with him.

These are in brief the two episodes. We can see clearly now that the number of coincidences is so high that we cannot attribute them just to Kṛṣṇa's and Heracles' common membership of the class of the heroes. We may conclude our survey of the Kṛṣṇa legends by looking at this series of parallels between Kṛṣṇa and Heracles and asking ourselves if mutual influence is possible. First we have to accept the point made in Chapter Three that there is a basic hero story found both in Asia and in Europe. Heroes following this general pattern share various traits essential to the story. Many of the similarities in the Kṛṣṇa and Heracles legends may be accounted for in this way. Nobody knows where this hero story originated or how it spread to so many countries, but apparently both the Kṛṣṇa and the Heracles stories grew separately, both having antecedents in their own tradition—Heracles in Zeus and Apollo, Kṛṣṇa in Indra. Another source of similarities we have in the myth of killing of the dragon as outlined by Fontenrose; several other traits shared in common by Heracles and Kṛṣṇa may be derived also from this myth.

But still we have coincidences like the Bāṇa-Geryon episodes and others that we feel cannot be attributed to anything but direct contact. It is well known that there was ample room for this direct contact. The Greeks arrived in North West India with Alexander the Great in the fourth century B.C. and stayed there until the first century B.C., when they were overrun by the Scythians. Their presence had a great influence in Indian art, which was felt all over the subcontinent, but was especially important in that it developed an important school of art in the territory of the former Indo-Greek kingdom of Gandhāra. Even while the Greeks were still there, and on a greater scale when they disappeared from the North West, regular commercial intercourse was taking place between the Mediterranean countries, especially Rome and Alexandria, and India. Trading posts of Greek and Roman merchants were established on both the coasts of the Arab Sea and the Bay of Bengal.[1] Pliny the Elder, writing in the middle of the first century A.D., says: 'In no year does India drain us of less than five hundred and fifty millions of sesterces, giving back her own wares, which are sold among us at fully a hundred times their first cost.'[2] The numerous hoards of Roman coins found in India witness to these words of Pliny.[3] In these conditions we cannot rule out, and rather prefer to postulate, a direct borrowing, in what exact circumstances, when and where, it is absolutely impossible to determine. Most probably mutual interchange of themes, motifs and even episodes started from the time that Megasthenes wrote about the worship of Heracles at Mathurā, and continued till the last Roman trading posts were closed. In the Bāṇa episode we feel that the borrowing was made from the Greek legend, but this need not necessarily be the case in all instances. The Heracles legends may also have felt Indian influence; for instance the Roman cult of Heracles and the Muses sounds very alien to the traditions of that hero, especially if we consider that there was already a recognised and indisputable leader of the Muses in Apollo. This could perhaps be due to influence from the Kṛṣṇa stories. But this is only a feeling, not even a conjecture, and, of course, someone may show that Heracles Musagetes is totally Classical. At any rate we know that the Hellenistic period in the Mediterranean as well as the age of the Roman Empire were epochs of great cultural effervescence, and syncretism was rampant. The Hellenistic Greeks and the Romans would have no scruples in taking foreign legends into the stories of their gods and heroes. In the same way in Indian religion a process of assimilation has always occurred.

To end all this, let us state clearly that Kṛṣṇa is not Heracles. Some stories may have been borrowed or adapted but we do not believe that the Indian people ever thought that the two heroes were identical. There is a statue of Heracles in the Indian Museum, Calcutta, proceeding from Mathurā.[1] There Heracles is depicted in the regular Classical fashion as killing the Nemean Lion. He wears his customary lion pelt around the shoulders as in all its Greek and Roman representations. This proves that Heracles was known in India, not only as a hero of whom stories were heard from merchants and who might be imagined as a local hero, but that he was well known in his fullfledged personality as a popular hero and demigod of the foreigners. That Kṛṣṇa was never given the attribute of a lion pelt nor was ever made to fight a lion proves to us that the Indians never purposefully took Heracles and fully identified him with Kṛṣṇa. Some stories interchanged naturally during the centuries of mutual intercourse, but Kṛṣṇa always remained an Indian god and was never changed into a Greek hero.

1. McCrindle, *The Periplus of the Erythrean Sea*, *IA*, v.8, 1879; Warmington, *Commerce Between India and The Roman Empire* (1928), rep., Curzon Press, London, 1974; M. Wheeler, *Rome Beyond the Imperial Frontiers*, Thames and Hudson, London, 1954.

2. Pliny, *Natural History* 6.26.101, quoted in W.H. Schoff, *The Periplus of the Erythraean Sea*, McKay, New York, 1916, p. 219.

3. M. Wheeler, *Rome beyond....*, pp. 137-45.

1. B. Rowland, *The Art and Architecture of India*, Penguin, Harmondsworth, 1970, I 11.103.

TABLE 6—THEMES OF THE COMBAT MYTH

1. The Enemy was of divine origin.
   - 1A. He was son of the primordial mother: chaos demoness or earth goddess.
   - 1B. He was son of a father god : chaos demon or deposed father god or ruling father god.
   - 1C. He had a wife or female companion of like origin and character.
2. The Enemy had a distinctive habitation.
   - 2A. The feature of geographical correspondence: the Enemy lived in a region in which myth tellers were wont to place the dwelling of monsters and demons in general.
   - 2B. He lived in a cave, hut, or tree.
   - 2C. He occupied a god's temenos.
   - 2D. He was guardian or spirit of a spring.
   - 2E. He lived in sea, lake, or river.
3. The Enemy had extraordinary appearance and properties.
   - 3A. He was gigantic.
   - 3B. He had nonhuman form: most often that of a snake, but also lizard, crocodile, scorpion, fish, hippopotamus, boar, lion, wolf, dog, horse, bull, eagle, vulture, hawk, etc.; sometimes a mixed form of various combinations of bestial and human members.
   - 3C. He had several heads, arms, legs, etc.
   - 3D. He sent death by fire, glance, or breath : fire from his nostrils, mouth, or eyes, death-dealing glances from his eyes or countenance, poison-laden breath from nostrils or mouth.
   - 3E. He could change his shape at will.
   - 3F. He was a death spirit, evil demon, spectre, rising from the lower world.
   - 3G. He was wind, flood, storm, plague, famine, drought.
4. The Enemy was vicious and greedy.
   - 4A. He plundered, robbed, murdered, made war.
   - 4B. He was a despotic ruler or master who oppressed his subjects and imposed tribute.
   - 4C. He carried off the young of man and beast.
   - 4D. He was gluttonous, devouring whole herds, and a maneater.
   - 4E. He was a lecher and ravisher, demanding that maidens be offered to him.
   - 4F. He commanded a road and killed travelers upon it, often in a contest that he forced upon them.
   - 4G. He blockaded rivers or springs to keep men from water; or he drained rivers in his thirst.
5. The Enemy conspired against heaven.
   - 5A. He wanted to rule the world.
   - 5B. His mother or wife or female companion incited him.
6. A divine Champion appeared to face him.
   - 6A. The weather god or sky god went forth to fight him.
   - 6B. It was his first exploit : he was then a boy or youth.
7. The Champion fought the Enemy.
   - 7A. The Champion, using his favorite weapons, fought and killed the Enemy.
   - 7B. He had to use numerous missiles; for the Enemy was formidable, or had an invulnerable hide.
   - 7C. The other gods were panicstricken : they appeased the Enemy or fled.
   - 7D. The Champion's sister, wife, or mother, helped him.
   - 7E. The Champion was helped by another god or hero.
   - 7F. The Enemy fled during the combat.
   - 7G. The combat was the central encounter of a gigantomachy.
8. The Champion nearly lost the battle.
   - 8A. He suffered temporary defeat or death.
   - 8B. The Enemy removed a potent organ from his body, or took a potent object from him.
   - 8C. The Enemy overcame him after luring him to a feast.
   - 8D. The Enemy's consort seduced the Champion to his destruction, or entered into a liaison with him (Venusberg theme).
   - 8E. The dead Champion was lamented.
9. The Enemy was finally destroyed after being outwitted, deceived, or bewitched : he was especially susceptible to lures of (a) food, and (b) sex; he was easily taken in by (c) disguise; (d) magic was employed against him.
10. The Champion disposed of the Enemy and celebrated his victory.
    - 10A. He punished the Enemy, even after killing him, by imprisoning him in the lower world or under a mountain, or by mutilating or cutting up or exposing his corpse.
    - 10B. He celebrated his victory with a banquet and other festivities; he was cheered by gods and men.
    - 10C. He was purified of blood pollution.
    - 10D. He instituted cult, ritual, festival, and built a temple for himself.

from J. Fontenrose, *Python,* pp. 9-11.

TABLE 7. CORRESPONDENCE OF FONTENROSE'S THEMES TO INDRA, HERACLES, AND KṚṢṆA EPISODES

Themes	Vṛtra	Geryon	Cacus	Kāliya	Aghāsura	Śaṅkhacūḍa	Jarāsaṃdha	Śambara	Bāṇa	Naraka	Vajranābha	Pañcajana	Nikumbha	Keśi	Pralamba	Kaṃsa	Ariṣṭa
1A	X	X	X				X			X							
1B	X	X	X						X							X	
2B	X	*x*	X										X				
2D	X	X	*x*	X													
2E	X	X		X								X					
3A	X		X		X			X	X	X							
3B	X	*x*	X	X	X							X		X	X	X	
3C		X	*x*	X					X	*x*							
3D			X	X	X												
3E								X				X	X				
3F	X	X	X						X								
4A	X		X				X										
4B	X		*x*													X	
4C			X		X	X						X				X	
4D	X		X		X	X											
4E										X							
4F	X						X						X				
4G	X			X													
5A	X										X					X	
6A	X	X	X	X	X	X	X	X	X	X	X	X	X	X	X	X	
6B	X			X	X	X								X	X	X	
7A	X	X	X						X	X	X		X			X	
7B	X		*x*								X		X				
7C	X			X	X					X							
7E	X	X	X	X							X		X			X	
7F			X							X			X				
8A	X			X	X						X		X				
8E	X			X									X				
9	X				X												
10B				X	X	X											
10C	X																X*x*

x indicates that the motif does not occur clearly.

TABLE 8 — ONE PARTICULAR EXAMPLE OF PARALLELISM

A. KṚṢṆA. BĀṆA'S EPISODE	B. HERACLES. GERYON'S EPISODE
1. K goes to Śoṇitapura (City of Blood) to rescue Aniruddha and to get Bāṇa's wonderful cows.	H goes to Erytheia (Red Island) to get Geryon's wonderful cows.
2. Flies on Garuḍa, a solar bird.	Obtained from the Sun a vessel to cross the ocean.
3. On his way is attacked by Śiva and Fire. Defeats them.	On his way is attacked by Oceanus. Defeats him.
4. Once arrived defeats Jvara (fever), monster of three feet, three heads and nine eyes (see B6).	Once arrived kills a dog that guards the kine.
5. Defeats Śiva who protects Bāṇa.	Kills the herdsman that guards the kine.
6. Defeats Kārttikeya and spares him at the intervention of the Goddess.	Kills Geryon, monster of three bodies, three heads and six arms.
7. Defeats and spares Bāṇa by the intervention of the Goddess.	Wounded the Goddess Hera who intervened in defence of Geryon.
8. Installs Kumbhāṇḍa as King of Śoṇitapura.	Installs a new king in Erytheia.
9. Marries his grandson to the daughter of Bāṇa and takes her away.	Takes away with him the daughter of Geryon.
10. On his way back fights with Varuṇa who kept Bāṇa's cattle. Defeats him, spares him and leaves him the cows.	Takes the cattle. On his way back, two sons of the Ocean try to steal the cows; He kills them.

CHAPTER FIVE

The Kṛṣṇa Legends in Iconography

After reviewing some of the characteristic themes and motifs of the Kṛṣṇa legends in the texts, we can now turn to the plastic representations of those legends to see how the hero of the Purāṇas has found expression in iconography. This section of our research will serve a twofold purpose, first, to give a wide survey of Kṛṣṇa Iconography up to the tenth century, something that to this day has not been done properly—especially in reference to the narrative series—and second, to compare the stories as they appear in the sculptures and as they are narrated in the Purāṇas, in this way illuminating some obscure aspects of both the literature and the iconography.

We know of only two earlier attempts to survey the early Iconography of Kṛṣṇa. The first of these is one article by Hermann Goetz, published long ago, that, because of its small size and pioneering character, failed to solve, and in some cases even to recognise, many problems, and at the same time introduced several new mistakes as well as perpetuating others.[1] The second of these attempts is contained in a recent book by S.K. Bhattacharya[2] that dedicates about fifty pages to our subject: the Iconography of Kṛṣṇa up to the tenth century. It covers a much wider ground than Goetz's article but, considering the time elapsed since that pioneer attempt, it also proves itself inadequate. Since these are the only two works dealing with the theme and the period we shall refer to them with some frequency.[1] Other contributions to our subject appear either in more general works like Kalpana Desai's,[2] or in works of a more restricted scope like R.D. Banerji's,[3] or Vats's.[4]

As we have already stated, our subject is the stories of Kṛṣṇa, and so we will pay particular attention to series of sculptures depicting these narrative scenes. We will also deal, however, to a certain extent, with isolated images. The fact is that the first extant images of Kṛṣṇa are considerably later than the first mentions of him in the literature. From the accepted time of the *Chāndogya Upaniṣad* to the date of the recently discovered coins of Agathokles, supposedly the earliest of all images of Kṛṣṇa, we have a span of at least five hundred years. Bhattacharya speculates that this may have been the case because 'the wealth and the social status of the Bhāgavatas were not sufficient to provide sculptural expression for the literary cult until early in the Christian Era.'[5] This is an interesting observation but it is very un-

1. H. Goetz, 'The Earliest Representations of the Myth-cycle of Kṛṣṇa-Govinda', *JOIB*, v. 1, 1951, pp. 51-59.

2. *Kṛṣṇa-Cult*, Associated Publishing House, New Delhi, 1978.

1. Lately it has come to our notice that in 1977 a thesis was submitted to Harvard University dealing with Kṛṣṇa as Butter Thief. We are unable to procure a copy of this work but it seems that it also deals to some extent with Iconographic matter up to the fifteenth century. What its contributions can be on this subject we must of necessity ignore. (J. S. Hawley, 'Krishna's Cosmic Victories', *JAAR*, v.47, 1979.)

2. *Iconography of Viṣṇu*, Abhinav, Delhi, 1973.

3. *Basreliefs of Badami*, *MASI*, no. 25, 1928.

4. *The Gupta Temple at Deogarh*, *MASI*, no. 70, 1952.

5. S. K. Bhattacharya, *Kṛṣṇa-Cult*, p. 40.

likely to be true, if we take into account the several inscriptions of royal personages who call themselves Bhāgavatas.[1] The absence of sculptural remains of the Kṛṣṇa religion is more likely due to the general scarcity of sculptural remains of any type in the centuries previous to the Christian Era. In fact the first sculptural representations we have after the Indus Valley Culture are the Mauryan animal emblems and, later, Mauryan ornamental sculpture using the human figure, all of it strongly influenced by Iranian models. Perhaps the Indo-Aryans had a very strong an-iconic of anti-iconic tradition, or it may be that, although images were made, they were shaped of perishable material like wood. We have to remember the account of Porus's army advancing against Alexander carrying an image of Heracles in front,[2] and the epigraphical reference to 'the images of the five heroes of the Lord Vṛṣṇi'.[3]

The Agathokles coins were discovered at Ai-Khanum, on the Oxus River in Afghanistan in 1970 by a French Archaeological Expedition. They are six pieces of one drachma each minted by the Indo-Greek king Agathokles, who lived in the first half of the second century B.C. They have the figure of a warrior on each side.[4] These figures were at first identified with Viṣṇu and Śiva but have been later supposed to represent Kṛṣṇa and his brother Balarāma, because of the emblems that they are carrying in their hands.[5] The figure in plate 1 is dressed as a Greek warrior and carries in his left hand a *cakra* and in his right hand an object that could very well be a *śaṅkha*. He wears boots with upward folded points, a helmet of Greek fashion but with two strange appendages protruding from the sides, and he also wears big round earrings. To the sides of the coin the Prakṛit legend *rajine agathuklayesa* can be seen. This figure is supposed to be that of Vāsudeva-Kṛṣṇa. On plate 2 we see his brother Balarāma who can be identified by the plough he wields in his left hand. In his right hand he has a sword. He is dressed in the same manner as Kṛṣṇa on the other side, and here we can read the Greek legend *BASILEOS AGATHOKLEOUS*. The identification of the two figures becomes more plausible if we examine other images of Kṛṣṇa and Balarāma and compare some of their features. It should be noted that the side with the Greek legend seems to have been considered the most important ('obverse'), since it normally bore the king's head. This suggests that Agathokles' mint masters looked on Balarāma as more important than Kṛṣṇa. After all, Balarāma was older. In plates 3, 4, 24, 25, 43, 58, 61, 63 and 65 we can see representations of Balarāma's plough that agree very closely with the one on the coin. Possibly the appendages of the sides of the figures' heads are intended to represent a peculiar hair style called *kākapakṣa* (crows' wings). This and big round earrings can also be seen in plates 3, 4, 6, 15, 16, 18, 19, 20, 33, 37 and 38. After looking at these other figures we may be more strongly convinced that indeed the Agathokles coins bear representations of Kṛṣṇa and Balarāma, as was first proposed by Jean Filliozat.

Our next image comes from Mathurā, is dated first century B.C. and is now kept at the Lucknow Museum. It represents Balarāma (plate 3). The figure is rather bulky. It has a canopy of serpent heads and holds a plough and a mace. The figure wears a loin-cloth tied at the hips with a knot in front and the end piece hanging between the legs. He appears to be wearing a cape falling from his shoulders. The face is much worn out but a pair of small, protuberant eyes, are still visible.

On our plate 4 we have three figures found not long ago at the village of Navangarh, near Gayā in Bihar. They represent from left to right Balarāma, Ekānaṃśā and Kṛṣṇa and are dated in the second century A.D., belonging to the Kuṣāṇa period and style.[1] The images are all standing in the typical fashion of Kuṣāṇa sculpture; all three have their right hands raised in the gesture of *Abhayamudrā*. The two males have a similar hair-style and big round earrings: their sister also has large earrings. Balarāma has his usual canopy of snake heads and a plough very similar to that wielded by one of the

1. See above, p. 23.
2. See above, p. 21.
3. See above, p. 24. It must be remembered that in the Gangetic Valley stone suitable for sculpture had to be brought from long distances, while hardwood timber was plentiful everywhere, since all the evidence goes to show that the Valley was much more thickly forested than it later became. Megasthenes speaks of Candragupta's fine wooden palace at Pāṭaliputra. Wooden images may well have existed. Monumental stone sculpture seems to have begun at the Mauryan court and then to have been taken up by Buddhists (Bhārhut) and devotees of popular cults (Yakṣas).
4. See plates 1 and 2.
5. J. Filliozat, 'Représentations de Vāsudeva et Saṃkarṣaṇa au IIe Siècle avant J. C.', *Arts Asiatiques*, v.26, 1972, pp. 113-23.

1. C. R. P. Sinha, 'Some Important Sculptural Acquisitions of the Patna Museum', *JBRS*, v.53, 1967, pp. 157-59; P. L. Gupta, 'Ekānaṃśā and her Images', *JBRS*, v.54, 1968, pp. 242-44.

figures in the Agathokles coin. Kṛṣṇa is represented with four arms and seems to be holding a *cakra* in his lower left hand. In his upper left hand there is an unidentified object, perhaps a *śaṅkha*, and in his upper right hand a *gadā*. These sculptures are very important, being some of the earliest representing the three divinities together. From their size and postures they seem to have been made for cultic purposes. They do not represent any scene in the life of Kṛṣṇa, but the trio presupposes the story of the birth of Kṛṣṇa, Ekānaṃśā being the Goddess Yoganidrā who protected the baby from Kaṃsa and died in his stead. Other representations of the trio are shown in plates 35 and 54.

Next we have in plate 5 a piece that deserves some comment because it has been claimed to be, and it is still being called, the first representation of Kṛṣṇa.[1] It is a fragment of a slab from Mathurā, where we see a man with uplifted arms standing in water surrounded by fish and other acquatic animals. On the left side and facing away from the first figure is a *nāga* with his hands together as if saluting somebody who is not to be seen in the extant fragment of the sculpture. Daya Ram Sahni, the first to describe this sculpture in 1925[2] wrote:

> The incident represented is the carriage of the baby Kṛṣṇa across the Jumnā immediately after his birth in the prison in which Devakī and her husband, Vasudeva, had been confined by Kaṃsa. Several of their children had been destroyed by the tyrant and in order to protect their new baby from the same fate, Vasudeva decided to exchange him for the daughter of Yaśodā and Nanda who had been born at the same moment. It was raining heavily and the river was in full flood when Vasudeva descended into the water to cross over to the opposite bank. The baby was placed in a winnowing basket (*sūpa*) which he carried on his head and the snake deity Śesha advanced in front to drive away water with his many hoods. In this way Vasudeva safely crossed over to the other side of the river to the village of Gokula. The representation in this sculpture faithfully follows the description of the event given in the Bhāgavata purāṇa and elsewhere.[3]

If we turn to the original Sanskrit texts of the *Harivaṃśa*, the *Viṣṇu Purāṇa* and the *Bhāgavata-Purāṇa*, already quoted, the most influential works on the biography of Kṛṣṇa, we find that nowhere is this scene described in the manner of Sahni's account. We may ignore inexactitudes, such as Sahni's assertion that 'Vasudeva decided to exchange Krishna for the daughter of Yaśodā and Nanda who had been born at the same time', when, from Sahni's own words, it is clear that Vasudeva had no means of knowing that another child had been born at the same time. We will concentrate on the description of the scene that, according to Sahni 'faithfully follows ... [that] given in the Bhāgavata-purāṇa and elsewhere.'

Firstly, neither the *Viṣṇu Purāṇa* nor the *Harivaṃśa*, the older texts, mention the 'winnowing basket' referred to by Sahni, and the same is true of the *Bhāgavata Purāṇa*. These texts only mention that Vasudeva took the child and not the basket. It is only in the early nineteenth century Hindi adaptation of the tenth book of the *Bhāgavata*, the *Prem Sāgar*, that we find the 'winnowing basket' (the Hindi word *sūpā*). From this we would infer that Sahni used only the Hindi version and did not consult the Sanskrit originals, but on going through the description given in the *Prem Sāgar* we find that in that work there is no mention of the Nāga that 'advanced in front'. The serpent is mentioned only in the *Viṣṇu* and the *Bhāgavata Purāṇas*— the *Harivaṃśa* treating the whole episode only summarily..and there the description is completely different. The Nāga does not 'advance in front to drive away water' as Sahni claims, in order to fit his interpretation of the relief, but follows Vasudeva, covering him with his hoods to protect the child from the rain, as we can see from the Sanskrit words: *saṃvṛtyānuyayau śeṣaḥ phaṇairānakadundubhiṃ*, 'Śeṣa followed Ānakadundubhi covering [him] with his hoods', (i.e. Vasudeva), in the *Viṣṇu Purāṇa*,[1] and: *śeṣo'nvagād vāri nivārayan phaṇaiḥ*, 'Śeṣa followed holding back the water with his hoods' in the *Bhāgavata Purāṇa*.[2] As we see Daya Ram Sahni modified the description given in the Purāṇas in order to make it agree with the scene represented in the relief.

It is surprising that this interpretation was accepted without any criticism, and from then on the relief was recognised as the earliest image representing a scene of the life of Kṛṣṇa. So D.B. Diskalkar in an article entitled 'Some Brahmanical Sculptures in the

1. S. K. Bhattacharya, *Kṛṣṇa-Cult*, p. 41.
2. *ASIAR*, 1925-26, p. 184, pl..lxvii-c.
3. Sahni, *ibid.*, p. 184.

1. 5.3.17b.
2. 10.3.49b.

Mathura Museum'[1] says about it: 'it may be said to be the earliest sculpture referring to the Kṛṣṇa legend, which must have been already well known from the Harivaṃśa Purāṇa and thus found representation by the first or second century AD' (p. 28). And V.S. Agrawala in an article called 'Brahmanical Images in Mathura Art'[2] accepts the same interpretation: 'I agree with this view [Sahni's] and think that the relief is the earliest representation of a scene from Krishna's life.' However, as we have seen from the Sanskrit texts, this interpretation is wrong, and it is very unlikely that the relief has anything to do with Kṛṣṇa. In 1977 we went to Mathurā specially to see this relief and discussed the matter with the Curator of the Museum, who insisted on the identification of the piece as a scene of Kṛṣṇa's life, but his only reason for this was the authority of V.S. Agrawala. Our own unbiased view, after carefully examining the relief, is that the extant fragment belonged to a bigger sculpture. From what we can see now it is most probable that in the complete piece there was a figure to which the Nāga in our fragment is paying respect, as is evident from the position of his hands. The other figure in the slab, the one with raised arms, seems to be sustaining something, but this is not certain since that part has also disappeared. He could very well be simply standing in a very common ascetic posture, but, as we have seen, whatever the figure is holding it cannot be a basket carrying a baby, since that basket is not to be found in the early texts, nor is it depicted in the relief. In any case, it is now clear that this supposed first representation of a Kṛṣṇa-līlā without Kṛṣṇa is but a case of wrong interpretation.

What then is the first representation of the Kṛṣṇa-līlā or adventures of Kṛṣṇa? We find it in the so-called Maṇḍor Pillars, now kept at the Jodhpur Museum in Rajasthan, considered to date from the fourth century A.D. These are two large pillars (almost four metres high) forming part of a door jamb, carved with scenes of the life of Kṛṣṇa (see plates 6 to 9). They were first described by D.R. Bhandarkar and Sir John Marshall in the Reports of the Archaeological Survey of India for the years 1905-6 and 1909-10 respectively, although they failed to identify all the eight scenes depicted in the pillars. The episodes identified by them are: Govardhanadhārī (pl. 6), Dugdhaharaṇa and Śakaṭabhaṅga (pl. 7) of the first pillar, and Dhenukavadha, Kāliyadamana (pl.8), Ariṣṭāsuravadha and Keśiniṣūdana (pl. 9) of the second pillar. As we see, they failed to identify the central scene of the second pillar (bottom one in pl. 8). In it we see from left to right a female figure leaning on a male figure at the centre of the scene, and then two more figures, one mounted on the shoulders of the other.[1] From this last detail we can say that the scene depicted here is Pralambāsuravadha, already described.[2] One very interesting detail here is the presence of the female figure to the left. She is not mentioned in the texts, but from the context we can say that she must be one of the *gopīs*, and from the familiarity with which she leans on the shoulder of Kṛṣṇa we can guess that she is one of his very close associates, perhaps Rādhā. This may seem an adventurous conclusion but we are considering the evidence of the Tamil poem *Śilappadikāram*, dated at around the same time as these pillars, that mentions the loves of Kṛṣṇa with one girl called Napinnai whom we may consider a prototype of Rādhā,[3] and, more important still, in the Prakrit anthology of Hāla called *Sattasāī*, traditionally considered as dating from the first century A.D., but most probably belonging to the period of the fourth to the seventh centuries, we find a verse where Rādhā is specifically mentioned: 'Kṛṣṇa, in removing the cow-dust from Rādhikā with the breath of your mouth / you even sweep away the high esteem of these other cowherd women.'[4] This verse is then almost contemporary with the Maṇḍor Pillars and lends plausibility to our newly identified central panel as containing the earliest known representation of Rādhā.

Another very important point to note in the Maṇḍor Pillars is in the bottom panel of pillar one (plate 7 bottom), that Bhandarkar described as: 'Kṛṣṇa as an infant lying on a bed, with his right hand clutching a bird apparently as a plaything, and his left pulling one of his mother's breasts.' And he concludes:

1. *JUPHS*, v.5, 1932.
2. *JISOA*, June-Dec., 1937.

1. We have been able to identify this panel thanks to a photograph in the collection of the American Committee for South Asian Archives (classified Meister 69-1/7) edited by Susan L. Huntington in Microfiche card no. (I-1102).
2. See above, pp. 71-72.
3. *Śilappadikāram*, tr. by J. Danielou, Allen and Unwin, London, 1967, pp. 112-21.
4. muhamāarueṇa tam kaṇha goraaṃ rāhiāe avaṇento / etāṇaṃ vallavīṇaṃ aṇṇāṇaṃ vi goraaṃ harasi; *Sattasāī*, 1.89; tr. B. S. Miller, 'Rādhā: Consort of Kṛṣṇa's Vernal Passion', *JAOS*, 95.4, 1975, p. 660.

'This is doubtless the scene of Śakaṭabhaṅga.'[1] Śakaṭabhaṅga it well may be, but what is that bird the baby clutches and what is Yaśodā doing there, since, as we have seen, neither she nor anyone else was present at that time and only some boys saw what happened from a distance?[2] At first we thought this could just be due to the fact that the sculptor did not know the Purāṇic texts very well. We then thought of the bird mentioned in the *Harivaṃśa*, in which shape Pūtanā came to kill the baby,[3] and deduced that the sculptor had combined both accounts, the Pūtanāvadha and the Śakaṭabhaṅga. Since a similar image occurs at Deogarh (see pl. 14), this made our supposition more firm. A third image from Pattadakal tended to confirm this (see pl. 43). We then discovered an episode in the *Padma Purāṇa* that is not mentioned elsewhere, and thought we had finally found the textual source for the image. This account states that after the baby Kṛṣṇa had destroyed the cart, another demon came in the form of a cock and this also was killed by Kṛṣṇa with his own hands.[4] The three sculptures could thus be identified for the first time. Finally we found this passage in a Jaina work of the twelfth century:

> Then from inherited hostility Sūrpaka's two daughters, Śakuni and Pūtanā, unable to injure Vasudeva, went to Gokula, like witches most evil, to kill Kṛṣṇa, who was alone without Yaśodā and Nanda. Śakuni, standing on a cart, cried out sharply to Kṛṣṇa standing below and Pūtanā thrust her breast smeared with poison into Kṛṣṇa's mouth. Instantly the deities attending on Kṛṣṇa struck them both with the same cart and killed them.[5]

Here for the first time we have all the elements in the sculpture: the bird, the suckling woman and the cart, that in the other texts do not appear together. This Jaina text separates the bird and Pūtanā, that in the Purāṇas were confused, and also introduces the cart. The similarities between the text and the sculpture seem to guarantee an identification. The problem lies in their dates, for they are separated by a 700 to 800 year gap. This would lead us to suppose either that the Jaina tradition of the life of Kṛṣṇa is indeed very old, or that there were other Kṛṣṇa stories that have been lost long ago, perhaps even that the sculpture in this case gave origin to the text.

From the Maṇḍor Pillars we can pass to the terracottas found at Rang-Mahal in the North West of Rajasthan, in an area that geographically belongs to the East Punjab. These pieces were probably originally attached to temples that have since disappeared, so that we cannot now know the original position of the sculptures. They have been dated as belonging to the fifth century.[1] Two of these pieces concern us here. The first clearly represents Govardhanadhārī (plate 10). In it we see Kṛṣṇa represented in a rather stiff pose. He is a stout fellow with short and almost imperceptible neck and very rounded cheeks: he also displays a moustache and his hair is arranged in plaits tied at the back of the head forming a kind of turban shape. He holds the mountain with a very short right arm and, if we judge by the size of the bulls and cows at his feet, he must be of gigantic stature. The mountain is represented with realistic effects such as some animals, one peeping out of a cave, and a tree. S.K. Bhattacharya proposes a novel idea in respect of the bull mounting a cow in the foreground, and by referring to the *Bṛhadāraṇyaka Upaniṣad* (1.4.4) he tries to prove the divinity of Kṛṣṇa in this particular relief. He says: 'That this ancient iconic idea is associated with Kṛṣṇa certainly elevates him from the status of hero to that of divinity in Art for the first time.'[2] This is a very strange assertion. How can the copulation of kine have to do with the divinisation of Kṛṣṇa, even with quotations from the Upaniṣads?

Next we have in plate 11 what has been identified as a representation of Dāna-Līlā, or that incident when Kṛṣṇa exacts a toll from the *gopīs* to let them cross the forest. This piece, like the one already mentioned, is now at the Bikaner Museum. It was first described by Spooner as 'a representation of an idyllic scene between a man and a woman standing under a tree.'[3] However, Goetz was not as cautious and in 1950 he put forward its identification as a Dāna-Līlā. His opinion was accepted without reserve and the piece has since been always described as Kṛṣṇa in Dāna-Līlā.[4] What Goetz and his followers

1. *ASIAR*, 1905-6, p. 137.
2. See above, pp. 67-68.
3. See above, pp.56, 59-60.
4. jānubhyāmatha hastabhyāṃ ramamaṇau viceratuḥ / māyāvī rākṣasaḥ kaścittatra kukkuṭaveṣadhṛk // kṛṣṇaṃ hantuṃ samārabdho vicacāra mahītale / jñatvā kṛṣṇastu tadrakṣo nijaghāna talena vai; *PP Utt.* 272.87-88.
5. Hemacandra, *Triṣaṣṭiśalākāpuruṣacaritra*, 8.5.121-25; tr. H. M. Johnson, *GOS*, Baroda, 1962, v.5, pp. 160-61.

1. R. C. Agrawala, 'Rājaputānā through the Ages', *JBRS*, v. 41-3, 1956, p. 313.
2. S. K. Bhattacharya, *Kṛṣṇa-Cult*, p. 44.
3. D. B. Spooner, *ASIAR*, 1917-18, pt. 1, p. 22.
4. H. Goetz, *Art and Architecture of Bikaner*, Oxford

did not consider was that there is nothing in the piece itself that points to it representing Kṛṣṇa. In fact, the sculptures were found scattered over a large area and therefore the location does not help to identify them. But, even more important, Goetz also overlooked that the Dāna-Līlā episode is not mentioned in any of the Purāṇas and only appears very late in the Medieval period in the vernacular languages. So we seriously question that this terracotta represents a scene in the life of Kṛṣṇa. In the relief itself we see only a man and a woman standing in front of each other. The man holds a stick in his left hand, and the woman carries a pot on her head, sustaining it with her left hand, while a right hand finger touches her lips. They seem to be engaged in conversation. At their back there is a tree depicted with some elegance, and we note the care taken in the depiction of the folds in the lady's skirt; they are very un-Indian and could be inspired by the Gandhāra school.

We come now to a very important series of sculptures from the Gupta period. They are from the Viṣṇu temple at Deogarh, dating from the fifth century A.D. The first one of those dealing with Kṛṣṇa's legend is in our plate 12. This very fine relief is now kept at the National Museum, New Delhi. It represents Devakī handing her new-born baby, the little Kṛṣṇa, to her husband Vasudeva to be taken to Gokula where he will be safe from the evil designs of Kaṃsa. Here we can appreciate Gupta art at its best, the modelling of the bodies is full of grace and softness, sensual and restrained at the same time. The clothes are depicted with extraordinary mastery; one can almost feel the delicate texture of the fine muslins draped over Devakī's and Vasudeva's thighs. These clothes are held in place by a jewelled girdle in the case of Devakī and a long piece of cloth tied at the waist of Vasudeva. They also wear bracelets, armlets, necklaces, diadems and earrings, all of very fine workmanship. Their headdresses are equally well and carefully depicted: Vasudeva's coiffure is of many plaits that fall over his shoulders, and Devakī's is short and curled in the front and the sides and tied in a long and elaborate tress at the back. Vasudeva is taking the baby from Devakī, who touches the little one on the head one last time with her left hand.

In our plate 13 we can see the interchange of the babies, on the left Vasudeva holding Kṛṣṇa and on the right either Yaśodā or the goddess Yogamāyā in disguise, holding Yaśodā's little daughter. This scene cannot be interpreted as Nanda and Yaśodā fondling Kṛṣṇa and Balarāma, as M.S. Vats believed,[1] since we can easily see that the figure on the left is exactly the same personage as the male of the previous plate, i.e. Vasudeva. Yaśodā is wearing a long skirt of a thick material that does not reveal the contour of her thighs; she also seems to be wearing a sort of chemise not found in any other sculpture that we can remember from other sites. Her coiffure is also less elaborate than that of Devakī in the previous plate. At the feet of the couple we see three recumbent cows, which indicates that the scene takes place at Gokula. The piece is *in situ*. Next we have the Śakaṭabhaṅga episode depicted in plate 14. This sculpture also is now kept at the National Museum, New Delhi. It represents the baby Kṛṣṇa lying on a bed kicking away a wooden cart full of pots. To the right a woman is observing the scene with surprise and she raises her right hand to her mouth in a gesture of astonishment. She wears the same kind of clothes as the female of the previous plate, but with an over-elaborate headdress. The baby Kṛṣṇa is strangling a bird with his right hand. We have already referred to this bird before.

Finally we have in plate 15 a Kṛṣṇa Govardhanadhārī. This piece is kept at the Deogarh archaeological godown and was not illustrated by Vats in his short monograph on the Gupta temple. Again we see Gupta sculpture in one of its best examples. The figure of Kṛṣṇa is serene and dignified at the same time, rather than majestic. He holds the mountain on his left palm and keeps the other hand on his hip. He wears his hair arranged in the *kākapakṣa* fashion that we mentioned before. Two cows can be seen to the left.[2]

We can compare this last sculpture with three other depictions of the same episode. These are in

University Press, 1950, p. 5; R. C. Agrawala, *JBRS*, v.41, 1956, p. 317; U. P. Shah, 'Terracottas from Former Bikaner State, *Lalit-kalā*, no. 8, 1960, pl.xxi, fig.2; V. S. Agrawala, 'The Religious Significance of the Gupta Terracottas from Rang Mahal', *ibid.*, p. 65; J. C. Harle, *Gupta Sculpture*, Oxford University Press, 1974, p. 53.

1. M. S. Vats, *The Gupta Temple at Deogarh*, *MASI*, no.70, 1952, pp. 18-19.

2. Besides these four sculptures there are other fragments found around the temple that can be identified as forming part of other sculptures on the legend of Kṛṣṇa. They are: Cīraharaṇa, Dhenukavadha or Ariṣṭavadha, Kaṃsavadha, two other scenes with Vasudeva and the baby Kṛṣṇa, and, perhaps, a *gopī*. All these fragments are illustrated in plate XXI of Vat's monograph (*MASI*, no.70, 1952).

plates 16, 17 and 19, and come respectively from Sarnath, near Banaras, Vat Koh in Kampuchea, and Kara in the Allahabad District. The first one, now kept at the Bharat Kala Bhavan, Banaras Hindu University, is a monumental piece originally close to four metres high. It is also a masterpiece of Gupta sculpture. Its dress is very similar to the one in the previous plate, only with the knot being at the back and not at the front. We can also appreciate the modelling of the abdomen, derived from some Gupta Buddha images from Sarnath and from Mathurā. The jewelry is represented with great care and so is the headdress, still following the *kākapakṣa* fashion but tied with a costly diadem and not just with a cord over the forehead, and the side appendages formed by smaller plaits. The mountain also follows the convention represented in the previous plate. The big size of this sculpture and the fact that Kṛṣṇa for the first time wears a crown suggest that he may be here definitely considered a god and perhaps that the image had some cultic use. This piece is dated in the fifth century.

Then in plate 17 we see a marvellous piece from Kampuchea. In it are preserved again the best qualities of Gupta art. The sculpture has been badly damaged but it is still possible to appreciate the delicacy of the modelling, especially in the left arm that is fully extended and, compared with the two previous examples, much more natural. The fashion in the loin cloth is the same but its depiction varies, perhaps in accordance to local usage; it is tied around the hips in a thick roll as in the other cases but here the knot is at the left back side and the cloth falls freely from the back. The mountain is not visible but the headdress can be compared with our other examples; this is totally different, being derived from the Buddha's headdress consisting of nothing but very short curls, in this case crowned by three tufts of hair and not just by one. The ears are also elongated like the Buddha's. The image belongs to the fifth or sixth centuries, and is, or was, kept at the National Museum, Pnomh Penh.

Finally we can examine together with these other Govardhanadhārī images one kept at the Allahabad Museum (pl.19). It comes from Kara, Allahabad District, and is dated in the early sixth century. Now, this sculpture is totally different from our last three examples, all the grace and elegance being lost. The craftsman still tried to follow the Gupta idiom but his is a stiff figure lacking that supple and soft modelling of the best Gupta art. This image can be compared rather to the Rang Mahal terracotta (pl. 10) than to any of the three previous examples. The cows here very much resemble those of the Rang Mahal piece. The figure is effaced but it is still possible to recognise the *kākapakṣa* hair style. The mountain is represented with some realism and garlands can be seen hanging from it. One very interesting detail in this piece is a lion represented at the bottom left. We have never seen a lion like this in Indian art, except perhaps for some Pallava pillar figures, although this one looks more like some Chinese seated lion.

In plate 18 we have a fragmentary piece of sculpture representing the Kāliyadamana. It is very badly damaged but we can see that this was a round composition with Kṛṣṇa in a very lively pose riding on the back of Kāliya whom he dominates like a horse with a rein. It is a most peculiar arrangement only found much later in some Cālukyan art from Gujarat and Rajasthan.[1] The characteristic Kṛṣṇa coiffure can still be recognised in spite of the damage. The piece is kept at the Mathura Archaeological Museum and is dated in the fifth century.

In plate 20 we have a beautiful terracotta composition representing the Pralambāsuravadha. On the left we can see Kṛṣṇa cheering his elder brother, who is mounted on the back of the demon and is hitting him with his right fist. Pralamba's face is distorted by the pain and the children's faces are beaming with pleasure. The *kākapakṣa* hair style is here depicted somewhat differently from the other examples we have seen. It looks as though the children's heads have been shaven except for three long tufts of hair, two on the sides falling freely and one tied on top. This sculpture is at the Allahabad Museum and dates from the sixth century.

The Kṛṣṇa reliefs in the Badami caves do not follow a narrative sequence, so we have arranged them to fit more or less the order in which the events are narrated in the Purāṇas. In plate 21 we see nine panels from Cave Three as they were drawn for James Burgess in the 1870's and published in *The Indian Antiquary*, v.6, 1877.[2] In the first panel we see, from left to right, Nārāyaṇa-Viṣṇu lying on the serpent Śeṣa with Brahmā issuing from his navel seated on a lotus, and the demons Madhu and Kaiṭabha with swords drawn, ready to pounce upon him. Next we can see these two demons in flight, and in

1. See J. S. Hawley, *JAAR*, v.47, p. 205.
2. In plates inserted between pages 364-365.

front of them is Garuḍa flying to the right; we do not know if as a part of that scene or of the next, which depicts two men fighting, interpreted by Burgess as: 'two royal personages who are struggling ... these perhaps represent the wicked kings who oppressed the earth and rendered a new *avatāra* necessary'.[1] To the right of these two figures we can see two other men watching two bulls fighting. According to the opinion of Pandit Bhagavan Lal Indraji as reproduced by Burgess,[2] this shows 'two persons ... oppressing an ox ... a representation perhaps of Dharma ... and a cow or Pṛthvī—the earth';[3] that is, however, not clear. Finally, at the extreme right, we have Viṣṇu facing two personages who appear to be supplicating. As Banerji puts it: 'On the whole this basrelief seems to be connected with the Kṛṣṇa-Līlā', perhaps representing the deputation of the gods to Viṣṇu to ask for his descent to earth.

This first panel is on the lintel to the right, or west, of the colonnade. On the second lintel from the right we find represented the killing by Kaṃsa of Yoganidrā, the daughter of Yaśodā, substituted for Kṛṣṇa. There seem to be three different scenes in the panel. First we see on the left a seated man flanked by two female attendants with fly-whisks, who is talking to another man seated in front of him. This scene appears to take place between two pavilions. Banerji interprets it as Kaṃsa talking to Vasudeva,[4] and Burgess, to our mind more accurately, thinks that the two are Kaṃsa and Nārada.[5] To the right of this scene are two male figures facing right, the front one with a raised right arm, and then a half-kneeling figure with four arms on a platform between two trees. This most probably represents the dashing of the girl Yoganidrā against a stone and her rising as a divine figure. Next we have four standing figures that, according to Burgess,[6] represent the apologising of Kaṃsa to Devakī and Vasudeva, the fourth figure perhaps being Nārada.

The following panel, according to the sequence of the story, should be the one on the lintel at the extreme left, or east, of the colonnade. In it we see five episodes in the life of Kṛṣṇa. Starting from the left we have the Pūtanāvadha, the Śakaṭabhaṅga, the Ariṣṭāsuravadha, the Yamalārjuna and the Dhenukavadha episodes. The first three are represented in the usual manner in the style of Badami, although the Ariṣṭāsuravadha does not narratively belong there. The Yamalārjuna does not follow the usual convention, showing Kṛṣṇa standing and threatening the anthropomorphic trees with his raised fist, instead of representing him crawling and dragging the mortar. The drawing that we reproduce here did not include the palmyra tree on the extreme right of the panel, which permits the identification of the last scene as the killing of Dhenuka by Balarāma. The drawing of the third lintel from the left, the fourth in our plate no.21, is also incomplete, probably owing to the bad state of preservation of the panels, their high position and the poor illumination inside the cave. These factors also prevented our getting good photographs of the panels both here and in Cave Two. The relief represents the birth of Kṛṣṇa and his transfer to Gokula, and because of this we should have placed it as second in our plate 21. Burgess was mistaken in identifying the recumbent figure as Kṛṣṇa,[1] and Banerji is right in describing the panel as Yaśodā on the delivery bed being attended by three figures[2] (one of these does not appear in the drawing). Next we see five cows (one is missing in the drawing), and seven standing figures and a cow.[3] The scene represents the exchange of the babies, since the first of the figures to the right of the cows holds a child, as does the last figure on the right of the panel, although we are unable to see the latter in the photograph presented by Banerji and we have to take his word for it. These two figures do not appear in the drawing, where they should be flanking the four figures that do appear.

The fifth panel shown in plate 21 is also the next one to that we have just described. It represents, according to Banerji,[4] the mock coronation of Kṛṣṇa, when he was anointed by Indra after the Lifting of Mount Govardhana.[5] In it we see first six standing figures and a seated figure, representing Kṛṣṇa being anointed and the *gopīs* attending the ceremony. Next we see a group of cows and a human figure standing

1. J. Burgess, 'Rock-cut temples at Badami', *IA*, v.6, 1877, p. 365.
2. R. D. Banerji, *Basreliefs of Badami, MASI*, no.25, 1928.
3. Banerji, *Basreliefs*...., p.42.
4. Banerji, *Basreliefs*...., p. 53.
5. Burgess, *IA*, v.6, 1877, p. 365.
6. Burgess, *ibid.*

1. Burgess, *ibid.*
2. Banerji, *Basreliefs*....p.53.
3. In the drawing there appear only four figures and no cow, and Banerji (*ibid*) speaks only of five personages here. A photograph of the panel can be seen in pl.xxiv, fig. d, of Banerji's monograph.
4. Banerji, *ibid.*, p. 54.
5. *HV* 62.58; *BhP* 10.27.

in the middle of them, and finally two seated figures that we cannot identify. The figure standing among the cows must be that of Kṛṣṇa. We have to note that in this panel the modelling of the cows is very delicate, in contrast to that of the human figures and also to that of the other panels.

In the next relief we have representations of four episodes of the Kṛṣṇa story. First we see on the right Kṛṣṇa holding Mount Govardhana, then we see a figure holding a cow from the back in what could be a representation of *HV* 63.17 where Kṛṣṇa plays at surprising the cows and catching them as a crocodile would do. Next we can see the Keśiniṣūdana and, at the extreme right, the killing of the elephant Kuvalayāpīḍa. In plate 22 we present a photograph of this same lintel which gives an idea of the relation of the drawings to the originals.

The seventh panel in plate 21 depicts two more events in the life of Kṛṣṇa, separated by a vertical partition that does not appear in the drawing. The scene to the left represents the Kāliyadamana with Kāliya almost at the centre, begging forgiveness with joined hands, and Kṛṣṇa trampling on the right side of his body (that part of the body of Kāliya is not depicted in the drawing). To the left of Kṛṣṇa we see Balarāma and some *gopīs* and *gopas* alarmed to see Kṛṣṇa fighting the monster. To the right of Kāliya we see two *nāginīs* also begging for compassion. To their right is the vertical division that separates the next scene that represents the combat of Kṛṣṇa and Balarāma against Kaṃsa's wrestlers.[1]

Finally we have two more panels. The first represents the story of the Pārijāta tree that Kṛṣṇa took forcibly from heaven, defeating the armies of Indra the king of the gods. The narrative starts on the right of the lintel, where we can see Indra mounted on his elephant Airāvata surrounded by his soldiers and fighting with Kṛṣṇa, whom we see to the left mounted on Garuḍa and shooting arrows at Indra. To the left we have a small division where Kṛṣṇa is shown flying on Garuḍa, possibly transporting the divine tree to Dvārakā. To the left again we see Kṛṣṇa with four arms seated relaxedly, attended by a *chaurī* bearer. To the left there is a small figure, then the Pārijāta tree being worshipped by Satyabhāmā, and finally two standing female figures.

The other panel represents an advancing army trampling upon the bodies of the defeated enemy. Besides many human figures we see from left to right two elephants and two horses charging towards the left, and behind them, on the extreme right, the smaller figures of Agni, Yama and Varuṇa, who can be recognised by their *vāhanas*, the goat, buffalo and *makara*. Burgess[1] thinks that this panel represents another scene of the legend of Pārijātaharaṇa, but Banerji denies this saying:

> The paper was evidently written long after Dr. Burgess's visit to Badami, when he had forgotten the exact arrangement of the basreliefs, from the drawings. In fact this battle scene cannot have any reference to the basrelief in the last lintel, on the left in the rear on (*sic.*) which the *Pārijātaharaṇa* is depicted, because in the first place we have the same subject depicted in the same place in Cave no. II where the *Pārijātaharaṇa* has not been represented and in the second place, the basrelief in Cave no.III[2] represents the gods led by Indra, Yama, Agni and Varuṇa as victorious over their opponents, a fact which proves that it cannot have any connection with the *Pārijātaharaṇa*, where, according to the Viṣṇu Purāṇa and the Harivaṃśa, the gods were defeated by their opponent, Kṛishṇa.[3]

Banerji's argument is very cogent and it suggests that the scene represented in this panel could very well be one of the battles between gods and demons that led to the churning of the ocean. In Cave Two at Badami, as Banerji mentions, a complete series of Kṛṣṇa stories is depicted on the lintels of the colonnade. This series we are unable to reproduce owing to the difficulties encountered when we tried to photograph them. Later we were also unable to procure photographs of them from the Archaeological Survey of India, and drawings were equally unavailable. They can be examined, however, in plate

1. There is one more panel that we do not reproduce in plate 21 because it is not given in Burgess's article. It probably again represents the encounter of Kṛṣṇa and Balarāma against Kaṃsa's wrestlers. It is divided into two parts by a sort of pillar or column in the centre. To the left we see first Balarāma holding his plough, and then Kṛṣṇa with four arms, and one more figure watching the fight of two pairs, one of two standing men, giving and receiving blows with their fists, the other a fallen figure with a second one over it. To the right of the pillar we see four standing armed male figures and a seated one flanked by two female figures. This is in all probability king Kaṃsa and his men ready to apprehend the two cowherd boys in case they escape from the two powerful gladiators. (Banerji, *ibid.*, plate xxv, d.)

1. *IA*, v.6, 1877, p. 365.
2. Banerji sometimes calls Cave Four, Cave Three as other authors do.
3. R. D. Banerji, *Basreliefs....*, p. 47.

xii of Banerji's monograph. Their style is very much like that of those in Cave Three and the rest of the series at Badami, if a little less finished. One episode which appears in these basreliefs of Cave Two and is not present in those of Cave Four, is the Dugdhaharaṇa,[1] in a scene full of charm where Kṛṣṇa is really represented as a baby as in all Cālukyan art.

Badami is an extremely important place for Kṛṣṇa iconography because, besides these two series in the caves, we have several other series in the Cālukyan temples of the same epoch. The best known of these series is that first discovered at the North Fort of Badami. Part of a long-destroyed temple that had been used for building material, it had been incorporated in one of the doorways to the Fort, where it remained for many long years, but has now been taken to the new Archaeological Museum close by, where we obtained the photographs presented in our plates 23, 24 and 25. The style of these panels is, as we said, very similar to that of those in the caves, especially those of Cave Four, and they must therefore date just a few years after the caves were built, i.e. they belong to the early seventh century.[2]

In our plate 23 we see first, from left to right, a palace divided into two sections; in the first one there is a standing male figure leaning on a long mace, in the second we see a king seated comfortably, attended upon by a dwarf, to the right, and three other figures behind him. The first scene must represent Kaṃsa in his inner apartments waiting for the news of the birth of Devakī's eighth child, and, on the left, a guard sleeping under the spell of Yoganidrā. Next we see two standing male figures facing each other and holding small bundles in their arms; to the right are some cows and female figures, one of them churning milk, and in the back what is intended to be the representation of a village. The two men are, of course, Vasudeva and Nanda exchanging the babies, and the cows indicate that they are in Gokula. To the right of the churning *gopī*, three episodes are represented in a very crowded composition: they are first Pūtanāvadha, then Śakaṭabhaṅga, and in the background the uprooting of the Yamalārjuna trees. There also appear in these compositions one cow and three human figures, amongst them Yaśodā praying.

In plate 24 we see the next section of the panel which represents on the left the Tṛṇāvartāsuravadha, a very interesting fact since this may be an indication of the date of the *Bhāgavata Purāṇa*. As we have mentioned, this Purāṇa is the only text that has that episode, which is actually a copy of the Pralambāsuravadha, where Balarāma kills the demon Pralamba who was carrying him away on his shoulders. That we have here a representation of the Tṛṇāvartavadha, and not of Pralambavadha is clear from the figure to the extreme left which is none other than Balarāma, since he carries the *hala*, the plough emblematic of Kṛṣṇa's brother. So, as Balarāma is standing there, we can safely assume that the small figure on the shoulders of the flying giant is Kṛṣṇa, and that, therefore, the episode of the *Bhāgavata Purāṇa* was known in the kingdom of the Cālukyas in the early seventh century.

To the right of the Tṛṇāvartavadha we see the killing of the elephant Kuvalayāpīḍa in a scene full of movement. The stature of the elephant, although described in the Purāṇas as enormous, is here represented as minuscule as compared with that of Kṛṣṇa, who is trampling on the elephant's head and brandishing on high one of the tusks he has just uprooted from the beast, which he is about to strike and kill with its own tusk. Next to this scene there is a powerful standing male figure with his right arm raised and holding a quadruped by the tail. We say quadruped because the species of the animal is not very evident, and there are actually three different episodes with which this scene could be identified. It could either be the Dhenukavadha or the Vatsāsuravadha already described[1] or, considering the situation (in a space separated from the rest of the panel by two vertical divisions and together with the killing of the elephant), it is more probably the dragging of the same elephant by Kṛṣṇa or Balarāma.[2] This last suggestion seems more plausible if we look closer at the animal hanging from the mighty arm of the hero and notice its elephantine head and its stout legs. Goetz inexplicably identifies this scene with the killing of Vyomāsura.[3]

Finally, on the extreme right of the panel, we have

1. Banerji, *ibid.*, plate xii b; contrary to the affirmation of Charlotte Vaudeville, who says that this scene is not found at all at Badami. We also have it in the panels of the Surali temple. (Ch. Vaudeville, 'Aspects du Mythe de Kṛṣṇa-Gopāla dans l'Inde Ancienne', *Mélanges d' Indianisme à la Memoire de Louis Renou*, Boccard, Paris 1968, p. 751.) See our plate 30.

2. See H. Goetz, 'The Earliest Representations of the Myth-Cycle of Kṛṣṇa Govinda', *Journal of the Oriental Institute*, Baroda, v.1, 1951, p. 56.

1. See above, pages 72-73

2. *HV* 74.36; *BhP* 10.43.38.

3. Goetz, 'The Earliest Representations....', *JOIB*, v.1, p. 59.

a representation of Govardhanadhārī. In it we can see from left to right two calves and a human figure behind them. Next is the powerful figure of Kṛṣṇa holding aloft the mountain, and then four human figures, a bull and a cow. We should note here that Kṛṣṇa is holding the mountain with his right hand, contrary to the literary and iconographic tradition that specifies that he actually used his left arm.[1] This seems to be a peculiarity only found in the Deccan, since the only other examples of it are from Badami itself (see plate 27), Pattadakal (pl. 44), and Ellora (pl. 52). In the example from Cave Four at Badami (see above p.109; and plate 22), it looks as if Kṛṣṇa were supporting Govardhana with his two hands. Other images where Kṛṣṇa does not follow the traditional depiction represent him as multi-armed, as in Ellora (pl. 51), Pattadakal (pl. 49), and Pāhārpur (pl. 39).

In plate 25 we see the next panel in this Badami series. Starting from the right we see first the Keśini-ṣūdana. This is a very vigorous composition with Kṛṣṇa valiantly receiving the attack of the vicious horse, stopping it with his left arm and raising his right arm to strike the horse's head. Four other figures appear in this scene, three standing ones holding maces or sticks, two at the back of Kṛṣṇa (the one on the extreme left is not visible in our plate), and the other behind the horse, with the fourth one lying down under the hoofs of Keśi. All these figures must represent the cowherds who were menaced by the demon-horse. Goetz interprets the scene as the slaying of Dhenuka.[2] This interpretation cannot be accepted, because the manner of the fight is very different in both episodes and the description of the killing of Keśi in the Purāṇas is in complete agreement with this scene[3] as well as with other examples of the same episode in the iconography.[4]

Starting immediately to the right of the horse we have the next scene that occupies the best part of the panel and represents the Kāliyadamana. First we see Balarāma holding his plough and attentively watching Kṛṣṇa's battle. Then we see a female figure standing behind some lotus plants that conceal from our eyes the lower half of her body; she is probably Yaśodā alarmed at the sight of her child fighting the serpent. To the right we see a *nāginī* with joined palms imploring compassion, and then, at the very centre of the panel, the heroic figure of Kṛṣṇa standing on the coils of Kāliya who is also begging for pardon. Finally we have another imploring *nāginī* and a seventh figure looking on from behind her hoods. Goetz, very strangely, identifies the left half of this scene as 'Devakī and Rohiṇī with the children Kṛṣṇa and Balarāma at Gokula'[1] without any justification whatsoever. The scene follows very closely the composition of the depictions of the same episode in Cave Four (see pl. 21, sec. 7) and in Cave Two[2] of Badami, as well as that of the image in Bhuvanesvar Museum.[3]

To the right of this scene is depicted the Ariṣṭāsuravadha, in a lively composition, as in all the rest of this panel. First there is a figure holding a mace or stick and, next to the right, Balarāma holding the plough, after which another man is represented, and then Kṛṣṇa grasping the bull by one horn with his right hand and by the lower jaw with his left, and twisting the beast's neck. The composition of this scene follows that of the same episode in Cave Four at Badami (see pl. 21, sec. 3), Surali temple, also of Badami (pl. 32), and the Maṇḍor pillars (pl. 9). Behind the bull we see Balarāma again, forming part of the next scene that is not included in our plate 25. That scene represents, according to Goetz,[4] the dragging of Kaṃsa, but we seriously doubt this interpretation since the depiction does not follow in the least the accounts of this episode in the Purāṇas. What one sees in that last scene on the panel is a man kneeling with his face to the ground in a submissive attitude; over him there are two standing armed figures. We cannot accept Goetz's identification, but neither can we identify the scene with any certainty. Reproductions of the full panel can be examined in plate ii of Goetz's article and figure 12 of Aschwin Lippe's 'Early Chalukya Icons'.[5]

The last fragment in the Badami Museum that we have to examine does not belong to the same series as those in plates 23-25. This one (pl.26) must have belonged to a different temple of around the same period and has not been described or reproduced before. It represents the Pūtanāvadha episode in the same fashion as the one in the series we have just described (pl. 23) and as in the other example at Badami, that of the Surali temple (pl.30), and similar also to the examples at the Virūpākṣa temple

1. *HV* 61.30.
2. Goetz, *ibid.*, p. 59.
3. *HV* 81; *VP* 5.16; *BhP* 10.37.
4. See our plates 9, 22, 31 and 37.

1. Goetz, 'The Earliest....', p. 59.
2. Banerji, *Basreliefs....*, pl. xii c.
3. Goetz, *ibid.*, fig. 2.
4. Goetz, *ibid.*
5. *Artibus Asiae*, v. 34, 1972.

in Pattadakal (pl.43), and at the Lakṣmaṇa temple, Khajuraho (pl.66), i.e. we see the fiend seated in *lalitāsana* with both arms raised on high and a baby on her lap clasping her breast. The relief is very badly weathered and so we cannot see the finer details. Besides the figures of Pūtanā and Kṛṣṇa, there are in the fragment other figures completing the scene. We see first on the right a wooden cradle hanging from the ceiling and, under it, two seated persons, the one on the right being a female, breast-feeding a baby. Behind the other seated figure there are two standing figures and next to it is Pūtanā being killed. We can interpret the relief, following the account in the *Bhāgavata Purāṇa*, as the house of Nanda, with him and his wife Yaśodā sitting with the baby Kṛṣṇa at the moment when Pūtanā comes in disguise and asks to suckle the baby. The fourth figure would be one of the *gopīs* startled by the stranger's unearthly beauty.

We come now to the last of these four series from Badami, in the place with the largest number of early reliefs depicting the Kṛṣṇa legends. This is the series found at the Surali or upper Sivalaya Temple built on the northern ridge of the town. The temple was built before A.D. 640 according to Lippe,[1] and it was he who first referred to this series although without describing or illustrating them. Goetz had illustrated the Govardhanadhārī image on the south wall,[2] but did not refer to the panels with the Kṛṣṇa stories found on that same wall and on the west wall. This Govardhanadhārī is an image independent of those in the smaller friezes, being much bigger and occupying the most prominent place on the south wall in a separate niche. As we have said, this is one of the very few representations of this episode in which Kṛṣṇa is depicted holding the mountain with his right hand. The composition of the image follows the established models of this, one of the two episodes in the legend of Kṛṣṇa that obtains a prominent place in Indian iconography during our period, the second one being the Kāliyadamana with much fewer examples. The group is much worn, but it is still possible to appreciate the fine details of the carving such as the careful depiction of the pearl threads, chains, garlands and necklaces, as well as the beautifully sculpted crown that antedates by several centuries the very similar examples in Hoysaḷa art. In this Cālukya example the style is still close to that of the Guptas, the differences marked by the emphasis in the ornamentation. This is clear when we compare it to the two Gupta examples from Deogarh and Banaras (pls. 15 and 16). In these the cloth waist-knot is represented with fine detail, and other ornaments too, but they do not break the line of the body: on the contrary, they enhance it. In our example the line is still there but its importance is getting lost because of the profusion of ornamentation, especially on the legs. The depiction of the mountain is comparable to that in the Rang Mahal terracotta (pl.10) with its cave sheltering a lion. This image from the Surali temple may be the first that represents Kṛṣṇa with a crown.

We come now to the panels with the actual narrative scenes. As we have said the panels have not been described or illustrated before. J.S. Hawley refers to them in a recent article but does not provide any evidence of his close acquaintance with them.[1] The first panel in the series we present in plate 28, where we see the scene of the transfer of Kṛṣṇa to Gokula. From right to left we have first the inside of a chamber with three figures, two seated and one standing to the left. They are Vasudeva and Devakī seated on a couch just after the birth of Kṛṣṇa—who is not represented here—and the goddess Yoganidrā, shown with two arms and holding a *triśūla*, who has just put to sleep everybody in the palace. Next to the left we see the outside of the chamber, with a sleeping guard leaning on his spear and an open door. And finally on the extreme left of the panel we have Vasudeva carrying the baby in a bundle that he holds aloft with his right hand. In plate 29 we have the continuation of the narrative. Again from right to left we see first a house, inside which there are a standing male, a seated female, and a baby lying on the ground. They can be identified as Nanda, Yaśodā and their still-born daughter. To the left and outside the house we see a man leaning on a cow (he is probably Vasudeva), and then the same Vasudeva carrying a baby in his arms. Then we see in the very centre of the panel the goddess Yoganidrā who is protecting the whole enterprise; she is represented with four arms. To the left, a female is holding another child in her arms. She is probably Yaśodā

1. *Ibid.*, p. 273.
2. Goetz, *JOIB*, fig. 3.

1. J. S. Hawley, 'Krishna's....', *JAAR*, v.47, 1979, p.207; the same author has an unpublished doctoral thesis (*The Butter Thief*, Harvard University 1977) where he presents illustrations of Kṛṣṇa Iconography. This work we have been unable to consult, and therefore do not know if he illustrates or discusses these panels.

or Yoganidrā who has lost two of her arms in her human manifestation. Finally we see, on the extreme left, three *gopīs*, two of them standing and the third seated churning butter.

Next we have in pl.30 a part of the relief that is very badly worn, but in which we can still recognise three scenes in the story of Kṛṣṇa, the other two being unidentifiable. From left to right we see first two standing figures —the first one appears to be a man standing with open legs, the second a woman holding a child on her left hip—possibly Yaśodā holding Kṛṣṇa. Then we see Kṛṣṇa uprooting the Yamalārjuna trees, his little figure to the left of the bending trees which tower over him. To the right of this scene is represented the Dugdhaharaṇa, the stealing of butter-milk. Although very damaged, we see a seated female, her extended arms churning the milk in a pot with a churning-stick, to the right a little pot-bellied fellow reaches with his hand to take the butter from the jar. Next, to the right, we can identify the Pūtanāvadha in its usual form: the seated fiend with her arms raised in despair and the child sitting on her lap clinging tenaciously to her breast. In a separate section of the panel there is an unidentified scene. We see the inside of a palace and a figure approaching a bed holding a baby. It would appear to have something to do with the birth of Kṛṣṇa but we are not sure which part of the legend it represents.

In our plate 31 we can see two more scenes from the legend. They are also badly weathered but it is still possible to identify them. They are from left to right Keśiniṣūdana and the Wrestling match. The killing of Keśi is a very vigorous composition; we see the figure of Kṛṣṇa to the left bending forward and raising his right arm to strike the final blow to the horse-demon who is biting Kṛṣṇa's left arm; the position of the horse is very strange, being seated in human fashion. A curious detail is a big human head that is at the back of Keśi and that cannot be identified. The next scene is obviously a part of the wrestling match but the figures are so damaged that we cannot tell if it is Kṛṣṇa or Balarāma fighting one of Kaṃsa's wrestlers.

The final panel of this series of the Surali temple can be seen in our plate 32. It is also very much damaged by the elements but its fine modelling is still visible and we can appreciate it as one of the finest pieces, if not the finest, in all the Badami series, including those of the two caves and that of the Museum. It was obviously realised by a master craftsman and an artist. It can even be compared to some Gupta reliefs, especially 'Kṛṣṇa fighting the bull'. The panel contains two scenes: Pralambāsuravadha and Ariṣṭāsuravadha. To the left we have the scene of the Killing of Pralamba; the demon is fleeing with the boy Balarāma mounted on his shoulders and two figures observe what is happening. These two figures have been effaced but one of them must be that of Kṛṣṇa, probably the second figure from Pralamba, since it has four arms although his right upper arm has disappeared. The second scene is the killing of Ariṣṭa, the bull-demon. In it we see one figure standing by while the formidable battle rages between Kṛṣṇa and the fierce bull. As we said, the figure of Kṛṣṇa is of classical proportions, and the whole presence of his body reflects a sense of majestic divinity, of a force that does not need to exert itself even at this moment of supreme peril. Full of restraint and with complete mastery and control over his own might and that of his adversary, Kṛṣṇa breaks the neck of the bull who hangs from the hero's hands with his front legs scarcely touching the ground. With the presentation of this fine piece, which with the others of the Surali temple we review and illustrate here for the first time, we leave Badami and go back to Mathurā.

In plates 33 and 34 we have two Govardhanadhārī images that are important to us because both have been supposed to be the earliest images of Kṛṣṇa. The first one is kept at the Archaeological Museum, Mathurā and shows a highly stereotyped figure. Everything in it is stereotyped—from the attending figures to the cows standing on special supports, and the mountain that has become a mere symbol—as if following long established models. If we compare this image with those of plates 10, 15, 19 and 27, we see that this is a stereotype, almost a mass-produced figure. Coomaraswamy, without any basis whatsoever, ascribed it to the Kuṣāṇa Period,[1] and, we suspect that following him, Dandekar gave to it a date in the first century, converting it into the first of the Kṛṣṇa story images, also without foundation.[2] V.S. Agrawala, with a greater sense of the differing styles, dated it in the seventh century.[3] One can clearly see in the image, not the imperfections of a pre-Gupta piece, which indeed it does not have, but

1. A. K. Coomaraswamy, *History of Indian and Indonesian Art*, Goldston, London 1927, pl.xxix, fig. 102.
2. R. N. Dandekar, 'Vaiṣṇavism and Śaivism', in *R. G. Bhandarkar as an Indologist*, *BORI*, Poona 1976, p. 39.
3. *JUPHS*, v.22, 1949, p. 119.

the decadence of the Gupta style evident especially in the posture, which makes an attempt at being graceful but which, nevertheless remains stiff. Clearer proof of it being post-Gupta is to be found in the facial features. No piece of the first century has such features. The Museum authorities date it to the sixth century.

The other image, kept at the Indian Museum, Calcutta, is that little piece known as the Jātipāra image, after the place near Mathurā where it was found. This sculpture was considered by Goetz to be the earliest image of Kṛṣṇa, as stated in his article mentioned before. He says: 'the earliest representation we know of Kṛṣṇa Govinda is the Jātipāra image which belongs to the reigns of the Kṣatrapas of Mathurā.'[1] Obviously such an affirmation coming from such an authority must have a certain basis, but all that Goetz provides is a footnote giving his source as the *Annual Report of the Archaeological Survey of India* for the years 1921-22, p.104. Unfortunately, on checking his reference we found that Goetz made a mistake in his reading and that the piece in question belongs in fact to a quite later age. What the *Report* actually says is:

> ... forty-two pieces of fragmentary sculptures ... have been purchased at Mathura ... Most of these are of red sandstone and belong to the Kṣatrapa-Kushān period (1st and 2nd centuries A.D.). There are a few pieces of grey sandstone belonging to the mediaeval period. One of these pieces represents the child Kṛishṇa lifting up Mount Govardhana on his left hand. This piece was found at Jātipāra, near the village called Govardhana in the Muttra District.[2]

As we see, Goetz overlooked a whole sentence and that is how he arrived at the mistaken identification that crept into his article. The *Report* puts it vaguely in the Medieval Period and Rene Grousset dates it in the ninth-tenth centuries.[3]

Next we have in plate 35 another example of the trio Balarāma-Ekānaṃśā-Vāsudeva as in plate 4. This panel was first thought to be a representation of Lakṣmaṇa, Sītā and Rāma,[4] but it was later rightly identified by J.C. Ghosh.[5] D.B. Pandey questioned

1. *JOIB*, v.1, 1951, p. 54.
2. *ASIAR*, 1921-22, p. 104.
3. R. Grousset, *L'Inde*, Plon, Paris, 1961, fig. 130.
4. P. Dayal, 'Important sculptures added to the Provincial Museum, Lucknow, during the last decade', *JUPHS*, v.7, 1934, pp. 74-75.
5. 'Ekānaṃśā and Subhadrā', *JRASB*, v.2, 1936.

this identification, and suggested that the image represented Balarāma, Rukmiṇī and Kṛṣṇa,[1] but in our opinion without being very convincing. We believe it to depict Balarāma, Ekānaṃśā and Kṛṣṇa, and with S.C. Mukherji prefer to date it to the tenth-eleventh centuries rather than the seventh, as do the Lucknow Museum authorities and Kalpana Desai.[2] In it we see the three figures with two attendants each, Balarāma with his serpent heads canopy, Ekānaṃśā with a halo and holding a lotus, and Kṛṣṇa also with a halo and four arms.

Before discussing our next plate we can mention here a series of images of Kāliyadamana, copies of which we were unable to secure for reproduction. These images are all roughly contemporary, dated as they are in the seventh century. Three of them are Pallava and can be seen at Kanchipuram and Mahabalipuram in Tamil Nadu. The other one is at the other extreme of the subcontinent in Nepal. The first is at the Kailāsanātha temple in Kanchipuram,[3] and is a very strange image. Kṛṣṇa is shown with eight arms and not actually dancing upon Kāliya but hurling him around while dancing in a pose rather reminiscent of Śiva's dance. The other image from Kanchipuram is at the Vaikuṇṭha Perumāl temple,[4] and is a more conventional image, Kṛṣṇa being shown with two arms and trampling on Kāliya whom he has caught by the tail. This pose is typical of South Indian Kāliyadamana images, and the other example that we mentioned from Mahabalipuram follows that model. It is found on the second floor (*tala*) of the Dharmarāja Ratha, one of the monolithic temples on the shore in Mahabalipuram.[5] It represents Kṛṣṇa holding Kāliya by the tail and pushing him down with his right foot; the nāga king is shown as very distressed, but not saluting Kṛṣṇa as in other South Indian images. Finally the other Kāliyadamana image of the seventh century is found in Kathmandu at the old Vasantpur Palace.[6] This

1. D. B. Pandey, 'Identification of a Sculpture in the Provincial Museum, Lucknow', *JBRS*, v. 27, 1941.
2. K. Desai, *Iconography....*, p. 138.
3. A. Rea, *Pallava Architecture*, *ASI*, New Imperial Series, v.34, rep. Indological Book House, Varanasi 1970, pl. 39, fig. 5.
4. Rea, *ibid.*, pl. 83, fig. 3.
5. K. R. Srinivasan, *The Dharmaraja Ratha and its Sculptures*, Mahabalipuram, Abhinav, New Delhi 1975, pl. 20a.
6. S. Kramrisch, *The Art of Nepal*, Asia House Gallery, New York 1964, pl. iv; P. Pal, *Vaiṣṇava Iconology in Nepal*, Asiatic Society of Bengal, Calcutta 1970, fig. 51 (where he dates it sixth century); and P. Pal, *The Arts of Nepal*, Brill, Leiden 1974, figs. 90-91 (where he corrects his date to seventh century).

is a very strange image, Kāliya being represented as if he were at the top of a mountain formed by his own coils and those of his wives, and brandishing the body of a serpent to defend himself from the blows that Kṛṣṇa is giving him with his feet and with a lotus. Kṛṣṇa is here represented as a child and not as a man as in the three examples that we have just mentioned.

We can now present the Govardhanadhārī from Mahabalipuram, as portrayed in plate 36. This is truly one of the most powerful images in Kṛṣṇa Iconography and in the whole realm of Indian art. It is an enormous panel carved out of the living rock and our photograph only includes about half of it. In the plate we can see from left to right Balarāma reclining on the shoulder of an old man, probably Nanda, and next to them a lady, probably Yaśodā. At their backs a number of cows can be seen. Then we have the towering figure of Kṛṣṇa sustaining the mountain on his left hand. His right hand instead of resting on his hip or on his thigh as the convention demands is in *varadamudrā*, the granting boons sign. To the right we have three other female figures, two holding children by the hand, and one old man carrying a child on his shoulders. More cows can be seen in the background. The woman next to Kṛṣṇa on the right, has been identified as Rādhā.[1] This identification seems probable in view of the *mukuṭa* crown that the lady is wearing, although Yaśodā could also wear a crown, and also in view of the Tamil earlier tradition of a girl Napinnai who made love with Kṛṣṇa at Vṛndāvana.[2]

We will discuss now some very interesting pieces found at the Buddhist *stūpa* at Pāhārpur, now in Bangladesh. The site was most probably originally Hindu, and many of the sculptures and terracottas were taken either from the original temple or from other places and attached to the basement of the stūpa at random.[3] It is thus very difficult, not to say impossible, to determine the date, or dates, of the sculptures. S.K. Saraswati[4] has divided them into three groups according to style and has assigned dates to them ranging from the 6th to the 8th centuries. However, this is all very subjective and even Saraswati himself admits that the proposed dates

1. O. C. Gangoly, 'Indra-cult *versus* Kṛṣṇa-cult' *JGJRI*, v.7, 1949, p. 2.
2. *Śilappadikāram* 16.
3. See K. N. Dikshit, *Paharpur*, *MASI*, v. 55, Delhi 1938, pl. 26 c, d, e.
4. *Early Sculpture of Bengal*, Sambodhi, Calcutta, 1962.

are uncertain: "we may propose the following chronology for the Pāhārpur sculptures—sixth century for the first group, seventh for the second, and eighth for the third. It is possible that the first and the second groups belong to the same epoch, namely the seventh century A.D."[1] There are in Pāhārpur twelve pieces identified as scenes in the Kṛṣṇa legends; of these twelve four are doubtful identifications. The twelve scenes are: Vasudeva carrying the baby Kṛṣṇa; the uprooting of Yamalārjuna; Pralambāsuravadha; Keśiniṣūdana; Govardhanadhāraṇa; Balarāma; the wrestling match; the killing of Kaṃsa; the abduction of Subhadrā; Veṇugopāla; Rādhā and Kṛṣṇa; and Devakī giving Kṛṣṇa to Vasudeva.

We believe that there is nothing to guarantee that the pieces said to represent the killing of Kaṃsa, the abduction of Subhadrā, Veṇugopāla, and Rādhā and Kṛṣṇa indeed represent those scenes. We have not been able to obtain copies for reproduction of all twelve panels and we are therefore presenting in our plates 37 to 40 only four of them, the others may be seen in S.K. Saraswati's monograph.[2] The episode of the killing of the horse-demon is, as we said in the fourth chapter, one of the most popular of Kṛṣṇa's adventures and one that is often represented in the iconography. In plate 37 we have one of the best of these images, both for its dramatic force and its plastic qualities. In it we see the figure of Kṛṣṇa valiantly receiving the vicious attack of Keśi. The hero is in an upright posture, raising his right arm to strike a blow to the demon's face. Keśi is biting Kṛṣṇa's elbow, but in spite of his ferocious looks he is seen here as a small figure in comparison with the hero. Both the horse and Kṛṣṇa are trampling on an unidentified figure crouching on the ground. The dress of Kṛṣṇa consists of a loin cloth fastened by a girdle, and a waist-band, tied in a knot at his right side, the ends of which fall freely in an elegant pattern that enhances greatly the line of the hip. His hair is in the *Kākapakṣa* style, and he wears big round ear-rings. Two palm trees flank the composition, and in the background another tree can be seen.

In plate 38 we present the uprooting of the Yamalārjuna trees. The representation of this episode in Pāhārpur is an iconographic transformation of the South-Indian depictions of Kāliyadamana. There Kṛṣṇa is trampling over the hoods of the serpent while holding its tail in his hand.[3] If we could not

1. S. K. Saraswati, *ibid*, p. 47.
2. *Ibid.* plates 27, 28, 29, 33 and 36.
3. See H. Zimmer, *Art of Indian Asia*, V.2, pl. 423;

see in the Pāhārpur panel a faint resemblance to leaves in Kṛṣṇa's hands, we could take it to be the destruction of two serpents. Other representations of the scene depict the heads of Kubera's sons on the trunk of the trees and not at their roots as here (see plates 43 and 46). The composition of this relief is related to the depiction of the same episode at the Lakṣmaṇa Temple, Khajuraho (pl.68). S.K. Saraswati assigns this piece as well as the previous one to the 2nd group of his classification, i.e., 7th century.

In the next plate we have an extremely interesting image generally regarded as depicting the Govardhana-dhāraṇa,[1] but we can show that it represents the Aghāsuravadha. What we see in the panel is a four armed figure opening the jaws of a gigantic monster with his two upper arms, and protecting a pair of children with his other two arms. Now, this depiction perfectly agrees with the account of the *Bhāgavata Purāṇa* quoted earlier,[2] where the demon Aghāsura assumes the shape of an enormous python. The cowboys mistake this for a mountain and enter into his cave-like mouth, from where they are rescued by the hero who augments his own body in size to such an extent that he chokes the monster. After that, he took the children out of the demon's maw.[3] As we can see the text and plastic depiction are in very close agreement. One important point to note here is that this episode is found only in the *Bhāgavata Purāṇa* and in no other text. If we consider this, our new identification of that panel would presuppose the knowledge of the *Bhāgavata* account in Bengal during the 8th century, the date assigned to the piece by Saraswati who includes it in his third group.[4]

Next we have another very interesting piece in that it has also been claimed to be the earliest representation of Rādhā (plate 40). Dikshit was the first one to identify this couple as Rādhā and Kṛṣṇa[5] but this identification was disputed afterwards by Saraswati:

> There are....no definite data to identify the pair in the panel as Kṛishṇa and Rādhā. From the... features indicating divinity, from the frequency of the depiction of Kṛishṇaite scenes in Pāhārpur art and from its position in the same wall that contains the figures of Balarāma and Yamunā, Dikshit's interpretation may appear to be a probable one which, if correct, would give us perhaps the first plastic representation of a motif, so common and abundant in the neo-Vaishnavite art of Bengal.[1]

After this opinion he goes on to consider the position of Rādhā at the time of the probable date of the sculpture (6th-7th centuries), and concludes that it could not possibly represent her: "if the amatory couple at Pāhārpur have anything to do with the Kṛishṇa legend it would be better to describe them either as Kṛishṇa and Rukmiṇī or as Kṛishṇa and Satyabhāmā" (*ibid.* p.53). Saraswati's reasons for that possible identification are, however, far outweighed by his own reasonable doubts. Neither the frequency of the Kṛṣṇaite themes nor the position nearby of other panels that are not at their original location, are sufficient reasons to identify what is, most probably, just an amatory couple. If we were to identify every couple found as Rādhā and Kṛṣṇa we would have hundreds of them. The position is very similar to that of the supposed Dānalīlā of Rang Mahal (pl.11), another piece found out of its original context and therefore rendered unidentifiable in view of the lack of any other recognizable signs of identity. There are several other couples at Pāhārpur[2]; why are not they identified as Rādhā and Kṛṣṇa? Of course the same objections apply to the identification of this sculpture as Kṛṣṇa and Rukmiṇī or any other of his wives.

The futility of so many of these pseudo-identifications can be demonstrated by taking the example of the supposed Kṛṣṇa playing the flute of S.K. Bhattacharya[3]. He follows Dikshit's description of a figure (Dikshit, *Pāhārpur* pl.XXXVI, d) holding a flute, and hastily concludes that because of the strange position of the hands it must be Kṛṣṇa holding a flute. He could not see that the figure is in fact leaning on a staff whose lower part has been broken, as Saraswati has shown.[4] With this we can leave Pāhārpur and pass on to two other very important series. These ones, however, are in their original positions and can be dated with much more certainty. We are referring to the reliefs on two pillars of the Virūpākṣa and the Mallikārjuna temples at Pattadakal.

In plates 41 to 44 we present four panels found on

C. Sivaramamurti, *South Indian Bronzes*, Lalit Kalā Academy, Delhi 1963, pl. 44b; and our plate 59 from Prambanam, Java.

1. K. N. Dikshit, *Pāhārpur*, *MASI*, v.55, pl. XXVIII; S.K. Saraswati, *Early Sculpture....*, p. 82 ("an unmistakable representation of Krishna holding up mountain Govardhana").
2. See above p. 92.
3. *BhP* 10.12.
4. S. K. Saraswati, *ibid.*
5. K. N. Dikshit, *Pāhārpur* p. 44, pl. XXVII, c.

1. S. K. Saraswati, *ibid,*....pp. 51-52.
2. *Ibid,*....pls. 35, 45, 62.
3. *Kṛṣṇa-Cult*, p. 75 and p. 83.
4. S. K. Saraswati, *Early Sculpture....*, p. 87 and pl. 34.

the four sides of the first pillar in the southernmost row of the inside of Virūpākṣa temple. The first panel is that on the South face of the pillar (pl.41). It represents the exchange of the babies. From left to right we see first Devakī inside a palace, lying on the delivery bed with the baby Kṛṣṇa by her side. Next to the right we see Vasudeva taking the baby in his arms and then, further to the right, again Vasudeva and the baby with a second figure behind them, this last one could be a protecting deity. There is, however, no text that accords with this. In the centre of the panel there is the depiction of a temple with a *liṅga* inside, indicating that the whole operation is realized under the protection of Śiva, although this is also absent from the texts. To the right of the temple we have a similar scene being performed in the reverse direction. First Yaśodā giving her still-born daughter to Nanda and then Nanda approaching the temple with the baby and with a second figure at his back. At the extreme right of the relief there is a different scene. We see Yaśodā inside her house and the baby Kṛṣṇa outside putting his little hand in a pot of butter.

Plate 42 reproduces the East side of the pillar. In it we see the scene of the killing of Kaṃsa. First, from left to right, we have two figures observing how Kṛṣṇa drags Kaṃsa by one foot. At the back another seated figure is also watching the scene and on the right we see the image of the Goddess flying to the sky mounted on her lion, fulfilling her promise to Kaṃsa that she would be present at the time of his death.[1] This relief differs also from the texts since here Kṛṣṇa drags Kaṃsa by the foot and not by the hair as described in the Purāṇas.

Next we have on the West face of the pillar another very interesting panel. It has been described and illustrated by R.S. Panchamukhi but he failed to identify the first scene on the left.[2] In plate 43 we see that this particular scene corresponds narratively to that described by us in relation to the Maṇḍor pillars (pl.7) and a Deogarh panel (pl.14), based on the texts of the *Harivaṃśa*, the *Padma Purāṇa*, and especially the *Triṣaṣṭiśalākāpuruṣacaritra* (see above pp 104-5). In the Pattadakal version we have first the baby Kṛṣṇa lying in his cradle and the bird-demon over him. Immediately next we see a cart-wheel with a demonic face issuing from it, and then Kṛṣṇa sucking Pūtanā's breast until she dies. To the right of this scene there is a depiction of Kṛṣṇa dragging the mortar and uprooting the Yamalārjuna trees as he follows Yaśodā, who is standing with a pot of milk on her head. After this we have a representation of the killing of Keśi, where Kṛṣṇa is shown as an adult figure and not as baby as in the rest of the panel. The personage observing the battle is Balarāma as we can see from the plough he carries in his right hand.

Finally, on the North Face of the same pillar we can see three more scenes of the Kṛṣṇa story. They are from left to right, Kāliyadamana, Govardhanadhāraṇa and the wrestling match. In the first of these scenes Kṛṣṇa is dragging Kāliya by the tail instead of trampling on his hoods as in the standard representations. The Govardhanadhāraṇa also differs from the usual models since here, as we mentioned before, Kṛṣṇa holds the mountain on his right hand. The final episode depicted includes six figures, first those of Balarāma and Kṛṣṇa entering the arena and then the same two killing the two wrestlers Cāṇūra and Muṣṭika. This relief has been illustrated by Bruhn but has not been described in detail.[1] Cousens presented drawings of the four sides of the pillar,[2] but neither did he present a description of the panels.

At the Mallikārjuna temple there is also another pillar with scenes of the life of Kṛṣṇa. This temple is a contemporary of the Virūpākṣa, both being built within very few years of each other, or even at the same time, by the two queens of the Cālukya king Vikramāditya II.[3] The pillar is the fourth from the entrance in the row at the left of the central aisle and it is more elaborately carved than the other one at the Virūpākṣa temple, having two rows of figures plus a medallion on each face instead of only one row. The North face of the pillar even has three rows with scenes of Kṛṣṇa's life and a pair of supporting figures instead of a medallion. The reliefs on this side are extremely important and we reproduce them in plates 45, 46 and 47.

In plate 45 we see the two upper rows of the panel. The topmost one reproduces roughly the same scene as that of plate 41. In it we see a temple with a *liṅga* and Nanda and Vasudeva approaching from either

1. *HV* 48.35
2. R. S. Panchamukhi, "Pattadakal and its Sculptures—a Brief Outline", *Bulletin of the Deccan College Research Institute*, V.8, 1947, pl. VI.

1. K. Bruhn, "Classification in Indian Iconography", in *German Scholars on India*, v. 2, Nachiketa, Bombay 1976, fig. 4.
2. H. Cousens, *Chalukyan Architecture*, ASI, Calcutta 1926, pl. XLVI, drawings on the upper right corner.
3. R. S. Panchamukhi, "Pattadakal....", JDCRI, v.8, 1947, p. 63.

side, each one with a baby in his arms. Beside them there are other figures that must be divine protectors, especially the one on the extreme left which is of very high stature. In the second row can be seen three other episodes. Starting from the right we have the Śakaṭabhaṅga, then a scene where Yaśodā is suckling the baby Kṛṣṇa on a bed inside a house while two other figures are watching them, and finally a depiction of Kṛṣṇa stealing the butter from the *gopīs*. In plate 46 we can see the lower row with another two scenes. These are, from right to left, Pūtanāvadha, which is barely recognizable—the carving not being very good—and the dragging of the mortar and uprooting of the Yamalārjuna trees. In this last scene we see first the little boy tied to the mortar walking towards the left looking for Yaśodā. Then we see him past the two trees, pulling at the mortar that has been stuck between them and calling Yaśodā who can be seen together with other *gopī* on the extreme left.

In plate 47 we have a couple in dancing posture whom we can identify as Kṛṣṇa and Rādhā. In contrast with the supposed Dānalīlā of Rang Mahal (pl.11) and with the alleged Rādhā-Kṛṣṇa or Kṛṣṇa-Rukmiṇī (pl.40) of Pāhārpur, there are positive elements in this relief to identify the figures. In the first place we have the flute held by the man; in the other sculptures there is not a similar characteristic mark. In second place, and most importantly, the scene is depicted within an entirely Kṛṣṇaite context, the four sides of the pillar having depictions of Kṛṣṇa legends—the other two sculptures are not, as we said previously, in their original position. Thus we have here, perhaps for the first time, a representation of that famous motif, Kṛṣṇa eloping with Rādhā in the stations of the dance. There are only two other possible depictions of the couple, one of which is in the Govardhanadhāraṇa panel at Mahābalipuram (pl.36), as we said before. There, however, they are not represented together as here, and the identity of the lady is only a probability. The second is in the Maṇḍor pillars (pl.8), but that is also a speculation. This could also be the first depiction of a flute playing Kṛṣṇa.

On the East side of the pillar—very damaged by dampness—we have three more episodes, one in the medallion and two more in parallel registers under it. This side is illustrated in plate 48. There we can see the Kāliyadamana depicted on the medallion. Kṛṣṇa is shown fighting the serpent who is also fighting and not asking for compassion as in the usual depictions. The two enemies are of gigantic stature compared with the two onlookers on the lower left. The coils of the serpent form an enormous mass on which Kṛṣṇa is furiously trampling with his feet. The composition of this medallion is quite similar to that of the Kathmandu Kāliyadamana.[1] In the registers there can still be recognized—although only very faintly—the scenes of the killing of Yogamāyā, Yaśodā's little daughter, in place of Kṛṣṇa. In the first register, on the left, we see Devakī's lying-in chamber, and she is on the bed with the baby girl put there instead of her own child. In the background there are two figures with maces, perhaps the guards who were awaiting the birth so that they could communicate the news to Kaṃsa. Next we have a figure coming out of the chamber and giving the child to a man, perhaps Vasudeva. Then we see Vasudeva imploring Kaṃsa to spare the life of this only girl, while Kaṃsa rebukes him while holding the baby in his arms. Finally we see on the right Vasudeva watching horrified as Kaṃsa hurls the baby by the feet to dash her against the stone at the extreme right, and over this stone we see the goddess floating in the air, telling Kaṃsa of the birth of his mortal enemy. The scene on the second register is not very easily identifiable but we think it may represent the adoration of the Goddess by the Yādavas. On the left we see a figure on a throne being saluted by several seated and standing figures, and in the centre the Goddess appears dancing on a corpse and attended by two dwarfish figures to the right. At the extreme right there is another standing figure that can not be identified.

In plate 49 we see the South face of the pillar. The medallion presents a Govardhanadhārī image with four arms; no other human figures are shown but many cows are depicted. The first register includes four episodes of the Kṛṣṇa legend. From left to right we have the Dhenukavadha, where, differently from the texts, it is Kṛṣṇa who hurls this demon by the hind legs and throws him to the top of a tree while Balarāma watches the scene. Next we have Kṛṣṇa killing the elephant Kuvalayāpīḍa. The hero is shown in the moment that he uproots the right tusk of the elephant, which looks small compared with the divine stature of Kṛṣṇa. Then we have two more scenes of battles against beasts. These are Keśiniṣūdana and Ariṣṭāsuravadha, i.e., the killing of the horse-demon and of the bull-demon. In the background we see Balarāma again watching closely. In

1. P. Pal, *The Art of Nepal*, pl. 90.

the second register we see the wrestling match. First, from left to right, we see Kaṃsa seated on his royal seat at the arena, and then we see Kṛṣṇa and Balarāma jumping into the arena and, further, the several battles that took place on that occasion between the two brothers and Cāṇūra, Muṣṭika, Tośalaka, Andhra, etc.

Finally in plate 50 we have the West face of the pillar. In the medallion we see another couple that again could be identified as Rādhā and Kṛṣṇa. This identification is made possible because of the cow that is included at the bottom left. On the two registers we see more battle scenes that could be identified as part of the wrestling match.

In plates 51 and 54 we present some sculptures from Ellora, ranging from the 8th to the 10th centuries. The first one is a six armed Govardhanadhārī found at the Daśāvatāra cave, dated around A.D. 725.[1] Kṛṣṇa's figure is truly gigantic compared with the cows and the cowherds, and he holds some of Viṣṇu's emblems. In his upper right hand he has a lotus, and in his second one a *cakra*. In his lower left arm he holds a *śaṅkha*. The mountain is not depicted. In plate 52 we have another Govardhanadhārī. This one is at the Kailāsanātha temple, dated c.A.D. 754-773, and is also of gigantic stature, although it has only two arms. Kṛṣṇa wears here, like in the Pāhārpur Keśiniṣūdana a piece of cloth around the waist besides his regular loin-cloth. He holds the mountain with his right hand.

In plate 53 we have a narrative panel that depicts some scenes of the legend of the birth of Kṛṣṇa. This relief is also at the Kailāsanātha temple. It consists of two registers, one over the other, as at the Virūpākṣa temple in Pattadakal, but here they were not completely finished, and this, besides the weathering down, renders their identification very difficult. In the lower register, from right to left, there seems to be represented, first, the exchange of the babies. This identification is made on the strength of the two similar examples found at Pattadakal (plates 41 and 45), which also include the depiction of a temple as here, although the actions of the personages are not very clear. The next scene to the left apparently represents the killing of Pūtanā. We see a cradle hanging from a tree-branch and on it the demoness raising her arms while Kṛṣṇa clings to her bosom. On the other side of the tree we see a *gopī* churning milk and some cowherds taking the cows to graze. The figures are very badly damaged, and we cannot be sure if there is a broken figure of the little Kṛṣṇa stealing the butter, or if one of the cowherds could be he. In the upper register, from left to right, we have again the cows and the cowherds, but the scene is unidentifiable. In the second division of the register there seems to be depicted the Śakaṭabhaṅga, although the cart is almost invisible. We see Kṛṣṇa lying in his cradle with some object over him, and at the foot of the cradle a demon falling as though he has been pushed by the child. After this division with Śakaṭabhaṅga we see some other unidentifiable scenes. First, the goddess flying to the left. We know that she is the goddess because of the lion that can be seen behind her, waiting upon her. The other, and last, scene in the register includes several figures, the central one apparently being a man shooting arrows from a chariot, represented only by the two wheels. This could be any of the many battles fought by Kṛṣṇa.

Finally, in plate 54, we have another representation of the three deities, Balarāma, Ekānaṃśā and Vāsudeva. This one is found at Cave no.27 in Ellora, generally dated in the 9th-10th centuries A.D.[1], and is comparable, on many counts, to the Kuṣāṇa images at the Patna Museum, (pl.3). The posture and the position of the hands is exactly the same in both cases. Some differences being in the crowns worn by the Ellora images, absent in the ones from Bihar, and in the lack of Balarāma's serpent canopy, as well as in the lotus held by Ekānaṃśā in Ellora but not in Bihar. This image and the one in the Lucknow Museum (pl.35) roughly contemporary, prove that the cult of these three deities was still very popular in the tenth century, as it is even now in Orissa as the Jagannāth Puri proves.

Before coming to our two final series, Prambanam and Khajuraho, we have two more pieces in our plates 55 and 56. They are, first a Keśiniṣūdana, very traditional in its depiction of the episode, found at Abaneri, Rajasthan, dating from the 9th century and now kept at the Amber Museum. The second is a panel in the lintel of the Caturbhuja temple at Gwalior, Madhya Pradesh, dated in the late 9th century. This panel includes several scenes of the legends of Kṛṣṇa, among which we can identify the exchange of the babies, Pūtanāvadha, Śakaṭabhaṅga, and the uprooting of Yamalārjuna, an episode that here has been reduced to the removal of a sort of flowerpot. The photograph (kindly supplied by the Institute

1. A. Lippe, "Early Chālukya Icons" *Artibus Asiae* v. 34, 1972 p. 282.

1. K. Kumar, "An Ekānaṃśā Relief of Ellora", *Journal of Indian History*, v.44, 1966, pp. 831-838.

of American Studies, Varanasi) does not include the complete scenes at the extreme right and left of the panel, and so we are unable to identify them.

In plates 57 to 65 we have a series of panels found in the Viṣṇu temple of the Loro-Jongrang complex at Prambanam, Java. This series is of great importance, and this is the first time that it is discussed in the general context of the Kṛṣṇa Iconography. Even in the field of Indonesian Art it has not been much noticed.[1] The first panel has two scenes, the first one not found in the Purāṇas but that can be related to an episode in them. This represents, we believe, the finding of Kṛṣṇa by Nanda and Yaśodā after he has miraculously survived being cast away in the river by his true parents. On the left we see Nanda petting the baby while Yaśodā observes, and on the right we see Kṛṣṇa coming out of the water holding a fish in his hand. If we look at the next section of the panel, we could even think that in this first scene we actually have the two brothers, Kṛṣṇa and Balarāma, being found in the river, since in the Pūtanāvadha episode, represented in the second part of the panel, it is the two brothers who suck the demoness' breasts till she dies.

In plate 58 we have two more scenes of the Kṛṣṇa stories. The first one from the left is again very difficult to identify. It looks as if Balarāma is hitting a boy on the head, probably for cheating in the game that the latter is playing with the smaller boy on the right, who points to him as if accusing him. We do not know, however, which of the two seated boys would be Kṛṣṇa, the cheat being scolded by Balarāma, or the accuser. We recognize Balarāma, in the centre, by his ploughshare. To the right we have another scene. This one, it seems to us, represents the games of the two brothers at the cow-pens. We actually see three boys, but this could just be the conventional way of representing the same person twice or thrice in the same plastic space. The first boy is holding a calf on high, while the second boy pulls another calf by the tail, and the third boy hurls still another calf by a hind leg.

In plate 59 we have the Kāliyadamana represented on the left. Kṛṣṇa is shown holding the serpent by the tail and trampling on his head, in the manner of South Indian representations, while Balarāma encourages him from the river bank. One interesting detail to note here is that Kāliya is shown with only one head, different from the usual Indian seven-headed representation. To the right we have the killing of two demons. The first one is a very strange scene, with Kṛṣṇa tearing apart a demon by opening his legs widely with the right foot and the left hand, keeping him down with the right foot and, apparently, pulling the demon's penis. In the second one we see Kṛṣṇa killing either a horse or a bull, the species can not be ascertained, in the first case it could be the killing of Keśi, in the second that of Ariṣṭa. The depiction does not correspond, however, to any of these episodes as they are related in the Purāṇas. What we see is Kṛṣṇa pushing with his left foot on the animal's neck, and pulling at his tail and hind legs to kill him.

In plate 60 we have what seems to be a representation of Dhenukavadha and Ariṣṭāsuravadha. On the left we see Balarāma hurling the demon Dhenuka on high. Dhenuka is half human and half beast, his upper body resembling that of a man, and his lower body that of a donkey; we can see one of his hoofs to the left of Balarāma's head. Next to the right we see Kṛṣṇa trampling upon a second demon. We know that this is Dhenukavadha because of the palm-tree at the extreme left. To the right of the panel we see the scene of the killing of Ariṣṭāsura. Kṛṣṇa is standing on the body of the enormous bull who has fallen. The relief is badly damaged but we can see the bull's hump and Kṛṣṇa's right foot on the horn.

In plates 61 to 65 we see five different scenes of the wrestling match. We cannot identify each one of the wrestlers encountered by Kṛṣṇa and Balarāma in each scene, we only know that they have to be Cāṇūra, Muṣṭika, Tośalaka, Andhra, Śala or Kūṭa. In the first three scenes (plates 61, 62 and 63) Kṛṣṇa wrestles while Balarāma observes attentively. In plates 61 and 62 the fight is presented with great realism, but in plate 63 a fantastic element is admitted. There we see Kṛṣṇa breaking a giant's back and the body of the latter almost forms a circle around that section of the panel. In plate 64 we see Balarāma disposing of one of his adversaries holding him by the neck and hitting him on the face with the right fist. Finally

1. A. J. Bernet Kempers, *Ancient Indonesian Art*, van der Peet, Amsterdam 1959, presents a photograph of one of the panels (pl. 159). That is the only one of this series that we have been able to trace. His description of it does not go into any details to try to identify the scenes. On the other hand, we have not been able either to find a Javanese text that presents the Kṛṣṇa legends as found in these reliefs, (see P. J. Zoetmulder, *Kalangwan, A survey of Old Javanese Literature*, Martinus Nijhoff, The Hague, 1974, pp. 250-290, and 387-395). This perhaps indicates that the series is derived from a Sanskrit text, Indian or Javanese, now disappeared, since the sculptures do not always agree with the Purāṇic accounts.

in plate 65 we see another scene of wrestling but is too complicated to be described, four persons being apparently involved, and their bodies are intertwined.

We have to note, before leaving them, that the Prambanam reliefs are of a high artistic quality. This can be appreciated even in their present condition when they are badly weathered down. They are full of energy and action, and also of great realism expressed in extremely fine carving. The faces of the dying demons are notable for their emotive expression. In the context of the Kṛṣṇa Iconography we can note especially the absence of the Govardhanadhāraṇa episode, and also of the Dugdhaharaṇa, Śakaṭabhaṅga and Yamalārjuna trees, the episodes most often encountered in the Indian images. We have already noted the scenes found in these reliefs but not in India, specially the finding of Kṛṣṇa in the river. The Prambanam panels are witnesses, together with the Vat Koh Govardhanadhārī (pl.17), of some four hundred years before, of the enormous territorial expanse covered by the Kṛṣṇa legends, and of their popularity.

We come now to the final series that we will consider in this survey of iconographic depictions of the Kṛṣṇa stories up to the 10th century. This last one is that found in the Lakṣmaṇa temple of Khajuraho. Different from other series that we have treated here, this one is not in panels with various scenes represented one after the other, but it consists of separate scenes represented in individual sculptures and attached in separate niches. All the sculptures are highly stereotyped and appear to be following standard models for each scene. They are found on the *Pradakṣiṇāpatha*, i.e. ambulatory corridor around the sanctum of the temple, interspersed with figures of *apsaras* and guardian deities.

In Plate 66, we have a depiction of Pūtanāvadha, and another of Vatsāsuravadha.

The Pūtanāvadha representation is one of the most forceful that we have of this episode, its detail and expressiveness is only matched by the energy and action of the same scene in the panels of Prambanam, Java, nearly contemporaries of the Khajuraho sculptures (see pl. 57).

This sculpture is the panel no. 8 in the North side of the exterior of the *garbhagṛha*. It follows exactly the same design as the ones at Badami of two hundred years before, only that being inside a temple it is much better preserved, and we are able to appreciate the detailed realism of the carving—as well as the force in the expression so carefully conveyed by the artist. However, the piece is still stereotyped, and all the action seems to be frozen forever, the faces looking like masks as in all the rest of the series. We see Pūtanā seated on a low seat in *lalitāsana*. She raises both her arms with alarm and her face reflects the great pain she is suffering while Kṛṣṇa, who is standing at her left side, clings to her left breast with both hands and sucks intently. The baby Kṛṣṇa keeps a serene pose despite the dramatic situation and in contrast with the agonizing image of the demoness. The body of Pūtanā is emaciated by pain and we can see her veins, junctures and ribs under the parched skin. In contrast, the body of Kṛṣṇa is plump, soft and tender. Her head-dress resembles very much that of Kṛṣṇa in the Maṇḍor and Pāhārpur panels (*kākapakṣa*).

This is the only Khajuraho sculpture where we actually see Kṛṣṇa as a boy. In all others he is represented as being of superhuman stature, including the one representing the Śakaṭabhaṅga.

The Vatsāsuravadha in the same plate is the panel no.10 on the North face of the sanctum. There we see Kṛṣṇa as having four arms, passing his right leg over the back of the calf and holding him by the nose. The composition is cold and rigid, and this may be the poorest piece in all the series.

In plate 67 we have the Śakaṭabhaṅga. This is the panel no.10 on the West face of the sanctum. Again, as in the last scene, Kṛṣṇa is shown here as having four arms. Unlike other representations of this scene (plate 7 and 14 specially), we do not see Kṛṣṇa under the cart kicking and upsetting it, but here he holds it with his two lower hands and, pushing it down with his right foot, tries to break it. The cart looks more like a toy than like the big cart described in the Purāṇas. The next scene, the uprooting of the Yamalārjuna trees, is in panel no. 4 of the North face of the sanctum. We present it in plate 68, where we see Kṛṣṇa, with two arms only, pulling the trees (here become more like small plants) by the stem. He entwines his legs around the two trunks and there is no sign of the mortar. This statue is, as we have said before, compositionally related to the depiction of the same scene in Pāhārpur (pl. 38).

In plate 69 we have what may be the finest of all the statues in this Khajuraho series, and even in the whole of the Kṛṣṇa Iconography. It is the Kāliyadamana of the second panel of the West face of the sanctum. The composition is full of energy and vitality, and the lines balanced, elegant and refined. The torso of Kṛṣṇa is a masterpiece of design with the raised arm's line continued by the cordon on the chest, and the bent forearm balanced at the bottom by Kāliya's arm and tail. The entire piece transpires a sort of controlled might and force that reflects in the stone what the texts express as the essence of Kṛṣṇa's activities. The whole battle is more like a performed dramatic dance, a *līlā*. The face of Kāliya shows no fear or dejection and defeat, but deep, profound devotion to the Lord who chastises him. He has really awakened to the meaning of Divine Might and fully surrenders himself to God's will. This statue has no stylistic parallels to any other Kāliyadamana that we have shown here, the only remote approximation that we can think of is in a panel at the Harihara temple no.1 of Osian, Jodhpur District, Rajasthan, dating from the 9th century.[1]

The next scene is in plate 70; it represents the Ariṣṭāsuravadha, and is in the panel no. 2 on the North face of the sanctum. It is again a lifeless image very much like the Vatsāsuravadha (pl. 66). The demon is diminutive and Kṛṣṇa does not seem to have much trouble, not even much interest, in holding him by one horn and pushing his face to break his neck. In plate 71, the fourth panel on the South face of the sanctum, we have a depiction of the Pralambāsuravadha. This must be a work by the same master who produced the Kāliyadamana, since again we can see that energy at play and that equilibrium of lines in the composition. Balarāma rides on the shoulders of the demon, who is half kneeling, and pulling his hair with the left hand, prepares to strike him with his right hand.

In plate 72 we have the only known representation of Trivakrānugraha. This is the 8th panel on the West face of the sanctum, in it we see both Kṛṣṇa and Balarāma, besides the small figure of Trivakra, who is offering them Kaṃsa's perfumed ointments. Kṛṣṇa and Balarāma appear to be walking together, and Kṛṣṇa turns his face to say something to his brother as he dips his fingers in the oil jar presented by the little hunchback. The woman's body is sensuously delineated, suggesting the erotic episode that follows her cure. She turns up her face in adoration to Kṛṣṇa. The sculpture is again refined and full of zest.

In panel 12, on the South face of the sanctum, we have a depiction of Kuvalayāpīḍa. This again may be by the same master who produced the Kāliyadamana and the Pralambāsuravadha—the force of the composition indicates that this is so. As in most of the other pieces in the series, this one portrays Kṛṣṇa as of gigantic stature; he virtually tramples on the elephant, who compared to the hero looks like a toy animal. Kṛṣṇa has four arms here. With his two lower ones he clasps the elephant's trunk and with his upper right he raises a mace to strike the beast. The other arm is missing.

Finally, in plates 74 and 75 we have Balarāma and Kṛṣṇa wrestling with Cāṇūra and Muṣṭika. In plate 74, the 4th panel on the West face of the sanctum Balarāma is striking Muṣṭika with his right fist. In plate 75 we see Kṛṣṇa with four arms killing Cāṇūra. With his two lower arms he grips the athlete's right leg, and with his upper left hand he strangles him, while with his upper right hand he brandishes a mace to annihilate him.

To end this survey of the Kṛṣṇa Iconography we should mention a few images, copies of which could not be secured for reproduction here, but which have to be taken into consideration. These are firstly those reproduced in figures 6, 7 and 8 of an excellent article on our subject written in Gujarati by U.P.Shah.[1] They are one of Keśiniṣūdana from Saurāṣṭra, dated 4th century AD[2], and one of Veṇugopāla and Govardhanadhārī, from Khotan, Central Asia, dated also 4th century, and kept at the Hermitage Museum, Leningrad[3]. These last, however, are, in our opinion, very doubtful identifications. We have then a Kāliyadamana, dated 5th-6th century, kept at the Baroda Museum.[4] We can also mention here an identification of a fragment of Nāgārjunakoṇḍa *stūpa* as a scene from the *Ghaṭa Jātaka*[5], this identification has not been discussed by anybody else, and this is perhaps because it is extremely doubtful that it is indeed a depiction of the *Ghaṭa Jātaka*.

Also to be mentioned are a relief in the Berlin Museum of Indian Art, stylistically classified as Gupta, representing Kṛṣṇa and Arjuna watching the fight between Bhīma and Jarāsaṃdha[6], and a series in Garhwa that unfortunately we have been unable to study. This series apparently includes depictions of the exchange of the babies, Pūtanāvadha, Śakaṭa-

1. K. Desai, *Iconography*....fig. 92.

1. U. P. Shah, "Śrī Kṛṣṇa Bālalīlā", *Svādhyay*, Baroda, v. 10-4, 1973, pp. 483-505.
2. U. P. Shah, *ibid*, fig. 6.
3. *Ibid.*, figs. 7-8.
4. Goetz, "Earliest Representations...." *JOIB*, v.1, 1951, pl. 1, fig. 1.
5. S. Kramrisch, *The Art of India through the Ages*, Phaidon, London 1965, pl. 35 and p. 201.
6. K. Bruhn, "Classification in Indian Iconography" fig. 1.

bhaṅga, Yamalārjuna, Dugdhaharaṇa, Kāliyadamana, Govardhanadhāraṇa, Kuvalayāpīḍavadha, and the wrestling match.[1] This series also belongs to the Gupta period. Perhaps some idea of how they look can be had from a fragment now in a private collection in France[2], and from another fragment kept in the Allahabad Museum.[3] One of these two fragments is a depiction of Kāliyadamana, and the second of Ariṣṭāsuravadha.

Another important sculpture which we should mention although it does not directly refer to the Kṛṣṇa legends, is a panel from Kandamotu, Guntur District, Andhra Pradesh[4] depicting Narasiṃha flanked by Kṛṣṇa and other members of his family: Balarāma, Pradyumna, Sāmba and Aniruddha. It is dated as 4th century. There is also, according to Hawley[1], a Śakaṭabhaṅga in the Svarga Brahma temple at Alampur, Andhra Pradesh, dated 7th century. Some more Kṛṣṇa stories are represented in the temple at Sirpur, Eastern Madhya Pradesh, of the 7th-8th centuries[2], and in the contemporary Kośaleśvara temple, at Baidyanath, Orissa[3].

Finally there is the recently discovered miniature shrine in Varanasi, dated c. 900 AD. It includes representations of the three deities Balarāma, Ekānaṃśā and Vāsudeva, and of Govardhanadhārī Kṛṣṇa lifting the mountain with the right hand and flanked by two female figures.[4]

1. B. H. Bourdillon, "Krishna Obelisks at Garhwa", *JUPHS*, v. 1, 1918, pp. 30-40.
2. M. Benisti, *Rapports entre le premier art Khmer et l'art Indien*, EFEO, Paris 1970, v. 2, fig. 141.
3. P. Chandra, *Stone Sculpture in the Allahabad Museum*, American Institute of Indian Studies, Poona 1970, pl. 250.
4. A Eschmann, H. Kulke and G. C. Tripathi eds., *The Cult of Jagannath and the Regional Tradition of Orissa*, Manohar, Delhi 1978, fig. 53.

1. *JAAR*, v. 47, p. 216, n. 4.
2. K. Desai, *Iconography*,. . . ., p. 133.
3. D. R. Das, "Kośaleśvara temple at Baidyanath" *Artibus Asiae*, v. 38, 1976, figs. 12, 13 and 14; Das makes a mistake in the identification of figs. 12 and 13; 12 should be Ariṣṭāsuravadha, and not Keśiniṣūdana as he says, and 13 is not Kuvalayāpīḍa but Keśiniṣūdana, as one can easily see by comparing the position of the figures with that in other depictions of this episode.
4. P. K. Agrawala, "Some Varanasi images of Ganapati, and their Iconographic Problem". *Artibus Asiae*, v. 39, 1977 figs. 6-8.

Conclusion

The main subject of our work has been the stories of Kṛṣṇa, their origins and their formation, the themes and motifs that constitute them, and their representation both in art and literature, specifically in the Purāṇas, up to the tenth century.

We start our survey of these legends by looking at the Vedic gods of whom Kṛṣṇa is said to be an incarnation: Viṣṇu and Nārāyaṇa. Viṣṇu is essentially a divinity of pervasiveness and spatial extensiveness. His most characteristic trait is his three steps and therefore he is called *urugāya* and *urukrama*, 'the wide stepping one' or 'he of ample paces'. Within his three steps the whole Universe is comprehended, and it is several times repeated that this striding-out over the cosmic expanses was done for the benefit of humanity and for creation. Viṣṇu is constantly associated with Indra and helps him in his cosmogonic battle against the demon of chaos and restraint. He is also a protector and a saviour, and is connected with the sun, especially with the solar light, and with fertility also. In his most famous Vedic incarnation as the dwarf Vāmana he prefigures the little Kṛṣṇa who also encompasses the whole Universe. All of these traits are incorporated in one way or another in the Kṛṣṇa stories.

Nārāyaṇa, a deity of the *Brāhmaṇas*, is identified with the Puruṣa of the *Ṛg Veda*, the Universal Giant from whose body the Universe was formed. He is also identified with the Golden Germ, Hiraṇyagarbha, the Primeval embryo who sustained the origins of everything within himself while floating in the cosmic waters. This again is a prefiguration of the image of the child Kṛṣṇa containing the worlds in his little body. The main connections with Kṛṣṇa found in the Veda are therefore in these two images, Universal manifestation, developing and protection; and Universal origin or possibility, i.e. Cosmic manifestation in potency, in latent state as it were. These traits we shall find again in the Kṛṣṇa cycle.

Next we review the occurrence of the name Kṛṣṇa in the *Ṛg Veda*, and the allegations of some scholars that we have there the same personage as the later Purāṇic hero. Their arguments are proven to be groundless and we conclude that the name Kṛṣṇa in the *Ṛg Veda* does not refer to the hero of our legends and, therefore, cannot be used to argue an aboriginal origin of the Kṛṣṇa of the Purāṇas. The first chapter's conclusion is that the Kṛṣṇa legends are not yet present in the *Ṛg Veda*, but that essential traits of the Kṛṣṇa figure exist there in Viṣṇu and Nārāyaṇa, the two deities that mythologically are connected with him.

After looking at the Vedic material we examine some of the earliest evidence on Kṛṣṇa, the Kṛṣṇa cult and the Kṛṣṇa stories. First we address ourselves to the references to Kṛṣṇa in the *Chāndogya Upaniṣad*, and in The Grammar of Pāṇini, as well as in other texts like the *Nirukta* and the *Arthaśāstra* and especially in the *Mahābhāṣya* of Patañjali. We then discuss some epigraphical material that, because it can be dated with more certainty, gives us our first chronological data. All this evidence is then taken together with the assessments of various scholars and examined in detail to try to find, with a degree of certainty, about the image of Kṛṣṇa that was prevalent at the time when most probably the

Purāṇas had not yet been written, i.e. when the legends were in their formative stage, and also about the spreading and the evolution of this image. It is concluded that from the sixth century B.C. onwards, stories about Kṛṣṇa were known and that possibly even from that time or a little later he was a divine figure also. Four different episodes of the life of Kṛṣṇa are found to be documented previous to the Christian Era, these are: the birth of Kṛṣṇa, the killing of Kṛṣṇa, the Syamantaka episode, and the death of Kṛṣṇa. By the beginning of the Christian Era Kṛṣṇa was already considered by many as the Supreme God.

We proceed then to examine the legend itself and employ some of the methods used by folklorists in their analyses of folk-stories and fairy-tales, materials very similar in content to the Purāṇic legends. We start by looking for a type-story and find that several scholars have investigated hero-stories and found out that a common pattern can be discerned in many of them. We make a summary of their findings and include Kṛṣṇa within the number of heroes who share many common characteristics in their legends. Having established this, we select a number of important and characteristic themes and motifs of the Kṛṣṇa story and try to analyse their occurrence in the *Harivaṃśa*, the *Viṣṇu*, *Bhāgavata* and *Devī Bhāgavata Purāṇas*, as well as in the *Ghaṭa Jātaka* and the *Bālacarita*. We also compare these motifs in the Kṛṣṇa cycle with their parallels in the stories of two other heroes, one from India and one from Greece: Indra and Heracles, to find out if the parallelisms are due only to the common hero pattern or to mutual influence.

We start our survey of the Kṛṣṇa stories by looking at the themes of the birth of the hero and find several characteristic motifs like the cast-away child, the baby floating on the waters and the suckling beast, that are of extreme importance in the analysis of the legends of Kṛṣṇa. These motifs are also traced in the myths of Indra and the Heracles saga. We then analyse one particular motif related to the birth of Kṛṣṇa, the eighth child, and find its origins in Vedic Mythology, and follow its development up to the Purāṇas. Parallels to this motif are also pointed out from European folklore.

In the next chapter we examine further themes and motifs essential to the understanding of the legends. First, in our study of the themes of the wonderful child and of the cosmic child, we find that whereas the wonderful child has parallels in the myths of Indra and the legends of Heracles, the cosmic child is a development exclusive to the Kṛṣṇa story. Next we analyse other adventures of Kṛṣṇa and find that most of them fall under the heading of: the deeds of a strong man. We pay particular attention to an aspect of Kṛṣṇa's personality hitherto very little studied, the wrestler. A survey of his wrestling activities is made, and it is shown that this trait is essential to an interpretation of the Kṛṣṇa image. Two other aspects of Kṛṣṇa as a strong man considered by us are his erotic capacity as a great lover and the strong man's ability to consume enormous amounts of food as the great eater.

In this survey of typical themes and motifs of the Kṛṣṇa stories we finally examine two of Kṛṣṇa's most characteristic aspects: the monster killer, and the dragon slayer. As in the other themes and motifs we make a point here of bringing out the parallels with the legends of Heracles and these become more and more striking until, with the analysis of the Bāṇa episode in the Kṛṣṇa legend and the Geryon episode in the cycle of Heracles, we can make a case for direct influence between the two. With this we conclude our research on the Kṛṣṇa stories in the Purāṇas and pass on to their representation in sculpture.

In the last chapter we examine thoroughly the iconographical evidence of the stories. We look for the narrative episodes in the plastic art and therefore concentrate on series of sculpture more than on isolated images, although some of these are also considered, especially if they have a relation to the stories. Important new identifications are made and correspondences between the images and the texts are found. We discuss the problem of Kṛṣṇa's earliest representation and of the stories' earliest representations also. We present for the first time a whole new series found by us at the Surali temple, Badami. We also present what could be the first representation of Rādhā and discuss in detail for the first time the Kṛṣṇa-līlā reliefs found at Pattadakal. Another very important series presented and for the first time discussed here, comparing it with the rest of the Kṛṣṇa iconography, is that of the Lara Jongrang temple at Prambanam, Java. With the survey of the plastic representation of the Purāṇic legends of Kṛṣṇa we conclude our study which, it is hoped ,will shed new light on diverse aspects of the stories, their origin and development, and, not the least, their relationship to other hero stories.

KEY TO MAP

1 Abaneri
2 Ai Khanu
3 Alampur
4 Allahabad
5 Badami
6 Baidyanath
7 Besnagar
8 Delhi
9 Deogarh
10 Devangarh
11 Dvaraka
12 Ellora
13 Etah
14 Ghosundi
15 Guntur
16 Gwalior
17 Kanchipuram
18 Kathmandu
19 Khajuraho
20 Lucknow
21 Mahabalipuram
22 Mandor
23 Mathura
24 Nanaghat
25 Paharpur
26 Pattadakal
27 Rang Mahal
28 Sirpur
29 Taxila
30 Varanasi

MAP OF INDIA
with main sites mentioned in the text.

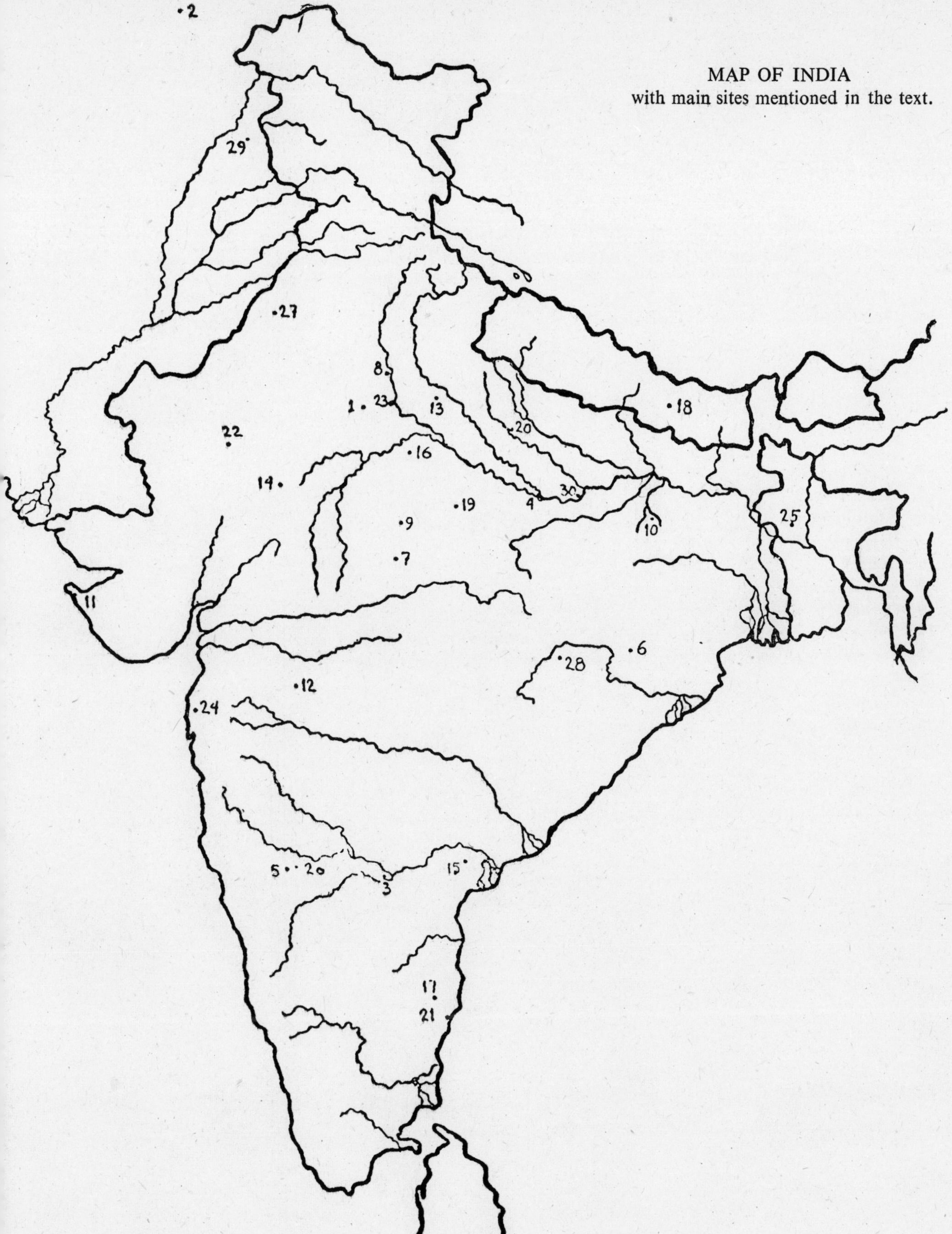

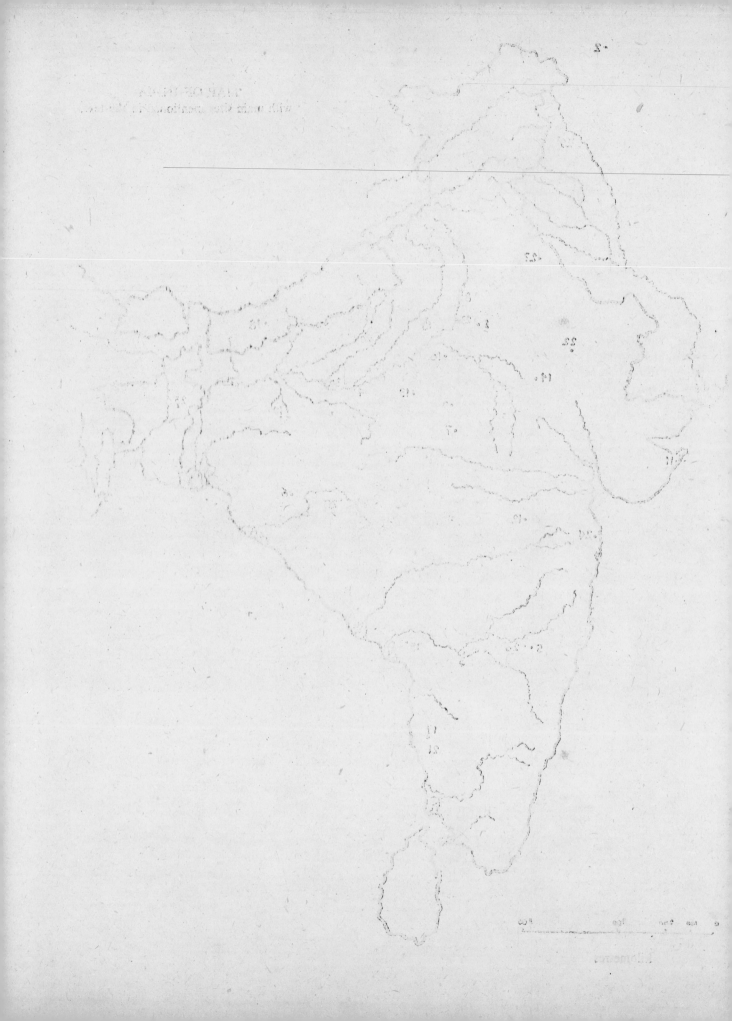

LIST OF PLATES

Calcutta; from R. Grousset, *L'Inde*, fig. 130.

Plate 35. Balarāma-Ekānaṃśā-Vāsudeva. Gangetic Valley, 7th century A.D., Lucknow Museum; from Kalpana Desai, *Iconography of Viṣṇu*, fig. 102.

Plate 36. Kṛṣṇa Govardhanadhārī. Mahabalipuram, Tamil Nadu, 630-668 A.D., Kṛṣṇa maṇḍapa.

Plate 37. Kṛṣṇa Keśiniṣūdana. Pāhārpur, Bangladesh, 7th-8th centuries A.D., Pāhārpur; from S. K. Saraswati, *Early Sculpture of Bengal*, pl. VI-16.

Plate 38. Kṛṣṇa Yamalārjuna. Pāhārpur, Bangladesh, 7th-8th centuries A.D., Pāhārpur; *ibid.*, pl. VI-17.

Plate 39. Kṛṣṇa Aghāsuravadha. Pāhārpur, Bangladesh, 7th-8th centuries A.D., Pāhārpur; from K.N. Dikshit's *Excavations of Paharpur*, pl. xxix-c.

Plate 40. Rādhā-Kṛṣṇa (?) Rukmiṇī-Kṛṣṇa (?) Pāhārpur, Bangladesh, 7th-8th centuries A.D., Pāhārpur; from S.K. Saraswati, *Early Sculpture of Bengal*, pl. III-10.

Plate 41. Kṛṣṇa Līlā. Pattadakal, Karnataka, c.745 A.D., Virūpākṣa Temple.

Plate 42. Kṛṣṇa Līlā. Pattadakal, Karnataka., c.745 A.D., Virūpākṣa Temple.

Plate 43. Kṛṣṇa Līlā. Pattadakal, Karnataka, c.745 A.D., Virūpākṣa Temple.

Plate 44. Kṛṣṇa Līlā. Pattadakal, Karnataka, c.745 A.D., Virūpākṣa Temple.

Plate 45. Kṛṣṇa Līlā. Pattadakal, Karnataka, c.745 A.D., Mallikārjuna Temple.

Plate 46. Kṛṣṇa Līlā. Pattadakal, Karnataka, c.745 A.D., Mallikārjuna Temple.

Plate 47. Rādhā Kṛṣṇa. Pattadakal, Karnataka, c. 745 A.D., Mallikārjuna Temple.

Plate 48. Kṛṣṇa Līlā. Pattadakal, Karnataka, c.745 A.D., Mallikārjuna Temple.

Plate 49. Kṛṣṇa Līlā. Pattadakal, Karnataka, c.745 A.D., Mallikārjuna Temple.

Plate 50. Kṛṣṇa Līlā. Pattadakal, Karnataka, c.745 A.D., Mallikārjuna Temple.

Plate 51. Kṛṣṇa Govardhnadhārī. Ellora, Maharashtra c.725 A.D., Cave 15.

Plate 52 Kṛṣṇa Govardhanadhārī. Ellora, Maharashtra, c.754-773 A.D., Kailāsanātha Temple.

Plate 53. Kṛṣṇa Līlā. Ellora, Maharashtra, c.754-773 A.D., Kailāsanātha Temple.

Plate 54. Balarāma-Ekānaṃśā-Vāsudeva. Ellora, Maharashtra, 9th-10th centuries A.D., Cave 27. Colour neg. Professor A.L. Basham.

Plate 55. Keśiniṣūdana. Abaneri, Rajasthan, 9th century A.D., Amber Museum; from Kalpana Desai, *Iconography of Viṣṇu*, fig. 93.

Plate 56. Kṛṣṇa Līlā. Gwalior, Madhya Pradesh, 875 A.D., Caturbhuja Temple; courtesy American Institute of Indian Studies, Varanasi.

Plate 57. Kṛṣṇa Līlā. Prambanam, Java, c.900-30 A.D., Loro Jongrang Temple.

Plate 58. Kṛṣṇa Līlā. Prambanam, Java, c.900-30 A.D., Loro Jongrang Temple.

Plate 59. Kṛṣṇa Līlā. Prambanam, Java, c.900-30 A.D., Loro Jongrang Temple.

Plate 60. Kṛṣṇa Līlā. Prambanam, Java, c.900-30 A.D., Loro Jongrang Temple.

Plate 61. The Wrestling Match. Prambanam, Java, c.900-30 A.D., Loro Jongrang Temple.

Plate 62. The Wrestling Match. Prambanam, Java, c.900-30 A.D., Loro Jongrang Temple.

Plate 63. The Wrestling Match. Prambanam, Java, c.900-30 A.D., Loro Jongrang Temple.

Plate 64. The Wrestling Match. Prambanam, Java, c.900-30 A.D., Loro Jongrang Temple.

Plate 65. The Wrestling Match. Prambanam, Java, c.900-30 A.D., Loro Jongrang Temple.

Plate 66. Vatsāsuravadha and Pūtanāvadha. Khajuraho, Madhya Pradesh, 953-954 A.D., Lakṣmaṇa Temple.

Plate 67. Śakaṭabhaṅga. Khajuraho, Madhya Pradesh, 953-954 A.D., Lakṣmaṇa Temple.

Plate 68. Yamalārjuna. Khajuraho, Madhya Pradesh, 953-954 A.D., Lakṣmaṇa Temple.

Plate 69. Kāliyadamana. Khajuraho, Madhya Pradesh, 953-954 A.D., Lakṣmaṇa Temple.

Plate 70. Ariṣṭāsuravadha. Khajuraho, Madhya Pradesh, 953-954 A.D., Lakṣmaṇa Temple.

Plate 71. Pralambāsuravadha or Tṛṇāvartavadha. Khajuraho, Madhya Pradesh, 953-954 A.D., Lakṣmaṇa Temple.

Plate 72. Kubjānugraha. Khajuraho, Madhya Pradesh, 953-954 A.D., Lakṣmaṇa Temple.

Plate 73. Kuvalayāpīḍavadha. Khajuraho, Madhya Pradesh, 953-954 A.D., Lakṣmaṇa Temple.

Plate 74. Salavadha or Muṣṭikavadha. Khajuraho, Madhya Pradesh, 953-954 A.D., Lakṣmaṇa Temple.

Plate 75. Cāṇūravadha. Khajuraho, Madhya Pradesh, 953-954 A.D., Lakṣmaṇa Temple.

Bibliography

Aarne, A.A., *The Types of the Folktale*, ed. and tr. by S. Thompson, Suomalainen Tiedeakatemia, Helsinki, 1961.

Agarwal, U., *Khajuraho Sculptures and Their Significance*, S. Chand, Delhi, 1964.

Agni Purāṇa, ed. Jivananda Vidyasagara, Kalikata (Calcutta), 1882.

Agni Purāṇa, Chowkhambha, Varanasi, 1966.

Agni Purāṇa, A prose English Translation by M.N. Dutt, Chowkhambha Sanskrit Series Office, Varanasi, 1967.

Agrawala, P.K., "Some Varanasi Images of Gaṇapati, and their Iconographic Problem", *Artibus Asiae*, v. 39, 1977.

Agrawala, R.C., "Rajputana through the Ages", *Journal of the Bihar Research Society*, v. 41, pt. 3, 1956.

Agrawala, V.S., "Brahmanical Images in Mathurā Art", *Journal of the Indian Society of Oriental Art*, 1937.

——— "A Note on Pūtanā and Yaśodā", *Purāṇa*, v. 2, 1960.

——— "Brahma, Viṣṇu and Śiva in Mathurā Art", *Journal of the United Provinces Historical Society*, v. 22, 1949.

—— "Hiraṇyagarbha", *Purāṇa*, v. 2, 1960.

——— "Puruṣa Sūkta", in *Felicitation Volume presented to Dr. V.V. Mirashi*, ed. by G.T. Deshpande and others, Vidarbha Samshodhan Mandal, Nagpur, 1965.

Aiyangar, K., *Some Contributions of South India to Indian Culture*, University of Calcutta, Calcutta, 1942.

American Committee for South Asian Art Archives, Microfiche Photographic Collection, ed. by S.L. Huntington and W. Spink, Ann Arbor, 1976.

American Institute of Indian Studies, Photographic Archives, Varanasi.

Ansari, Z.D. and Mate, M.S. *Excavations at Dwarka*, Deccan College Postgraduate and Research Institute, Poona, 1966.

Apollodorus Atheniensis, *The Library*, with an English translation by Sir James George Frazer, The Loeb Classical Library, Heinemann, London, 1921.

Archer, W.G., *The Loves of Krishna*, MacMillan, New York, 1962.

Armstrong, R.P., "Content Analysis in Folkloristics", in *Mythology*, ed. by Pierre Maranda, Penguin Modern Sociology Readings, 1972.

Arora, U.P., "Birth of Karṇa", *K.C. Chattopadhyaya Memorial Volume*, Allahabad, 1975.

Atharva Veda Sanhitā, ed. by R. Roth and W.D. Whitney, 3rd. ed., Ferd. Dumlers Verlag, Bonn, 1966.

Atharva Veda Sanhitā, tr. and comm. by W.D. Whitney, *HOS*, vols. 7-8, rep. Motilal Banarsidass, Delhi, 1962.

Auboyer, J., *Daily Life in Ancient India*, Asia Publishing House, London, 1967.

Hymns of the Atharva Veda, tr. by M. Bloomfield, *SBE*, v. 42, rep. Motilal Banarsidass, 1964.

Banerjea, J.N., *The Development of Hindu Iconography*, Calcutta University Press, Culcutta, 1956.

——— *Paurāṇic and Tantric Religion*, University of Calcutta, Calcutta, 1966.

Banerjea, J.N. and Majumdar, R.C. "Two Inscribed

images of Imadpur", *Journal of the Asiatic Society of Bengal*, v. 16, 1950.

Banerjee, P., *Early Indian Religions*, Vikas, Delhi, 1973.

——— "Some Observations on the Interpretation of the Pāṇini Sūtra Vāsudevārjuna-bhyām-vun and the Antiquity of the Bhāgavatas", *Journal of the Bihar Research Society*, v. 40, 1954.

Banerji, A., "Some Sculptures of Qutb Mosque", *Indian Culture*, vol. 2, 1935.

Banerji, R.D., *Basreliefs of Badami*, Archaelogical Survey of India, Memoir no. 25. Calcutta, 1928.

Barnett, L.D., *Hindu Gods and Heroes*, Murray, London, 1922.

——— "Review of *Notes sur la Bhagavad-Gītā* by Étienne Lamotte", *Bulletin of the School of Oriental Studies*, University of London, v. 5, 1928-30.

——— "Review of *The Bhagavad-Gītā* tr. by W.D.P. Hill", *Journal of the Royal Asiatic Society*, 1929.

Barth, A., *Les Réligions de L'Inde*, (1885), rep. in *Oeuvres Complètes d'Auguste Barth*, Ernest Leroux, Paris, 1914.

Basham, A.L., *The Wonder that was India* (1954), Fontana, London, 1971.

——— "Review of Jan Gonda's *Viṣṇuism and Śivaism*", *Indo-Iranian Journal, v.* 18, 1976.

Bayet, J., *Les Origines de l'Hercule Romain*, Boccard, Paris, 1926.

Benisti, M., *Rapports entre le premier art Khmer et l'art Indien*, École Française de l'Extreme Orient, Paris, 1970, 2 vols.

Bergaigne, A., *La Réligion Vedique*, (1878-83), rep. Bibliothèque de l'École des hautes Études, Paris, 1963.

Bernard, P. (Ed.), "Fouilles d'Aï Khanoum I", *Memoires de la Délégation Archéologique Française en Afghanistan*, v. 21, Editions Klincksieck, Paris, 1973.

Bernet Kempers, A.J., *Ancient Indonesian Art*, van der Peet, Amsterdam, 1959.

Die Bhagavadgītā, tr. into German by R. Garbe; Haessel, Leipzig, 1905.

The Bhagavad Gītā, tr. and notes by W.D.P. Hill, Oxford University Press, Oxford, 1928.

Bhagavad Gītā, tr. and comm. by R.C. Zaehner, Oxford University Press, Oxford, 1969.

Bhāgavata Purāṇa, Nirnaya Sagar Press, Bombay, 1950. Rep. 1983 Motilal Banarsidass.

Bhāgavata Purāṇa, text and tr. by C.L. Goswami, Gita Press, Gorakhpur, 1971, 2 vols.

Bhāgavata Purāṇa, tr. by J.M. Sanyal, Munshiram Manoharlal, Delhi, 1973, 2 vols.

Bhāgavata Purāṇa, ed. J.L. Shastri, Motilal Banarsidass, Delhi, Eng. Tr. 4 vols., 1978.

Bhandarkar, D.R., "The Date of Kauṭalya", *Annals of the Bhandarkar Oriental Research Institute*, v. 7, 1925-26.

——— "Non-Vedic Origin of Vaiṣṇavism", *Journal of the Gujarat Research Society*, v. 1, 1939.

——— "Notes on Ancient Indian History", *Indian Culture*, v. 1, 1934-35.

——— *Some Aspects of Ancient Indian Culture*, University of Madras, Madras, 1940.

——— "Two Sculptures at Mandor", *Archaeological Survey of India, Annual Report*, 1905-6.

Bhandarkar, R.G., "Allusions to Kṛṣṇa in Patañjali's Mahābhāṣya", *Indian Antiquary*, v. 3, 1874.

——— *Vaiṣṇavism, Śaivism and Minor Religious Sects* (1931), rep. Indological Book House, Varanasi, 1965.

——— "Vāsudeva of Pāṇini, 4.3.98", *Journal of the Royal Asiatic Society*, 1910.

Bhāsa, *Bālacarita*, text, intro., and Hindi tr. by S.R. Sehgal, Munshiram Manoharlal, Delhi, 1959.

Bhāsa, *Bālacarita*, in *Bhāsa's two plays*: *Avimāraka and Bālacarita*, tr., intro., and notes by B. Kunbae, Meharchand Lacchmandas, Delhi, 1968.

Bhattacharjee, U.C., "The Evidence of Pāṇini on Vāsudeva Worship", *Indian Historical Quarterly*, v. 1, 1925 and v. 2, 1926.

Bhattacharji, S., *The Indian Theogony*, Cambridge University Press, Cambridge, 1970.

Bhattacharya, S.K., *Kṛṣṇa-Cult*, Associated Publishing House, New Delhi, 1978.

Bhattacharya, V., "The Besnagar Inscription of Heliodorus", *Indian Historical Quarterly*, v. 8, 1932.

Bhattacharyya, S.P., "The Approximate Date of the Harivaṃśa", *Journal of the Asiatic Society of Bengal*, v. 22, 1956.

Bhattacharyya, S.P. "Kālidāsa and the Harivaṃśa", *Journal of the Oriental Institute, Baroda*, v. 7, 1958.

Bhusari, R.M., "A Note on Bhakti in Pāṇini", *Annals of the Bhandarkar Oriental Research Institute*, v. 8, 1927.

Bloomfield, Maurice, "The Story of Indra and Namuci", *Journal of the American Oriental Society*, v. 15, 1891.

Bosch, F.D.K., *The Golden Germ*, Mouton, The Hague, 1960.

Bourdillon, B.H., "Kṛishṇa Obelisks at Garhwa" *Journal of the United Provinces Historical Society*, v. 1, 1918

Brahma Vaivarta Purāṇa, ed. Jivanand Vidyasagara, Kalikata (Calcutta), 1888.

Brahma Vaivarta Purāṇa, tr. by R.N. Sen, *SBH*, v. 24, Panini Office, Allahabad, 1920-22.

Brown, W.N. "The Creation Myth of the Ṛig Veda", *Journal of the American Oriental Society*, v. 62, 1942.

——— "Indra's Infancy According to Ṛg Veda 4.18", *Siddha Bharati or The Rosary of Indology, Siddheshwar Varma Presentation Volume*, Vishveshvarananda Vedic Research Institute, Hoshiarpur, 1950.

———"Theories of Creation in the Ṛig Veda", *Journal of the American Oriental Society*, v. 85, 1965.

Bruce, Lincoln, "The Indo-European Cattle Raiding Myth", *History of Religions*, v. 16, 1976.

Bruhn, K., "Classification in Indian Iconography", in *German Scholars on India*, v. 2, Nachiketa Publications Limited, Bombay, 1976.

——— "Distinction in Indian Iconography", *Bulletin of the Deccan College Research Institute*, v. 20, 1960.

Bühler, G., "Further Pabhosa Inscriptions", *Epigraphia Indica*, v. 2.

——— *The Sacred Laws of the Aryas*, *SBE*, vols. 2 and 14, 1879 and 1882, rep. Motilal Banarsidass, Delhi, 1964.

Burgess, J., "Rock-cut Temples at Badami, in The Dekhan", *Indian Antiquary*, v. 6, 1877.

Campbell, J., *The Hero with a Thousand Faces*, (1949), Bollingen Series, v. 17, Princeton, 1968.

Carpenter, E.E., *Theism in Medieval India*, Williams & Norgate, London, 1921.

Chakravarti, A.C., *The Story of Kṛiṣṇa in Indian Literature*, Indian Associated Publishing Co., Calcutta, 1976.

Chakravarti, S.C., *Philosophical Foundation of Bengal Vaiṣṇavism*, Academic, Calcutta, 1969.

Chanda, R.P., *The Indo-Aryan Races*, (1916), rep. *Indian Studies Past and Present*, Calcutta, 1968-69.

——— "Archaeology and Vaiṣṇava Tradition", *Archaeological Survey of India, Annual Report*, 1920.

Chandra, P., *Stone Sculpture in the Allahabad Museum*, American Institute of Indian Studies, Poona, 1970.

Chāndogya Upaniṣad, text and tr. by Swami Swahananda, Sri Ramakrishna Math, Madras, 1965.

Chatterji, S.K., "Purāṇa Legends and the Prākrit Traditions in new Indo-Aryan", *Bulletin of the School of Oriental Studies*, University of London, v. 8, 1935-1937.

——— "Kṛishṇa Dvaipāyaṇa Vyāsa and Kṛishṇa Vāsudeva", *Journal of the Royal Asiatic Society of Bengal*, v. 16, 1950.

Chattopadhyaya, S., *Evolution of Hindu Sects*, Munshiram Manoharlal, Delhi, 1970.

Chaudhuri, N.M., "The Indian Cowherd-God", *Journal of the Bihar Oriental Research Society*, v. 28, 1942.

——— "Some Aspects of the Worship of Nārāyaṇa", *Indian Historical Quarterly*, v. 20, 1944, and v. 22, 1946.

Chaudhury, B.C., "Some Vaiṣṇava Legends in Vedantic test-tube", *Annals of the Bhandarkar Oriental Research Institute*, v. 18, 1961-62.

Choudhury, M., "The Ābhīras of ancient India and their contemporary remnants", *Man in India*, v. 54, 1974.

Choudhury, M.C., "Besnagar Garuda Pillar Inscription of Heliodorus—An Assessment", *Visvesvarananda Indological Journal*, v. 2, 1964.

Cohen, A. (tr)., "The Soṭah", in *The Babylonian Talmud*, ed. by I. Epstein, Soncino Press, London, 1936.

Colebrooke, H.T., *Miscellaneous Essays* (1837) rep. as *Essays on the Religion and Philosophy of the Hindus*, Williams and Norgate, London, 1858.

Combaz, G., *L'Inde et L'Orient Classique*, Geuthner, Paris, 1937.

Coomaraswamy, A.K., *Yakṣas* (1931), rep. Munshiram Manoharlal, Delhi, 1971.

——— *History of Indian and Indonesian Art*, Goldston, London, 1927.

Cousens, H., *Chālukyan Architecture*, Archaeological Survey of India, New Imperial Series, v. 42, Calcutta, 1926.

Crooke, W., "The Legends of Kṛishṇa", *Folk-lore*, v. 11, London, 1900.

Cunningham, A., *Coins of Ancient India*, Reprint, Indological Book House, Varanasi, 1963.

Dahlquist, A., *Megasthenes and Indian Religion*, Motilal Banarsidass, Delhi, 1977.

Dandekar, R.N., "The Beginnings of Vaiṣṇavism", *Indologica Taurinensia*, vols. 3-4, 1975-76.

——— "Vaiṣṇavism and Śaivism", in *Ramakrishna Gopal Bhandarkar as an Indologist, a Symposium*, ed. by R.N. Dandekar, Bhandarkar Oriental Research Institute, Poona, 1976.

——— "Viṣṇu in the Veda", in *Studies in Indology*,

Commemorative Volume in Honour of P.V. Kane, Poona Oriental Series, no. 76, Poona, 1941.

Das, B., *Kṛṣṇa, a Study in the Theory of the Avatāras*, Bharatiya Vidya Bhavan, Bombay, 1962.

Das, D.R., "Kośaleśvara Temple at Baidyanath", *Artibus Asiae*, v. 38, 1976.

Dasgupta, M., "Early Viṣṇuism and Nārāyaṇīya Worship", *Indian Historical Quarterly*, v. 7, 1931 and v. 8, 1932.

De, S.K., *Early History of the Vaiṣṇava Faith and Movement in Bengal*, K.L. Mukhopadhyay, Calcutta, 1961.

——— "The Vedic and the Epic Kṛṣṇa", *Indian Historical Quarterly*, v. 18, 1942.

——— "Sects and Sectarian Worship in the Mahābhārata", *Our Heritage*, University of Calcutta, v. 1, 1953.

De, S.K., "Bhagavatism and Sun-worship", *Bulletin of the School of Oriental Studies*, University of London, v. 6, 1931.

Desai, K., *Iconography of Viṣṇu*, Abhinav, New Delhi, 1973.

Deva, K., "Kṛiṣṇa-līlā scenes in the Lakṣmaṇa temple at Khajuraho", *Lalit Kalā*, no. 7, 1960.

Devī Bhāgavata Purāṇa, Pandit Pustakalaya, Kasi,1969.

Devī Bhāgavata Purāṇa, tr. Swami Vijnanananda, *SBH*, no. 26, rep. Oriental Reprint, New Delhi, 1977.

Dikshit, K.N., *Excavations at Pāhārpur. Memoirs of the Archaeological Survey of India*, v. 55, Delhi, 1938.

Dikshitar, V.R.R., "Kṛiṣṇa in Early Tamil Literature", *Indian Culture*, v. 4, 1937-38.

Diodorus Siculus, *The Library of History*, tr. by C.H. Oldfather, Loeb Classical Library, Harvard University Press, 1961.

Diskalkar, D.B., "Some Brahmanical Sculptures in the Mathura Museum", *Journal of the United Provinces Historical Society*, v. 5, 1932.

Douglas, M., "The Meaning of Myth", in *The Structural Study of Myth and Totemism*, ed. by Edmund Leach, London, 1967.

Demézil, G., *Heur et Malheur du Guerrier*, Presses Universitaries de France, Paris, 1969.

——— "Karṇa et les Pāṇḍava", *Orientalia Suecana*, v. 2, 1954.

——— *Mythe et Epopée*, Gallimard, Paris, vols. 1 and 2, 1968-69.

——— "Les Pas de Kṛṣṇa et l'exploit d'Arjuna", in *Orientalia Suecana*, v. 5, 1957.

——— "La Transposition des Dieux Souverains Mineurs en heros dans le Mahābhārata", *Indo-Iranian Journal*, v. 1, 1959.

Dunlop, J., *History of Prose Fiction*, rev. and ed. by H. Wilson, Bell and Sons, London, 1888.

Dupont, P., *La Statuarie pre'-angkorienne*, Ascona, 1955.

Eschman, A.C., Kulke, H., and Tripathi, G.C., *The Cult of Jagannath and the Regional Tradition of Orissa*, Manohar, Delhi, 1978.

Esnoul, A.M., "Le Courant affectif á l'interieur du Brahmanisme Ancien", *Bulletin de l'École Française de l'Extrème Orient*, t. 48, 1956.

Farnell, L.W., *Greek Hero Cult and Ideas of Immortality*, Clarendon Press, Oxford, 1921.

Filliozat, J., "Dates du Bhāgavata Purāṇa and Bhāgavata Māhātmya", in *Indological Studies in Honor of W.N. Brown*, ed. by E. Bender, American Oriental Society, New Haven, 1962.

——— "La Dévotion Vishnouite au Pays Tamoul", *Conference del Instituto Italiano per il medio ed estremo Oriente*, v. 2, 1954.

——— "Representations de Vāsudeva et Saṃkarṣaṇa au siecle IIe avant J.C.", *Arts Asiatiques*. 26, 1973.

Flacelière, R. and Devambez, P., *Heracles, Images & Recits*., Boccard, Paris, 1966.

Fontenrose, J., "The Hero as Athlete", *California Studies in Classical Antiquity*, v. 1, 1968.

——— *Python: A Study of Delphic Myth and its Origins*, (1959), 2nd. ed., Biblo and Tannen, New York, 1974.

Galinsky, G.K., *The Herakles Theme*, Blackwell, Oxford, 1972.

Gangoly, O.C., "Indra-cult versus Kṛṣṇa-cult", *Journal of the Ganganatha Jha Research Institute*, v. 7, 1949.

Ganguli, R., "Cattle and cattle rearing in Ancient India", *Annals of the Bhandarkar Oriental Research Institute*, v. 12, 1931.

Garbe, R., "Bhagavad Gītā", in *Encyclopaedia of Religion and Ethics*, ed. by J. Hastings, T. & T. Clark, Edinburgh, v. 2, 1909.

——— *India and Christendom*, Open Court, Chicago, 1959.

Gardiner, K. and de Rachewiltz (trs)., *The Historia Langobardorum of Paul the Deacon*, unpublished.

Gardiner, K. and de Crespigny, R., "T'an-shih-huai and the Hsien-pi tribes", *Papers on Far Eastern History*, Australian National University, 1977.

Ghosh, A., "A note on Ekānaṃśā", *Indian Culture*, v. 4, 1937-38,

Ghosh, J.C., "Ekānaṃśā and Subhadrā", *Journal of the Royal Asiatic Society of Bengal*, new series, v. 2,1936.

——— "Notes on the Ghosūndī stone Inscription", *Indian Historical Quarterly*, v. 9, 1933.

Goetz, H., *The Art of Architecture of Bikaner*, Oxford University Press, Oxford, 1950.

——— "Earliest representation of the Myth-cycle of Krishṇa-Govinda", *Journal of the Oriental Institute*, Baroda, v. 1, 1951.

——— "Imperial Rome and the genesis of Classical Indian Art", *East-West*, Rome, v. 10, 1959.

——— *Studies in the History, Religion and Art of Classical and Mediaeval India*, ed. by H. Kulke, Steiner, Wiesbaden, 1971.

Gonda J., "Ancient Indian Kingship from the Religious point of view", Brill, Leiden, 1966.

——— *Aspects of Early Viṣṇuism*, (1954), rep. Motilal Banarsidass, Delhi, 1969.

——— *Viṣṇuism and Śivaism*, Athlone Press, London, 1970.

——— "Viṣṇu's name Aniruddha", in *Selected Studies* by Jan Gonda, v. 4, Brill, Leiden, 1975.

Gopinatha Rau, T.A., *Elements of Hindu Iconography* (1914-16), rep. Paragon, New York, 1968.

Goswami, A., "The Monogamist Kṛṣṇa", *Charudeva Shastri Felicitation Volume*, C. Shastri Felicitation Volume Committee, Delhi, 1974.

——— "Rādhā", *Journal of the Department of Sanskrit*, Delhi University, v. 1, 1972.

Goswami, K.G., *A Study of Vaiṣṇavism*, Oriental Book Agency, Calcutta, 1956.

Grant, M., *Myths of the Greeks and Romans*, Mentor, London, 1962.

Grassmann, H., *Wörterbuch zum Ṛig-Veda*, Reprint, Harrassowitz, Wiesbaden, 1964.

Graves, R., *The Greek Myths*, Penguin, Harmondsworth, 1976, 2 vols.

Greimas, A.J., "Comparative Mythology", from *Mythology*, ed. by Pierre Maranda, Penguin Modern Sociology Readings, 1972.

Grierson, G., "Bhakti Marga", in *Encyclopaedia of Religion and Ethics*, ed. by J. Hastings, T. & T. Clark, Edinburgh, v. 2, 1909.

——— "The Nārāyaṇīya and the Bhāgavatas", *Indian Antiquary*, v. 37, 1908.

——— "A note on Vāsudeva of Pāṇini", *Journal of the Royal Asiatic Society*, 1910.

Griswold, H.W., *Religion of the Ṛgveda*, (1923) rep., Motilal Banarsidass, Delhi, 1973.

Grousset, R., *L'Inde*, Plon, Paris, 1961.

Gupta, P.L., "Ekānaṃśā and her Images", *Journal of the Bihar Research Society*, v. 54, 1968.

Halliday, W.R., *Indo-European Folk-Tales and Greek Legend*, Cambridge University Press. 1933.

Harivaṃśa, Text critically ed. by P.L. Vaidya, Bhandarkar Oriental Research Institute, Poona, 1969.

Harivaṃśa, Text and Hindi tr. by R.N. Datta, Gita Press, Gorakhpur, 1967.

Harivaṃśa, tr. M.N. Dutt, Elysium Press, Calcutta, 1897.

Harivaṃśa, ou histoire de la Famille de Hari, French tr. by A. Langlois, Oriental translation Fund of Great Britain and Ireland, Paris, 1834, 2 vols.

Harle, J.C., *Gupta Sculpture*, Clarendon Press, Oxford, 1974.

Hawley, J.S., "Thief of Butter, Thief of Love", *History of Religions*, v. 19, 1979.

——— "Krishna's Cosmic Victories", *JAAR*, v. 47, 1979.

Hazra, R.C., "The Bhāgavata Purāṇa", *Indian Historical Quarterly*, v. 14, 1938.

——— "The Date of the Viṣṇu Purāṇa", *Annals of the Bhandarkar Oriental Research Institute*, v. 18, 1936-37.

——— "The Devī Purāṇa", *New Indian Antiquary*, v. 4, 1942.

——— "Vāsudeva Worship as known to Pāṇini", *Our Heritage*, v. 18, 1970.

Hein, N., *The Miracle Plays of Mathura*, Yale University Press, New Haven, 1972.

Held, G.J., *The Mahābhārata; an Ethnological Study*, uitgeversmaatschappij, Amsterdam, 1935.

Hemacandra, *Triṣaṣtiśalākāpuruṣacarita*, tr. by H.M. Johnson, v. 5, Gaekwad Oriental Series no. 139, Oriental Institute, Baroda, 1962.

Herbert, J. "Śakaṭa and Pūtanā", *Purāṇa*, v. 2, 1960.

Hiltebeitel, A., *The Ritual of Battle, Kṛishṇa in the Mahābhārata*, Cornell University Press, Ithaca, N.Y., 1976.

Hopkins, E.W., *The Great Epic of India* (1901), rep. Punti Pustak, Calcutta, 1969.

——— *The Religions of India* (1885), 2nd. ed. Ginn & Co., Boston, 1891.

——— "Mythological Aspects of Trees and Mountains in the Great Epic, *Journal of the American Oriental Society*, v. 30, 1910.

——— "Gleanings from the Harivaṃśa", *Festschrift Ernst Windisch zum Siebzigsten Geburtstag*, Leipzig, 1914.

——— *Epic Mythology*, Rept. 1974 Motilal Banarsidass Delhi.

Ilangōradigaḷ, *Shilappadikaram*, tr. by Alain Danielou, Allen and Unwin, London, 1967.

Ingalls, D.H.H., "The Harivaṃśa as a Mahākāvya", *Melanges d'Indianisme a la Mémoire de Louis Renou*, Ecole Française de l'Extrême Orient, Paris, 1968.

Irwin, J., "The Heliodorus Pillar at Besnagar", *Puratattva*, no. 8, 1976-77.

Jacobi, H., "Incarnation (Indian)", in *Encyclopaedia of Religion and Ethics*, ed. by J. Hastings, T. & T. Clark, Edinburgh, v. 7, 1914.

——— "Über Viṣṇu-Nārāyaṇa-Vāsudeva", *Kleine Schriften*, v. 1, Franz Steiner Verlag, Wiesbaden, 1970.

——— "Die Jaina Legende von dem untergang Dvāravatī's und von dem Tode Kṛishṇa's", *ZDMG*. v. 42, 1888.

Jaiminīya Upaniṣad Brāhmaṇa, Sarasvati Vihara Series no. 31, Nagpur, 1954.

Jaiminiya Upanisad Brahmana, tr. by H. Oertel, *Journal of the American Oriental Society*, vols. 18-28, 1896-1906.

Jaiswal, Suvira, *The Origin and Development of Vaiṣṇavism*, Munshiram Manoharlal, Delhi, 1967.

Jātakas, ed. by V. Fausboll, Pali Text Society, Luzac, London, 1962-64. 7 vols.

Joshi, N.P., "Some Kuṣāṇa Passages in the Harivaṃśa", *Indologentagung*, 1971.

Jouveau-Dubrevil, G., *Iconography of Southern India*, Geuthner, Paris, 1937.

Jung, C.G., and Kerenyi, C., *Essays on a Science of Mythology: the Myths of the Divine Child and the Divine Maiden*, Harper and Row, New York, 1963.

Kakati, B., *Viṣṇuite Myths and Legends*, Gauhati, Assam, 1952.

Kane, P.V., "The Arthaśāstra of Kauṭilya", *Annals of the Bhandarkar Oriental Research Institute*, v. 7, 1925-26.

Karmakar, A.P., "Some Nude gods in Hindu Pantheon", *Annals of the Bhandarkar Oriental Research Institute*, v. 23, 1942.

Kashalikar, M.J., "The Origin of the Pāṇḍavas", *Journal of the Oriental Institute, Baroda*, v. 16, 1966-67.

Katre, S.L., "Kṛṣṇa, gopas, gopīs, and Rādhā", in *Prof. P.K. Gode Commemorative Volume*, ed. by H.L. Hariyappa and M.M. Patkar, pt. 3, Oriental Book Agency, Poona, 1960.

——— "Kṛṣṇa and Jarāsandha", *Indian Historical Quarterly*, v. 8, 1932, and v. 9, 1933.

Kauṭilya, *Arthaśāstra*, tr. by R. Shamasastry, 4th edn., Raghuveer Printing Press, Mysore, 1951.

The Kauṭilīya Arthaśāstra, ed. and tr. by R. P. Kangle, University of Bombay, Bombay, 1963, 2 vols.

Keith, A. B., "The Child Kṛṣṇa", *Journal of the Royal Asiatic Society*, 1908.

——— "Reviews of *History of Religions* by G. F. Moore, and *Indian Theism* by N. McNicol", *Journal of the Royal Asiatic Society*, 1915.

——— *The Sanskrit Drama* (1924), Oxford University Press, London, 1954.

——— *Religion and Philosophy of the Veda and Upanishads*, *HOS*, vols. 31-32, rep. Motilal Banarsidass, Delhi, 1976.

Kennedy, J., "The Child Krishna, Christianity, and the Gujars", *Journal of the Royal Asiatic Society*, 1907.

——— "The child Krishna and his Critics", *Journal of the Royal Asiatic Society*, 1908.

——— "Gospels of the infancy, the Lalita Vistara, and the Visnu Purana", *Journal of the Royal Asiatic Society*, 1917.

Keny, L. B., "The Iconography of Viṣṇu-Nārāyaṇa. A Study with Historical Perspective", *Proceedings of the 22nd All India Oriental Conference*, v.2, Gauhati, 1966.

——— "The Origin of Nārāyaṇa", *Annals of The Bhandarkar Oriental Research Institute*, v. 23, 1942.

Khare, M. D., "Comments on Irwin's 'The Heliodorus Pillar' ", *Puratattwa*, no. 8, 1976-77.

Khuddak Nikāya, Nalanda Devanagari Pali Series, Nalanda, 1960.

Keilhorn, F., "Bhagavat, Tatrabhavat and Devanampriya", *Journal of the Royal Asiatic Society*, 1908.

Kinsley, D. R., *The Divine Player. A Study of Kṛiṣṇa Līlā*, Doctoral thesis, Motilal Banarsidass Delhi 1978.

——— "Without Kṛiṣṇa there is no song", *History of Religions*, v. 11, 1972.

Kirfel, W., "Kṛṣṇa's Jugendgeschichte in den Purana", *Beitrage zur Literaturwissenschaft und Geistesgeschichte Indiens. Festgabe Hermann Jacobi zum 75 Geburtstag*, Bonn, 1926.

Kirk, G. S., *Myth : its Meaning and Functions in Ancient and other Cultures*, Cambridge University Press, 1973.

Konow, Sten & Tuxen, Paul, *The Religions of India*, G. E. C. Gad, Copenhagen, 1949.

Kosambi, D. D., *An Introduction to the Study of Indian History*, Popular Book Depot, Bombay, 1956.

Kosambi, D. D., "Autochtonous Elements in the Mahābhārata", in *Journal of the American Oriental Society*, v.84, 1964.

——— *Myth and Reality*, Popular Prakashan, Bombay, 1962.

——— "The sources of the *Bhagavad-Gītā*, and the Avatāra syncretism", *Journal of the Bombay Branch of the Royal Asiatic Society*, v.24-25, 1948-49.

Kramrisch, S., *The Art of India Through the Ages*, Motilal Banarsidass, Delhi, Rep. 1983.

——— *The Art of Nepal*, Asia House Gallery, New York, 1964.

Krappe, E. H., *The Science of Folklore*, Methuen, London, 1930.

Kuiper, F. B. J., "The Three Strides of Viṣṇu", *Indological Studies in Honor of W. N. Brown*, ed. by. Ernest Bender, American Oriental Society, New Haven, Conn. 1962.

Kulke, H., "Some Remarks about the Jagannatha Trinity", *Indologentagung*, 1971.

Kumar, K., "An Ekānaṃśā relief of Ellora", *Journal of Indian History*, v. 44, 1966.

Kūrma Purāṇa, tr. by A. B. Bhattacharya, ed. by A. S. Gupta, All India Kashiraj Trust, Varanasi, 1972.

Lalluji Lal, *The Prem Sāgar*, tr. by W. Hollings, Nawul Kishore Press, Lucknow, 1871.

Lalye, P. G., *Studies in Devī Bhāgavata*, Popular Prakashan, Bombay, 1973.

Larson, G. J., "The Study of Mythology and Comparative Mythology", *Myth and Indo-European Antiquity*, ed. by G. J. Larson, University of California Press, 1974.

Law, B. C., "Mathurā in Ancient India", *Journal of the Royal Asiatic Society of Bengal*, 3rd series, v.13, 1947.

Lévi, Sylvain, *Le Théatre Indien*, 2nd ed., Reprint, College de France, Paris, 1963.

Lincoln, B , "The Indo-European Myth of Creation", *History of Religions*, v. 15, 1975-76.

Lippe, A., "Early Chālukya Icons", *Artibus Asiae*, v. 34-4, 1972.

Lüders, H., "Die Jātakas und die Epik, 1. Die Kṛṣṇa-Sage," *ZDMG*, v.58, 1904.

Machek, V., "Origin of the God Viṣṇu", *Archiv Orientalni*, v. 28., 1960.

Mahābhārata, crit. ed. by various scholars, Bhandarkar Oriental Research Institute, Poona 1933-1959, 19 vols.

Mahābhārata, tr. by M. N. Dutt, Elysium Press, Calcutta, 1895-1905, 18 vols.

Mahābhārata, tr. by K. M. Ganguly, ed. by P. C. Roy, Reprint, Oriental Publishing Co., Calcutta, 1952, 12 vols.

Mahābhārata, tr. by J. A. B. van Buitenen, University of Chicago Press, Chicago, 1973-1978, 3 vols. (incomplete).

Majumdar, A. K., "Note on the Development of Rādhā Cult", *Annals of the Bhandarkar Oriental Research Institute*, v. 36, 1955.

Majumdar, B. B., *Kṛṣṇa in History and Legend*, University of Calcutta, 1969.

Majumdar, R. C., *The Classical Accounts of India*, Firma K. L. Mukhopadhyay, Calcutta, 1960.

Mānavadharmaśāstra (1886), tr. by G. Bühler, *SBE*, 25, Motilal Banarsidass, Delhi, 1964.

Mani, V., *Purāṇic Encyclopaedia*, Motilal Banarsidass, Delhi, 1975.

Maranda, P., "Qualitative and Quantitative Analysis of Myths by Computer", from *Mythology*, ed. by Pierre Maranda, Penguin Modern Sociology Readings, 1972.

Mārkaṇḍeya Purāṇa, ed. Jivananda Vidyasagara, Kalikata (Calcutta), 1896.

Mārkaṇḍeya Purāṇa, tr. and ann. by F. E. Pargiter, Asiatic Society, Calcutta, 1904.

Marshall, J. H., "Excavations at Maṇḍor", *Archaeological Survey of India Annual Report,* 1909-10.

Masson, J. L., "The Childhood of Kṛṣṇa: Some Psychoanalytic Observations", *Journal of the American Oriental Society*, v.94, 1974.

Matsya Purāṇa, ed. Jivananda Vidyasagara, Kalikata (Calcutta), 18 ?

Matsya Purāṇa, tr. a Taluqdar of Oudh, *SBH*, v.17 (1916-17), rep. Oriental Publishers, Delhi, 1972.

Mazumdar, B. C., "Vāsudeva of Pāṇini", *Journal of the Royal Asiatic Society*, 1910.

Mehendale, M. A., "Nirukta Notes IV: Yāska's Etymology of *daṇḍa*", *Journal of the American Oriental Society*, v.80, 1960.

Miller, B. S., "Rādhā: consort of Kṛṣṇa's vernal passion", *Journal of the American Oriental Society*, v.99, 1975.

Mirashi, V. V., "The date of the Original Harivaṃśa", in *Studies in Indology*, by V. V. Mirashi, v.5, V. S. Mandal, Delhi, 1975.

Monier-Williams, M., *Sanskrit-English Dictionary* (1889), rep. Motilal Banarsidass, Delhi, 1969.

Muir, J., *Original Sanskrit Texts* (1858) rep. of 1872 ed., Oriental Press, Amsterdam, 1967, 5. vols.

Mukherji, S. C., "The Cult of Ekānaṃśā", *Indian Historical Quarterly*. v.35, 1959.

Mukhopadhyaya, B. S., "The Śiśupālavadham and its sources", *Bharati, Bulletin of the College of Indology, BHU*, no. 9, 1965-66.

McNicol, N., *Indian Theism* (1915) rep. Munshiram Manoharlal, Delhi, 1968.

Mackenzie, M. W., *Hercules in the Early Roman Empire with particular reference to Literature*, unpublished Thesis, Cornell University, New York, 1967.

McCrindle, J.W., *Ancient India as Described by Megasthenes and Arrian* (1887), Chuckervertty, Chaterjee & Co., Calcutta, 1960.

——— *The Invasion of India by Alexander the Great* (1896), rep. Barnes & Noble, New York, 1969.

——— tr. "Periplus of the Erythrean Sea", *Indian Antiquary*, v.8, 1879.

The Bṛhad-devatā attributed to Śaunaka, ed. and tr. by A. A. MacDonell (1904), rep. Motilal Banarsidass, Delhi, 1965.

MacDonell, A. A., *History of Sanskrit Literature* (1899), rep., Motilal Banarsidass, Delhi, 1959, 2 vols.

——— *The Vedic Mythology*, (1897), rep. Motilal Banarsidass, Delhi 1979.

MacDonell, A. A., and Keith, A. B., *Vedic Index of Names and Subjects*, (1912). rep. Motilal Banarsidass, Delhi, 1958, 2 vols.

Macnicol, N., "The Origin of the Kṛṣṇa Cult", *Journal of the Royal Asiatic Society*, 1913.

Narain, A. K., *The Indo-Greeks*, Oxford University Press, 1957.

Neve, F., "Des éléments Étrangers du Mythe et du Culte Indiens de Krichna", *Annales de Philosophie Chrétienne*, t.11, 1876.

Nilakanta Sastri, K. A., Ed., *A Comprehensive History of India*, v. 2, Orient Longmans, Bombay, 1957.

——— *Development of Religion in South India*, Orient Longmans, Bombay, 1963.

Nutt, A., "The Aryan Expulsion and Return formula in the Folk and Hero tales of the Celts", *Folklore Journal*, v.4, 1886.

O'Flaherty, W., *The Origins of Evil in Indian Mythology*, University of California Press, Berkeley, 1976.

Oldenberg, Hermann, *Die Religion des Veda*, Cotta'sche Buchhandlung Nachfolger, Stuttgart, 1923.

Pal, P., *The Arts of Nepal*, E. J. Brill, Leiden, 1974.

——— *Vaiṣṇava Iconology in Nepal*, Asiatic Society, Calcutta, 1970.

Padma Purāṇa, Anandasrama, Poona, 1893-94.

Panchamukhi, R. S., "Pattaḍkal and its Sculptures", *Bulletin of the Deccan College Research Institute*, v.8, 1947.

Pandey, D. P., "Identification of a sculpture in the Provincial Museum, Lucknow", *Journal of the Bihar Oriental Research Society*, v.27, 1941.

Pargiter, F. E., "Review of H. C. Raychaudhuri's Materials....", *Journal of the Royal Asiatic Society*, 1923.

Le Paripatal, Intr., tr. et notes par François Gros, Publications de l'Institut Française d'Indologie No. 35, Pondichery, 1968.

Patañjali, *Vyākaraṇamahābhāṣya*, ed. by F. Kielhorn, *Bhandarkar Oriental Research Institute*, Poona, 1962.

Pathak, K. B., "The Divine Vāsudeva different from the Kṣatriya Vāsudeva", *Journal of the Bombay Branch of the Royal Asiatic Society*, v.23, 1909-14.

Pathak, V. S., "Early Vaiṣṇava Pantheon", *Journal of the Uttar Pradesh Historical Society*, v.24-25, 1951-52.

Penner, H. H., *Myth and Ritual in the Viṣṇu Purāṇa*, unpublished Thesis, University of Chicago, 1965.

Prakash, B., "Govardhana Pūjā", *Poona Orientalist*, v.18, 1953.

——— "Kṛishṇa, an Ethnological Study", in *Prof. P. K. Gode Commemorative Volume*, ed. by H. L. Ḥariyappa and M. M. Patkar, pt. 3, Oriental Book Agency, Poona, 1960.

——— "On Pāṇini's sūtra 4.3.98", *Kurukshetra University Research Journal*, v.l, 1967.

——— "The Ābhīras, their Antiquity, History and Culture", *Journal of Bihar Research Society*, v.40, 1954.

——— "Vṛtra", *Annals of the Bhandarkar Oriental Research Institute*, v. 30, 1949.

Prayag, Dayal, "Important Sculptures added to the Provincial Museum, Lucknow, during the last decade", *Journal of the United Provinces Historical Society*, v.8, 1934.

Propp, V., *Morphologie du Conte*, Seuil, Paris, 1973.

Przyluski, J., "La Legende de Kṛṣṇa dans les Bas-reliefs d'Angkor-Vat", *Révue des Arts Asiatiques, Annales du Musée Guimet*, v.5, 1928.

——— "The name of the God Viṣṇu, and the Kṛṣṇa-legend", *Quarterly Journal of the Mythic Society*, v.25, 1934-35.

Pusalker, A.D., "The Problem of the Bālacarita", in *A Volume of Studies in Indology in Honour of P. V. Kane*, Poona Oriental Series, no.76, 1941.

——— *Studies in the Epics and Purāṇas*, Bharatiya Vidya Bhavan, Bombay, 1955.

Radhakrishnan, S., *Indian Philosophy* (1923), rep. Allen and Unwin, London, 1962, 2 vols.

Raglan, Lord, "The Hero of Tradition", *Folklore,* v.45, 1934.

——— "Myth and Ritual", in *Myth: a Symposium,* ed. by T. A. Sebeok, American Folklore Society, Bloomington, Ind., 1958.

——— *The Hero,* Methuen, London 1936.

Ramanujan, A. K., "The Indian Oedipus", from *Indian Literature,* ed. by A. Podder, Institute of Advanced Studies, Simla, 1972.

Randhawa, M. S., *Kangra Paintings of the Bhāgavata Purāṇa,* National Museum of India, New Delhi, 1960.

——— *The Kṛiṣṇa Legend in Pahari Paintings,* Lalit Kalā Akademi, New Delhi, 1956.

Rank, O., *The Myth of the Birth of the Hero* (1914), Vintage Books, New York, 1964.

Rau, W., "Twenty Indra Legends", from *German Scholars on India,* v.1, Chowkhamba, 1973.

Rawlinson, H. G., "Foreign Influences in the Civilization of Ancient India, 900 B.C.—400 A.D.", *Journal of the Bombay Branch of the Royal Asiatic Society,* v. 23, 1909-1914.

Ray, A., "Domicile of the author of the Bhāgavata Purāṇa", *Indian Historical Quarterly,* v.8, 1932.

——— "Interpolations in the Bhāgavata Purāṇa", *Indian Historical Quarterly,* v.8, 1932.

——— "Śrīkṛṣṇa and the source of the Bhagavadgītā", *Indian Historical Quarterly,* v.9, 1933.

Ray, H. C., "Allusions to Vāsudeva Kṛishṇa Devakīputra in the Vedic Literature", *Journal of the Royal Asiatic Society of Bengal,* New Series, v.19, 1923.

Raychaudhuri, H. C., *Materials for the Study of the Early History of the Vaiṣṇava Sect* (1921). University of Calcutta, 2nd. rev. ed., 1936.

——— "The Mahābhārata and the Besnagar Inscription", *Journal of the Royal Asiatic Society of Bengal,* v.18, 1922.

Rea, A., *Pallava Architecture,* Archaeological Survey of India, New Imperial Series, v.34, Southern India, v.11, rep. Indological Book House, Varanasi, 1970.

Rees, A. D. "The Divine hero in Celtic Hagiology", *Folk-lore,* v. 47, 1956.

Renou, L., *Anthologie Sanskrite,* Payot, Paris, 1961.

——— "Indra dans L'Atharvaveda", *New Indian Antiquary,* v.8, 1946.

——— *Études Védiques et Pāṇineennes,* Publications de l'Institut de Civilization Indienne, E. de Boccard, Paris, 1955-1969, 17 vols.

Hymnen des Ṛigveda, ed. by T. Aufrecht (1877) rep. Harrazowitz, Wiesbaden, 1968.

Der Ṛig Veda, tr. in German by K. F. Geldner, *HOS,* vols. 33-35, Cambridge, Mass., 1951-53.

Vedic Hymns, tr. by F. M. Müller, and H. Oldenberg, *SBE,* vols. 32 and 36, rep. Motilal Banarsidass, Delhi, 1964, 2 vols.

The Hymns of the Ṛig Veda, tr. with a popular comm. by R. T. H. Griffith (1889), rep., Motilal Banarsidass, Delhi, 1973.

Le Ṛig-Veda, tr. in French by M. Langlois, Firmin Didot, Paris, 1848-1851.

Rose, H. J., *A Handbook of Greek Mythology* (1928), Methuen, London, 6th ed., 1958.

Rowland, B., *The Art and Architecture of India,* Penguin, Harmondsworth, 1970.

Ruben, W., "The Kṛṣṇacarita in the Harivaṃśa and certain Purāṇas", *Journal of the American Oriental Society,* v.61, 1941.

——— *Kṛishṇa. Konkordanz und Kommentar der Motive seines Heldenlebens,* Istanbuler Schriften no.17, Istanbul, Yazilari, Istanbul, 1944.

——— "On the original text of the Kṛṣṇa-epic", in *A Volume of Eastern and Indian Studies presented to Prof. F. W. Thomas,* Bombay, 1939.

Sahni, D. R., "A Stone sculpture representing an incident from the life of Kṛishṇa", *Archaeological Survey of India, Annual Report,* 1925-26.

Sankalia, H. D., "Antiquity of Modern Dwarka", *Journal of the Asiatic Society,* Bombay, v.38 1963.

Saraswati, S. K., *Early Sculpture of Bengal,* Sambodhi, Calcutta, 1962.

Śatapatha Brāhmaṇa, ed. by A. Weber, Chowkhamba, Varanasi, 1964.

Śatapatha Brāhmaṇa, tr. by J. Eggeling, *SBE,* vols. 12, 26, 41, 43, 44, Motilal Banarsidass, Delhi, 1963.

Schoff, W. H., *The Periplus of the Erythrean Sea,* tr. and comm. McKay, New York, 1916.

Schoo, J., *Hercules' Labors, Fact or Fiction?* Argonaut, Chicago, 1969.

Schrader, F. O., *Introduction to the Pāñcarātra and the Ahirbudhnya Saṃhitā,* Adyar Library, Madras, 1916.

Sedgwick, L. J., "Bhakti", *Journal of the Bombay Branch of the Royal Asiatic Society,* v.23, 1909-1914.

Shah, U. P., *Śrīkṛṣṇāni Bālalīlā,* Svādhyay (University of Baroda), v.10-4, 1973.

Sharma, B. N. K., "The Date of the Bhāgavata Purāṇa", *Annals of the Bhandarkar Oriental Research Institute,* v.14, 1932-33.

Sharma, M. M., *Inscriptions of Ancient Assam,* Gauhati University, Gauhati, 1978.

Sharma, V. M., "Kṛṣṇa Theme in Sanskrit Kāvyas", *Kurukṣetra University Research Journal,* v.2, 1968.

Shastri, A. M., "Herakles in front of the infantry of Porus", *Journal of Indian History,* v.42, 1964.

Shende, N. J., "The Puruṣa-Sūkta in the Vedic Literature", reprint from *Journal of the University of Poona, Humanities Section,* no. 23, University of Poona, 1965.

Simon, M., *Hercule et le Christianisme,* Universite de Strasbourg, Strassburg, 1955.

Singer, M. (Ed.), *Kṛishṇa : Myths, Rites and Attitudes,* University of Chicago Press, Chicago, 1968.

Sinha, C. P., "Some important sculptural acquisitions of the Patna Museum", *Journal of the Bihar Research Society,* v.53, 1967.

Sircar, D. C., *Select Inscriptions bearing on Indian History and Civilization,* University of Calcutta, 2nd. ed., 1965.

——— *Studies in the Religious Life of Ancient and Medieval India,* Motilal Banarsidass, Delhi, 1971.

Sivaramamurti, C., *The Art of India,* Harry N. Abrams, New York, 1977.

——— *South Indian Bronzes,* Lalit Kala Academy, Delhi, 1963.

Solomon, T. J., "Early Vaiṣṇava Bhakti and its Autochtonous Heritage", *History of Religions,* v.10, 1970.

——— *The Origin and Development of Early Indian Bhakti. The Autochtonous Heritage of Vaiṣṇavism,* unpublished Thesis, University of Chicago, 1966.

Soundara Rajan, K. V., "Bhāgavata cult in Rajasthan temples", in *Studies in Indology, Memorial Volume to U. Mishra,* Commemorative Volume Committee, v.1, Allahabad, 1967.

——— "The Iconic development of the early Tamils", *Journal of Indian History,* v.31, 1953.

Sorensen, S., *Index to the Names of the Mahābhārata,* rep. Motilal Banarsidass, Delhi, 1963.

Spink, W. M., *Kṛishṇa Maṇḍala. A Devotional Theme in Indian Art,* University of Michigan, Ann Arbor, 1971.

Srinivasan, K. R., *The Dharmarāja Ratha and its Sculptures : Mahabalipuram,* Abhinav Publications, New Delhi, 1975.

Subrahmanyam, K. C., "A Note on the Evidence of Pāṇini on Vāsudeva Worship", *Indian Historicai Quarterly,* v.2, 1926.

Suhr, E., "Kṛishṇa and Mitra as Messiahs", *Folklore,* v.77, 1966.

Suryavanshi, B., *The Ābhīras, their History and Culture,* University of Baroda, Baroda, 1962.

Suśrutasaṃhitā, Nirnaya Sagara, Bombay, 1945.

Svamin, G., "Two Vāsudevas", *Indian Antiquary,* v.39, 1910.

——— "The Name Vāsudeva", *Indian Antiquary,* v.40, 1911.

Tadpatrikar, S. N., "The Kṛishṇa Problem", *Annals of the Bhandarkar Oriental Research Institute,* v.10, 1929-30.

Taittirīya Brāhmaṇa, ed. by R. L. Mitra, Asiatic Society, Calcutta, 3 vols., 1859-1890.

Taittirīya Sanhtiā, ed. by A. Weber, Brockhaus, Leipzig, 2 vols., 1871-72.

The Veda of the Black Yajus School entitled Taittiriya Sanhita, tr. and ann. by A. B. Keith, *HOS,* vols. 18-19, rep. Motilal Banarsidass, 1967.

Tarn, W. W., *The Greeks in Bactria and India* (1938), Cambridge University Press, 1951.

Thapar, R., "Puranic Lineages and Archaeological Cultures", *Puratattva,* no. 8, 1976-77.

Thompson, S., *The Folktale,* Holt, Rinehart and Winston, New York, 1946.

——— "Myth and Folktales", in *Myth : a Symposium,* ed. by T. A. Sebeok, American Folklore Society, Bloomington, Ind., 1958.

Tonnelat, E., "Teutonic Mythology", in *Larousse Encyclopedia of Mythology,* Hamlyn, London, 1968.

The Upaniṣads, tr. by F. M. Müller, SBE, 1, 15 (1879-84) Motilal Banarsidass, Delhi, 1965.

The Thirteen Principal Upanishads, tr. by R. E. Hume (1921), Oxford University Press, rep. 1968.

Vāmana Purāṇa, with Engl. tr. by S. M. Mukhopadhyaya, All India Kashiraj Trust, Varanasi, 1968.

Vājasaneyī Sañhitā, ed. by A. Weber, Ferd. Dumler Verlag, Berlin, 1852.

Hymns of the Yajur Veda, tr. and comm. by R. T. H. Griffith (1898), rep. Chowkhamba, Varanasi, 1963.

Varenne, J., *La Mahānārāyaṇa Upaniṣad,* Boccard, Paris, 1960.

Vats, M. S., *Gupta Temple at Deogarh, Memoirs of the Archaeological Survey of India,* v.70, Delhi, 1952.

Vaudeville, Ch., "Aspects du Mythe de Kṛṣṇa-Gopāla dans l'Inde Ancienne", in *Mélanges d'Indianisme a la Mémoire de Louis Renou,* École Française de l'Extrème Orient, Boccard, Paris, 1968.

——— "The Govardhan Myth in Northern India", *Indo-Iranian Journal,* v.22, 1980.

Vaidya, C. V. "The date of the Bhāgavata Purāṇa", *Journal of the Bombay Branch of the Royal Asiatic Society,* v.l, 1925.

Viennot, O., "Typologie du Makāra et essai de Chronologie", *Arts Asiatiques,* v.l, 1954.

Viṣṇu Purāṇa, text and Hindi tr. by M. L. Gupta, Gita Press, Gorakhpur, 1969.

Viṣṇu Purāṇa, tr. by H. H. Wilson (1840), rep. Punthi Pustak, Calcutta, 1972.

Vitsaxis, V. G., *Hindu Epics, Myths, and Legends in Popular Illustrations,* Oxford University Press, Delhi, 1977.

Walcot, P., "Cattle Raiding, Heroic Tradition and Ritual : the Greek evidence", *History of Religions,* v.19, 1979.

Waldschmidt, E., "Illustrations de la Kṛṣṇa-Līlā", *Revue des Arts Asiatiques,* 4-6, 1931.

Warmington, E. H., *The Commerce between the Roman Empire and India,* Curzon Press, London, 1974.

Weber, A., *The History of Indian Literature* (1852), Chowkhamba, Varanasi, 1961.

——— "On the Kṛishṇajanmāshtamī, or Kṛishṇa's birth-festival", *Indian Antiquary,* v.3, 1874, and v.6, 1877.

Wheeler, M., *Rome beyond the Imperial Frontiers,* Bell and Sons, London, 1954.

Winternitz, M., *A History of Indian Literature,* Russell & Russell, New York, 1971.

Yāska, *Nirukta,* Anandasrama, Poona, 1921-26.

Yāska, *The Nighantu and the Nirukta,* tr. by L. Sarup, Motilal Banarsidass, Delhi, 1967.

Zimmer, H., *The Art of Indian Asia,* Bollingen Series, v.39, Pantheon, New York, 1955.

Zoetmulder, P. J., *Kalangwan, A Survey of Old Javanese Literature,* Martinus Nijhoff, The Hague, 1974.

ERRATA

Page	*Column*	*Line*	*Incorrect*	*Correct*
14	L(eft)	7	Kṛṣṇa in	Kṛṣṇa as in
34	R(ight)	31	Kāṇvad ynasty	Kāṇva dynasty
49	R	1	prceise	precise
52	L	F. N. 3, last line	Jaya	Java
55	R	5	Uttaramdhura	Uttaramadhura
79	L	F.N. 1, line 3	match in	match kept in
87	L	23	divinised throughout his career,	divinised, throughout his career
125	L	10	Kṛṣṇa	Kaṃsa

Index

Q

R

S

PLATES

Plate 1. Kṛṣṇa. Agathocles coin, Ai Khanoum, Afghanistan; 2nd century B.C., from *Arts Asiatiques*, v. 26, 1973, p. 123.

Plate 2. Balarāma. Agathocles coin, Ai Khanoum, Afghanistan; 2nd century B.C., from *Arts Asiatiques*, v. 26, 1973, p. 123.

Plate 3. Balarāma. Mathura; 1st century B.C., Lucknow Museum, from Kalpana Desai, ***Iconography of Viṣṇu***, fig. 98.

←*Plate* 4. Balarāma-Ekānaṃśā-Vāsudeva. Devangarh, Bihar; 2nd century A.D., Patna Museum; from *JBSR*, v. 53, 1967, pl. 30.

Plate 6. Kṛṣṇa Govardhanadhārī. Mandor Rajasthan, 4th-5th century A.D., Jodhpu Museum.

←*Plate* 5. Transfer of Kṛṣṇa (?). Mathura, U.P., century A.D., Mathura Museum.

Plate 8. Kṛṣṇa Līlā. Mandor, Rajasthan, 4th-5th century A.D., Jodhpur Museum.

Plate 7. Kṛṣṇa Līlā. Mandor, Rajasthan, 4th-5th century A.D., Jodhpur Museum; from Kalpana Desai, *Iconography of Viṣṇu*, fig. 90.

←*Plate* 9. Kṛṣṇa Līlā. Mandor, Rajasthan, 4th-5th century A.D., Jodh Museum.

Plate 10. Kṛṣṇa Govardhanadhārī. Rang Mahal, Rajasthan, 4th-5th century A.D., Bikaner Museum; from *Lalit Kalā*, no. 8, 1960, pl. xxi-1.

←*Plate* 11. Kṛṣṇa in Dānalīlā (?) Rang Mahal, Rajasthan, 4th-5th century A.D., Bikaner Museum, from *Lalit Kalā*, no. 8, 1960, pl. xxi.

Plate 13. The Exchange of Babies. Deogarh, U.P., 5th century A.D., Gupta temple.

←*Plate* 12. Exposing of Kṛṣṇa. Deogarh, U.P., 5th century A.D., National Museum, New Delhi.

←*Plate* 14. Śakaṭabhaṅga. Deogar
U.P., 5th century A.D., Nation
Museum, New Delhi.

Plate 16. Kṛṣṇa Govardhanadh
Varanasi, U.P., 5th century A.I
Bhārat Kalā Bhavan, B.H.U.

Plate 15. Kṛṣṇa Govardhanadhārī. Deogarh, c. 5th century A.D., Deogarh Godown; courtesy American Institute of Indian Studies, Varanasi.

'late 17. Kṛṣṇa Govardhanadhārī. Vatkoh, Kampuchea, 5th century A.D., National Museum, Phnom Pehn; from P. Dupont, La Statuarie Preangkorienne, pl. 1-A.

Plate 18. Kāliyadamana. Mathura, U.P., 5th century A.D., Mathura Museum.

Plate 19. Kṛṣṇa Govardhanadhārī. Kara, Allahabad Dist., U.P., late 5th/early 6th century A.D., Allahabad Museum; courtesy American Institute of Indian Studies, Varanasi.

←*Plate* 20. Pralambāsurava(
Gangetic Valley, 6th century A
Allahabad Museum; from Kalp
Desai, *Iconography of Viṣṇu*, fig.

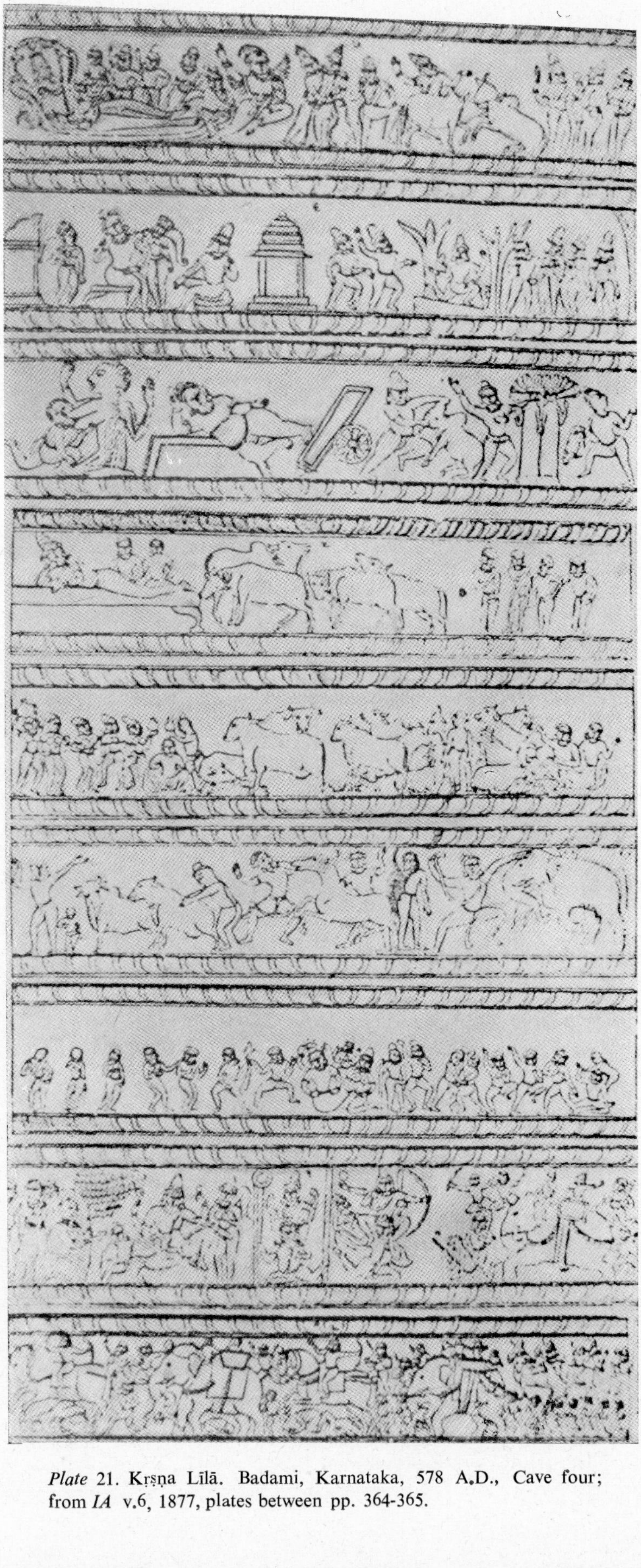

Plate 21. Kṛṣṇa Līlā. Badami, Karnataka, 578 A.D., Cave four; from *IA* v.6, 1877, plates between pp. 364-365.

←*Plate* 22. Kṛṣṇa Līlā. Ba
Karnataka, 578 A.D., Cave

Plate 23. Kṛṣṇa Līlā. Badami. Karnataka, North Fort, 7th century A.D., Badami Museum.

←*Plate* 24. Kṛṣṇa Līlā. B
Karnataka, North Fort
century A.D., Badami Mus

←*Plate* 25. Kṛṣṇa Līlā. Badami, Karnataka, North Fort, 7th century A.D., Badami Museum.

e 26. Pūtanāvadha. Badami, nataka, North Fort (?), 7th ury A.D., Badami Museum.

←*Plate* 27. Kṛṣṇa Govardhanadhārī. Badami, Karnataka, before 640 A.D., Surali Temple.

Plate 28. Transfer of Kṛṣṇa. Badami, Karnataka, before 640 A.D., Surali Temple.

Plate 29. Kṛṣṇa Līlā. Badami, Karnataka, before 640 A.D., Surali Temple.

Plate 30. Kṛṣṇa Līlā. Badami, Karnataka, before 640 A.D., Surali Temple.

Plate 31. Kṛṣṇa Līlā. Badami, Karnataka, before 640 A.D., Surali Temple.

Plate 32. Kṛṣṇa Līlā. Badami, Karnataka, before 640 A.D., Surali Temple.

Plate 33. Kṛṣṇa Govardhanadhārī. Mathura, U.P., 7th century A.D., Mathura Museum.

←*Plate* 34. Kṛṣṇa Govardhar
dhārī. Jatipara, Mathura Di
7th-10th (?) centuries A.
Indian Museum, Calcutta; fr
R. Grousset, *L Inde*, fig. 13

Plate 35. Balarāma-Ekānaṃśā-Vāsudeva. Gangetic Valley, 7th century A.D., Lucknow Museum; from Kalpana Desai, *Iconography of Viṣṇu*, fig. 102.

Plate 36. Kṛṣṇa Govardhanadhārī. Mahabalipuram, Tamil Nadu, 630-668 A.D., Kṛṣṇa maṇḍapa.

Plate 37. Kṛṣṇa Keśiniṣūdana. Pāhārpur, Bangladesh, 7th-8th centuries A.D., Pāhārpur; from S. K. Saraswati, *Early Sculpture of Bengal*, pl. VI-16.

'late 39. Kṛṣṇa Aghāsuravadha. Pāhārpur, Bangladesh. 7th-8th :nturies A.D., Pāhārpur; from K. N. Dikshit's *Excavations of 'aharpu* ı p .XXIX-C.

←*Plate* 38. Kṛṣṇa Yamalārjuna. Pāhārpur, Bangladesh, 7th-8th centuries A.D., Pāhārpur; *ibid.*, pl. VI-17.

←*Plate* 40. Rādhā-Kṛṣṇa (?) Rukmiṇī-Kṛṣṇa (?) Pāhārpur, Bangladesh
7th-8th centuries A.D., Pāhārpur; from S. K. Saraswati,
Early Sculpture of Bengal, pl. III-10

Plate 41. Kṛṣṇa Līlā. Pattadakal, Karnataka, c. 745 A.D., Virūpākṣa Temple.

Plate 43. Kṛṣṇa Lilā. Pattadakal, Karnataka, c. 745 A.D., Virūpākṣa Temple.

←*Plate* 42. Kṛṣṇa Līlā. Pattadakal, Karnataka., c. 745 A.D., Virūpākṣa Temple.

Plate 45 & 46. Kṛṣṇa Līlā. Pattadakal, Karnataka, c. 745 A.D., Mallikārjuna Temple.

Plate 44. Kṛṣṇa Līlā. Pattadakal, Karnataka, c. 745 A.D., Virūpākṣa Temple.

Plate 47. Rādhā Kṛṣṇa. Pattadakal, Karnataka, c. 745 A.D., Mallikārjuna Temple.

Plate 48. Kṛṣṇa Līlā. Pattadakal, Karnataka, c. 745 A.D., Mallikārjuna Temple.

←*Plate* 49. Kṛṣṇa Līlā. Pattadakal, Karnataka, c. 745 A.D., Mallikārjuna Temple.

←*Plate* 50. Kṛṣṇa Līlā. Pattadakal, Karnataka, c. 745 A.D., Mallikārjuna Temple.

Plate 51. Kṛṣṇa Govardhanadhārī. Ellora, Maharashtra c. 725 A.D., Cave 15.

←*Plate* 52. Kṛṣṇa Govardhanadhārī. Ellora, Maharashtra, c. 754-773 A.D., Kailāsanātha Temple.

Plate 53. Kṛṣṇa Līlā. Ellora, Maharashtra, c. 754-773 A.D., Kailāsanātha Temple.

Plate 54. Balarāma-Ekānaṃśā-Vāsudeva. Ellora, Maharashtra, 9th-10th centuries A.D., Cave 27. Colour neg. Professor A. L. Basham.

Plate 55. Keśiniṣūdana. Abaneri, Rajasthan, 9th century A.D., Amber Museum; from Kalpana Desai, *Iconography of Viṣṇu*, fig. 93.

Plate 56. Kṛṣṇa Līlā. Gwalior, Madhya Pradesh, 875 A.D., Caturbhuja Temple; courtesy American Institute of Indian Studies, Varanasi.

Plate 57. Kṛṣṇa Līlā. Prambanam, Java, c. 900-30 A.D., Loro Jongrang Temple.

Plate 58. Kṛṣṇa Līlā. Prambanam, Java, c. 900-30 A.D., Loro Jongrang Temple.

Plate 59. Kṛṣṇā Līlā. Prambanam, Java, c. 900-30 A.D., Loro Jongrang Temple.

Plate 60. Kṛṣṇa Līlā. Prambanam, Java, c. 900-30 A.D., Loro Jongrang Temple.

Plate 61. The Wrestling Match. Prambanam, Java. c. 900-30 A.D., Loro Jongrang Temple.

Plate 62. The Wrestling Match. Prambanam, Java, c. 900-30 A.D., Loro Jongrang Temple.

Plate 63. The Wrestling Match. Prambanam, Java, c. 900-30 A.D., Loro Jongrang Temple.

Plate 64. The Wrestling Match. Prambanam, Java, c. 900-30 A.D., Loro Jongrang Temple.

Plate 65. The Wrestling Match. Prambanam, Java, c. 900-30 A.D., Loro Jongrang Temple.

Plate 66. Vatsāsuravadha and Pūtanāvadha. Khajuraho, Madhya Pradesh, 953-954 A.D., Lakṣmaṇa Temple.

Plate 67. Śakaṭabhaṅga. Khajuraho, Madhya Pradesh, 953-954 A.D., Lakṣmaṇa Temple.

Plate 68. Yamalārjuna. Khajuraho, Madhya Pradesh, 953-954 A.D., Lakṣmaṇa Temple.

←*Plate* 69. Kāliyadamana. Khajuraho, Madhya Pradesh, 953-954 A.D., Lakṣmaṇa Temple.

Plate 70. Ariṣṭāsuravadha. Khajuraho, Madhya Pradesh, 953-954 A.D., Lakṣmaṇa Temple.

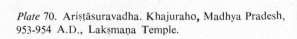

←*Plate* 71. Pralambāsuravadha or Tṛṇāvartavadha. Khajuraho, Madhya Pradesh, 953-954 A.D., Lakṣmaṇa Temple.

Plate 72. Kubjānugraha. Khajuraho, Madhya Pradesh, 953-954 A.D., Lakṣmaṇa Temple.

Plate 73. Kuvalayāpīḍavadha. Khajuraho, Madhya Pradesh, 953-954 A.D., Lakṣmaṇa Temple.

Plate 74. Salavadha or Muṣṭikavadha. Khajuraho, Madhya Pradesh, 953-954 A.D., Lakṣmaṇa Temple.

Plate 75. Cāṇūravadha, Khajuraho, Madhya Pradesh, 953-954 A.D., Lakṣmaṇa Temple.

P74